AI Use Cases for Diplomats

In today's rapidly changing world, diplomacy is undergoing a revolutionary transformation. Imagine ambassadors using artificial intelligence (AI) to analyze millions of social media posts in real time, crisis responses guided by predictive analytics, and complex negotiations enhanced by unprecedented data-driven insights. This isn't the future—it's diplomacy today, reimagined through AI.

Drawing on over 21 years of experience integrating technology into foreign affairs, Donald Kilburg, a retired U.S. diplomat, reveals how AI is revolutionizing diplomatic engagement, crisis management, and public diplomacy. From enhancing communication strategies to optimizing consular services, each chapter presents a vivid exploration of AI's potential to amplify the effectiveness of diplomatic missions across the globe.

Readers will discover practical strategies for implementing AI in diplomatic operations, gain insights into the future of AI-driven global governance, and learn when—crucially—not to use AI at all. Through vivid case studies and real-world examples, this book illuminates both the opportunities and ethical complexities at the intersection of technology and international relations.

Whether you're a diplomatic practitioner, a student of international affairs, or fascinated by technology's impact on global relationships, this groundbreaking guide charts the course for diplomacy's next evolution—where human wisdom and AI converge to address our world's most pressing challenges.

Donald Kilburg is a retired U.S. diplomat, global strategist, and psychologist with a Ph.D. in Experimental Psychology, who has spent over 30 years applying social science and technology to foreign affairs. He lived, studied, and worked across five continents, bringing an interdisciplinary approach to international policy and governance.

A U.S. Foreign Service officer from 2003 to 2025, Dr. Kilburg specialized in public diplomacy and strategic communication, with diplomatic assignments spanning public affairs, consular services, logistics, intelligence, and research. He served as Spokesperson for the Energy Resources Bureau and Assistant Spokesperson for the U.S. Embassy in Beijing, China, engaging on critical issues at the intersection of policy, energy, and international relations. His diplomatic career included formal training in Japanese, Spanish, Chinese, and Russian. His innovations in diplomacy and technology earned him multiple Superior and Meritorious Honor Awards from the U.S. Department of State.

A U.S. Army veteran and former university professor, Dr. Kilburg is a strong advocate for the scientist-practitioner approach and remains an active thought leader, contributing to academic research, public discourse, and innovation in governance, while mentoring the next generation of professionals at the intersection of technology and diplomacy.

AI Use Cases for Diplomats
Applying Artificial Intelligence to Diplomacy

Donald Kilburg

CRC Press
Taylor & Francis Group
Boca Raton London New York

CRC Press is an imprint of the
Taylor & Francis Group, an **informa** business

A CHAPMAN & HALL BOOK

Designed cover image: Shutterstock_2058908708

First edition published 2026
by CRC Press
2385 NW Executive Center Drive, Suite 320, Boca Raton FL 33431

and by CRC Press
4 Park Square, Milton Park, Abingdon, Oxon, OX14 4RN

CRC Press is an imprint of Taylor & Francis Group, LLC

© 2026 Donald Kilburg

ISBN: 978-1-041-00926-9 (hbk)
ISBN: 978-1-041-00835-4 (pbk)
ISBN: 978-1-003-61230-8 (ebk)

DOI: 10.1201/9781003612308

Typeset in Times
by codeMantra

To my parents, for showing me that virtue is its own reward.

To the diplomats who operate in good faith
despite conflicting signals around them.

And to those who embrace technology as a bridge
to dialogue, understanding, and democracy.

Contents

AI can magnify diplomacy, but only authenticity gives it meaning—a truth as valid today as it will be a thousand years from now.

Foreword

I still remember the early mornings in Beijing—adrenaline filled, caffeinated, and huddled around a whiteboard with my colleague and friend, the author of this book, as we worked through drafts of a speech for then-U.S. Ambassador Gary Locke and developed strategies for messaging disagreements among two of the world's great powers. It was 2011, and I had just stepped into the role of Chief of Staff at the U.S. Embassy in Beijing. We were navigating a complex media landscape, a shifting U.S.–China relationship, and a rising tide of global information flows. At the time, our tools and windows on those information and communication flows were email chains, an early phase of messaging wars over social media, briefing binders, and the finely honed instincts and experience of a talented diplomatic team. The U.S. and China were navigating the historically perilous period of relations between a rising power and an existing one, with precarious fronts in trade, military relations and deployments, and ongoing disputes over human rights. Among the most sensitive disputes was over the entry into the embassy of Chinese dissident Chen Guangcheng.

AI wasn't on the table. Not yet.

Fast forward a decade, the world of diplomacy has transformed. Protests once delivered via diplomatic channels are now just as likely to come through aggressively worded tweets from China's "wolf warrior" diplomats and cleverly produced TikTok videos. Information moves faster than ever, disinformation spreads in seconds, and geopolitical decisions increasingly rely on the ability to process, analyze, and respond to data in real time. As CNN's Chief National Security Analyst and Anchor of CNN Newsroom, I've seen firsthand how artificial intelligence is no longer a future concern—it's a present force. Intelligence officials across the globe have told me how AI has become a force multiplier on numerous fronts from influence operations to cyber weapons to drone warfare. Moreover, from detecting deepfakes and monitoring military buildups to analyzing global sentiment and forecasting instability, AI is reshaping the very terrain on which diplomacy operates.

That's why this book is so timely—and so necessary.

AI Use Cases for Diplomats doesn't just describe what AI can do; it shows how AI is already being used, misused, and, in the best cases, thoughtfully integrated into the craft of diplomacy. It's a playbook for modern statecraft. But more than that, it's a reminder that the human element—judgment, empathy, cultural fluency—remains irreplaceable. In fact, working diplomats play an essential role not only in maximizing the benefits of AI but in mitigating the risks as well.

I know the author understands that, because we've lived it. Together, we worked on messaging strategies under pressure, balancing nuance with clarity, translating values across cultural lines, and never forgetting the people on the other end of the message. Reading this book, I recognize that same mindset: tech-savvy but ethically grounded and forward-looking but rooted in the timeless principles of public service.

What I appreciate most is how this book steers away from AI hype and techno-utopianism. That's a rarity in the current public discussion of this new and transformative technology. It's honest about the risks—bias, overreach, the temptation to automate away empathy—and clear-eyed about the opportunities. It offers diplomats a toolkit that includes not just technologies but also a mindset, which enables them to lead in this new era with confidence, clarity, and conscience.

Diplomacy is about building trust in uncertain times. It's about choosing words carefully, understanding your audience, and navigating gray areas with integrity. AI can assist with that. But it cannot replace the core of what diplomacy truly is: human connection.

If you're a diplomat, this book will help you navigate the changes ahead. If you're a policymaker, it will sharpen your sense of what's possible—and what's at stake. And if you're simply someone who believes, as I do, that truth and trust still matter in a noisy world, you'll find in these pages a thoughtful, urgent call to action.

This isn't just a guidebook. It's a reflection of where diplomacy is headed—and a challenge to shape that future, wisely.

Jim Sciutto
CNN Chief National Security Analyst
Anchor, CNN Newsroom
Former Chief of Staff, U.S. Embassy Beijing (2011–2013)
Author, *The Return of Great Powers*

Preface: Diplomacy in the Age of AI

In 1999, hunched over a hulking computer at the U.S. Department of State in Washington, DC, I watched as my monitor—the size of a microwave oven—slowly flickered to life. As a new intern, I learned my first lesson in diplomatic patience: our computers took so long to boot up that it made sense to turn them on and go grab coffee while waiting for the login screen to appear. Email was a novelty, smartphones were science fiction, and the internet was in its infancy.

Fast forward to today, where diplomatic missions worldwide have transformed into sophisticated digital hubs. What once required physical presence, paper trails, and days of preparation now happens in virtual meeting rooms, collaborative digital spaces, and instant communication channels. Secure collaboration platforms, data analytics dashboards, and digital tools have fundamentally altered how diplomats gather information, communicate across borders, and make decisions.

Yet amidst this technological revolution, the heart of diplomacy beats unchanged. It remains the art of finding common ground with someone whose worldview or tangible goals might be fundamentally different from your own. It demands crafting messages with the precision of a poet, preparing for high-stakes meetings with the discipline of an athlete, and reading subtle cultural nuances like a master anthropologist.

Above all, diplomacy requires what no machine can replicate: empathy, intuition, and deep cultural understanding. Diplomats must be skilled at "reading the room"—not because they are necessarily concerned with everyone's welfare (though many are), but because advancing their country's agenda demands sensing and understanding social dynamics, emotional atmospheres, and unspoken cues in every gathering and meeting.

While diplomatic technology has advanced, the challenges diplomats face have also intensified. Today's diplomats confront climate change that threatens to displace populations, cyberattacks that can destabilize governments in minutes, and pandemics that spread globally with unprecedented speed. Economic crises now travel across continents as quickly as digital transactions. Additionally, malicious actors increasingly use technology to spread disinformation and manipulate public opinion for strategic advantage or to consolidate power.

These global challenges demand solutions that transcend traditional approaches. Artificial intelligence (AI) has emerged as a powerful ally in this mission, offering tools that can process vast amounts of information, identify patterns in global trends, and illuminate connections that might otherwise remain hidden. From predicting refugee movements to spotting early warning signs of conflict, AI systems are becoming essential components of the diplomatic toolkit.

During my career as a diplomat, psychologist, and educator, I have observed how technology has increasingly influenced international relations. While AI tools show promise in areas like identifying potential agreement points in negotiations, they can also amplify biases or oversimplify complex cultural contexts. The diplomatic community continues to explore AI applications ranging from crisis response coordination to public diplomacy campaigns, revealing both the potential and limitations of AI in practice. This book examines these developments, offering a practical guide for those navigating an increasingly digital diplomatic landscape.

Within these pages, you will discover concrete examples of AI use cases in diplomacy that are already becoming reality at missions worldwide. You will learn how AI has the potential to support trade negotiations by analyzing vast datasets of economic indicators, enhance humanitarian responses through predictive modeling of population movements, and amplify public diplomacy efforts via sentiment analysis and social media monitoring.

You will also encounter forthright discussions about critical challenges: How do we address algorithmic bias when AI systems are trained primarily on Western diplomatic traditions? What happens when AI-powered translation misses crucial cultural nuances in high-stakes negotiations? Who bears responsibility when automated systems make recommendations that influence international relations? These questions demand not just technical solutions but ethical frameworks rooted in diplomatic principles.

Those entering the field of international relations today will define how these technologies shape global cooperation. This book aims to equip readers with both practical knowledge and critical perspectives on the intersection of AI and diplomacy. My hope is that readers will finish these pages with greater technical understanding, as well as greater ability to thoughtfully evaluate when AI can enhance diplomatic work and when human judgment must prevail.

Together, let us reimagine the art (and science) of diplomacy for the Age of AI— one where technology amplifies our capacity for understanding, without replacing the human connections at the heart of international relations.

Acknowledgments

Special thanks and appreciation for reviewing early drafts of this book: Virginia Blaser, David Nguyen, Dan Spokojny, Jeff Ogren, Travis Feuerbacher, Brian Razzino, and David Levi.

Statement on AI Use in Writing This Book

In writing this book about AI use cases for diplomats, I made a deliberate choice to "practice what I preach" and thereby embrace various AI tools throughout my writing process, including ChatGPT, Claude, Gemini, and Perplexity. Using AI helped me to expand my thinking about the subject matter and to write this book quickly, in hopes of forging new knowledge at a pace that could keep up with AI advancement. I recognize that there is currently lively debate over the extent to which writers should use AI in their writing process, including for diplomacy.

I would therefore like to be specific about how AI assisted in creating this book, as I believe transparency about AI use in writing can help advance an important discussion in our field. I used AI tools as my thought partners and editorial assistants. The tools helped me to brainstorm ideas, organize research, create structured outlines, improve clarity, and ensure consistent formatting. Throughout my AI-assisted writing process, I found myself reflecting on how such collaborative approaches might benefit diplomatic work. My experience came with careful consideration about where to draw the lines, particularly in balancing innovation with tradition, efficiency with deliberation, and technological capability with my own human judgment. Did I always succeed? Probably not.

Nevertheless, I have come to see AI-assisted writing on a spectrum, with different tools and approaches being appropriate for different tasks and contexts, rather than a simple yes/no choice for authors. Some aspects of writing and diplomacy (or any field) may benefit greatly from a degree of AI assistance, while others may require more traditional human-centered approaches. As AI tools continue to evolve, I believe authors, diplomats, and professionals should share their experiences openly and engage in constructive dialogue about best practices. I feel no guilt about openly using AI as a writing assistant—if anything, avoiding AI while writing a book on conscientious AI adoption would be disingenuous.

While I am confident in the value this human-AI collaboration has brought to the project, I also recognize that we are all walking unique paths as these technologies evolve. I invite you to engage critically with the ideas presented here, drawing on your own experiences and perspectives. My hope is that by being transparent about my own approach, while remaining open to diverse viewpoints, we can collectively develop thoughtful frameworks for integrating AI tools into diplomatic practice. The future of diplomacy will likely be neither purely human nor predominantly automated, but rather a careful synthesis of human wisdom and technological capability. I look forward to exploring this path forward together!

Introduction

By far the greatest danger of Artificial Intelligence is that people conclude too early that they understand it.

—Eliezer Yudkowsky, AI Researcher, Machine
Intelligence Research Institute (2008)

The rise of powerful AI will either be the best or the worst thing ever to happen to humanity. We do not yet know which.

—Stephen Hawking, theoretical physicist,
University of Cambridge (2016)

Humanity is at the edge of a revolution driven by artificial intelligence. It has the potential to be one of the most significant and far-reaching revolutions in history...

—Henry Kissinger, former U.S. Secretary
of State (in Kissinger et al. 2019)

Think back to your first conversation with an AI language model or "chatbot" such as ChatGPT. Perhaps, you started with something simple—a question that had been on your mind, a playful request for a poem, or maybe just a quick language translation you needed. But then something unexpected happened. As the AI responded with remarkable thoughtfulness, adapted to match your own conversational style, and built meaningfully on each of your exchanges, you likely found yourself experiencing a subtle but profound shift in perspective. That moment may have suggested to you this wasn't just another tech tool, but something that could engage with you in ways that potentially reshape how we think about the relationship between humans and machines. If you work in diplomacy or international relations, this revelation might have sparked even deeper questions about how AI could transform the very nature of global dialogue and cooperation. Your initial skepticism may have given way to curiosity about how these new forms of intelligence might reshape the diplomatic landscape you navigate every day—for better or worse.

VIGNETTE   An AI-Enhanced Embassy in the Republic of Z

Picture an AI-enhanced embassy in the fictional Republic of Z, in the Age of AI. It's mid-morning in the embassy, and the day was supposed to be routine. You're at your workstation in the secure communications center, reviewing reports and preparing for a scheduled briefing. The embassy hums with its usual rhythm—diplomatic staff moving between meetings, AI systems quietly processing data in the background. Then suddenly everything changes.

An encrypted alert floods the screens. A catastrophic explosion has rocked a major port facility in a neighboring country, and within moments, the world

---

is watching. Social media erupts with speculation, news agencies scramble to launch live coverage, and inside the crisis room, you and your team shift into high gear. AI-enhanced systems begin sorting through a deluge of real-time information, pulling in satellite imagery, security feeds, and sentiment analysis from social media in multiple key languages.

Your ambassador steps in, his usual schedule instantly upended. He studies multiple AI-powered dashboards at once. One screen highlights a growing wave of coordinated disinformation across various platforms. Another analyzes satellite images, comparing thermal signatures from the blast site with historical data. A third screen presents a predictive model mapping out potential diplomatic responses, each assigned probability scores based on past crises and current political alignments.

As your team studies the incoming data, something catches your attention in a foreign ministry statement. While the AI translation seems accurate, you notice subtle diplomatic language that carries special weight in regional politics—something the algorithms missed. The ambassador, drawing on decades of experience, confirms your observation. The choice of certain formal titles and traditional phrases suggests this crisis may be more serious than initially apparent.

This fictional vignette illustrates how diplomatic work is rapidly evolving, requiring human expertise and AI to work as essential partners. Throughout this book, we will use such vignettes to introduce each chapter's exploration of potential diplomatic futures. Our opening vignette raises a crucial question: How do traditional diplomatic functions adapt in an era transformed by advanced technology? To understand AI's role in reshaping diplomacy, we must first examine diplomacy's core functions and guiding principles.

WHAT IS DIPLOMACY?

Imagine a world where countries are like neighbors in a global community. Just as neighbors need ways to communicate, resolve disagreements, and work together, nations need diplomacy—the art and practice of managing relationships between countries. At its heart, diplomacy is about building bridges between nations through dialogue and negotiation, much like how you might work things out with a neighbor over a cup of coffee or tea.

Modern diplomacy operates through a network of embassies and consulates—think of them as your country's homes away from home in foreign lands. These diplomatic missions serve seven core functions, which we'll unpack in Chapter 1 and then in more detail in dedicated chapters of this book. The core functions are political affairs, economic affairs, management affairs, consular affairs, public affairs, diplomatic security, and diplomatic technology. For now, here is a taste of each:

1. Political affairs officers serve as the diplomatic corps' eyes, ears, and voice in foreign countries. They're like skilled political analysts and negotiators who spend their days decoding the local political landscape and its implications for their home country. When they're not meeting with local political figures or

attending important policy discussions, they're writing detailed analyses that help shape their nation's foreign policy. As their careers advance, these officers often take on leadership roles, managing large political sections, advising ambassadors, and leading international negotiations. Their deep understanding of local culture and history becomes invaluable in crafting effective diplomatic responses to complex situations. (See Chapter 3.)

2. Economic officers are the bridge-builders between nations' economies. While you might think they all have economics degrees, what they really need is sharp analytical skills and strong relationship-building abilities. Through comprehensive training, they become experts in economics, trade, commercial diplomacy, energy, and environmental issues. These officers spend their days developing networks within government ministries, business communities, and international organizations. When your country needs to understand how another nation's economic policies might affect trade relations, these are the experts who provide those crucial insights. (See Chapter 4.)

3. Management officers are the unsung heroes who keep diplomatic missions running smoothly. Think of them as the chief operating officers of embassies with an international twist. They manage multi-million dollar budgets, maintain diplomatic facilities, and coordinate high-profile visits. When crises strike, these action-oriented leaders develop quick, effective solutions. Beyond their executive responsibilities, they negotiate with host governments on diplomatic privileges, tax reciprocity, and operational agreements—critical functions that keep embassies running effectively. (See Chapter 5.)

4. Consular officers are often called the frontline diplomats, serving as a crucial link between nations and their people. They're the ones who help citizens in crisis abroad, whether it's a lost passport or a natural disaster requiring evacuation. But their role goes beyond helping citizens—they're also on the front lines of preventing human trafficking, facilitating international adoptions, and making visa decisions that can change lives. Their work requires not just quick thinking under pressure, but also the ability to make fair decisions while showing compassion in difficult situations. (See Chapter 6.)

5. Public diplomacy officers are the storytellers and bridge-builders of the diplomatic world. They work to explain their country's values, history, and policies to foreign audiences in ways that resonate and build understanding. These officers might be organizing cultural programs one day and coordinating educational exchanges and scholarships the next. They serve as embassy spokespersons, manage digital communication strategies, and build the kind of lasting relationships that turn diplomatic agreements into genuine international friendships. (See Chapter 7.)

6. Diplomatic security service agents combine the roles of federal law enforcement officers and international security professionals. Unlike typical law enforcement roles, these agents must understand both security protocols and diplomatic sensitivities. They protect diplomatic personnel and facilities worldwide, advise ambassadors on security matters, investigate passport and visa fraud, and even protect visiting foreign dignitaries. Their work

requires constant vigilance and adaptation to evolving global security challenges. (See Chapter 8.)
7. Diplomatic technology officers represent the technological backbone of
modern diplomacy. In an age where a cyberattack could compromise sensitive diplomatic communications or a technical glitch could disrupt a crucial presidential visit, these officers ensure that the complex machinery of
diplomacy runs smoothly. They manage everything from secure networks
to the technical support for high-level diplomatic events. Their role requires
constant learning and adaptation as technology evolves, combining technical expertise with diplomatic sensitivity. (See Chapter 9.)

These seven functions work together seamlessly in modern diplomacy, each playing
a crucial role in maintaining international relationships and advancing national interests. While there are many other functions and aspects of diplomacy and numerous
government agencies involved in international relations, understanding these core
functions provides a strong foundation for exploring how AI can enhance diplomatic
work while preserving its essential human element.

As we stand on the cusp of a technological revolution, particularly in AI, it's
crucial to understand how these new tools can augment traditional diplomatic practices. But before we explore this intersection, let's first understand what AI is, how
it works, and why it's particularly well-suited to address the complex challenges of
international relations.

WHAT IS AI AND WHAT DOES IT MEAN FOR DIPLOMACY?

For modern diplomats, AI isn't just another technological trend to monitor—it's
rapidly becoming as essential to their toolkit as diplomatic immunity or secure
communications. But what exactly is AI, and why should diplomats care about its
evolution?

At its core, AI functions somewhat like having numerous specialized assistants,
each capable of processing and analyzing certain types of information at speeds that
typically exceed human capabilities. But unlike traditional computer programs that
simply follow predetermined rules, AI systems can learn from data and adapt certain
behaviors—in a limited parallel to how junior diplomats develop specific expertise
through their service.

Modern AI systems excel in three key areas that are particularly relevant to diplomatic work. First, through machine learning, they can analyze vast troves of historical diplomatic communications, trade data, and international agreements to identify
patterns and predict potential outcomes. Imagine being able to rapidly analyze many
trade agreements your country has signed to help identify potential precedents for a
current negotiation—that could be the power of advanced AI-driven analysis.

Second, natural language processing allows AI to work with human language in
sophisticated ways. When a diplomatic mission receives thousands of messages in
different languages during a crisis, AI could potentially translate, categorize, and
help identify the most urgent communications. For instance, during a natural disaster, AI could help consular officers quickly identify and prioritize messages from

citizens in immediate danger while automatically translating emergency instructions into multiple languages.

Third, computer vision—AI's ability to interpret visual information—offers new possibilities for diplomatic work. From potentially analyzing satellite imagery to detect possible treaty violations to assisting with processing visa application photos for security concerns, these capabilities might extend human oversight in significant ways.

Recent years have witnessed a remarkable evolution in AI's language capabilities through Large Language Models (LLMs), such as ChatGPT, Gemini, Claude, or DeepSeek. These sophisticated systems represent a giant leap in AI's ability to understand and generate human language, but their role in diplomacy requires careful consideration. While they can draft initial responses to routine diplomatic communications or summarize lengthy policy documents in seconds, they lack the nuanced understanding of diplomatic protocol and cultural sensitivities that experienced diplomats possess.

For example, when analyzing a diplomatic note, an LLM might accurately summarize its content but miss subtle diplomatic signals conveyed through word choice or formatting—signals that could indicate a shift in bilateral relations. This underscores why these tools should augment rather than replace human diplomatic expertise. Consider them as highly capable research assistants who can handle routine tasks and provide initial analyses, allowing diplomats to focus on the nuanced aspects of international relations that require human judgment.

For today's diplomats, AI serves dual roles: it's both a powerful tool for enhancing diplomatic work and a crucial topic for international negotiation and cooperation. When a diplomat needs to understand public sentiment in their host country, AI systems might analyze large volumes of social media posts and news articles to offer valuable insights. Similarly, when preparing for complex multilateral negotiations, advanced AI systems could eventually simulate different scenarios and help identify possible areas of agreement or conflict.

However, the rise of AI also presents new diplomatic challenges. Nations are increasingly competing for AI supremacy, raising questions about data sovereignty, algorithmic fairness, and the ethical use of AI in international relations. Who owns the data that AI systems learn from? How do we ensure AI-driven decisions don't perpetuate international inequalities? These questions require diplomatic solutions that balance innovation with responsibility.

It's crucial to understand that AI's role in diplomacy is fundamentally supportive rather than replacive. The core skills of diplomacy—building trust, navigating cultural sensitivities, and negotiating complex agreements—remain uniquely human capabilities. AI can't replicate the intuition developed through years of diplomatic experience or the emotional intelligence required to build lasting international relationships.

Consider a diplomatic reception: while AI might help analyze the guest list and suggest talking points, it can't read the room, sense tensions, or build the personal connections that often lead to diplomatic breakthroughs. Instead, AI serves as an enabler, handling time-consuming analytical tasks so diplomats can focus on these essential human elements of their work.

DIPLOMACY AND AI NEED EACH OTHER

The relationship between diplomacy and AI represents more than just a technological upgrade to traditional diplomatic practices—it marks the beginning of a transformative partnership that could well reshape how nations interact in the 21st century. To understand how these two domains "need" each other, let's explore how they complement and enhance each other's strengths while addressing their respective limitations.

Think of modern diplomatic challenges as complex puzzles with countless moving pieces. Climate change negotiations, for instance, require understanding not just environmental science, but also economic impacts, political feasibility, and social implications across different cultures and regions. While AI can rapidly analyze climate data, economic trends, and public sentiment across multiple countries, only skilled diplomats can transform these insights into actionable agreements that consider each nation's unique circumstances and concerns.

The limitations of both AI and traditional diplomacy become clear when we examine complex diplomatic situations. Take, for example, a delicate negotiation following a border dispute between two nations. An AI system might excel at:

- Analyzing historical border conflicts and their resolutions
- Monitoring real-time troop movements through satellite imagery
- Assessing economic implications of different boundary proposals
- Tracking public sentiment in both countries

However, only human diplomats can:

- Read subtle body language during face-to-face meetings
- Understand the personal histories and relationships between key leaders
- Recognize when cultural or historical sensitivities require special handling
- Build the trust necessary for parties to make difficult compromises

This complementarity extends to crisis management. During a humanitarian emergency, AI can rapidly process information from multiple sources—social media, news reports, satellite imagery, and ground sensors—to provide a comprehensive situation assessment. But the decision to intervene, the delicate task of coordinating with multiple governments, and the crucial work of building international consensus require human judgment and diplomatic skill.

Perhaps, the most crucial aspect of this partnership lies in how diplomacy shapes the future of AI itself. As AI systems become more powerful and pervasive, the international community faces pressing questions about their governance:

- How can we ensure AI development benefits all nations, not just the technologically advanced?
- What ethical principles should guide the deployment of AI in sensitive areas like surveillance or military applications?

- How can we protect privacy and human rights in an age of increasingly sophisticated AI systems?

These questions cannot be answered by any single nation or through purely technical solutions. They require careful diplomatic negotiation, cultural sensitivity, and a deep understanding of different national perspectives. Diplomats become the bridge builders, helping create frameworks that balance innovation with responsibility, competition with cooperation.

As this partnership develops, we're seeing the emergence of new diplomatic practices that combine human wisdom with AI capabilities. For instance, modern diplomatic missions might use AI to:

- Simulate complex multilateral negotiations to better prepare for actual talks
- Identify emerging international issues before they become crises
- Provide real-time translation and cultural context during diplomatic exchanges
- Analyze vast amounts of data to support evidence-based policymaking

Yet, these tools remain firmly in service of human diplomatic goals: building understanding, fostering cooperation, and promoting peace and prosperity.

The future of international relations will therefore increasingly depend on what we might call "collaborative intelligence" or "co-intelligence" (Mollick 2024)—the thoughtful integration of human wisdom with AI capabilities. This doesn't mean replacing traditional diplomatic skills with technology, but rather enhancing them to meet the challenges of an increasingly complex world.

For example, future peace negotiations might combine:

- AI-powered scenario modeling to understand potential outcomes
- Data-driven analysis of economic and social impacts
- Traditional face-to-face diplomacy to build trust and understanding
- Human insight into cultural and historical sensitivities

As we move forward, the key will be maintaining the right balance—using AI to enhance diplomatic capabilities while preserving the essentially human nature of diplomacy itself.

EXPLORING DIPLOMACY IN THE AGE OF AI

This book examines the integration of AI into diplomatic practice—a transformation that is already reshaping international relations. Rather than offering merely a technical manual, we provide a comprehensive analysis of how AI technologies are being applied across the full spectrum of diplomatic functions. Through detailed case studies, practical frameworks, and evidence-based assessments, we map the evolving landscape where technology meets the ancient art of diplomacy.

The diplomatic world is rapidly adopting diverse AI applications. LLMs draft and analyze diplomatic communications, reducing time spent on routine correspondence while extracting insights from vast document collections. Predictive analytics tools forecast political instability, economic trends, and emerging crises with increasing accuracy. Computer vision systems monitor border movements and verify compliance with international agreements. Natural language processing algorithms track global sentiment across multiple languages, providing real-time insights into how diplomatic initiatives are perceived worldwide.

Each of these technologies brings specific capabilities to diplomatic work. Consider how embassy political sections could process hundreds of local news sources, potentially identifying emerging political narratives that might otherwise go unnoticed. Economic officers may leverage AI tools to help model potential impacts of trade negotiations across multiple sectors. Consular operations use pattern recognition to process visa applications more efficiently while flagging potential security concerns for human review.

The practical applications extend throughout the diplomatic enterprise. During multilateral negotiations, AI systems might help analyze the stated positions of multiple stakeholders, potentially identifying areas for compromise. In crisis response, these tools could help diplomatic teams filter important information, creating visualizations of complex situations to support more informed decision-making. For public diplomacy, AI-powered analytics could measure the effectiveness of outreach efforts across diverse cultural contexts and digital platforms.

Yet, understanding AI's limitations is just as important as recognizing its capabilities. The technology excels at pattern recognition, data processing, and certain types of prediction—but it cannot replicate the uniquely human dimensions of diplomatic craft. An AI system can identify statistical anomalies in visa applications, but it cannot assess the fear in an asylum seeker's eyes. It can analyze negotiation transcripts for inconsistencies, but it cannot build the personal trust essential for breakthrough agreements. It can draft talking points based on policy positions, but it cannot read the subtle body language across a negotiating table.

This complementary relationship forms the foundation for effective integration. When properly implemented, AI handles routine analysis and information processing, allowing human diplomats to focus their attention on relationship building, cultural understanding, ethical judgment, and the creative problem-solving that defines diplomatic excellence. The most successful diplomatic missions will need to find this balance—leveraging technology to enhance human capabilities rather than attempting to replace them.

As subsequent chapters will demonstrate, AI in diplomacy is not a distant possibility but a present reality that is evolving rapidly across all diplomatic functions. From enhancing political analysis to transforming consular operations, from supporting economic negotiations to amplifying public diplomacy, these tools are reshaping how diplomatic missions pursue their objectives in the digital age.

PREPARING FOR THE FUTURE: LEADING IN THE AGE OF AI

We stand at the starting line of an unprecedented race, and the starter pistol has already been fired without much advance notice or public preparation or consensus.

Unlike traditional competitions with a single finish line, we're simultaneously running multiple critical races in the development and governance of AI. Nations sprint for technological supremacy while civil society races to establish ethical frameworks. Meanwhile, humanity as a whole races against time to ensure our values guide AI development before these systems potentially become too complex to meaningfully influence.

This multi-track competition carries immense stakes for humanity's future. If we wait until AI reaches more advanced states of development, we may find ourselves unable to shape its fundamental nature and behavior. The time for action is now, while we can still embed human values, create adaptive governance frameworks, and ensure AI serves humanity's best interests. For perspective, consider how rapidly smartphones and social media have become integrated into daily life, and the challenges many now face in managing their influence or shaping how these technologies affect society—particularly for younger generations who have grown up with these tools and never known life without them (the so-called "digital natives").

Diplomats are uniquely positioned to lead this crucial effort of influencing AI's development, drawing on centuries of experience in bridging seemingly insurmountable divides. Throughout history, diplomats have helped nations with opposing worldviews find common ground and build lasting peace. Now they must apply these same skills to perhaps their most challenging task yet: helping humanity come to terms with AI as an emerging force in global affairs.

Think of AI as a new kind of global actor, one with its own unique "cultural" logic and rules of operation. Just as diplomats learn to decode the subtle nuances of different societies—understanding how history, values, and traditions shape behavior—they must now develop a deep understanding of how AI systems "think" and make decisions. This isn't merely an academic exercise; it's essential for creating frameworks that ensure AI development aligns with human values and interests.

The traditional diplomatic role of representing national interests abroad must evolve to meet this challenge. Consider climate change as a precedent: it demonstrated that some challenges transcend national boundaries and benefit from collaborative approaches. AI similarly presents governance challenges that extend beyond individual nations. When negotiating AI governance or establishing ethical guidelines, diplomats must balance immediate national interests against our collective human future.

This balancing act becomes particularly crucial as AI systems begin to shape how human values and interests are understood and implemented in automated systems. Imagine, for instance, an AI system designed solely to maximize one nation's economic advantage. It might recommend actions that, while beneficial to that country, could undermine global stability or human welfare. We've seen similar dynamics play out in areas like environmental protection, where short-term national gains often conflict with long-term global needs.

To prevent such scenarios, diplomats must help create frameworks that ensure AI systems recognize and respect universal human values—principles like human dignity, privacy, and self-determination—while acknowledging legitimate national interests. This requires building bridges between:

- Technology developers and policymakers
- Competing national interests and universal human values
- Technical capabilities and ethical constraints
- Short-term advantages and long-term humanitarian concerns

The path forward requires embracing what might appear paradoxical: becoming more technologically sophisticated while simultaneously becoming more deeply human. As AI systems grow more capable, the distinctly human aspects of diplomacy—empathy, ethical judgment, cultural understanding, and the ability to build trust—become more crucial, not less.

Diplomats must call for a new humanism in our practice. This isn't about opposing regional heritage or technological progress; rather, it's about ensuring that as we harness AI's tremendous potential, we do so in ways that enhance rather than diminish our shared humanity as one species. Diplomats must lead in articulating and defending our core human values in an age where machines increasingly shape our world and AIs are being developed in geographic or ethnographic isolation.

The future effectiveness of diplomacy—and potentially the trajectory of international relations—will be significantly influenced by how thoughtfully we navigate these technological changes. By combining technological innovation with timeless diplomatic principles and a renewed commitment to common human values, we can work toward a future where AI serves as a tool for fostering understanding, cooperation, and human flourishing, even if nation-state borders are an inevitable part of the human experience.

We now turn our attention to a brief look at some of the literature at the intersection of AI and diplomacy. Here, we take a scientist-practitioner approach, to establish a framework for this book that emphasizes both rigorous analysis and practical application.

SELECTED LITERATURE REVIEW: HOW THIS BOOK FITS IN

The rapid advancement of AI is fundamentally reshaping many aspects of global governance, including the practice of diplomacy. As Kissinger, Schmidt, and Huttenlocher (2021) suggest in *The Age of AI: And Our Human Future*, the rise of AI marks a pivotal moment in human history, one that will not only enhance existing diplomatic tools but may also introduce entirely new dynamics in global power relations. AI technologies enable diplomats to process vast amounts of data, predict certain geopolitical trends, and automate decision-making processes, offering the potential to address some of the world's most pressing challenges. However, alongside these opportunities, the growing presence of AI in diplomacy also introduces significant ethical concerns, governance issues, and geopolitical risks.

This literature review aims to explore the current landscape of AI in diplomacy, highlighting key themes such as the transformative role of AI, the ethical and governance challenges, and the geopolitical implications of AI's integration into diplomatic practice. Drawing from a diverse set of works—including foundational theories on diplomacy, seminal contributions to AI ethics, and case studies of AI's practical use in diplomacy—the review touches on current knowledge and identifies gaps in the literature on applied AI. By doing so, this review sets the stage for this book's contribution, offering actionable insights and practical frameworks that diplomats can apply as they navigate the AI-driven future of global relations.

Diplomacy has always been shaped by the technologies available to states, from the invention of the telegraph to the advent of digital communication. As Black (2010) and Berridge, Keens-Soper, and Otte (2001) outline in their foundational works on the history of diplomacy, each technological revolution has introduced new tools that expand the reach, efficiency, and impact of diplomatic activities. The telegraph, for example, revolutionized communication between distant capitals by enabling near-instant negotiation and decision-making—a parallel that highlights how each technological innovation brings unique opportunities and challenges to diplomacy. Today, we stand on the precipice of another such revolution: the widespread adoption of AI technologies.

In *The Age of AI*, Kissinger et al. discuss how AI could enhance traditional diplomatic tools by providing predictive capabilities, though they caution that its transformative potential must be tempered by ethical considerations and human oversight. While earlier technological advances were primarily about speed and efficiency, AI introduces a new dimension of predictive power and decision augmentation, making it a potentially disruptive force in diplomacy. This shift is already evident in applications such as AI-driven decision-support systems that assist diplomats in navigating complex issues like economic stability, public diplomacy, and geopolitical forecasting (Bjola et al. 2019, 2022; Bjola 2020, 2024; Kurbalija 2024).

AI's potential to transform diplomatic practice is vast, with applications ranging from predictive analysis to real-time decision-making and crisis management. AI technologies allow diplomats to synthesize and analyze large volumes of information at speeds far beyond human capabilities, providing valuable insights into complex international issues. As Bjola and Kornprobst (2024) discuss, AI-driven models could help diplomats anticipate potential crises or conflicts, enabling more effective early intervention strategies.

At the same time, AI offers new tools for enhancing public diplomacy, such as sentiment analysis, which can help gauge the mood of foreign populations and assist in shaping communication strategies (Stanzel & Voelsen 2022). AI's ability to process and analyze social media data offers diplomats valuable insights into global sentiment and communication trends, but human expertise is essential to contextualize these findings and craft culturally appropriate responses (Putri et al. 2020). While AI-based tools for sentiment analysis are useful, they should be understood as part of a broader set of capabilities to enhance diplomatic communication and engagement.

In *The Oxford Handbook of Digital Diplomacy* (2024), Bjola and Manor explore AI's role in augmenting traditional diplomacy, particularly through advanced data analysis, sentiment mapping, and predictive modeling. Their multidisciplinary approach highlights how diplomats are leveraging AI to address the evolving challenges of the digital age and enhance foreign policy objectives, reinforcing AI's role in reshaping diplomatic practices and institutional logic.

Yet, as Kissinger, Schmidt, and Mundie (2024) note in *Genesis*, while AI offers tremendous potential, it is crucial that it does not overshadow the human aspects of diplomacy, such as empathy, cultural understanding, and trust-building. Diplomats must remain at the helm of diplomatic negotiations, using AI as a tool to augment their decision-making, not replace the human dimension that remains central to diplomacy. The integration of AI into diplomatic processes requires a careful balance between technology and human judgment. This theme of effective human-AI collaboration is further developed in Mollick's *Co-Intelligence* (2024), which provides practical frameworks for working alongside AI systems while maintaining human agency and judgment. Mollick's emphasis on AI as an enhancing rather than replacing force particularly resonates in diplomatic contexts, where human discernment remains paramount.

As AI becomes more integrated into diplomatic processes, it raises profound ethical and governance challenges that must be addressed to ensure that these technologies are used responsibly. One of the most pressing issues is algorithmic bias, where AI systems may inadvertently reinforce existing social, political, or economic biases present in the data they are trained on. As Crawford (2021) and Konovalova (2023) caution, this risk is particularly significant in diplomacy, where AI-driven decisions could have far-reaching consequences for global equity and stability. For example, AI systems used in conflict resolution must be developed with a sensitivity to cultural nuances and the complexity of international negotiations.

Another significant ethical issue is transparency. Many AI systems function as "black boxes," where their decision-making processes are opaque even to developers, making transparency and explainability crucial for fostering trust and accountability in diplomatic applications (European Commission 2019, 2025). In diplomacy, where decisions can impact national security or international relationships, transparency and accountability are critical to maintaining trust. As Bjola and Kornprobst (2023) emphasize, ensuring that AI systems are explainable should be a priority to ensure that diplomats and their stakeholders can confidently rely on AI tools without compromising the integrity of the decision-making process.

Additionally, data sovereignty is an emerging concern in the context of AI in diplomacy. As AI systems increasingly rely on cross-border data, countries must navigate issues related to data ownership and the protection of national information (Rafik 2021). Global governance frameworks are necessary to address these concerns and ensure that AI technologies are developed and implemented in ways that respect national sovereignty while promoting international cooperation (Garcia 2021).

The rise of AI is also reshaping global power dynamics, as nations compete for technological dominance. As Horowitz (2018) and Keskin and Kiggins (2021) explain, AI is not only a tool for economic growth but also a critical component of national security. Countries that lead in AI development, including the United States, China, and the European Union, will have strategic advantages in areas such as military innovation, cybersecurity, and economic diplomacy, while the Global South's participation is crucial to ensuring equitable global AI governance. This competition is already visible in the rivalry between the United States and China, where both nations are heavily investing in AI to enhance their geopolitical influence (Horowitz 2018, Horowitz et al. 2018a, 2018b, Rauf & Iqbal 2023).

AI's dual-use nature further complicates this competition. While AI can be used for peaceful purposes, such as improving international cooperation or predictive diplomacy, it can also be weaponized for cyberattacks, surveillance, or disinformation campaigns (Jensen, Whyte, & Cuomo 2020). This poses a significant challenge for diplomats, who must navigate the risks of AI-fueled escalation while promoting cooperation and stability. As Kissinger, Schmidt, and Huttenlocher (2021) emphasize, the global governance of AI must account for these risks, establishing norms to ensure AI is used responsibly across borders.

As Roumate (2024) discusses in *Artificial Intelligence and the New World Order*, AI is now central to shaping international security strategies, including AI-powered military assets, autonomous weapons systems, and surveillance mechanisms. Additionally, as noted by the U.S. Department of State (2023), AI is also playing a critical role in operational diplomacy, including AI-powered machine translation and real-time data processing for enhanced consular services and multilateral negotiations.

Despite the growing body of research on AI in diplomacy, several key areas remain underexplored. One of the most significant gaps is the practical integration of AI into everyday diplomatic functions. While much of the literature discusses the theoretical potential of AI, there is limited exploration of how diplomats are actually using these tools in their daily work. This includes practical applications in embassy operations, consular services, and bilateral negotiations, particularly in regions that may not have access to cutting-edge AI technology (Miegbam & Bariledum 2022).

Another gap is the underexplored issue of how AI can complement the human aspects of diplomacy—such as negotiation, cultural sensitivity, and empathy—which remain essential for maintaining effective diplomatic relations. This requires further research into how AI can be integrated in ways that preserve these human-centric dimensions of diplomacy.

Finally, there is a significant need for more research into the Global South's role in the AI-diplomacy discourse. Much of the literature has focused on AI in developed nations, but countries in the Global South face unique challenges and opportunities in adopting AI technologies. These nations are often excluded from global discussions on AI governance, despite their growing need for AI to address developmental challenges (Garcia 2021). This book aims to help bridge this gap by offering frameworks and specific use cases and tools that show how AI can be applied in diplomatic contexts in these regions.

Note: for a more comprehensive review of related literature, see "Bibliography" at the end of this book. Please forgive any mischaracterizations or omissions; none are intentional.

HOW THIS BOOK IS ORGANIZED: A READER'S GUIDE

Sections

There are six main sections of this book that are aimed at walking you through different analytic frames so you can develop a broad appreciation for applied AI in diplomacy.

1. Foundation (Chapters 1 and 2): Understanding AI's role in modern diplomacy
2. Core Functions (Chapters 3–7): AI applications in specific diplomatic areas
3. Technical Focus (Chapters 8 and 9): Security and technology considerations
4. Integration (Chapter 10): Cross-functional and interagency applications
5. Critical Thinking (Chapter 11): Understanding when not to use AI
6. Capacity-Building (Chapter 12): Developing the mindset and capabilities for success

CHAPTERS

The chapters are largely mapped out across different sections of a typical embassy, including various professional roles in diplomacy.

1. Diplomacy in the Age of AI—A foundational overview exploring how AI is reshaping diplomatic practice through enhanced analysis, automation, and decision support
2. Executive Leadership—How Chiefs of Mission and Deputy Chiefs of Mission can leverage AI for strategic leadership and decision-making
3. Political Affairs—AI's role in analyzing political dynamics, monitoring public sentiment, and managing international relationships
4. Economic Affairs—Using AI to advance trade negotiations, attract investment, and strengthen economic cooperation
5. Management Affairs—Transforming embassy operations through AI-enhanced resource management and administrative efficiency
6. Consular Affairs—Optimizing visa processing, enhancing citizen services, and managing crises with AI support
7. Public Affairs—Amplifying diplomatic messaging and measuring influence through AI-driven analytics and engagement
8. Diplomatic Security—Using AI to protect missions, detect threats, and ensure cybersecurity
9. Diplomatic Technology—Leveraging AI-powered tools and infrastructure across diplomatic functions
10. Interdisciplinary Diplomacy—Breaking down silos with AI to enable whole-of-government approaches
11. When Not to Use AI—Critical examination of AI's limitations, risks, and situations requiring human judgment
12. Building AI Capacity—Developing the mindset, skills, and organizational capabilities for effective AI use

CHAPTER FORMAT

The chapters all have the following format, designed to stimulate thought at different levels of analysis and in different diplomacy contexts.

1. Opening Quotes—Insights from leaders in technology and diplomacy

2. Republic of Z Vignette—A continuing narrative showing AI in diplomatic practice
3. Core Content—Detailed exploration of AI applications and implications
4. Historical AI Use Cases—Real-world examples and lessons learned
5. Large Language Models Section—Practical guidance for using ChatGPT, Claude, and other LLMs
6. Advanced AI Use Cases—Detailed implementation guidance with success metrics
7. Limitations and Future Research Directions
8. Discussion Questions—Thought-provoking scenarios for practical learning

APPENDICES AND GLOSSARY

There are two appendices and a Glossary at the end to round out your understanding.

- Appendix A: 100 AI Use Cases for Diplomats—A comprehensive collection of practical applications across all diplomatic functions
- Appendix B: Introduction to the AI Landscape—Current tools and platforms, from language models to specialized diplomatic applications
- Glossary of AI Terms—Essential terminology explained in diplomatic context

VIGNETTES

Each chapter has a vignette covering the fictional Republic of Z where you will be introduced to the following diplomats, chapter by chapter. (The names are entirely fictional and any connection to real diplomats is coincidental and unintended.)

- Ambassador to the Republic of Z—Daniel Grant, Chapter 1
- Deputy Chief of Mission—Sofia Tan, Chapter 2
- Political Officer—Sarah Chen, Chapter 3
- Economic Officer—Elena Moretti, Chapter 4
- Management Officer—Amir Qureshi, Chapter 5
- Consular Officer   Maria Santos, Chapter 6
- Public Affairs Officer—David Kim, Chapter 7
- Diplomatic Security Officer—Jim Thompson, Chapter 8
- Diplomatic Technology Officer—Anya Novak, Chapter 9

DISCLAIMER: THIS BOOK IS NON-TECHNICAL AND PROSPECTIVE

This book provides a foundational overview for exploring AI in diplomacy, but it intentionally simplifies many technical concepts to make them accessible. Technical readers will likely find the explanations lack the depth and precision they expect—the simplifications of how AI systems work deliberately prioritize reader accessibility over technical completeness. This approach reflects the goal of providing diplomatic practitioners with practical insights rather than a comprehensive technical education.

This book serves as an entry point for those who need operational understanding without requiring expertise in computer science. (Please see appendices for additional technical clarification.)

This book also recognizes the vital importance of responsible AI development and appropriate safeguards. While it presents opportunities for AI application in diplomacy, this should not be interpreted as advocating for uncritical or hasty adoption. Diplomatic institutions are stewards of sensitive international relationships and must approach technological change with appropriate caution. Throughout this book, the continued centrality of human judgment, the need for careful testing in non-critical contexts before wider deployment, and the importance of transparency in AI systems that support diplomatic functions are emphasized. The exploration of use cases is not a call for immediate implementation, but rather an invitation to thoughtful consideration.

The practical challenges of implementing AI in diplomatic settings extend beyond technical hurdles to include vital ethical and governance considerations. Many important questions about AI governance remain unresolved at both national and international levels. Rather than attempting exhaustive coverage of these complex and rapidly evolving topics, this book aims to equip readers with sufficient knowledge to participate meaningfully in these important conversations. Responsible AI adoption requires ongoing learning, careful deliberation, and balanced assessment of both opportunities and risks—a journey that extends well beyond the introductory framework this book provides.

1 Diplomacy in the Age of AI
Leveraging Smart Machines to Build Relationships

We will not only use the machines for their intelligence, we will also collaborate with them in ways that we cannot even imagine.

—Fei-Fei Li, Stanford Institute for Human-Centered AI (2015)

AI Is the New Electricity.

—Andrew Ng, Co-founder of Coursera (2017)

With the emergence of the increasingly powerful AI systems, the stakes for global cooperation have never been higher.

—Sam Altman, CEO of OpenAI (2023)

Diplomacy has entered a transformative era where artificial intelligence (AI) is fundamentally reshaping how nations interact and pursue their interests. From analyzing vast troves of data to enhancing decision-making and automating routine tasks, AI offers unprecedented capabilities that extend far beyond traditional diplomatic tools. This evolution represents one of the most significant changes in diplomatic practice since the advent of modern telecommunications. Yet while AI can process information at superhuman speeds and identify patterns invisible to human analysts, it cannot replace the judgment, cultural sensitivity, and ethical reasoning that define effective diplomacy. The challenge facing diplomatic missions lies not in choosing between human expertise and AI, but in finding ways to combine their respective strengths to advance international cooperation and understanding.

VIGNETTE   AI-Enhanced Embassy in the Republic of Z

As dawn streams through the windows, Ambassador Daniel Grant reviews the daily intelligence dashboard on his secure monitor at the AI-enhanced embassy in the Republic of Z. A red alert catches his eye: the system has flagged troubling patterns across three separate data streams—unusual volatility in Z's currency trading, a spike in social media discussions about food prices, and a surge in critical coverage of economic issues in the local news.

DOI: 10.1201/9781003612308-1

The predictive analytics deepen his concern. Drawing from historical data on similar situations in neighboring countries, the system forecasts a high likelihood of protests within two weeks. Encrypted messages flood Grant's inbox as his political and economic teams exchange rapid updates. The economic counselor highlights recent reductions in agricultural subsidies, while the political counselor reports mounting tensions in parliament. Meanwhile, the public affairs section's AI-enhanced media monitoring uncovers growing criticism of Z's government policies across major outlets, signaling a brewing storm.

Throughout the embassy, AI tools hum in the background, aiding each team in responding to the escalating situation. The consular section notes a slight uptick in visa applications, possibly reflecting unease among the business community. The public affairs team leverages AI-generated sentiment analysis to evaluate the effectiveness of recent messaging, while the security team monitors unusual activity patterns—both physical and cyber—around the embassy perimeter. In every section, AI enhances human efforts, providing early warnings and detailed analysis, but never replacing the critical judgment of experienced diplomats.

As Ambassador Grant drafts messages to key contacts in Z's government, he reviews AI-suggested talking points but tailors them with his deep understanding of local political dynamics and his trusted personal relationships. He convenes an emergency country team meeting, relying on AI-driven data to inform the briefing but knowing that the decisions ahead will demand human wisdom, strategic thinking, and diplomacy.

This morning in the fictional Republic of Z illustrates how AI can transform modern diplomacy—not by replacing human expertise but by amplifying it. By enhancing capabilities across every facet of embassy operations, AI has the potential to enable diplomats to act with greater foresight and precision while preserving the essential human judgment at the heart of their craft.

REDEFINING THE DIPLOMATIC LANDSCAPE

For centuries, diplomacy has been anchored in human skills: careful negotiation, idea exchange, and behavioral understanding (Berridge 2022). AI could transform this traditional craft, not by replacing these fundamental elements but by enhancing diplomats' capabilities and expanding their reach. This evolution would mark a shift from purely intuitive diplomacy to a hybrid approach that combines human expertise with data-driven insights, potentially changing how nations interact and negotiate on the global stage.

Diplomatic work could benefit from unprecedented technological support in managing international relationships, shaping policy, and negotiating agreements (Stanzel & Voelsen 2022, Pokhriyal & Koebe 2023). Diplomats might utilize AI-powered dashboards providing comprehensive monitoring capabilities, including real-time tracking of geopolitical hotspots, early warning systems for political instability, predictive analytics for potential crises, and sentiment analysis of diplomatic communications (DiploFoundation 2019, Buch, Eagleman, & Grosenick 2022, Pokhriyal & Koebe 2023). For example, during periods of regional instability, AI systems could detect patterns suggesting potential upheaval, enabling proactive diplomatic intervention before crises escalate (Pokhriyal & Koebe 2023). For instance, an AI system could analyze financial transactions, identify unusual currency fluctuations, and cross-reference them with increased social media mentions of unemployment. Such a pattern, historically linked to political unrest in the region, could prompt diplomats to engage local governments or offer mediation before protests materialize. Such capability would transform diplomacy from a reactive art into a proactive science, where anticipation and prevention become possible (Bjola 2020, Pokhriyal & Koebe 2023).

The integration of AI has the potential to revolutionize diplomatic decision-making processes (Bano, Chaudhri, & Zowghi 2023, Pokhriyal & Koebe 2023). While traditional diplomacy has relied heavily on experience and intuition, modern diplomats could complement these skills with sophisticated data analysis of complex global situations (Buch, Eagleman, & Grosenick 2022, Berridge 2022). They would be able to track sentiment in political statements, recognize patterns in international relations, and assess diplomatic communications in real time (Manor 2017, Kissinger, Schmidt, & Huttenlocher 2019, 2021). These enhancements could allow for more nuanced and informed responses in diplomatic exchanges, helping to either build trust or defuse tensions with greater precision.

The adoption of AI in diplomacy would likely face resistance from traditionalists who may view it as potentially disruptive to established practices (Horowitz et al. 2018). Addressing these concerns would require a multifaceted approach (Roumate 2024). Foreign ministries would need to develop comprehensive AI literacy programs for diplomatic staff while establishing transparent governance frameworks (U.S. Department of State 2023, 2024a, 2024b, 2024c, 2024d, 2025a, 2025b). Success would depend on maintaining a delicate balance between technological innovation and diplomatic tradition, demonstrating the concrete benefits through careful implementation that shows how AI could augment rather than diminish traditional diplomatic skills (Stanzel et al. 2022).

The COVID-19 pandemic has already accelerated the emergence of hybrid diplomacy, where virtual and physical engagements coexist (Akdenizli 2024). This new paradigm, supported by AI, could revolutionize diplomatic practices through enhanced virtual communication capabilities (Bjola & Manor 2024a, 2024b). Diplomatic missions might enjoy broader reach in their relations, greater flexibility in international engagement, and more efficient resource allocation (Roumate 2021a, 2021b). These technological adaptations could prove that effective diplomacy can transcend physical boundaries while maintaining its essential human elements (Bouchard 2024).

As international relations continue to evolve in complexity and scope, AI could serve as a crucial tool in expanding diplomatic capabilities while preserving the fundamental human elements of statecraft (U.S. Department of State 2024a, 2024b, 2024c, 2024d). This transformation promises more effective, informed, and proactive diplomatic engagement (Alder 2024). By carefully embracing technological advancement while honoring diplomatic traditions, modern diplomacy could become more capable of addressing complex global challenges. The future of international relations might lie in this careful integration of AI with time-tested diplomatic practices, creating a more responsive and effective global diplomatic framework that could better serve our interconnected world.

In the Introduction chapter, we briefly introduced seven core areas essential to modern diplomacy: political affairs, economic affairs, management affairs, consular affairs, public diplomacy, diplomatic security, and diplomatic technology. Here in this chapter, we will unpack each of these areas in greater detail, laying the groundwork for deeper explorations in subsequent chapters dedicated to each core area.

AI AND POLITICAL AFFAIRS: ENHANCING POLITICAL ANALYSIS AND BILATERAL RELATIONS THROUGH DATA-DRIVEN INSIGHT

Political officers serve as the diplomatic corps' primary analysts and negotiators, interpreting host country political landscapes and their implications for national interests. Their work demands deep understanding of local politics, culture, and history to maintain relationships with key figures and advise on policy decisions. AI now offers unprecedented capabilities to enhance this traditional craft without replacing the essential human judgment at its core.

AI transforms political analysis through advanced data processing and pattern recognition. Modern political officers can leverage AI systems to monitor vast amounts of information sources—from social media and news outlets to economic indicators and satellite imagery—to identify emerging trends and potential flashpoints. For example, AI platforms can analyze changes in political rhetoric across multiple languages, detect subtle shifts in coalition dynamics, or flag unusual patterns in government activities that might signal policy changes. These tools don't replace an officer's judgment but rather provide additional context and early warning indicators that might otherwise be missed.

In bilateral relationship management, AI serves as a powerful support tool for tracking and analyzing diplomatic engagements. AI systems can maintain comprehensive relationship maps showing connections between political figures, summarize past interactions, and suggest optimal timing for diplomatic outreach based on historical patterns. Throughout negotiation periods, AI can provide analysis of discussion points, cross-reference historical agreements, and identify potential areas of common ground—all while the political officer focuses on the nuanced human elements of the exchange.

Implementation challenges include ensuring data privacy, managing algorithmic bias, and maintaining the primacy of human judgment in sensitive political matters. Political officers must be trained to effectively integrate AI insights into their analysis while recognizing its limitations. Success requires balancing technological capabilities with traditional diplomatic skills—using AI to enhance rather than replace the cultural understanding and relationship-building that define effective political work.

Looking ahead, emerging AI capabilities in predictive analytics and scenario modeling offer new possibilities for political officers. These tools could help simulate the potential impacts of policy decisions, forecast political developments with greater accuracy, and identify opportunities for diplomatic engagement before they become apparent through traditional analysis. However, the core of political work remains fundamentally human—AI serves as an enabler for more informed, proactive, and effective political diplomacy.

We'll explore how AI is transforming political analysis and bilateral diplomacy in Chapter 3, where we'll examine the intersection of AI and political affairs in detail.

AI AND ECONOMIC DIPLOMACY: STRENGTHENING TRADE NETWORKS AND ECONOMIC ANALYSIS FOR POLICY FORMATION

Economic officers focus on building and maintaining positive economic and trade relations between nations, analyzing market conditions, and promoting commercial interests. While their role traditionally relies on economic expertise and relationship-building within government ministries and business communities, AI now provides powerful tools to enhance their analytical capabilities and decision-making processes.

AI transforms economic analysis through its ability to process complex market data and identify subtle economic trends. Economic officers can leverage AI systems to analyze trade flows, monitor currency fluctuations, and detect early warning signs of market instability. For example, AI platforms can simultaneously track multiple economic indicators across different markets, identify supply chain vulnerabilities, and forecast potential economic impacts of policy changes. These capabilities help officers provide more precise and timely economic recommendations to their missions.

In trade promotion and negotiation, AI serves as a valuable support tool by modeling complex trade scenarios and identifying optimal negotiating positions. AI systems can analyze historical trade data, simulate the effects of proposed agreements, and highlight potential opportunities for mutual benefit. During trade discussions, AI can provide real-time analysis of proposed terms, evaluate their potential impact across different economic sectors, and suggest alternative approaches based on successful past agreements.

Implementation challenges include ensuring data accuracy, managing information overload, and maintaining human oversight in complex economic decisions. Economic officers must learn to effectively integrate AI insights while recognizing that local market knowledge and relationship-building remain essential. Success requires balancing technological capabilities with traditional economic diplomacy skills—using AI to enhance rather than replace the nuanced understanding of market dynamics and business relationships.

Looking ahead, emerging AI capabilities in predictive economics and automated market analysis offer new possibilities for economic officers. These tools could help simulate long-term economic impacts, identify emerging market opportunities, and optimize resource allocation for trade promotion activities. However, the fundamental role of building trust and understanding between economic partners remains distinctly human—AI serves as a tool to enable more informed and effective economic diplomacy.

We'll provide an in-depth analysis of AI's impact on economic diplomacy in Chapter 4, where we'll examine everything from trade negotiations to financial forecasting and development planning.

AI AND MANAGEMENT AFFAIRS: STREAMLINING MISSION OPERATIONS AND RESOURCE MANAGEMENT

Management officers serve as the operational backbone of diplomatic missions, handling everything from real estate and personnel to budgets and logistics. As action-oriented leaders who develop solutions in fast-paced environments, their role increasingly benefits from AI's ability to streamline complex operations and predict resource needs.

AI can transform mission management through automated systems that optimize resource allocation and facility operations. Management officers can leverage AI platforms to monitor building systems, track inventory, forecast maintenance needs, and manage personnel schedules. For example, AI systems have the potential to analyze patterns in facility usage to optimize energy consumption, predict equipment failures before they occur, and suggest adjustments to staffing levels based on workload patterns. These capabilities could help officers maintain efficient operations while reducing costs and preventing disruptions.

In budget and personnel management, AI serves as a powerful planning tool by analyzing spending patterns and workforce needs. AI systems can process complex financial data, identify potential cost savings, and suggest optimal resource allocation strategies. During budget planning cycles, AI can provide real-time analysis of spending trends, forecast future needs based on historical patterns, and identify areas where resources might be better utilized. The technology can also assist in HR functions by analyzing staffing patterns, predicting turnover, and optimizing training programs.

While implementation challenges include system security, data privacy, and balancing automation with human oversight in diplomatic decisions, emerging AI capabilities in predictive maintenance and workflow management offer opportunities to create more resilient and efficient diplomatic facilities with reduced costs—though the core responsibility of ensuring smooth mission operations remains human-centered, requiring judgment and cultural sensitivity.

We'll comprehensively examine how AI is revolutionizing diplomatic mission management in Chapter 5, where we'll explore these operational transformations in detail.

AI AND CONSULAR AFFAIRS: ADVANCING CITIZEN SERVICES AND VISA PROCESSING WHILE COMBATING FRAUD

Consular officers provide vital services to both citizens abroad and foreign nationals seeking entry, handling everything from emergency assistance to visa processing. While their role demands strong interpersonal skills and quick thinking in crises, AI now offers powerful tools to enhance service delivery while maintaining security and fraud prevention.

AI transforms visa processing and document verification through advanced pattern recognition and fraud detection. Consular officers can leverage AI systems to screen visa applications, verify supporting documents, and identify potential security concerns. For example, AI platforms can analyze biometric data, cross-reference multiple databases simultaneously, and flag suspicious patterns that might indicate fraudulent applications. These capabilities can help officers process legitimate requests more efficiently while maintaining robust security screening.

In citizen services and crisis response, AI has great potential as a critical support tool for managing emergencies and coordinating assistance. AI systems can monitor global events affecting citizens abroad, predict potential crisis areas, and optimize emergency response resources. During crises, AI can help track affected citizens, coordinate evacuation plans, and manage communication with multiple stakeholders. The technology can also assist in routine services by automating appointment scheduling, document processing, and general inquiries through intelligent chatbots.

Implementation challenges include ensuring algorithm fairness, protecting sensitive personal data, and maintaining the human touch in citizen services. Consular officers must balance automation with the need for human judgment in complex cases. Success requires integrating AI capabilities while preserving the empathy and cultural sensitivity essential to consular work, particularly in emergency situations or cases involving vulnerable individuals.

Looking ahead, emerging AI capabilities in predictive analytics and automated processing offer new possibilities for consular operations. These tools could help create more efficient and accessible consular services while strengthening security measures. However, the core mission of protecting and serving citizens remains fundamentally human—AI serves as an enabler for more effective and secure consular operations.

We'll delve deeper into the intersection of AI and consular operations in Chapter 6, where we'll examine innovations in citizen services, visa processing, and crisis response.

AI AND PUBLIC AFFAIRS: AMPLIFYING CULTURAL ENGAGEMENT AND STRATEGIC COMMUNICATIONS ACROSS GLOBAL AUDIENCES

Public diplomacy officers serve as the voice and face of diplomacy abroad, explaining values, policies, and culture to foreign audiences through media engagement and cultural programs. While their role centers on building human connections and understanding, AI now provides sophisticated tools to enhance outreach effectiveness and measure public engagement.

AI can transform public communication through advanced sentiment analysis and content optimization. Public diplomacy officers can leverage AI systems to monitor global media coverage, analyze public sentiment across multiple languages, and identify emerging narratives. For example, AI platforms can track social media discussions, assess the impact of public diplomacy initiatives, and suggest optimal timing and channels for message delivery. These capabilities help officers craft more effective communication strategies while maintaining authentic engagement with local audiences.

In cultural and educational program management, AI serves as a valuable tool for targeting outreach and measuring impact. AI systems can analyze participation patterns, identify underserved communities, and optimize program delivery for maximum effect. During cultural events or educational exchanges, AI can help track engagement metrics, suggest program modifications based on participant feedback, and identify opportunities for expanding reach. The technology can also assist in managing alumni networks and maintaining long-term relationships with program participants.

Implementation challenges include avoiding algorithmic bias in audience targeting, maintaining message authenticity, and balancing automation with personal engagement. Public diplomacy officers must ensure AI tools enhance rather than diminish the human element of cultural diplomacy. Success requires integrating technological capabilities while preserving the genuine relationship-building that defines effective public diplomacy.

Looking ahead, emerging AI capabilities in predictive analytics and personalized content delivery offer new possibilities for public diplomacy. These tools could help create more targeted and impactful outreach while better measuring program effectiveness. However, the core mission of building cross-cultural understanding remains distinctly human—AI serves as an enabler for more strategic and effective public diplomacy.

We'll provide an extensive analysis of how AI is reshaping public diplomacy in Chapter 7, where we'll examine everything from digital engagement to cultural exchange programs.

AI AND DIPLOMATIC SECURITY: INTEGRATING LAW ENFORCEMENT AND SECURITY OPERATIONS FOR MISSION PROTECTION

Diplomatic security service agents combine law enforcement duties with diplomatic security management, protecting personnel, facilities, and information worldwide. While their role demands hands-on security expertise and quick decision-making, AI now provides advanced capabilities to enhance threat detection and emergency response.

AI is transforming security operations through integrated surveillance and threat analysis. Security officers can leverage AI systems to monitor multiple data streams simultaneously, from physical security cameras to cyber threat indicators. For example, AI platforms can analyze patterns in facility access, detect unusual behavior, and correlate physical and digital security events that might signal coordinated threats. These capabilities can help agents identify potential security risks before they materialize while reducing false alarms.

In investigations and protective operations, AI serves as a critical support tool for threat assessment and resource deployment. AI systems can process vast amounts of intelligence data, identify patterns in criminal behavior, and optimize security coverage based on risk analysis. During high-profile events or crisis situations, AI can help coordinate response teams, track multiple threat vectors simultaneously, and provide real-time situational awareness. The technology can also assist in passport and visa fraud investigations by detecting sophisticated forgery patterns and tracking criminal networks.

Implementation challenges include ensuring system reliability, maintaining operational security, and balancing automation with human judgment in critical security decisions. Security officers must integrate AI capabilities while preserving the flexibility to respond to unexpected threats and unique security situations. Success requires combining technological tools with traditional security expertise and cultural awareness.

Looking ahead, emerging AI capabilities in predictive threat analysis and automated response systems offer new possibilities for diplomatic security. These tools could help create more resilient and proactive security operations while optimizing resource allocation. However, the core mission of protecting diplomatic personnel and facilities remains fundamentally human—AI serves as an enabler for more effective and comprehensive security operations.

We'll explore AI's role in enhancing diplomatic security operations in-depth in Chapter 8, where we'll examine these critical developments in detail.

AI AND DIPLOMATIC TECHNOLOGY: SECURING GLOBAL COMMUNICATIONS AND INFRASTRUCTURE FOR MODERN DIPLOMACY

Diplomatic technology professionals manage the technological foundation of modern diplomacy, overseeing everything from secure communications networks to cybersecurity systems. While their role traditionally focuses on maintaining technical infrastructure, AI now offers powerful tools to enhance network security, optimize systems, and predict technological needs.

AI transforms infrastructure management through predictive maintenance and automated system monitoring. Diplomatic technology professionals can leverage AI systems to analyze network traffic patterns, detect potential system failures, and optimize performance across multiple platforms. For example, AI can monitor communication systems for anomalies, predict bandwidth requirements during high-traffic periods, and automatically adjust system configurations to maintain optimal performance. These capabilities allow for more reliable and secure diplomatic communications and can help prevent disruptions to service.

In cybersecurity and information protection, AI serves as a critical defense tool by identifying and responding to threats in real time. AI systems can analyze patterns in network activity, detect potential breaches, and automatically implement security protocols. During cyber incidents, AI could help to isolate affected systems, track attack vectors, and coordinate response efforts across multiple locations. The technology also has the potential to assist in managing secure communications during high-level diplomatic events by dynamically adjusting security measures based on threat levels.

Implementation challenges include maintaining system integrity, ensuring compatibility across diverse platforms, and balancing security with accessibility. Diplomatic technology professionals must carefully integrate AI capabilities while preserving the reliability and security essential to diplomatic operations. Success will require combining technological innovation with strict security protocols and operational requirements.

Looking ahead, emerging AI capabilities in autonomous system management and advanced threat detection offer new possibilities for diplomatic technology. These tools could help create more resilient and adaptive technological infrastructure while strengthening cybersecurity measures. However, the core responsibility of maintaining secure and reliable diplomatic communications remains human-centered—AI serves as an enabler for more effective and secure technological operations.

We'll provide a comprehensive analysis of how AI is transforming diplomatic technology infrastructure and cybersecurity practices in Chapter 9.

AUTONOMOUS SYSTEMS: CLARIFYING AI VS. AUTOMATION IN DIPLOMACY

At this point, some readers—especially those familiar with technology—may have already noticed something important: not every diplomatic use case described as "AI" in popular conversations truly requires AI. In fact, as technical specialists often remind us, many embassy functions can be effectively addressed by simpler "automation" —systems that rely on clearly defined, repetitive tasks without advanced AI capabilities.

Why does this technical distinction matter for diplomats? Simply put: using AI where automation would suffice might unnecessarily complicate operations, inflate budgets, or introduce avoidable risks. Conversely, misunderstanding what genuinely demands AI's adaptive and predictive strengths could mean missing opportunities for valuable foresight and agility.

Given this practical concern, let's briefly clarify the difference between AI and automation—and why recognizing this difference can significantly benefit diplomatic decision-makers.

Many diplomatic innovations indeed rely heavily on automation, not necessarily AI. Automated systems handle structured, rule-based tasks, improving efficiency without requiring AI's adaptive capabilities (Kiggins 2018). However, when tasks involve uncertainty, pattern recognition, or assisting decision-making in complex scenarios, AI becomes essential. Understanding this distinction can help diplomatic technology officers assess when AI is truly necessary.

Automation excels in high-volume, repetitive tasks with clear parameters (Kiggins 2018). For instance, visa and passport processing can be streamlined through rule-based systems that verify documents, cross-check databases, and flag discrepancies without requiring AI. Similarly, crisis communication alerts can be managed through automated protocols that distribute emergency messages across an embassy network. Operational logistics, including scheduling diplomatic meetings, tracking resources, and managing consular requests, can also be handled effectively by automation without the need for AI-driven adaptation.

However, AI becomes critical when situations require pattern recognition, adaptability, or predictive insights in uncertain conditions. Crisis forecasting, for example, relies on AI's ability to analyze satellite imagery, news reports, and social media trends to identify statistical patterns correlated with political instability or humanitarian crises (Manor 2017, 2019, 2024). In security operations, AI-powered surveillance can flag unusual patterns in embassy activity, assisting security teams in identifying potential threats (Kiggins 2018). Public diplomacy also benefits from AI, as sentiment analysis tools can process large-scale digital discourse, detecting shifts in public opinion that influence diplomatic strategy (Manor 2017, 2019, 2024).

While automation enhances efficiency, AI adds foresight and adaptability, allowing diplomats to anticipate crises, improve security, and engage in data-driven decision-making (Kiggins 2018). The key question is whether a given task requires AI or whether automation is sufficient. Those responsible for procuring and building technology infrastructure for diplomats must make strategic choices, ensuring that AI is applied where it provides real value rather than being used in cases where automation alone would be effective.

Since this book is largely exploratory, we will not explicitly distinguish between automation and AI in every use case. However, readers should recognize that many innovations can be implemented with just automation rather than AI. Over time, these innovations may evolve, blending into AI developments as diplomatic technology advances. The examples provided assume an understanding that AI and automation are often interconnected, with automation serving as a foundation upon which AI capabilities are built.

THE ETHICAL IMPERATIVE: BALANCING PROGRESS WITH PRINCIPLES

The integration of AI into diplomacy presents both unprecedented opportunities and significant ethical challenges. This intersection demands a careful balance between technological innovation and moral responsibility, guided by clear principles and robust oversight.

At the heart of AI deployment in diplomacy lies the fundamental question of governance: Who holds the authority to determine how these powerful tools should be used? This decision-making process must prioritize human dignity, privacy protection, and equitable access. Success requires the collaborative expertise of ethicists, technologists, and diplomats working together to design systems that are transparent, inclusive, and fair. Otherwise, we must carefully consider the purpose of integrating AI into diplomacy—ensuring that it augments human decision-making rather than replacing it entirely.

AI-driven diplomatic systems have the potential to routinely process vast amounts of sensitive information, from classified documents to personal consular data (Haseley et al. 2023, Collins 2024). This creates an imperative for robust data security protocols and privacy safeguards. Moreover, these systems must be protected against potential breaches that could compromise diplomatic operations or individual privacy.

AI systems can inherit biases from their training data, potentially leading to skewed diplomatic decisions (Höne et al. 2019, Kiggins 2018). Consider a scenario where AI monitors human rights abuses: false positives could trigger unnecessary interventions, while missed violations could result in failed humanitarian responses.

To address these risks, organizations would surely need to implement regular audits and maintain consistent human oversight of AI tools.

The path forward requires establishing a comprehensive framework that ensures AI serves diplomacy's highest ideals. This means:

- Developing transparent systems that can be scrutinized and understood
- Creating accountability mechanisms for AI-driven decisions
- Maintaining human judgment in critical diplomatic processes
- Regularly assessing and updating ethical guidelines as technology evolves

By embracing these principles, diplomats can harness AI's potential while ensuring it remains a force for good in international relations, elevating rather than compromising diplomatic work.

International frameworks, such as the Organisation for Economic Co-operation and Development (OECD) AI Principles, the European Union's (EU) AI Act, and the United States' Executive Order on Safe, Secure, and Trustworthy Artificial Intelligence, have sought to offer guidelines on transparency, fairness, and accountability in AI deployment. By adopting similar principles, diplomatic institutions can mitigate risks associated with bias and misuse of AI, ensuring that technological advancements align with universal human values and ethical standards. Establishing such governance frameworks will be critical for maintaining trust in AI-driven diplomatic processes. The process is ongoing and likely to be in constant evolution.

HISTORICAL AI USE CASE EXAMPLES IN DIPLOMACY

AI is rapidly evolving from a speculative technological frontier to an applied tool in diplomacy. Over the past two decades, governments worldwide have begun to integrate AI into their workforce policies and procedures, leveraging its capabilities to navigate complex global challenges. From augmenting decision-making processes in executive leadership to enhancing operational efficiency in consular services, AI has shown great potential as a versatile and powerful asset. However, its adoption has not been without ethical and operational challenges, including concerns over transparency, data privacy, and algorithmic bias (Manor 2023).

The historical integration of AI into diplomacy can be broadly categorized into several key areas which will come up throughout this book. In executive leadership, AI is being designed to support leaders by providing predictive analytics, streamlining resource allocation, and optimizing decision-making during crises (State Department AI Inventory 2024). In political affairs, AI is being applied to empower governments to counter disinformation campaigns, track public sentiment, and manage the nuances of public diplomacy (Pearson & Burgess 2023). Similarly, in economic diplomacy, AI is being brought to bear on facilitating trade negotiations, improving resource distribution, and supporting sustainable development initiatives (United Nations Development Programme [UNDP] 2020).

The U.S. government is increasingly using AI to advance its diplomatic and foreign policy objectives. In December 2024, the White House reported over 2,000 AI use cases across 41 federal agencies, including the Department of State and the

Department of Homeland Security. The State Department employs AI for managing international communication, streamlining visa processing, and enhancing fraud detection, while Homeland Security leverages it for border security and trade monitoring (Office of Management and Budget 2024, State Department AI Inventory 2024). AI is also playing a growing role in diplomatic security—both physical and cyber—by safeguarding sensitive information and protecting personnel (Kello 2023). Additionally, it supports embassy management and crisis communication, further integrating AI into core diplomatic operations (State Department AI Inventory 2024).

These efforts reflect the U.S. government's commitment to using AI responsibly and transparently, ensuring technologies support both domestic and international goals. To protect these systems, the Cybersecurity and Infrastructure Security Agency (CISA) has introduced new guidelines for securing cloud environments, an essential step in safeguarding sensitive data used in diplomatic and international operations (Alder 2025). For diplomats, this growing reliance on AI highlights its potential to streamline operations, improve decision-making, and enhance international engagement, making it a powerful tool for advancing U.S. foreign policy.

As reported in FedScoop, "StateChat," launched by the U.S. Department of State in August 2024, is an AI-powered chatbot designed to enhance operational efficiency and streamline routine tasks for the department's 75,000-strong global workforce (Alder 2024). Developed in collaboration with Palantir and powered by Azure OpenAI, StateChat operates within a secure, unclassified environment tailored to the department's unique requirements, ensuring sensitive data remains protected. The chatbot assists employees with drafting emails, translating documents, summarizing information, and brainstorming policy ideas, saving the workforce tens of thousands of hours since its introduction. This initiative reflects the Department's continued efforts to integrate AI into daily operations, allowing staff to focus on high-value diplomatic tasks.

In addition to StateChat, the State Department has deployed other AI tools as part of its broader modernization agenda. "Northstar," an AI tool designed for media monitoring, processes up to a million articles daily in over 100 languages. It synthesizes and translates content to provide real-time insights into the global information space, aiding public diplomacy officers in countering disinformation and shaping narratives. Another tool, "FamSearch," offers employees quick access to the department's Foreign Affairs Manual and related policies, making it easier to find critical information efficiently (U.S. Department of State 2025a, 2025b).

Despite these promising developments, applied AI's integration into diplomacy is just in its infancy and raises critical questions about its limitations. Historical cases reveal scenarios where over-reliance on AI has led to unintended consequences, underscoring the necessity of retaining human oversight (Huang 2022). Lessons from these experiences highlight the importance of ethical governance, interdisciplinary collaboration, and capacity-building to ensure AI is deployed responsibly and effectively (Kello 2024).

Throughout this recurring section of this book, we will look at some historical AI use cases across key dimensions of diplomacy, drawing on examples from around the globe. By examining these AI applications, we can get an early glimpse of AI's transformative potential while acknowledging its challenges and limitations.

AI'S TRANSFORMATION OF DIPLOMACY: A GLOBAL SHIFT

The integration of AI into diplomacy is more than just a technological shift—it represents a profound evolution in how nations interact, cooperate, and address global challenges (Kissinger, Schmidt, & Huttenlocher 2021, Kissinger et al. 2024). AI has already transformed decision-making, negotiations, and intelligence gathering, but as the technology advances, it opens the door to even more groundbreaking possibilities, including quantum AI, decentralized governance models, and AI-powered outer space diplomacy.

One of the most promising frontiers is quantum AI, which combines the power of quantum computing with AI (Viggiano 2023, Der Derian & Wendt 2022). Unlike traditional AI, quantum AI can process massive datasets at an unprecedented scale, one day allowing diplomats to simulate and optimize complex multilateral negotiations. For instance, in global trade negotiations, a quantum AI platform could model thousands of potential scenarios simultaneously, factoring in economic, geopolitical, and cultural considerations to craft agreements that maximize long-term stability.

As international relations grow increasingly complex, AI-powered governance models are reshaping how nations collaborate on critical challenges like climate change, cybersecurity, and global health (Lebedeva & Zinovieva 2023). AI platforms could accelerate climate negotiations by analyzing satellite data to verify compliance with emission targets or pinpointing regions where Sustainable Development Goals (SDGs) are falling behind (Spry 2024, United Nations 2015, Buch et al. 2022). In cybersecurity, a decentralized AI governance system could act as a global clearinghouse for threats, collecting and analyzing security risks across borders (Kello 2023, Minchev 2023, Simić 2021).

As humanity ventures deeper into space, AI could become an essential tool for interplanetary governance (Kissinger, Schmidt, & Huttenlocher 2021, Kissinger et al. 2024). AI-driven platforms could help mediate agreements on asteroid mining rights, ensuring fair distribution of extraterrestrial resources through analysis of satellite imaging, geological surveys, and international treaties. Science fiction is fast becoming science fact.

While these AI-driven innovations could reshape diplomacy, they also introduce new risks and ethical dilemmas surrounding bias, fairness, accountability, and unintended consequences (Höne 2019, Kiggins 2018). International institutions must establish robust oversight frameworks to ensure AI-driven diplomacy remains ethical, transparent, and aligned with democratic values. Yet, the heart of this transformation remains human. Diplomats, as stewards of trust and cooperation, must navigate this new terrain with integrity, empathy, and strategic vision—using AI as a tool to enhance decision-making while preserving the human relationships that underpin global engagement (Kissinger, Schmidt, & Huttenlocher 2021, Kissinger et al. 2024).

HOW DIPLOMATS MUST ADAPT TO AI

While the tools of diplomacy are evolving rapidly, the heart of diplomacy remains unchanged: its reliance on human values, judgment, and connection (Baines 2024,

Kissinger et al. 2021). For diplomats to thrive in this AI-enhanced world, they must adapt their skill sets and embrace a mindset that balances technological innovation with ethical responsibility. This begins with building AI literacy. Training programs must equip diplomats with the knowledge to understand AI's capabilities, limitations, and broader implications (Baines 2024, Broustau & Neihouser 2021, Grottola 2021). Workshops and scenario-based exercises can prepare them to use AI tools effectively, whether analyzing geopolitical trends, crafting public messages, or responding to global crises.

Ethical considerations must also take center stage from the outset. As AI becomes more embedded in diplomatic processes, the potential for misuse or unintended consequences grows rapidly (Roumate 2021a, 2021b). For example, an AI tool designed to monitor refugee movements should ideally be transparent and fair, ensuring that it respects privacy and human dignity. Diplomatic missions can address these challenges by collaborating with technologists, ethicists, and civil society to design systems that prioritize inclusivity, accountability, and the protection of vulnerable populations.

LARGE LANGUAGE MODELS: TRANSFORMING DIPLOMATIC WORK

Let's shift gears and discuss a range of practical tools for immediate use. Large Language Models (LLMs) represent a breakthrough in AI with particular relevance for diplomacy. These sophisticated AI systems—including ChatGPT, Claude, Gemini, and DeepSeek—learn from vast amounts of text data to understand and generate human-like language. Unlike earlier AI tools, LLMs can engage in nuanced dialogue, understand context, and adapt their responses to diplomatic needs.

These systems excel at processing large volumes of information, working across multiple languages, and supporting content generation. Their ability to analyze policy documents, media reports, and historical treaties while maintaining awareness of diplomatic protocol makes them particularly valuable for foreign affairs work. In strategic planning, LLMs can synthesize geopolitical trends, identify patterns in successful negotiations, and generate scenarios for consideration. During crises, they assist by analyzing open-source information in real time and helping draft preliminary response options.

In communication, LLMs enhance diplomatic efforts through translation support, message drafting, and cultural context adaptation. Tools like Perplexity AI, with its focus on delivering fact-based answers and citations, could also prove invaluable for verifying information and ensuring accuracy in high-stakes scenarios. Additionally, systems like Gemini are well-suited for multilingual tasks, while Claude's strength lies in analyzing and synthesizing long, complex documents.

As LLMs evolve, they are beginning to integrate multimodal capabilities, like those found in OpenAI's GPT-4, which can process both text and visual information. This trend could prove transformative for diplomacy, enabling AI to analyze maps, charts, and other visual materials alongside textual data to provide a more comprehensive understanding of critical issues.

However, their effectiveness depends on understanding their limitations. LLMs operate based on training data that may not reflect current events, require verification of outputs, and should never handle classified or sensitive diplomatic information—unless your organization has a proprietary system that permits it. Additionally, ethical considerations—such as bias, misinformation, and the environmental impact of AI training—must be addressed to ensure their responsible use in diplomacy.

To maximize benefits while managing risks, diplomatic institutions should treat all LLM outputs as drafts requiring human review, restrict usage to what could wind up as public information, and maintain clear protocols for appropriate tasks. Regular training ensures diplomatic staff can effectively leverage these tools while preserving security and confidentiality.

The role of LLMs is to augment rather than replace diplomatic judgment. By handling routine analysis and drafting tasks, they free diplomats to focus on essential relationship-building, complex negotiations, and cultural engagement. As these systems evolve into more autonomous, goal-directed tools, their support role will likely expand, but always under the guidance of skilled diplomatic professionals who understand both their capabilities and limitations. Success lies in balancing technological advantages with the human elements that remain central to diplomatic work.

PUTTING LLMS TO WORK IN DIPLOMACY

Now that we understand what LLMs like ChatGPT, Claude, and Gemini are capable of, the question becomes: how do we actually use them effectively in diplomatic work? The key lies in how we communicate with these AI tools—a practice known as prompt engineering. Think of it as the diplomatic protocol for interacting with AI.

Just as diplomatic communication requires clarity and structure, so does interacting with LLMs. When you open ChatGPT, Claude, or Gemini, you're essentially beginning a conversation with a highly capable digital assistant. The quality of its help will depend largely on how you frame your requests. Consider a common diplomatic task: preparing talking points for a bilateral meeting. A diplomat might open ChatGPT and type: "Give me talking points for my meeting." This is akin to walking into your office and asking a colleague, "Help me with my meeting," without providing any context.

Instead, you might say:

> I need to prepare for a bilateral meeting with [Country X] about technology cooperation. This is our first high-level meeting on this topic. Our goals are to establish a framework for cybersecurity collaboration while addressing their recent concerns about data privacy. Please help me draft talking points that acknowledge their concerns, highlight our capabilities, and suggest concrete areas for cooperation while leaving room for negotiation.

Let's see how this works in practice. Imagine you need to draft a response to public criticism about your embassy's visa processing times. You might begin by telling the LLM:

> Our embassy is facing public criticism about visa processing delays. The average wait time has increased from 2 weeks to 6 weeks due to staffing shortages and a 50% increase in applications. We need to acknowledge the problem while maintaining public confidence.

After receiving an initial draft, you can refine it by asking for more specific time-lines, warmer language, or relevant statistics.

While ChatGPT, Claude, and Gemini share many capabilities, they each have their strengths. ChatGPT excels at creative approaches to diplomatic challenges and can search the web for resources and answers. Claude is particularly good at careful analysis of complex diplomatic documents and nuanced language. Gemini is integrated with Google Suite and demonstrates strength in working across multiple languages and analyzing visual materials, while tools like Perplexity AI offer accuracy through fact-based responses and citations.

To use these tools effectively, provide clear context about the diplomatic situation, specify your audience, and treat their outputs as drafts rather than final products. These LLMs are assistants, not replacements for diplomatic judgment. They can help generate initial drafts, analyze situations from multiple angles, brainstorm approaches to negotiations, and prepare briefing materials—but always under human oversight.

Consider a final example in crisis communication. When preparing a response to a natural disaster affecting your citizens abroad, you might tell the LLM:

> We need to prepare crisis communications regarding an earthquake affecting our citizens in [Country X]. We have confirmed 3 citizens are injured and 50 are displaced. Help me draft a public announcement that is factual, empathetic, and includes clear action points.

After receiving the draft, you can refine it by requesting specific additions or adjustments to tone and content.

The power of tools like ChatGPT, Claude, Gemini, and Perplexity AI in diplomacy comes not from their ability to replace human judgment but from their capacity to enhance it. By approaching them with clear purpose and attention to detail—just as you would any diplomatic interaction—they can become valuable allies in your work, helping you analyze situations, draft communications, and prepare for engagements more effectively. The key is to be clear in your requests, iterative in your approach, and always mindful that these tools are meant to support, not replace, diplomatic expertise.

ADVANCED AI USE CASES FOR AN AI-ENHANCED EMBASSY

Advanced AI has the potential to revolutionize diplomatic work beyond what current language models can do. In this section, we explore practical examples of how AI could transform diplomacy, examining each case through three lenses: its core purpose, specific capabilities, and implementation challenges. We focus on how AI can address common diplomatic challenges like managing overwhelming amounts of information, coordinating fragmented communications, and accelerating decision-making processes. For example, AI systems could provide real-time analysis of diplomatic exchanges, track international sentiment automatically, and synthesize data from multiple sources to support faster, better-informed decisions.

Practical implementation of these tools involves thoughtful integration into diplomatic workflows. Success depends on identifying appropriate technologies, training staff, and aligning AI functionality with specific diplomatic needs. These systems have immense potential to streamline operations, improve responsiveness, and enhance strategic planning. However, challenges such as data biases, system errors, and ethical dilemmas must be addressed through careful oversight and regular evaluation.

Central to these use cases is the collaboration between human diplomats and AI systems. While AI excels at processing vast datasets and identifying patterns, human expertise ensures that these insights are applied with cultural sensitivity, strategic vision, and ethical judgment. AI tools amplify human capabilities, enabling diplomats to focus on nuanced tasks such as negotiation and relationship-building.

Equally important are the ethical and governance frameworks that guide the responsible use of AI. Transparency, accountability, and fairness must be at the core of these deployments to maintain trust and align with diplomatic values. Safeguards, including audits and compliance with privacy standards, are vital to ensuring AI systems uphold these principles.

These use cases were selected on the basis of their near-term to mid-term adoption potential. Hopefully, they will inspire you to consider other use cases to suit your unique circumstances. The possibilities are endless. This is just a starting place.

COMPREHENSIVE PREDICTIVE ANALYTICS FOR CRISIS MANAGEMENT

It's like having a crystal ball that warns embassies about upcoming crises by analyzing news, social media, and internal reports.

Anticipating crises is a persistent challenge for embassies, as traditional methods rely on fragmented data and human intuition. This limits timely decision-making in dynamic scenarios like political unrest, economic instability, or environmental crises. AI-powered predictive analytics addresses this by integrating diverse data sources—your internal mission reports or cables, financial trends, social media sentiment, and media coverage—to provide comprehensive and accurate forecasts.

Practical applications include identifying early signs of civil unrest or economic instability, enabling proactive engagement to mitigate risks. For instance, an embassy in a volatile region could use AI to detect emerging protests and engage stakeholders to prevent escalation. Implementation requires integrating AI tools into intelligence workflows, training staff, and validating accuracy through pilot programs tailored to regional contexts.

Challenges include data biases that can produce flawed predictions and the risk of overlooking cultural nuances. Ethical oversight is vital for transparency and trust, while human expertise ensures contextual understanding and effective action. By combining AI with diplomatic judgment, embassies can enhance crisis management, enabling timely and informed interventions that strengthen international stability.

REAL-TIME SENTIMENT AND PUBLIC OPINION MONITORING

A digital ear to the ground that tells embassies what people are really thinking and feeling about them right now.

Keeping pace with public sentiment is essential for managing a country's image and addressing misinformation effectively. Traditional methods of monitoring public opinion are slow and often insufficient for real-time challenges. AI-powered tools analyze social media, public forums, and news sources in real time, providing immediate insights into trends and sentiment shifts, enabling embassies to respond quickly and strategically.

Practical applications include identifying and countering misinformation or misunderstandings about embassy policies. For example, during a public diplomacy campaign, AI might detect rising negative sentiment around a specific initiative, prompting immediate adjustments to messaging. Implementation requires training communication staff to use sentiment analysis tools and integrating AI-generated insights into existing workflows for public engagement.

Challenges include the potential for AI to misinterpret cultural nuances, leading to flawed conclusions. Human oversight is crucial to refine AI findings and ensure responses are culturally appropriate and impactful. By combining AI with diplomatic expertise, embassies can enhance public engagement, adapt swiftly to public sentiment, and build trust through timely, informed communication strategies.

DYNAMIC ECONOMIC IMPACT ANALYSIS

Your embassy's financial weather forecast – predicting economic storms before they hit.

Economic diplomacy depends on accurate, real-time insights into market dynamics, which traditional methods often fail to provide. AI-powered tools analyze currency fluctuations, trade trends, and investment flows, equipping economic officers with timely data to recommend effective interventions. This enhances the ability of embassies to respond proactively to economic challenges and opportunities.

For example, an embassy could use AI to identify a sharp decline in commodity prices that threatens local economic stability, enabling swift recommendations for trade agreements or targeted investment strategies. Effective implementation requires partnerships with reliable financial data providers and ensuring AI tools integrate seamlessly into existing systems and workflows.

Challenges include potential inaccuracies during unprecedented market conditions and the need for careful contextual interpretation. Economic officers' expertise is essential to refine AI-driven insights and ensure balanced, ethical decisions that adhere to financial regulations. By integrating AI with their judgment, embassies can strengthen economic diplomacy, improve decision-making, and respond quickly to evolving market conditions.

AUTOMATED INFORMATION SYNTHESIS AND BRIEFING SUPPORT

TL;DR for diplomats – turning information overload into bite-sized briefings that matter.

Senior diplomats often face information overload, making it challenging to extract relevant insights quickly. AI addresses this by synthesizing data from diverse sources into concise, tailored briefings, enabling leaders to focus on strategic priorities rather than sorting through excessive details. This improves efficiency and supports better-informed decision-making.

For example, an ambassador preparing for negotiations can use AI to identify key developments in the host country's policies and highlight areas of mutual interest. Effective implementation requires integrating AI tools with existing information systems and training staff to interpret and apply AI-generated briefs effectively in their workflows.

Challenges include the risk of AI overlooking critical nuances or misinterpreting complex issues. Diplomatic expertise remains essential to validate and enhance AI findings, ensuring that briefings are accurate and contextually appropriate. By combining AI with human judgment, embassies can save time, improve situational awareness, and enhance the strategic impact of their diplomatic engagements.

AI-Driven Media Monitoring and Narrative Shaping

Your embassy's reputation guardian – spotting and shaping stories before they go viral.

Navigating and shaping narratives across diverse media landscapes is a vital function of public diplomacy. AI tools streamline this process by analyzing trending stories, assessing their alignment with embassy objectives, and suggesting effective messaging strategies. This enables embassies to respond to emerging narratives with precision and agility.

For example, during a cultural exchange program, AI might identify narratives misrepresenting the embassy's intent and recommend counter-narratives or amplify positive stories that align with diplomatic goals. To implement these tools effectively, media officers must receive training on AI capabilities and integrate them into comprehensive communication strategies.

Challenges include ethical concerns around influencing public opinion and the potential misuse of AI tools. Human oversight is critical to ensure that messaging adheres to diplomatic values and respects principles like free speech. By combining AI-driven insights with human judgment, embassies can enhance narrative control, improve public engagement, and foster trust through transparent and culturally sensitive communication.

Advanced Security Perimeter Monitoring

A super-smart security guard that watches both physical and digital threats simultaneously.

Embassies face complex physical and digital security threats that traditionally require separate monitoring systems. AI integrates these domains, combining surveillance data and cybersecurity analytics to identify unusual activity and potential threats in real time. This unified approach strengthens security and improves threat response capabilities.

For example, AI could flag a coordinated phishing attack targeting embassy staff while simultaneously detecting unusual movement patterns near the compound. Effective implementation requires integrating AI tools with existing security systems and providing thorough training for security personnel to interpret and act on AI-generated alerts.

Challenges include managing false positives, which can strain resources, and building staff trust in automated systems. Ethical oversight is critical to ensure compliance with privacy laws and local regulations while maintaining transparency. By integrating AI-driven insights with human expertise, embassies can enhance both physical and digital security, enabling proactive and informed threat mitigation.

STREAMLINED VISA AND CONSULAR OPERATIONS

The diplomatic fast lane – making visa processing smoother and smarter.

Consular sections often face high volumes of repetitive tasks, such as visa application reviews, which can result in delays and inefficiencies. AI addresses these challenges by automating processes, detecting anomalies, predicting demand surges, and streamlining workflows. This enables embassies to handle operations more efficiently and improve service delivery.

For example, during peak travel seasons, AI can anticipate spikes in visa applications and allocate resources to minimize bottlenecks. Successful implementation requires integrating AI tools with existing visa management systems, ensuring data accuracy, and providing staff training to oversee and refine automated processes.

Challenges include addressing privacy concerns and ensuring algorithmic fairness, particularly in sensitive decisions. Consular officers remain essential for handling complex cases that require empathy, cultural understanding, and judgment. By combining AI-driven efficiency with human expertise, embassies can enhance operational performance and provide a better experience for applicants.

DATA-DRIVEN POLICY RECOMMENDATIONS

Like having a policy advisor that can see the future impacts of today's decisions.

Formulating effective policy often involves analyzing complex, interdependent variables that traditional methods struggle to evaluate efficiently. AI addresses this challenge by using historical data and predictive analytics to simulate scenarios and provide data-driven insights. This enables embassies to anticipate outcomes and make evidence-based decisions with greater confidence.

For instance, an embassy negotiating a trade agreement could use AI to forecast the economic and political impacts of proposed terms, supporting more informed decision-making. Implementation requires integrating AI simulation tools into policy development workflows and training staff to interpret and apply model outputs effectively.

Challenges include ensuring the reliability of AI predictions, which depend on data quality and model transparency. Diplomatic judgment remains critical for balancing quantitative insights with qualitative factors such as cultural and political context. Ethical considerations, including transparency about AI's role in decision-making, are vital to maintaining trust. By combining AI with diplomatic expertise, embassies can enhance policymaking with robust, evidence-based recommendations.

CRISIS RESPONSE AND COORDINATION PLATFORMS

> Your embassy's emergency response command center – coordinating help when every minute counts.

During emergencies, embassies face significant pressure to coordinate resources and provide timely support. AI enhances crisis response by mapping affected areas, predicting resource needs, and optimizing evacuation routes. This enables embassies to respond more efficiently and effectively during critical moments.

For example, during a natural disaster, AI can analyze satellite imagery and social media data to identify areas requiring immediate assistance. Successful implementation involves investing in AI-driven crisis management platforms, ensuring integration with local systems, and training emergency response teams to leverage these tools effectively.

Challenges include ensuring interoperability with local infrastructure and maintaining the accuracy of real-time data. Ethical considerations focus on prioritizing aid distribution fairly and transparently to uphold trust and equity. By combining AI capabilities with human expertise, embassies can enhance coordination, save lives, and reinforce their role as dependable partners in crisis situations.

ETHICAL AI OVERSIGHT MECHANISMS

> The AI watchdog that makes sure all other AI systems play by the rules.

As embassies increasingly integrate AI into their operations, ensuring its ethical deployment is essential for maintaining credibility and trust. AI can be leveraged to establish oversight mechanisms that audit tools for transparency, accountability, and privacy compliance, ensuring responsible use of sensitive data and adherence to diplomatic values. These mechanisms help embassies address ethical challenges proactively while demonstrating leadership in responsible AI use.

For example, an embassy using AI for stakeholder mapping must rely on these frameworks to ensure sensitive data is managed responsibly and ethically. Effective implementation involves embedding AI tools into governance structures, conducting regular audits of their operations, and adapting frameworks to address emerging ethical challenges. This ensures AI use aligns with both diplomatic goals and ethical standards.

Challenges include maintaining consistency across diverse applications and keeping pace with evolving ethical norms. By utilizing AI to strengthen oversight and demonstrating leadership in its responsible application, embassies can mitigate risks, set international benchmarks for ethical AI use, and reinforce their reputation as trusted stewards of technology in global relations.

LIMITATIONS AND FUTURE RESEARCH DIRECTIONS

As AI reshapes diplomatic practice, we must acknowledge both the boundaries of our current understanding and the critical questions that remain unanswered. This examination of limitations and future research directions serves not just to highlight gaps, but to chart a course for the thoughtful development of AI in diplomacy. By organizing these challenges into interconnected themes, we can better understand how they influence each other and identify promising avenues for future research.

STRUCTURAL CHALLENGES IN THE GLOBAL DIPLOMATIC LANDSCAPE

The integration of AI into diplomacy raises fundamental questions about power, access, and equity in international relations. Just as the telegraph once transformed diplomatic communications while creating new disparities between nations, AI threatens to reinforce or even expand existing power imbalances in the international system. Wealthy nations can invest in sophisticated AI systems and extensive data collection networks, while smaller diplomatic missions or developing nations may struggle to access even basic AI tools. This technological divide could reshape diplomatic relationships in ways that merit careful study.

Consider how this disparity might affect multilateral negotiations: when some parties have AI-enhanced capabilities for real-time analysis and others do not, how does this impact the balance of diplomatic discussions? Future research must examine not only how to make AI tools more accessible to all diplomatic actors but also how to prevent these technologies from becoming another vehicle for diplomatic inequality. This investigation should extend beyond mere access to technology, considering how different cultural approaches to AI might influence its diplomatic application.

SYSTEMS, SECURITY, AND SOVEREIGNTY

The growing dependency on AI systems in diplomatic work introduces new vulnerabilities that demand careful consideration. While AI can enhance crisis response and decision-making, overreliance on these systems could prove dangerous. Drawing a parallel to modern navigation, consider how many drivers have lost basic wayfinding skills due to GPS dependency. Similarly, diplomatic missions must maintain robust non-AI capabilities alongside their technological tools.

Data sovereignty emerges as a particularly complex challenge at the intersection of diplomacy and AI. When diplomatic missions deploy AI to analyze local information, they essentially process massive amounts of data about host countries, raising delicate questions about ownership, privacy, and national sovereignty. This creates tension between diplomatic needs and host country concerns about data control and security. Future research must explore frameworks for balancing these competing interests, perhaps through new international agreements or technical solutions like federated learning that allow for data analysis without direct data access.

THE HUMAN DIMENSION: PRESERVING DIPLOMATIC ART IN AN AGE OF ALGORITHMS

At the heart of effective diplomacy lies a deep understanding of human behavior, cultural nuance, and the strategic value of time itself. While AI excels at efficiency and pattern recognition, it may struggle with the intentional "inefficiencies" that often serve diplomatic purposes. A pause in negotiations might allow tensions to cool; a deliberately paced exchange might give relationships time to develop. Future research must examine how to design AI systems that recognize and respect these human elements of diplomacy rather than always pushing for immediate resolution or optimal efficiency.

Cross-cultural understanding presents perhaps the most nuanced challenge in AI-enhanced diplomacy. While current systems can translate languages with increasing accuracy, they often miss the layers of meaning embedded in diplomatic discourse. Consider how the concept of "saving face" operates differently in East Asian diplomatic contexts compared to Western ones, or how time-related phrases like "soon" or "under consideration" carry different diplomatic weight across cultures. These nuances, essential to diplomatic practice, resist simple algorithmic interpretation. Future research must explore how AI can be trained to recognize and navigate these cultural complexities without reducing them to oversimplified rules.

INSTITUTIONAL TRANSFORMATION AND PROFESSIONAL DEVELOPMENT

The integration of AI into diplomatic services raises profound questions about skill development and institutional knowledge. Just as spell-checking technology has affected our relationship with spelling, AI might influence how diplomatic judgment develops. This concern becomes particularly acute for junior diplomats who are still developing their diplomatic instincts. Future research should examine how diplomatic training can evolve to ensure that AI enhances rather than replaces human judgment.

The question of accountability in AI-assisted diplomatic decisions demands particular attention. In complex scenarios involving multiple parties—human diplomats, AI systems, and oversight mechanisms—how do we determine responsibility for outcomes? This becomes especially crucial in crisis situations where decisions carry significant consequences. Research must develop frameworks for maintaining clear lines of accountability while leveraging AI's capabilities.

ENVIRONMENTAL AND ETHICAL IMPLICATIONS

The environmental impact of AI deployment in diplomatic services represents an understudied dimension that demands attention. As diplomatic missions increasingly rely on AI systems, their energy consumption and carbon footprint grow. This creates a potential contradiction: how can diplomatic services effectively engage in climate diplomacy while potentially contributing to the problem through their AI usage? Future research must examine how diplomatic services can balance technological capabilities with sustainability goals.

CONCLUSION

This chapter has explored how AI is reshaping diplomacy, offering tools to navigate international relations more effectively. From crisis prediction and enhanced negotiations to streamlined operations and real-time sentiment analysis, AI has the potential to empower diplomats in unprecedented ways. While these technologies complement rather than replace human diplomacy, their integration raises important questions about ethics, inclusion, and maintaining the essential elements of trust, empathy, and cultural understanding.

The scenarios presented here provide a foundation for understanding and applying AI in diplomatic practice. Success will depend on leveraging these tools thoughtfully while addressing the complex demands of the global stage. By combining AI's capabilities with diplomatic expertise, practitioners can create more effective approaches to international relations.

As diplomacy evolves, its future will be shaped by both technological advancement and enduring human values. The opportunity lies not just in adopting AI, but in using it to strengthen the connections and shared aspirations that drive meaningful international cooperation.

As AI continues to shape the landscape of diplomacy, leadership must evolve alongside it. In the next chapter, we explore how Chiefs and Deputy Chiefs of Mission can integrate AI into strategic decision-making, crisis management, and resource allocation to navigate the complexities of modern diplomacy.

DISCUSSION SCENARIOS AND QUESTIONS

Each chapter of this book concludes with discussion scenarios and questions, designed to encourage critical thinking and practical application of AI in diplomacy. This recurring section presents realistic scenarios followed by thought-provoking questions to help readers engage with the ethical, strategic, and operational challenges of integrating AI into diplomatic practice.

1. Generative AI for embassy staff communications

    Scenario: Your embassy adopts a generative AI tool for drafting routine communications like memos and policy briefs. You begin to notice something. While efficient, the AI occasionally misinterprets nuances, produces biased outputs, and prompts over-reliance by junior staff, risking erosion of their writing and analytical skills.

    Questions: How do we ensure the AI-generated outputs maintain the nuance and accuracy necessary for diplomatic communication? What safeguards can we implement to prevent over-reliance on AI tools, ensuring staff continue to develop critical skills? How can we address biases in the AI system to prevent them from influencing official communications or decision-making?

2. Predictive AI in crisis management

    Scenario: An embassy uses AI to analyze data from financial markets, social media, and satellite imagery to predict a political uprising. While the AI forecasts an 80% chance of unrest, human analysts disagree, citing previous false alarms.

    Questions: How do we balance AI-driven predictions with the judgment of human experts in decision-making? What risks might we face if our actions, based on AI predictions, inadvertently validate perceptions of instability? How can we ensure that AI incorporates nuanced, non-quantifiable cultural and political factors?

3. Autonomous systems in humanitarian crises

Scenario: An AI system manages resource allocation during a natural disaster, prioritizing urban areas due to higher data availability while neglecting rural communities with limited digital presence.

Questions: How do we ensure AI systems provide equitable aid distribution, especially to underserved communities? What protocols should we implement to validate AI-driven recommendations with on-the-ground input? How do we safeguard against systemic biases in data that could perpetuate inequalities in crisis response?

4. AI in trade negotiations

Scenario: During trade talks, AI analyzes decades of political and economic data and suggests a strategy that maximizes short-term benefits for our country. However, it overlooks long-term impacts on regional relationships, which are harder to discern.

Questions: How do we reconcile AI-recommended strategies with the broader, relationship-driven goals of diplomacy? What mechanisms should we use to ensure AI tools consider the long-term consequences of trade decisions? How do we address perceptions of bias if the AI appears to favor one side in negotiations?

5. Real-time sentiment analysis in public diplomacy

Scenario: AI tools monitor social media and news platforms to assess public sentiment about a new initiative by our embassy. The AI suggests a change in messaging to counter rising negative sentiment, but the proposed tone risks alienating key local stakeholders.

Questions: How do we balance AI-driven recommendations for public engagement with the need to maintain long-term trust with local partners? What role should we give local stakeholders in validating or refining AI-generated sentiment insights? How do we avoid over-reliance on AI in shaping our public diplomacy narratives?

2 Executive Leadership in Diplomacy

Guiding Missions in an AI-Driven World

Responsible AI is not just about liability—it's about ensuring what you are building is enabling human flourishing.

—Rumman Chowdhury, CEO of Parity AI (2023)

AI could supercharge existing human conflicts, dividing humanity against itself.

—Yuval Noah Harari, historian, Hebrew University of Jerusalem (2024)

AI is not unequivocally great; it is a dual-use technology with both benefits and risks.

—Gary Marcus, cognitive science professor emeritus at New York University (2024)

In the dynamic world of diplomacy, the roles of Chief of Mission (COM) and Deputy Chief of Mission (DCM) are central to balancing the complexities of international relations with the inspiration needed to lead effectively. These leaders serve as strategists and stewards, guiding their nation's interests abroad while managing political priorities, cultural sensitivities, and operational demands. As artificial intelligence (AI) reshapes the global landscape, these positions are undergoing profound transformation. AI offers data-driven insights, predictive capabilities, and tools that enhance decision-making, streamline coordination, and improve mission-wide efficiency. By integrating AI into their work, COMs and DCMs can better navigate challenges, foster innovation, and prepare for an increasingly complex future all while maintaining the human connections that remain essential to diplomacy. This chapter explores how AI is redefining these leadership roles, enabling diplomats to address the evolving demands of global relations with greater agility, insight, and impact.

VIGNETTE   AI-Enhanced Embassy in the Republic of Z

As the embassy mobilizes in response to the AI system's warnings, Ambassador Daniel Grant knows the mission's success will depend on teamwork. At the

---

DOI: 10.1201/9781003612308-2

center of this effort is his Deputy Chief of Mission, Sofia Tan, whose ability to coordinate across sections is invaluable. While Grant focuses on high-level engagement with Z's government officials, Tan ensures the embassy's operations—both human and digital—align to meet the evolving crisis.

Their partnership exemplifies modern diplomatic leadership. Grant leverages his trusted relationships with senior Z officials, quietly arranging meetings to address the economic and political tensions revealed by the AI. At the same time, Tan bridges the gap between the embassy's strategic objectives and its operational capabilities. She convenes section heads, ensuring each team's AI tools contribute to a unified understanding of the situation. From public affairs' sentiment analysis to security's risk assessments, she translates the wealth of data into actionable insights, empowering her teams to act decisively.

The division of labor proves essential. Grant tailors AI-suggested talking points with his nuanced understanding of Z's political climate, preserving the human touch that builds trust. Tan, in turn, streamlines internal workflows, resolving logistical bottlenecks and adapting AI tools to the embassy's immediate needs. Together, they maintain the delicate balance between technological sophistication and the judgment that defines effective diplomacy.

This collaborative approach reflects a new model of leadership in an AI-enhanced mission. Grant and Tan demonstrate how embassy leaders can harness technology to amplify their strengths without losing sight of the human connections at the heart of diplomacy. As the embassy navigates the growing tensions in the Republic of Z, their partnership sets a standard for integrating innovation with time-tested diplomatic wisdom.

INTRODUCTION TO EXECUTIVE LEADERSHIP IN DIPLOMACY

The complexity of modern diplomacy demands extraordinary leadership from COMs and DCMs. These executive leaders navigate an intricate landscape where traditional diplomatic challenges are beginning to intersect with technological transformation. COMs represent their nations as strategists and negotiators on the global stage, while DCMs serve as operational backbone leaders, ensuring mission success through careful management and coordination (Berridge, Keens-Soper, & Otte 2001). Together, they influence bilateral relationships, security outcomes, and the well-being of citizens both at home and abroad.

Traditional diplomatic leadership has faced persistent challenges: balancing long-term strategic planning with immediate crises, coordinating across multiple embassy sections, and making high-stakes decisions with incomplete information. In this environment, AI appears poised to become a transformative force, potentially offering new capabilities that could enhance rather than replace human judgment. Early experiments suggest that by delegating certain routine, data-intensive tasks to AI, leaders may be able to focus more intensively on strategy, relationship-building, and complex decision-making (Kello 2024).

Initial integrations of AI into diplomatic leadership are beginning to suggest new ways that COMs and DCMs might approach their core responsibilities (Pearson & Burgess 2023). Through its potential to analyze vast datasets, identify subtle patterns, and generate actionable insights, AI may soon empower leaders to make more informed and timely decisions while managing increasingly complex global relationships (Huang 2022). This technological evolution raises critical questions about the future of diplomatic leadership: How might we balance AI-driven efficiency with human judgment? What new risks could emerge as AI systems begin to inform critical diplomatic decisions? How do we ensure emerging technologies enhance rather than diminish the human connections at the heart of diplomacy (Buch, Eagleman, & Grosenick 2022)?

AI'S ROLE IN ENHANCING EXECUTIVE LEADERSHIP

AI appears positioned to serve multiple critical functions in supporting diplomatic leadership, each potentially addressing specific operational and strategic needs. At the decision-making level, early AI tools are being developed as support systems, which may eventually enable leaders to simulate scenarios and predict outcomes with greater precision (UNDP 2020). For instance, COMs might soon be able to use AI to model the potential impact of trade sanctions on bilateral relations, incorporating economic data, public sentiment analysis, and regional dynamics into comprehensive risk assessments (Stanzel & Voelsen 2022).

Predictive analytics capabilities are showing particular promise in crisis anticipation and response. Emerging AI systems are being designed to forecast various types of crises, from political unrest to natural disasters and economic shocks (State Department AI Inventory 2024). In practice, a DCM might eventually receive AI-generated alerts about rising tensions in their host country, potentially enabling preemptive measures to protect staff and citizens (Manor 2017, 2029, Russell 2022). These systems could draw upon decades of internal embassy reporting combined with intelligence sources and open-source media, potentially creating a more complete picture of emerging situations (Pokhriyal & Koebe 2023).

Communication and coordination tools are also evolving through experimental AI-driven dashboards that aim to aggregate real-time updates on political, economic, and security developments (Kello 2023). DCMs may soon be able to monitor reports from various embassy sections through unified interfaces, potentially ensuring better alignment of priorities and initiatives. The technology might even enable enhanced regional cooperation, with AI platforms potentially allowing neighboring embassies to coordinate responses to transnational challenges. For example, during future health crises, such systems could help synchronize response efforts across multiple missions, suggesting paths toward more unified and efficient approaches (Serhan 2024).

IMPLEMENTATION CHALLENGES AND ETHICAL CONSIDERATIONS

While AI offers promising capabilities, its implementation in diplomatic leadership requires careful consideration of both practical and ethical challenges. Leaders will likely need to develop new skills to effectively utilize these emerging tools (Yeo 2024), requiring a fundamental shift in mindset to view AI as a potential complement to, rather than a replacement for, human expertise. This adaptation may require comprehensive AI literacy programs for diplomatic leaders (United Nations Global Pulse 2019), including structured training in capabilities, limitations, and ethical considerations.

Early training programs are beginning to emerge that combine theoretical understanding with practical application. For instance, some diplomatic services are experimenting with scenario-based simulations where COMs can practice using AI tools to allocate resources during hypothetical crises, guided by AI-generated analyses (Höne et al. 2019a, 2019b). These programs aim to build both technical competency and critical judgment about when and how to apply AI insights effectively.

The risk of over-reliance on algorithmic decision-making presents a particular challenge, especially in areas requiring nuanced human judgment (Elgot & Booth 2025, Hern 2023). For instance, while AI might provide valuable data analysis for sentiment assessment, deploying such systems would require careful oversight and clear ethical guidelines to maintain trust and accountability (Zimmerman & Mathur 2025). Leaders must establish robust governance frameworks that balance technological capabilities with diplomatic sensitivity, particularly regarding data privacy and security (Baines 2024).

Crisis management scenarios illustrate both the potential and risks of AI integration. While AI may enhance emergency response by helping COMs anticipate and address crises more effectively (Alder 2025), leaders must ensure these systems don't inadvertently escalate tensions or override important cultural and political considerations. Success will likely require developing clear protocols for AI use, establishing oversight mechanisms, and maintaining human judgment as the final arbiter in diplomatic decisions (Rosen Jacobson, Höne, & Kurbalija 2018).

To address these emerging challenges, diplomatic missions are beginning to consider several key strategies:

1. Exploring the creation of ethical oversight committees to review AI deployments, with particular attention to privacy standards and cultural sensitivities
2. Developing preliminary training programs that emphasize both technical proficiency and ethical decision-making
3. Working toward clear guidelines for when and how AI recommendations should inform different types of diplomatic decisions
4. Considering feedback mechanisms to continuously assess and improve AI system performance while maintaining human oversight
5. Planning frameworks to ensure AI tools respect diplomatic protocols and cultural norms

Through these developing measures, diplomatic leaders may be able to harness AI's emerging capabilities while preserving the essential human elements of diplomatic leadership. The goal is not to automate diplomacy but to explore how AI-driven insights might enhance human judgment, potentially creating more effective and responsive diplomatic missions in the future (Konovalova 2023).

HISTORICAL AI USE CASE EXAMPLES IN EXECUTIVE LEADERSHIP

AI is increasingly playing a role in supporting executive leadership in diplomacy. By providing decision-makers with predictive analytics, real-time data insights, and operational support, AI has great potential to empower leaders to navigate complex global challenges. This section highlights key historical examples of AI deployments that are beginning to show direct influence on executive-level decision-making and leadership in diplomacy.

One of the earliest and most impactful examples of AI-driven leadership in diplomacy was the North Atlantic Treaty Organization (NATO)'s establishment of the Cooperative Cyber Defence Centre of Excellence (CCD-COE) in Tallinn, Estonia, following the 2007 cyberattacks on Estonia. These attacks, attributed to pro-Russian hacktivists, paralyzed critical infrastructure, including government systems and banking networks. In response, NATO launched the CCD-COE to develop advanced cyber defense mechanisms, including AI-driven tools for real-time threat detection and network traffic analysis (Kello 2023). These systems empowered NATO leaders to anticipate and neutralize cyber threats, laying the groundwork for collective cybersecurity strategies across member states. In November of 2024, NATO unveiled plans by Britain to set up a new Laboratory for AI Security Research to help create better defense tools and organize intelligence (Piper 2024). By fostering collaboration and knowledge sharing among allies, these initiatives demonstrate how AI can enhance executive decision-making in multinational contexts.

The European External Action Service (EEAS) demonstrated the utility of AI in executive leadership through its crisis response system, developed in 2019. This system aggregated real-time data from social media, news reports, and diplomatic communications, providing EU leaders with actionable insights during emergencies. During the early stages of the COVID-19 pandemic, the system proved instrumental in coordinating the repatriation of EU citizens and managing cross-border health responses (Manor 2023). By integrating AI into its crisis management framework, the EEAS highlighted how technology could support executive decision-making in dynamic and unpredictable scenarios.

Recently, the U.K. government created Parlex, an AI tool that predicts how MPs might react to new policies by analyzing their past statements in parliament (Elgot & Booth 2025). This helps ministers spot potential issues, build support, and adjust their approach before introducing policies. A similar tool could be adapted for ambassadors and embassy leadership, helping them anticipate responses from foreign officials or stakeholders and refine diplomatic strategies based on historical interactions and policy trends.

The U.S. Department of State has been at the forefront of integrating AI into diplomatic leadership. Through initiatives such as "StateChat" and "BudgetChat/BudgetSearch," AI systems seek to enable leaders to plan for how to best streamline information access and make data-driven decisions during crises. BudgetChat/BudgetSearch was envisioned as a way to consolidate budget documents and facilitate cross-referencing of financial data, with the goal of helping executives align resources with strategic priorities (State Department AI Inventory 2024). Similarly,

StateChat—a generative AI-powered chatbot—provides leaders with rapid processing of diplomatic cables, policy memos, and historical records, significantly enhancing situational awareness. These tools underscore the potential of AI to optimize resource allocation and support strategic planning at the highest levels of diplomacy.

These historical cases have established six critical lessons for executive leaders implementing AI in diplomacy:

1. Enhanced Situational Awareness: AI has proven essential for processing real-time data to identify emerging threats and opportunities, as NATO's CCD-COE demonstrates through integrated monitoring.
2. Strategic Resource Allocation: Tools like StateChat have established AI's capacity to align resources with policy objectives, optimizing decision-making under constraints.
3. Multinational Collaboration: NATO's CCD-COE has shown how AI strengthens collective governance frameworks through sustained information sharing and coordinated responses.
4. Balanced Human Oversight: While AI offers significant efficiencies, the EEAS's crisis response system has proven that robust human oversight remains essential for ethical and effective implementation.
5. Cultural Sensitivity: The United Kingdom's Parlex system demonstrated the critical importance of calibrating AI tools to local political and cultural contexts.
6. Robust Governance: Clear protocols for oversight, data protection, and ethical use have become indispensable as AI integration deepens.

AI's integration into executive leadership has established its transformative potential while reinforcing the importance of ethical standards and operational transparency. By applying these lessons, diplomatic leaders can ensure AI continues enhancing both strategic decision-making and global collaboration.

GLOBAL LEADERSHIP IN AI DIPLOMACY

AI is rapidly reshaping global affairs, prompting diverse actors to engage with its profound implications for diplomacy, security, and international cooperation. This engagement aims to steer AI's development and application toward contributing to global stability and human well-being, rather than exacerbating existing tensions or creating new forms of conflict. This overview highlights key figures, initiatives, and crucial issues shaping AI's role in international relations, acknowledging that this is a dynamic and contested field with numerous important contributors.

SCIENTIFIC PIONEERS AND THE ETHICAL IMPERATIVE

Scientists who have propelled AI's advancements have also played a crucial role in shaping the discourse around its ethical and societal implications.

- Yoshua Bengio has been a vocal advocate for robust international AI governance, emphasizing the need for safeguards to align AI development with human values. His contributions to the Montreal Declaration for Responsible AI and his calls for careful consideration of potential existential risks reflect a growing awareness of the need for ethical frameworks (Montreal Declaration for Responsible AI 2018).
- Geoffrey Hinton, while recognizing AI's potential benefits, has also cautioned about unforeseen risks, including systems acting beyond human control. His departure from Google in 2023 allowed him to speak more freely about these concerns (Hern 2023).
- Stuart Russell has focused on the dangers of autonomous weapons, advocating for their regulation and presenting arguments at the United Nations for a ban on lethal AI-driven systems (Russell 2022).
- Yi Zeng, based at the Chinese Academy of Sciences, has contributed to global discussions on AI safety and ethics, notably through his involvement with the Beijing Artificial Intelligence Principles (Zeng 2019).

These scientists have helped frame AI not just as a technological advancement but also as a transformative force requiring careful consideration of its societal and ethical impacts.

GOVERNMENT AND MULTILATERAL EFFORTS

Here is a concise overview of key developments in AI governance:

- OECD AI Principles: The first international AI guidelines promoting responsible and human-centric AI (OECD 2019a, 2019b).
- Rome Call for AI Ethics: A Vatican-led initiative emphasizing AI ethics, human dignity, and transparency, endorsed by tech and global leaders (Vatican Dicastery for the Doctrine of the Faith 2020).
- NATO introduced its inaugural AI Strategy (North Atlantic Treaty Organization [NATO] 2021).
- China's AI Regulations: Policies mandating AI-generated content labeling and integrating AI into national security and governance (Carnegie Endowment for International Peace 2023).
- Biden AI Executive Order: Established U.S. AI safety, security, and transparency standards (Biden 2023).
- U.K. AI Safety Summit: The first global AI safety summit, leading to the Bletchley Declaration on AI risk management (United Kingdom 2023).
- EU AI Act: The world's first comprehensive AI law, introducing strict oversight and risk-based regulations (European Commission 2024).
- NATO AI Security Framework: Integrated AI governance into defense and intelligence strategies (NATO 2024a, 2024b).

- UN AI Governance Initiative: Proposed global AI regulatory institutions to address emerging risks (United Nations 2024a, 2024b).
- Trump AI Executive Order: Shifted U.S. policy to prioritize AI innovation by rolling back certain regulations (Trump 2025).
- Vatican's *Antiqua et Nova* (2025): Warned against AI's risks to human dignity, misinformation (deepfakes), and autonomous weapons, urging ethical regulation (Vatican Dicastery for the Doctrine of the Faith 2025).
- Paris AI Action Summit: Highlighted growing regulatory divides between the United States, Europe, and China (Milmo 2025).

THE ROLE OF THE PRIVATE SECTOR

The private sector plays a dominant role in AI development and its governance:

- Sam Altman, CEO of OpenAI, has engaged with policymakers globally, advocating for AI governance models that balance innovation with public safety. However, OpenAI's approach has drawn criticism for potentially favoring large AI firms over smaller competitors and for a lack of transparency in its development processes.
- Sundar Pichai, CEO of Google, has emphasized responsible AI development and participated in regulatory discussions.
- Demis Hassabis, co-founder of DeepMind, has highlighted AI's potential for good while also cautioning against its misuse.
- Brad Smith, President of Microsoft, has called for a Digital Geneva Convention to establish international norms for cybersecurity, including AI governance in digital warfare.
- Anna Makanju, Vice President of Global Affairs at OpenAI, has worked to facilitate communication between tech companies and policymakers.
- Kay Firth-Butterfield, formerly of the World Economic Forum, has advised governments on AI governance frameworks.

THOUGHT LEADERS AND GEOPOLITICAL IMPLICATIONS

- Henry Kissinger, Eric Schmidt, and Daniel Huttenlocher, in *The Age of AI and Our Human Future*, discuss AI's profound impact on global decision-making, military strategy, and diplomacy.
- Eric Schmidt, through his work with the U.S. National Security Commission on AI, has been influential in shaping discussions on AI's implications for military strategy and international competition, particularly between the United States and China.
- U.S.-China AI Rivalry: U.S. export controls on AI chips (notably NVIDIA's) aim to limit China's access to cutting-edge AI capabilities. China is pursuing AI self-sufficiency through its New Generation AI Development Plan, reflecting an intensifying global technological competition.

The individuals, organizations, and issues highlighted here represent a fraction of those actively involved in shaping AI's role in international affairs. As AI evolves, continued dialogue, collaboration, and inclusion of diverse perspectives will be crucial to ensuring that AI serves humanity ethically and responsibly. Policymakers, diplomats, and stakeholders must remain engaged in ongoing discussions to navigate the rapid developments in this field.

THE FUTURE OF LEADERSHIP IN AN AI-DRIVEN WORLD

As AI continues to evolve, its role in diplomatic leadership appears likely to expand in both scope and sophistication. Chiefs and DCMs are beginning to explore ways to integrate AI capabilities into their workflows while considering how to champion responsible use across their missions (U.S. Department of State 2024a, 2024b, 2024c, 2024d). This transformation extends far beyond technological adaptation—it calls for a fundamental rethinking of how diplomatic leadership can preserve and enhance the human values at its core.

The challenge facing diplomatic leaders lies in balancing technological innovation with diplomatic tradition. While AI tools may offer increasingly sophisticated analytical capabilities, the foundational elements of diplomacy—trust-building, cultural understanding, and human empathy—remain irreplaceable (Konovalova 2023). As Stanzel and Voelsen (2022) argue, successful diplomatic leadership in an AI-enhanced environment requires developing new competencies while preserving time-tested diplomatic wisdom.

Looking ahead, those leaders who approach AI as a complementary tool rather than a replacement for human judgment may be better positioned to navigate the complexities of 21st-century diplomacy (Höne et al. 2019a, 2019b). This means developing frameworks for ethical AI deployment, establishing clear protocols for human oversight, and ensuring that technological capabilities enhance rather than diminish the personal relationships at the heart of diplomatic work. By thoughtfully integrating AI capabilities while maintaining focus on human-centered diplomacy, missions can work toward greater agility and insight in an increasingly interconnected world.

LARGE LANGUAGE MODELS: LEADERSHIP FACILITATORS

Building on our understanding of Large Language Models (LLMs) from Chapter 1, we now turn to their specific applications for Chiefs and DCMs. These tools take on particular significance in executive leadership roles, where strategic communication, rapid analysis, and efficient decision-making are paramount. While Chapter 1 explored the general diplomatic applications of LLM tools like ChatGPT, Claude, and Gemini, their value multiplies when applied to the unique challenges faced by mission leadership.

Senior diplomatic leaders must frequently synthesize complex information to make strategic decisions while maintaining numerous high-level relationships. LLMs can serve as valuable thought partners in this process, offering rapid analysis of complex scenarios and helping leaders consider multiple strategic angles. For instance, when preparing for a critical bilateral meeting, a COM might use these tools to analyze recent diplomatic exchanges, identify potential areas of alignment, and generate strategic approaches that balance multiple competing interests.

The communication demands on senior leaders are especially intense, requiring frequent shifts between different audiences and contexts. LLMs can help leaders maintain consistent messaging while adapting tone and content appropriately. A COM preparing for a series of engagements might use these tools to draft variations of key messages tailored for different stakeholders—from government officials to business leaders to civil society representatives. This capability proves particularly valuable during crises, when leaders must rapidly craft and adapt communications while maintaining diplomatic precision and cultural sensitivity.

Strategic planning and mission management also benefit from LLM support. DCMs can utilize these tools to analyze embassy operations, identify potential efficiencies, and draft preliminary guidance for different sections. For example, when preparing annual strategic planning documents, a DCM might use LLMs to analyze previous years' reports, identify emerging trends, and generate preliminary objectives for discussion with section heads.

However, the leadership context requires particular attention to certain limitations. The high-stakes nature of COM and DCM responsibilities means that LLM outputs must be treated with heightened scrutiny. Senior leaders should establish clear protocols for their teams regarding appropriate use cases, necessary human oversight, and security considerations. These tools work best when treated as sophisticated analytical aids rather than decision-makers, supporting rather than replacing the judgment that comes from years of diplomatic experience.

For mission leadership, the true value of LLMs lies in their ability to enhance strategic thinking and streamline routine aspects of high-level diplomatic work. By handling initial analysis and draft preparation, they free leaders to focus on the aspects of diplomacy that most require human judgment: building trust, navigating cultural nuances, and making critical decisions that shape bilateral relationships.

PUTTING LLMS TO WORK FOR CHIEFS AND DCMS

Building on the prompt engineering principles discussed in Chapter 1, let's explore how senior diplomatic leaders can craft effective prompts that address their specific responsibilities. The key for Chiefs and DCMs lies in framing requests that reflect the strategic nature of their roles and the complexity of their decision-making environment.

Consider how a COM might frame a request for analyzing an emerging bilateral challenge:

> We're experiencing heightened tensions with our host country over proposed technology export controls. Analyze recent public statements from both sides, identify potential areas of mutual interest, and suggest three strategic approaches that could

help de-escalate tensions while maintaining our core policy objectives. Consider impacts on: bilateral trade relationships, regional stability, and multilateral cooperation frameworks.

This type of prompt demonstrates how senior leaders can leverage LLMs for strategic thinking while maintaining focus on high-level diplomatic objectives. Similarly, a DCM coordinating mission-wide response to a developing situation might frame their request:

Our mission needs to coordinate responses to civil unrest in three major cities. Help me develop an integrated action plan that: 1) defines clear roles for political, economic, consular, and public affairs sections, 2) establishes coordination mechanisms across teams, and 3) outlines communication protocols for both internal updates and external engagement. Consider varying intensity levels of unrest and need for scalable responses.

These examples illustrate how mission leadership can move beyond basic prompt engineering to generate outputs that support executive decision-making. The focus should be on systemic thinking, strategic implications, and cross-sectional coordination—areas where Chiefs and DCMs add particular value.

When preparing for strategic discussions with country team members, leaders might craft prompts that help structure complex conversations:

Help me prepare for tomorrow's country team meeting addressing emerging economic and political risks. Generate a discussion framework that: examines interconnections between various risk factors, identifies potential blind spots in our current analysis, and suggests specific questions to pose to section heads to test our assumptions and planning scenarios.

The goal is to use these tools to enhance leaders' ability to guide strategic discussions and decision-making processes. While Chapter 1 established foundational approaches to working with LLMs, mission leadership must focus on prompts that:

- Frame issues within broader strategic contexts
- Consider implications across multiple sections and stakeholders
- Support integrated planning and coordination
- Maintain focus on high-level diplomatic objectives
- Generate insights that inform executive decision-making

By approaching LLMs with this strategic mindset, Chiefs and DCMs can better leverage these tools to support their unique leadership responsibilities while maintaining the diplomatic judgment that defines their roles.

ADVANCED AI USE CASES FOR CHIEFS AND DCMS

Building on Chapter 1's exploration of foundational AI applications in diplomacy, we examine how advanced capabilities specifically serve mission leadership. Chiefs and DCMs must maintain strategic oversight, coordinate across sections, manage host-country relationships, and guide their missions through complex challenges.

The integration of AI into executive workflows requires a comprehensive strategy that enhances mission-wide capabilities while preserving essential human judgment. Leaders must balance AI opportunities with their responsibilities as stewards of diplomatic relationships.

This section presents advanced use cases focused on enhancing executive decision-making, strategic planning, and mission-wide coordination.

AI-Enhanced Stakeholder Mapping

A digital map of who matters in diplomacy and how they're connected.

Managing relationships is at the core of diplomacy, yet traditional methods—relying on manual tracking, fragmented data, and personal networks—often struggle to keep pace with today's dynamic and interconnected world. The rise of new influencers and fast-changing political landscapes demands tools that provide a more comprehensive and adaptive approach. AI addresses this need by automating the collection and analysis of data from public records, news sources, and social media, generating detailed, real-time profiles of stakeholders. These profiles include policy priorities, public statements, and connections, equipping diplomats with actionable insights for strategic engagement.

The applications of AI-enhanced stakeholder mapping are extensive. Before a negotiation, an ambassador can consult AI-generated reports to understand their counterpart's recent actions and shared interests, fostering rapport. During public diplomacy campaigns, AI tools can identify influential figures, such as local journalists or NGO leaders, who can amplify messaging. In multilateral settings, AI maps influence within international organizations, allowing diplomats to prioritize impactful relationships. To implement these tools effectively, embassies should run pilot programs to test functionality, ensure data compatibility, and train staff to integrate AI insights into diplomatic workflows.

Challenges include ensuring data quality, addressing privacy concerns, and overcoming resistance to change among staff. Robust governance and ethical frameworks are critical to mitigate these risks and maintain trust. While AI offers precision and adaptability, human judgment remains essential for interpreting findings, engaging stakeholders with cultural sensitivity, and building meaningful relationships. By combining AI-driven insights with diplomatic expertise, embassies can enhance relationship management and adapt more effectively to complex geopolitical environments.

Decision Support Dashboards

A single screen showing everything a diplomat needs to know right now.

Decision-making in diplomacy often requires navigating vast amounts of fragmented information, a process that is time-consuming and prone to overlooking critical data. AI-powered decision support dashboards address this by aggregating real-time data from diverse sources, detecting patterns, and generating predictive insights. These dashboards simplify complex scenarios by presenting diplomats with clear, actionable overviews, whether through analyzing economic indicators, monitoring local sentiment, or summarizing security updates. Natural language processing further enhances their utility by condensing lengthy cables and policy briefs into concise, relevant insights.

The integration of AI dashboards enhances both preparation and responsiveness in diplomatic workflows. For instance, an ambassador preparing for negotiations could use the dashboard to access bilateral trade summaries and recent political developments, ensuring their approach aligns with host country priorities. During crises, such as political unrest, the dashboard could provide real-time updates on citizen safety, evacuation routes, and evolving local conditions. To implement these tools successfully, missions must focus on data reliability, seamless system integration, and thorough training for staff to interpret and act on AI-generated insights.

Challenges include the risk of overreliance on automation and potential data gaps that could skew conclusions. Regular audits and human oversight are essential to address these risks and ensure balanced decision-making. By combining AI-driven efficiency with the strategic judgment of diplomats, decision-support dashboards empower embassies to navigate complexity with greater precision, enabling timely and effective outcomes in high-stakes scenarios.

PUBLIC SENTIMENT ANALYSIS

A real-time window into what local communities are thinking and feeling.

Public opinion is a cornerstone of effective diplomacy, shaping the success of initiatives and the environment in which missions operate. Traditional methods of gauging sentiment, such as manual reviews of news and local media, are often slow and insufficient in today's fast-paced digital landscape. AI-powered public sentiment analysis addresses this challenge by automating the collection, translation, and evaluation of data from diverse platforms, including social media and news outlets. These tools analyze tone, detect trends, and identify misinformation, providing diplomats with real-time insights into public attitudes.

The practical benefits of sentiment analysis are significant. For example, before delivering a public address on climate policy, an ambassador could use AI-generated insights to identify topics—such as renewable energy or green job creation—that resonate with local audiences. In crises, such as political unrest, AI tools can pinpoint regions with the highest dissatisfaction, helping embassies prioritize outreach and assistance. To implement these systems effectively, missions must ensure accurate data inputs, culturally sensitive algorithms, and staff training to interpret results. Ethical considerations, such as privacy protections and transparency in data use, are critical to maintaining trust.

Challenges include managing potential biases in AI analysis and ensuring that tools are culturally nuanced. By pairing AI-driven insights with the contextual expertise of diplomats, missions can engage more meaningfully, aligning their actions and messaging with the priorities and concerns of the communities they serve.

This combination of technology and human judgment enhances responsiveness and fosters trust, strengthening the impact of diplomatic efforts.

SPEECH CRAFTING ASSISTANCE

A message builder that helps speeches connect with specific audiences.

Diplomatic speeches are vital tools for shaping perceptions and building relationships, but crafting impactful messages is often a time-intensive process that may overlook critical elements. Traditional methods depend on extensive research, staff input, and personal expertise, which can delay responsiveness in high-stakes scenarios. AI-powered speech crafting tools streamline this process by analyzing audience demographics, cultural contexts, and policy objectives to generate tailored drafts. These tools provide relevant data, suggest improvements in tone and structure, and ensure alignment with the occasion and audience expectations.

The applications of AI in speechwriting are diverse. For example, at a climate summit, AI could draft a speech integrating shared goals, local concerns, and recent policy developments, providing diplomats with a strong foundation to personalize further. In urgent situations, such as addressing a security crisis, AI tools can rapidly produce well-structured, effective statements, enabling diplomats to respond promptly while maintaining quality. Successful implementation requires integrating these tools into existing workflows, training staff to use them effectively, and being transparent about AI's role in the process.

Challenges include the risk of cultural inaccuracies or losing the authenticity that is essential in diplomatic communication. However, these risks are mitigated by ensuring human oversight throughout the process. By automating routine tasks, AI empowers diplomats to focus on the creative and strategic elements of their speeches, ensuring messages are impactful, credible, and aligned with the mission's goals.

CRISIS MONITORING AND ALERTS

An early warning system for spotting trouble before it escalates.

In times of crisis, such as natural disasters or political unrest, swift and decisive action is critical to saving lives and protecting interests. Traditional crisis response methods, which rely on manual monitoring and local authority communication, are often slow and reactive. AI-powered monitoring tools revolutionize this process by synthesizing data from diverse sources, such as social media, satellite imagery, and local reports, to provide real-time alerts and actionable insights. These systems detect emerging risks, prioritize affected areas, and recommend proactive measures, enabling diplomats to respond effectively to rapidly evolving situations.

The practical value of AI in crisis monitoring is clear. For example, during a natural disaster, AI can analyze satellite imagery to identify impacted zones, cross-reference reports to assess needs, and recommend optimized evacuation routes. In political crises, AI can track protest dynamics, flag high-risk areas, and provide real-time updates on security conditions. Implementing these tools effectively requires reliable data sources, comprehensive staff training, and adherence to ethical guidelines to ensure transparency and respect for privacy.

Challenges include ensuring data accuracy and addressing the limitations of AI in understanding local contexts. Human expertise remains critical to interpret AI findings and guide decision-making with nuance and cultural awareness. By combining AI's speed and scalability with diplomatic judgment, embassies can enhance crisis preparedness and response, ensuring timely and impactful actions in complex and high-stakes scenarios.

SOCIAL MEDIA MONITORING

A digital listening post for what people are saying about diplomatic issues.

In today's interconnected world, social media platforms play a pivotal role in shaping public opinion and influencing narratives. For senior diplomats, engaging with these platforms is essential for effective public diplomacy and crisis management. However, the sheer volume of content makes manual monitoring impractical and error-prone. AI-powered social media monitoring tools address this challenge by using natural language processing and machine learning to analyze sentiment, detect trends, and flag misinformation. These tools provide embassies with actionable insights by highlighting posts and discussions aligned with their diplomatic priorities.

The applications of AI in social media monitoring are wide-ranging. For example, during a public diplomacy campaign, AI can track trending hashtags and identify influential voices to guide outreach efforts effectively. In times of crisis, such as political unrest or natural disasters, these tools can detect misinformation campaigns and provide accurate, real-time updates to counter false narratives. To ensure success, missions must train staff to interpret AI findings, update models regularly for cultural relevance, and integrate these tools into communication strategies.

Challenges include managing data bias, addressing privacy concerns, and adhering to ethical standards. Transparent processes and robust governance frameworks are essential to mitigate these risks. By combining AI's scalability and analytical power with diplomats' interpretive expertise, embassies can enhance their engagement strategies, ensuring credibility, responsiveness, and alignment with the communities they serve.

EVACUATION PLANNING

A safety navigator for getting people out of danger quickly.

Evacuation planning is one of the most critical responsibilities for diplomats during emergencies such as natural disasters, political unrest, or security threats. Traditional methods relying on manual risk assessments and logistical planning often struggle to adapt to rapidly changing conditions. AI-powered tools address these challenges by integrating real-time data streams—such as traffic patterns, weather forecasts, and geopolitical risks—to recommend optimized evacuation routes and strategies. These systems analyze multiple variables simultaneously, ensuring plans are efficient and adaptive to evolving circumstances.

The practical applications of AI in evacuation planning are significant. During political unrest, for example, AI can monitor protest movements, identify safe evacuation corridors, and prioritize resource allocation for high-risk areas. In natural disasters, such as hurricanes, these tools can use satellite imagery to assess damage and recommend the fastest and safest evacuation routes. Effective implementation requires access to reliable data sources, thorough staff training, and strict adherence to ethical guidelines, particularly regarding sensitive information like geolocation data.

Challenges include ensuring the accuracy and reliability of data and addressing the limitations of AI in understanding on-the-ground realities. Human oversight remains essential to incorporate cultural nuances, manage complex dynamics, and make context-sensitive decisions. By combining AI's analytical power with the expertise and judgment of diplomats, embassies can execute evacuation efforts more effectively, saving lives and minimizing risks during crises.

Fraud Detection

A pattern spotter for catching suspicious visa and contract activity.

Fraud undermines the integrity of critical diplomatic processes, such as visa issuance, grant management, and procurement. Traditional methods, relying on manual reviews and standardized checks, are often time-consuming and prone to human error. As fraudulent schemes grow increasingly sophisticated, AI-powered fraud detection tools offer a transformative solution. These systems analyze large datasets to identify patterns, anomalies, and red flags that might go unnoticed during manual reviews, significantly enhancing the accuracy and efficiency of fraud prevention.

The applications of AI in fraud detection span various scenarios. For instance, an AI tool could flag visa applications where travel history conflicts with the stated purpose of the trip or detect duplicate grant applications submitted under different names. In procurement, AI can identify signs of bid collusion or inflated pricing, ensuring fair and transparent contract awards. To implement these tools effectively, missions must prioritize high-quality data inputs, provide comprehensive staff training, and run pilot programs to refine system functionality and accuracy.

Challenges include addressing privacy concerns and mitigating the risk of false positives that could unfairly penalize legitimate cases. Robust governance frameworks and ethical oversight are essential to ensure fairness and maintain trust. By combining AI's analytical power with human judgment, embassies can enhance efficiency, accountability, and transparency, allowing diplomats to focus on critical cases and uphold the integrity of their operations.

Cybersecurity Oversight

A digital shield protecting embassy computers and information.

In the digital age, cybersecurity threats present significant risks to diplomatic missions, including cyberattacks, data breaches, and espionage. These threats can compromise sensitive information, disrupt operations, and harm diplomatic credibility. Traditional cybersecurity approaches, often reactive in nature, struggle to counter increasingly sophisticated attacks. AI-powered tools provide a proactive solution by analyzing network activity, detecting anomalies, and predicting vulnerabilities. Using machine learning and behavioral analysis, these systems identify suspicious actions, such as unauthorized access attempts or malware in emails, allowing missions to respond swiftly and effectively.

The benefits of AI in cybersecurity oversight are considerable. For example, during heightened geopolitical tensions, an AI system can monitor embassy networks for unusual login patterns and alert the IT team to potential breaches. Similarly, it can detect phishing campaigns targeting embassy staff and neutralize threats before they escalate. To implement these tools effectively, missions must ensure compatibility with existing IT infrastructure, provide staff with comprehensive training, and establish ethical guidelines to maintain accountability and protect privacy.

Challenges include addressing false positives, ensuring AI systems adapt to evolving threats, and maintaining human oversight for evaluating flagged risks. By combining AI's speed and analytical power with the expertise of cybersecurity teams, diplomatic missions can strengthen their defenses, safeguard sensitive data, and ensure operational continuity in an increasingly interconnected and vulnerable world.

STRATEGIC SCHEDULING

A smart calendar that puts diplomatic priorities in the right order.

Time management is a critical challenge for senior diplomats, who must balance high-stakes negotiations, public appearances, and internal responsibilities. Traditional scheduling methods, reliant on human assistants, can be time-consuming and prone to conflicts, particularly in fast-changing environments. AI-powered scheduling tools address this by automating routine tasks, analyzing priorities, and providing data-driven recommendations. Using natural language processing and machine learning, these tools evaluate incoming requests, optimize meeting times, and dynamically adjust schedules to align with shifting priorities.

The practical applications of AI in strategic scheduling are significant. During an international summit, for instance, AI can analyze the availability of key stakeholders and propose the most efficient times for bilateral meetings. In crisis situations, these tools can reprioritize engagements to ensure urgent matters are addressed promptly. To implement AI scheduling tools effectively, missions must ensure data accuracy, integrate user-friendly interfaces, and train staff to interpret and adapt recommendations.

Challenges include safeguarding sensitive information, managing cultural considerations, and addressing unexpected developments. Human oversight remains essential to refine schedules and ensure they align with diplomatic priorities. By combining AI's efficiency with human judgment and flexibility, strategic scheduling tools help diplomats maximize their time, enabling them to focus on advancing their mission and achieving impactful results.

LIMITATIONS AND FUTURE RESEARCH DIRECTIONS

As AI reshapes diplomatic leadership, we must critically examine both the boundaries of our current understanding and the crucial questions that remain unanswered. This examination serves not only to acknowledge gaps in our knowledge but also to chart a course for future research that can enhance AI's effectiveness in diplomatic leadership while safeguarding its essential human elements.

THE EVOLUTION OF DIPLOMATIC AUTHORITY

One of the most profound limitations in our current understanding concerns how AI affects the nature of diplomatic authority itself. Traditional diplomatic leadership relies heavily on personal judgment, institutional knowledge, and the ability to build trust through face-to-face interactions. As AI systems become more sophisticated in their analytical and predictive capabilities, we must examine how this shifts the balance of authority within diplomatic missions.

Consider, for example, a situation where an AI system predicts civil unrest with 90% confidence, contradicting the assessment of experienced diplomatic staff. The COM must decide whether to trust human intuition or data-driven analysis. This scenario raises crucial questions about the future of diplomatic judgment: How do leaders maintain their authority while leveraging AI insights? How can we preserve the value of human experience in an increasingly data-driven environment? Future research must explore these questions, perhaps through longitudinal studies of diplomatic missions as they integrate AI systems.

LEADERSHIP DEVELOPMENT IN AN AI-ENHANCED ENVIRONMENT

The development of future diplomatic leaders represents another critical area requiring investigation. Traditional diplomatic training emphasizes experiential learning—the gradual accumulation of judgment through years of service. However, we don't yet fully understand how reliance on AI tools might affect this development process. Think of it like learning to navigate: while GPS provides immediate directions, it may prevent drivers from developing an internal sense of direction. Similarly, we must investigate how AI tools might help or hinder the development of diplomatic intuition.

Research is particularly needed on how to design training programs that effectively combine AI literacy with traditional diplomatic skills. This might include studying successful models from other fields where professional judgment must coexist with AI, such as medicine or aviation. We need to understand how to prepare diplomatic leaders who can both leverage AI capabilities and maintain the human judgment essential to their role.

CROSS-CULTURAL DYNAMICS AND AI INTEGRATION

The intersection of cultural understanding and AI capabilities presents unique challenges that our current research hasn't adequately addressed. While AI systems excel at processing data and identifying patterns, they may struggle with the nuanced cultural contexts that diplomatic leaders must navigate. For instance, an AI system might accurately translate words but miss crucial cultural subtexts that could affect diplomatic relationships.

Future research should examine how AI systems can be developed to better understand and incorporate cultural nuances. This might include studying how different cultures receive AI-driven diplomatic initiatives and developing frameworks for ensuring AI tools respect cultural sensitivities while supporting diplomatic objectives.

ETHICAL FRAMEWORKS AND ACCOUNTABILITY

The question of accountability in AI-assisted diplomatic leadership demands particular attention. When decisions involve multiple actors—human leaders, AI systems, and oversight mechanisms—determining responsibility becomes complex. Future research must develop clear frameworks for maintaining accountability while leveraging AI's capabilities, particularly in high-stakes diplomatic situations.

We need studies examining questions such as: How do we establish clear lines of responsibility in AI-assisted decisions? What protocols should govern the override of AI recommendations? How can we ensure transparency in AI-assisted diplomatic processes without compromising sensitive information?

ORGANIZATIONAL RESILIENCE AND TECHNOLOGICAL DISPARITIES

The impact of technological disparities on diplomatic relationships requires deeper investigation. As diplomatic missions adopt AI at different rates and with varying levels of sophistication, we must understand how these differences affect bilateral and multilateral relationships. Research should examine questions like: How do technological gaps between missions affect diplomatic equity? What strategies can ensure AI enhancement doesn't exacerbate existing power imbalances in international relations?

LEADERSHIP WELL-BEING AND COGNITIVE LOAD

The psychological impact of managing AI-enhanced diplomatic missions represents an understudied area. Leaders must simultaneously oversee human teams, interpret AI insights, and maintain traditional diplomatic relationships—a combination that could lead to increased cognitive load and potential burnout. Future research should examine how to support leaders in this complex environment, including studying optimal ways to present AI insights without overwhelming human cognitive capabilities.

PRIVACY AND SECURITY IN AI-ENHANCED DIPLOMACY

As diplomatic missions increasingly rely on AI systems, questions of data privacy and security become more complex. Future research must address how to protect sensitive diplomatic information while maintaining the benefits of AI-assisted leadership. This includes developing protocols for securing leadership communications and decision-making processes in an AI-enhanced environment.

CONCLUSION

AI is transforming diplomatic leadership by equipping COMs and their deputies with advanced capabilities in decision-making, crisis management, and strategic planning. Through AI-enhanced tools, including stakeholder mapping, predictive analytics, and LLMs, leaders can navigate diplomatic complexity with greater precision while maintaining essential human judgment. Key implementations like decision support dashboards, crisis monitoring systems, and sentiment analysis provide unprecedented insights for mission management and strategic planning.

This transformation requires balancing technological innovation with diplomatic tradition. Leaders must maintain authentic relationships and ensure AI enhances rather than diminishes the personal touch that builds diplomatic trust. Success demands implementing ethical governance frameworks and fostering AI-ready organizational cultures while viewing these technologies as enablers of better decision-making rather than replacements for diplomatic judgment.

The path forward requires leaders who can develop AI literacy while maintaining diplomatic intuition, implement ethical frameworks while preserving operational flexibility, and foster innovation while upholding diplomatic principles. By thoughtfully integrating AI while preserving core diplomatic elements, COMs can build more resilient and effective diplomatic missions that leverage technology's advantages while maintaining the human connections essential to diplomacy.

As AI continues to shape executive leadership in diplomacy, its impact extends to the realm of political affairs. In the next chapter, we explore how AI-driven insights are transforming political analysis, foreign policy decision-making, and diplomatic engagement with host governments.

DISCUSSION SCENARIOS AND QUESTIONS

The following scenarios examine how AI is transforming diplomatic leadership roles. They challenge readers to consider how Chiefs and DCMs can integrate AI into decision-making, crisis response, and resource management while maintaining ethical oversight and human-centered leadership.

1. Human oversight in AI-assisted decision-making

    Scenario: You rely on an AI system to streamline a routine but critical decision, only to find that the outcome damages relations with key stakeholders.

    Questions: How do you ensure accountability when AI systems play a significant role in decision-making? Should you delegate decisions to AI tools in time-sensitive scenarios or always prioritize human oversight? What safeguards can you establish to evaluate AI recommendations before they are implemented?

2. Privacy and surveillance in host countries

Scenario: Your embassy's AI-based security system inadvertently collects sensitive data from citizens of the host country. This sparks a media outcry and diplomatic tensions as the host government demands an explanation.

Questions: How do you handle the fallout while defending the operational needs of your security measures? What factors should influence your decision to delegate tasks to AI tools in time-sensitive scenarios while maintaining appropriate levels of human oversight? What protocols should you implement to ensure AI tools comply with the host nation's privacy expectations?

3. Ethics of AI-enhanced negotiations

Scenario: You use an AI system to analyze the preferences and negotiation styles of opposing diplomats, allowing you to craft tailored counterarguments. However, word of this leaks, and the host nation accuses you of using unethical tactics to manipulate the talks.

Questions: How do you respond to the accusation while maintaining the integrity of your negotiation process? Should AI tools be part of your negotiation strategy, or do they undermine the trust and transparency essential to diplomacy? What safeguards can you implement to ensure AI tools are used responsibly in negotiations?

4. AI-assisted crisis response

Scenario: During a natural disaster, your AI system recommends evacuation routes that bypass marginalized communities. While the plan is efficient, you face criticism for neglecting these groups.

Questions: Do you adjust the AI's plan to address equity concerns, even if it delays the response? How can you ensure AI tools incorporate considerations of fairness and inclusivity in emergencies? What processes should you establish to balance AI-driven efficiency with ethical imperatives in crisis management?

5. AI-driven diplomatic strategy

Scenario: An AI system at your disposal predicts imminent unrest in the host country, suggesting you issue a travel advisory for your citizens. However, acting on this recommendation could strain relations with the host government, which insists there's no cause for alarm.

Questions: How do you decide whether to trust the AI's prediction or rely on traditional diplomatic assessments? What steps do you take to balance the need for precaution with the potential diplomatic fallout? How do you ensure the AI system's predictions are reliable and not influenced by incomplete or biased data?

3 AI and Political Affairs
Advancing Foreign Policy with AI-Driven Insights

The real question is, when will we draft an artificial intelligence bill of rights? What will that consist of? And who will get to decide that?

—Gray Scott, Serious Wonder Media (2017)

We need governments urgently to work with tech companies on risk management frameworks for current AI development, and on monitoring and mitigating future harms.

—António Guterres, UN Secretary-General (2024)

Perhaps we could start from the observation that artificial intelligence is above all else a tool. And it goes without saying that the benefits or harm it will bring will depend on its use.

—Pope Francis, Vatican (2025)

In the quiet offices of embassies and consulates around the world, a transformation is reshaping the fabric of diplomacy. Long defined by intuition, handwritten memos, and whispered conversations, the art of diplomacy now embraces the power of cutting-edge technology. Artificial intelligence (AI), once the stuff of science fiction, is becoming an indispensable ally, helping political officers navigate the labyrinth of global politics with unprecedented precision and agility. These officers are no longer just interpreters of political landscapes; they are pioneers at the intersection of tradition and innovation, where algorithms and data magnify the reach and impact of human insight. AI doesn't diminish the timeless qualities of diplomacy—empathy, cultural understanding, and ethical reasoning. Instead, it acts as a force multiplier, enabling diplomats to decode complex signals, anticipate emerging trends, and respond with clarity and confidence. This chapter explores how AI is revolutionizing the role of political officers, offering tools and strategies that make the impossible feel achievable. Through this lens, we uncover a future where technology and human expertise converge to advance the art of diplomacy.

VIGNETTE   AI-Enhanced Embassy in the Republic of Z

It's 7:00 a.m. in the bustling capital of the Republic of Z, a country perched precariously on the fault lines of political instability. Political Officer Sarah

---

DOI: 10.1201/9781003612308-3

Chen reviews her AI-powered analytics dashboard while preparing for a series of critical meetings with opposition leaders. An overnight surge in social media activity has caught her attention—the AI system has flagged an incendiary speech by a prominent opposition figure that's sparking unrest in two key provinces.

Chen, who has spent months cultivating relationships across Z's political spectrum, recognizes the deeper implications. The AI's natural language processing algorithms have analyzed thousands of social media posts, news reports, and local government memos, revealing troubling patterns that align with her own ground-level observations. The system not only identifies protest hotspots but correlates them with underlying economic grievances she's been tracking—rising unemployment, energy costs, and wage stagnation.

As she prepares her morning briefing for the Ambassador, Chen appreciates how AI amplifies her traditional diplomatic skills. While the technology processes vast amounts of data, her deep understanding of Z's political dynamics and key relationships with party leaders allows her to contextualize the insights. The system has already drafted a preliminary demarche addressing the situation, which she refines based on her knowledge of what messages will resonate with local authorities.

The morning unfolds rapidly. Chen organizes an emergency country team meeting, sharing AI-generated analytics that map potential escalation scenarios. Her extensive network of contacts—developed through countless meetings and events—proves invaluable as she reaches out to political leaders across party lines. The AI system helps her craft tailored talking points for each conversation, considering each leader's past statements and positions while she adds the crucial personal touch that makes diplomacy effective.

By mid-morning, Chen is accompanying the Ambassador to meet with Z's Foreign Minister. The AI system provides real-time updates on developing situations across the provinces, but it's Chen's careful notes and intimate knowledge of the political landscape that guides the discussion toward concrete solutions. As they work to defuse tensions, she's already thinking ahead to how these developments might affect the broader diplomatic agenda, particularly the economic initiatives being developed by her colleagues in other sections.

DIPLOMACY IN THE AGE OF AI

The role of a political officer has always been both an art and a science, demanding a delicate balance of analytical precision and human intuition. For generations, these diplomats have served as their nations' eyes and ears abroad, decoding complex political dynamics and forging vital relationships that transcend borders. Their traditional toolkit consisted of careful observation, extensive networks of contacts, and the ability to synthesize vast amounts of information into actionable insights. Yet, in today's rapidly evolving digital landscape, this role is undergoing a profound transformation.

TRANSFORMING POLITICAL AFFAIRS WITH AI

The introduction of AI into diplomatic work hasn't simply added new tools to the political officer's arsenal—it is fundamentally reshaping how they understand and influence the political landscape. Where once they might have spent weeks poring over reports and meeting with contacts to gauge public sentiment, many now have access to AI-powered analytics that can process millions of social media posts, news articles, and public statements in real time. This technological revolution hasn't diminished the importance of human judgment; rather, it has amplified political officers' ability to identify patterns, anticipate developments, and respond with unprecedented precision.

Consider a political officer stationed in a country experiencing growing social unrest. In the past, they might have relied solely on local media reports and personal contacts to understand the situation's scope. Today, AI systems can analyze vast amounts of data to identify the root causes of dissatisfaction, map the geographic spread of protests, and even predict potential flashpoints before they erupt. This enhanced awareness enables the officer to engage more effectively with local authorities and community leaders, often preventing crises before they escalate.

The integration of AI into diplomatic work represents a carefully orchestrated partnership rather than a technological takeover. At its core, diplomacy remains a deeply human endeavor, built on trust, cultural understanding, and personal relationships. Political officers today find themselves navigating a hybrid landscape where AI amplifies their traditional strengths while opening new avenues for engagement and insight. This evolution demands a sophisticated understanding of both human nature and technological capabilities.

AI'S PRACTICAL APPLICATIONS IN DIPLOMACY

Take, for instance, the challenge of managing relationships within a complex coalition government. A political officer might leverage AI to build detailed profiles of key stakeholders, drawing from their public speeches, voting records, and media appearances. But the real art lies in how they use these insights. Rather than relying solely on data-driven analyses, skilled diplomats weave this information into their relationship-building strategy, using it to deepen conversations and demonstrate genuine understanding of their counterparts' perspectives, priorities, and constraints.

The power of this partnership becomes particularly evident in policy development and implementation. Modern political officers can utilize AI's predictive modeling capabilities to simulate the potential outcomes of various policy decisions, examining how different approaches might resonate across diverse populations and interest groups. For example, when working on a sensitive trade agreement, AI systems can analyze historical data, economic indicators, and public sentiment to identify potential sticking points and opportunities for mutual benefit. Yet it's the political officer's deep understanding of local politics, cultural sensitivities, and personal relationships that transforms these insights into effective diplomatic strategies.

When pairing public diplomacy and political affairs, this synthesis of human and AI proves especially powerful. AI-driven sentiment analysis tools can track how different communities respond to diplomatic initiatives, allowing political officers to tailor their messaging and engagement strategies with unprecedented precision. However, the success of these efforts still hinges on the diplomat's ability to craft authentic narratives that resonate with local values and aspirations. This human touch ensures that data-driven insights translate into meaningful connections and lasting partnerships.

The sheer complexity of modern diplomatic work demands tools and approaches that can match its scale and sophistication. Political officers increasingly find themselves processing information from a dizzying array of sources—social media feeds, satellite imagery, economic indicators, and diplomatic cables—all while maintaining the delicate balance of international relationships. AI serves as a crucial ally in this endeavor, helping diplomats cut through the noise to identify meaningful patterns and emerging opportunities.

Consider the challenge of monitoring compliance with international agreements, a task that has grown exponentially more complex in our interconnected world. Modern political officers increasingly have access to AI systems that can analyze satellite imagery, trade data, and emissions reports to verify adherence to treaty obligations. For instance, when monitoring a climate accord, these tools might flag unusual patterns in industrial activity or detect discrepancies between reported and observed emissions levels. This technological capability enables diplomats to address potential violations early, often through quiet diplomacy that preserves relationships while ensuring accountability.

The regional dynamics of political sentiment present another realm where AI's capabilities prove invaluable. Political officers must understand how different communities within a host country perceive policies and initiatives, a task that traditional polling and media monitoring could only partially address. Today's AI-powered sentiment mapping tools provide granular insights into public opinion across diverse regions and demographic groups. A diplomat might discover, for example, that support for a trade agreement varies significantly between urban and rural areas, allowing them to adjust their outreach strategies accordingly and address specific concerns before they become obstacles to progress.

Yet perhaps, the most transformative aspect of AI in political affairs lies in its predictive capabilities. By analyzing historical data patterns, diplomatic cables, internal reporting from missions worldwide, and current trends, these systems help diplomats anticipate potential crises and identify opportunities for constructive engagement. A political officer might receive early warning of growing social tensions based on subtle shifts in social media discourse, economic indicators, and local media coverage. This foresight enables them to initiate dialogue with key stakeholders and propose solutions before situations deteriorate into full-blown crises.

HISTORICAL AI USE CASE EXAMPLES IN POLITICAL AFFAIRS

The United Nations explored the early application of AI in political affairs through initiatives such as the U.N. Global Pulse program. This initiative utilized AI tools to analyze big data and assess political risks in member states. For example, AI models were used to detect early indicators of political instability, such as spikes in hate speech or protests, enabling U.N. diplomats to engage proactively in conflict prevention (United Nations Global Pulse 2019). This interdisciplinary approach underscored AI's potential to support multilateral collaboration in addressing complex political challenges.

According to reports from the U.S. Department of State's AI Use Case Inventory, the Bureau of Conflict and Stabilization Operations (CSO) was reportedly developing AI capabilities to enhance its conflict prevention and stabilization efforts globally. Five conflict analysis models reported showed integration of AI/machine learning (ML) technologies into global security monitoring. Three models focused on predicting civilian violence, analyzing stakeholder influence, and forecasting mass mobilizations using political and economic data. Two retired systems previously utilized satellite imagery for automated damage and burning assessments (U.S. Department of State 2024a, 2024b, 2024c, 2024d).

Recent years have seen the emergence of AI as a subversive tool in political affairs, with several state actors deploying AI technologies to advance their geopolitical objectives. Russia's deployment of AI during the Ukraine war represents one of the most significant examples of this trend. Russian operators utilized AI to generate deepfake videos, create synthetic news reports, and power extensive bot networks across social media platforms like Twitter and Telegram (Wikipedia Contributors 2024a, Hoffman 2023). These tools were specifically deployed to spread anti-Ukraine narratives and fabricate military successes (RAND 2024). However, Ukraine's response demonstrated the potential to counter such operations through preemptive "pre-bunking" strategies and coordinated media literacy initiatives (RAND 2024, Pearson & Burgess 2023, Kello 2023).

China has demonstrated perhaps the most comprehensive approach to AI deployment in political affairs, combining multiple technologies and strategies (Batke 2020). Chinese authorities created AI-generated news anchors to deliver state propaganda (The Guardian 2024a, 2024b, Thorne 2020) and deployed sophisticated networks of AI-powered fake social media accounts, particularly during the 2022 U.S. midterm elections (RAND 2024). In preparation for Taiwan's 2024 presidential election, China expanded these capabilities to include AI-generated fake news videos (CyberScoop 2024). Beyond direct influence operations, China pioneered the use of AI-powered sentiment analysis in diplomatic communications, particularly in support of its Belt and Road Initiative. This technology enabled Chinese officials to monitor global reactions to their initiatives and adjust their diplomatic messaging accordingly (Huang 2022).

Iran's deployment of AI technologies, while more focused, has shown similar sophistication in electoral influence operations. Iranian operators developed AI-driven sentiment analysis tools to optimize the impact of their propaganda efforts, particularly targeting elections in the United States and Middle East (OpenAI 2024). Their systems demonstrated the ability to tailor content for specific demographic groups, representing a significant advancement in targeted influence operations (The Guardian 2024a, 2024b).

These historical examples have fundamentally altered the landscape of international relations, with AI-powered disinformation becoming a standard component of modern political warfare. This shift has created significant ethical and operational challenges for election security and democratic institutions (RAND 2024). Russia's use of generative AI to create deepfake content during the Russo-Ukrainian War exemplifies these risks, as such disinformation erodes public trust and complicates diplomatic efforts to build consensus (Manor 2017, 2019). These cases underscore the critical importance of cautious AI integration in diplomatic contexts, emphasizing the need for transparency, rigorous testing, and robust governance frameworks. In response, nations have increasingly prioritized the development of AI-detection technologies and international cooperation frameworks to counter these emerging threats (The Guardian 2024a, 2024b).

Critical Lessons for Future Applications:

1. Proactive governance and early warning systems: Governments must establish ethical guidelines and transparency measures while leveraging AI for early detection of potential conflicts. The success of tools like the Violence Against Civilians Model demonstrates how AI can serve as an effective early warning system for political instability.
2. Collaboration across sectors: Partnerships between governments, academia, and private organizations are essential for developing AI tools that address political challenges without compromising ethical principles. The U.N. Global Pulse program illustrates how multi-stakeholder collaboration can enhance AI's effectiveness in political risk assessment and conflict prevention.
3. Cultural sensitivity: AI-driven political strategies must account for cultural and regional differences to avoid alienating target audiences or perpetuating stereotypes. China's experience with the Belt and Road Initiative highlighted the importance of tailoring AI-driven communications to specific regional contexts.
4. Rigorous testing and validation: Thorough testing is crucial before deployment in high-stakes diplomatic contexts. Premature deployment can damage credibility and undermine diplomatic efforts.
5. Balance between utility and ethics: The deployment of AI tools must be balanced against ethical considerations to maintain legitimacy and public trust.

By reflecting on these examples, diplomatic actors can better understand AI's role in political diplomacy and leverage it responsibly to address the complexities of global political engagement. Success requires not only technical capability but also careful consideration of ethical implications, cultural context, and the fundamental principles of diplomatic practice.

BALANCING HUMAN AND MACHINE INTELLIGENCE

As political officers stand at the frontier of AI-enabled diplomacy, they face both unprecedented opportunities and profound ethical challenges. The future promises even more sophisticated tools—AI systems that can simulate complex multilateral negotiations, predict the cascading effects of policy decisions across global systems, and facilitate cross-cultural understanding in ways previously unimaginable. Yet, this technological evolution demands careful consideration of how we preserve the essential human elements that make diplomacy effective.

The ethical dimensions of AI in political affairs cannot be overlooked. As these systems become more sophisticated in monitoring public sentiment and predicting political behavior, questions of privacy, consent, and transparency come to the fore. Political officers must navigate these concerns thoughtfully, ensuring that their use of AI tools aligns with diplomatic principles and respects the sovereignty and dignity of host nations. For instance, while AI-powered surveillance might offer valuable insights into emerging political movements, diplomats must carefully weigh the benefits of such monitoring against potential violations of privacy and trust.

Looking ahead, the integration of AI into political affairs will likely accelerate, driven by both technological advancement and the growing complexity of global challenges. Imagine AI systems that can instantly analyze the implications of a policy decision across multiple dimensions—economic, social, environmental, and geopolitical—while accounting for cultural nuances and historical contexts. Such capabilities could transform how diplomats approach negotiations and policy development, enabling more comprehensive and nuanced strategies.

Yet amid this technological evolution, the fundamental truth remains: diplomacy is, at its heart, about people. The most sophisticated AI systems cannot replace the intuitive understanding that comes from years of diplomatic experience, the trust built through personal relationships, or the nuanced judgment required in delicate negotiations. The political officers of tomorrow will need to be masters of both human interaction and technological capability, using each to enhance the other in service of their diplomatic missions.

LARGE LANGUAGE MODELS: ENHANCING DIPLOMATIC ENGAGEMENT

Following our exploration of Large Language Models (LLMs) in general diplomacy and leadership roles, we now turn to their specific applications in political affairs. Political officers face unique challenges in analyzing complex political developments, crafting diplomatic reporting, and supporting negotiations. While earlier chapters established how LLMs can enhance diplomatic work broadly and support mission leadership, their application to political analysis presents distinct opportunities and considerations.

In political affairs, the ability to quickly process and analyze vast amounts of information is crucial. LLMs excel at helping political officers parse through public statements, media reports, and policy documents to identify key trends and patterns. For instance, when analyzing a complex political development, an officer might use these tools to quickly compare multiple news sources, identify conflicting narratives, and highlight potential biases in reporting. This capability allows officers to spend less time on initial information gathering and more time on deeper analysis and relationship building.

Political reporting, a cornerstone of diplomatic work, benefits particularly from LLM support. These tools can help structure analytical frameworks, suggest alternative interpretations of events, and ensure reporting captures key elements while maintaining appropriate diplomatic tone. For example, when drafting an analysis of changing political dynamics, an officer might use an LLM to help outline key factors to consider, identify potential gaps in the analysis, and suggest additional angles to explore.

Negotiation support represents another valuable application. Building on the leadership applications discussed in Chapter 2, political officers can use LLMs to prepare for negotiations by analyzing historical precedents, mapping potential positions, and developing response strategies. This proves especially valuable when preparing for complex multilateral discussions where understanding multiple perspectives and potential outcomes is crucial.

However, political affairs work requires particular attention to certain limitations beyond those discussed in earlier chapters. The political sensitivity of many topics demands extra caution in how these tools are used. Officers must be especially mindful of potential biases in LLM outputs when analyzing political situations and ensure information used is not sensitive or classified, unless they have proprietary systems designed for that. The goal is to enhance, not replace, the careful political judgment that comes from years of diplomatic experience.

PUTTING LLMS TO WORK FOR POLITICAL OFFICERS

Building on the prompt engineering practices outlined in earlier chapters, let's explore how political officers can craft effective prompts for their specific analytical needs. While previous chapters covered general diplomatic applications and leadership uses, political affairs work requires particular attention to analytical frameworks and diplomatic reporting conventions.

When analyzing political developments, frame your prompts to encourage structured analysis. For example:

> Analyze recent developments in the parliamentary debate over electoral reform. Structure the analysis to address: 1) key positions of major political parties, 2) main points of contention, 3) potential compromises being discussed, 4) implications for upcoming elections, and 5) impact on our bilateral relationship. Base analysis only on publicly available information and maintain appropriate analytical distance.

For diplomatic reporting, help LLMs understand the expected format and tone:

> Help me structure a diplomatic cable analyzing growing tensions between the ruling party and opposition. Include: 1) summary of key developments in past month, 2) analysis of underlying drivers, 3) stakeholder positions and interests, 4) implications for regional stability, and 5) outlook and key indicators to watch. Maintain formal diplomatic style and clear separation between factual reporting and analysis.

For negotiation preparation, focus prompts on specific aspects requiring analysis:

> Based on publicly available statements and policy papers, analyze potential negotiating positions on the proposed regional security framework. Identify: 1) areas of likely agreement, 2) potential sticking points, 3) precedents from similar negotiations, and 4) possible compromise solutions. Consider domestic political constraints facing each party.

Political officers should particularly focus on prompts that:

- Encourage systematic analysis of complex situations
- Help identify patterns and connections in political developments
- Support structured diplomatic reporting
- Assist in preparing analytical frameworks for negotiations
- Generate alternative interpretations of political events

These applications build upon the foundational capabilities discussed in previous chapters while focusing specifically on the analytical needs of political affairs work. The key is maintaining appropriate diplomatic distance and analytical rigor while leveraging these tools to enhance understanding of complex political dynamics.

ADVANCED AI USE CASES FOR POLITICAL OFFICERS

Building on the foundational AI applications explored in Chapter 1 and the leadership-focused use cases discussed in Chapter 2, we now examine advanced AI applications specifically designed for political affairs work. While earlier chapters established how AI can enhance general diplomatic functions and support mission leadership, political officers face unique challenges that require specialized applications of these technologies. From real-time political event tracking to regional sentiment mapping and detecting disinformation, these use cases demonstrate how AI can transform the core functions of political work. Each application builds upon basic AI capabilities to address the sophisticated challenges of modern political affairs, where rapid analysis of complex situations and precise understanding of political dynamics are essential. As we continue through subsequent chapters examining AI applications across different diplomatic functions, these political affairs use cases provide important context for understanding how AI can enhance specific aspects of diplomatic work while maintaining the critical role of human judgment and expertise.

REAL-TIME POLITICAL EVENT TRACKING

A digital radar that spots important political changes as they happen.

Diplomats operate in fast-paced political environments where staying informed about unfolding events is crucial. Traditional methods, such as manual monitoring of news, diplomatic cables, and communications, can be slow and leave gaps, especially during crises. AI-powered real-time political event tracking offers a solution by using ML and natural language processing (NLP) to process vast amount s of data from news outlets, government announcements, and social media. These tools identify, prioritize, and summarize critical developments, such as policy shifts, protests, or elections, ensuring diplomats have actionable insights at their fingertips.

In practice, these systems enable ambassadors to remain agile during negotiations or crises. For instance, they can track public statements or social media trends in real time, providing critical context for decision-making. Implementation involves ensuring compatibility with existing workflows, access to reliable data sources, and staff training to interpret the outputs effectively. Pilot programs in volatile regions can refine tools and prove their value, with success measured by the timeliness and relevance of the insights provided.

While these tools enhance situational awareness and decision-making speed, challenges remain. Data biases or inaccuracies can mislead, and over-reliance on AI risks overlooking contextual nuances. Privacy concerns, especially when monitoring sensitive information, require clear ethical frameworks. Human expertise remains essential for interpreting findings and crafting responses aligned with diplomatic objectives. With robust governance and collaboration between AI and human judgment, real-time event tracking becomes an indispensable asset for modern diplomacy.

SENTIMENT MAPPING ACROSS REGIONS

A mood map showing how different communities feel about key issues.

Understanding regional sentiment is vital for tailoring diplomatic strategies and addressing public concerns. Traditional sentiment analysis methods, such as surveys and media reviews, are often slow and limited in scope, especially in regions with diverse and dynamic populations. AI-powered sentiment mapping uses NLP and ML to analyze vast datasets from sources like social media, local news, and forums, providing real-time insights into public attitudes and concerns. These tools visualize trends through heatmaps and sentiment graphs, offering diplomats a clear picture of public opinion.

The applications are extensive. For example, during a public diplomacy campaign, sentiment mapping can identify regions supportive of an initiative and areas requiring targeted outreach. In crises, it can highlight regions with heightened anxiety, guiding resource allocation and messaging. Implementation requires diverse data inputs, regular updates to algorithms, and culturally aware models to avoid biases. Training diplomats to contextualize AI-generated insights ensures their strategic application.

Challenges include interpreting language and cultural nuances, managing biased data sources, and addressing privacy concerns when analyzing public platforms. These tools must operate within ethical guidelines to maintain trust with host populations. AI cannot replace the human judgment required to understand complex social dynamics, but it complements diplomatic efforts by identifying patterns and trends that might otherwise go unnoticed. When integrated responsibly, sentiment mapping transforms how diplomats engage with and respond to public opinion.

DEEPFAKE DETECTION

A truth filter for spotting fake videos and manipulated media.

Deepfakes—manipulated audio, video, or images created using advanced AI—pose significant risks to diplomacy by spreading disinformation, undermining trust, and destabilizing negotiations. Traditional methods of detecting fakes are often inadequate, given the rapid sophistication of deepfake technology. AI-powered detection tools analyze multimedia content for inconsistencies, such as unnatural movements, mismatched audio, or lighting anomalies, providing diplomats with rapid assessments of authenticity. These tools are critical in identifying fabricated media before it causes harm.

Applications include verifying the authenticity of media during elections, countering disinformation campaigns, and protecting the integrity of diplomatic communications. For example, an embassy might use AI to debunk a viral deepfake video intended to discredit its host government. Successful deployment requires high-quality algorithms, regular updates, and integration into diplomatic workflows. Training programs ensure that users can effectively interpret outputs, while pilot programs in regions vulnerable to disinformation campaigns demonstrate their value.

Challenges include the pace of deepfake advancements, potential false positives or negatives, and ethical concerns over privacy and surveillance. AI tools must complement human judgment, as diplomats bring contextual expertise essential for determining appropriate responses. Transparent governance, adherence to ethical standards, and clear communication about these tools' purposes foster trust with stakeholders. Deepfake detection tools, when responsibly implemented, serve as a powerful defense against the growing threat of manipulated media.

FOREIGN MEDIA ANALYSIS

A news digest that reveals how different countries are covering stories.

Diplomats rely on understanding foreign media narratives to anticipate public sentiment, policy shifts, and emerging trends. Traditional media analysis—manual reviews of articles, broadcasts, and online content—is time-consuming and often insufficient to process the vast volumes of information generated daily. AI-powered foreign media analysis tools automate this process using NLP and ML to extract themes, sentiment trends, and key influencers from diverse media sources, including social media, news platforms, and blogs.

Practical applications range from tracking narratives on trade agreements to identifying shifts in public sentiment about diplomatic initiatives. For instance, an ambassador preparing for a speech might use AI insights to tailor messaging that aligns with public priorities. Implementation requires high-quality data inputs, language model updates, and training to contextualize AI findings. Pilot programs in regions with complex media landscapes help refine these tools and demonstrate their value in diplomacy.

Challenges include interpreting cultural nuances, managing biased data, and adhering to privacy regulations. Human oversight is critical for contextualizing and applying insights effectively, ensuring nuanced engagement with host populations. By integrating AI with diplomatic expertise, foreign media analysis tools enhance situational awareness, improve communication strategies, and strengthen bilateral relationships.

POLICY ANALYSIS VIA TEXT MINING

A document decoder that finds important patterns in complex policies.

Analyzing dense policy documents and legislation is a critical yet time-intensive task for diplomats. Traditional methods often involve manual reviews prone to oversight and inefficiencies, especially with the growing volume of international agreements and legal texts. AI-powered text mining tools address this by automating the extraction, comparison, and synthesis of information from large datasets. These systems use NLP and ML to identify key themes, flag inconsistencies, and provide actionable insights.

For example, during trade negotiations, an AI tool could analyze multiple agreements to identify overlapping clauses or contentious points. In multilateral discussions, text mining might compare policy positions to highlight potential areas of alignment. Implementing these tools requires ensuring compatibility with diplomatic workflows, validating data sources, and providing staff training. Success is measured by improved efficiency, accuracy, and the quality of insights.

Challenges include biases in input data, the contextual limitations of AI, and ethical concerns related to sensitive documents. Human expertise remains indispensable for interpreting findings and applying them strategically. Ethical guidelines ensure responsible use and build trust in AI outputs. When combined with diplomatic judgment, text mining transforms policy analysis into a more efficient and insightful process.

AI-Augmented Dossiers

A smart briefing book that updates itself with the latest information.

Dossiers are essential for diplomats to prepare for meetings, negotiations, and engagements, yet compiling and updating them can be time-intensive. Traditional methods involve manual research and synthesis, which often struggle to keep pace with rapidly changing information. AI-augmented dossiers streamline this process by using NLP and ML to automatically gather, organize, and analyze relevant data from vast sources such as news articles, social media, and government reports. These tools generate comprehensive, real-time profiles of individuals, organizations, or issues critical to diplomatic missions.

Practical applications include preparing detailed profiles of key stakeholders or identifying policy priorities before negotiations. For example, an AI tool could provide an up-to-date dossier on a foreign minister's recent statements and policy shifts ahead of a high-stakes meeting. Successful implementation depends on access to reliable data sources, regular updates to algorithms, and ensuring staff are trained to contextualize and apply the generated insights. Pilot programs targeting high-profile engagements can demonstrate the value of these tools.

Challenges include data biases, incomplete information, and ethical concerns, particularly around privacy. Human expertise is essential for validating and interpreting the insights, ensuring they align with diplomatic objectives. Clear ethical guidelines and transparent usage frameworks build trust with stakeholders and host-country authorities. AI-augmented dossiers, when integrated responsibly, enhance preparation, reduce administrative burdens, and empower diplomats to engage more effectively.

LOCALIZED POLITICAL SENTIMENT DASHBOARDS

A local opinion tracker showing what different neighborhoods think.

Understanding public sentiment across different regions is a cornerstone of effective diplomacy. Traditional approaches, like surveys and media reviews, are often slow and resource-intensive, limiting their ability to capture real-time shifts. AI-powered localized political sentiment dashboards aggregate and analyze data from social media, news outlets, and public forums to provide real-time, region-specific insights. These tools visualize sentiment trends through heatmaps or graphs, enabling diplomats to understand public attitudes at a granular level.

For example, during a contentious policy rollout, an ambassador could use the dashboard to identify regions where dissatisfaction is highest and adapt outreach strategies accordingly. Implementation requires high-quality data sources, updates to ensure cultural sensitivity, and training to interpret outputs effectively. Pilot programs in politically dynamic regions can refine these tools and highlight their impact on diplomatic engagement.

Challenges include linguistic and cultural nuances, biases in data sources, and privacy concerns related to public platform monitoring. While AI excels at processing vast datasets, human judgment is critical for contextualizing insights and applying them strategically. Ethical guidelines and transparent usage protocols ensure responsible implementation. When integrated into diplomatic workflows, sentiment dashboards enhance situational awareness and enable more targeted and effective public engagement.

ELECTION INTERFERENCE MONITORING

A watchdog system for protecting elections from outside manipulation.

Safeguarding election integrity is crucial for maintaining democratic stability, yet traditional monitoring methods often fail to detect sophisticated interference tactics such as disinformation campaigns or cyberattacks. AI-powered election interference monitoring tools analyze diverse data sources, including social media and digital infrastructure, to detect coordinated manipulation efforts in real time. These systems use ML and NLP to identify disinformation narratives, suspicious activity, and anomalies in voter behavior patterns.

Practical applications include monitoring social media for false claims about polling locations or detecting cyberattacks targeting voter databases. For instance, during a close election, an AI system could flag coordinated efforts to spread disinformation, enabling rapid countermeasures. Implementation requires high-quality algorithms, robust data inputs, and staff training to interpret and respond to findings effectively. Success is measured by the ability to detect threats early and mitigate disruptions.

Challenges include evolving interference tactics, data quality issues, and ethical concerns regarding privacy and surveillance. Human oversight ensures that findings are contextualized and appropriately addressed. Transparent frameworks and adherence to ethical guidelines are essential for building trust with stakeholders. AI-powered monitoring tools, when deployed responsibly, strengthen the ability of diplomats to protect electoral integrity and support democratic processes.

LANGUAGE AND TONE ANALYSIS FOR DIPLOMATS

A communication advisor for striking the right tone in messages.

Effective communication is a cornerstone of diplomacy, where the tone and language of messages can significantly influence outcomes. Traditional methods of crafting and reviewing communication rely on individual expertise, which can be subjective and time-consuming. AI-powered language and tone analysis tools enhance this process by analyzing drafts for tone, sentiment, and cultural appropriateness. Using NLP, these tools provide actionable suggestions, such as rephrasing to strike a conciliatory tone or simplifying language for broader accessibility.

Applications include refining speeches, correspondence, or negotiation statements to align with diplomatic objectives and cultural sensitivities. For instance, an ambassador preparing a press release could use AI insights to ensure the language is empathetic and non-confrontational during a sensitive crisis. Successful implementation requires culturally sensitive models, regular updates, and staff training to integrate the tool into communication workflows. Metrics for success include improved audience reception and reduced misunderstandings.

Challenges include interpreting idiomatic expressions, potential over-reliance on AI suggestions, and ethical concerns when analyzing private communications. Human judgment remains essential for contextualizing AI outputs and preserving authenticity. Transparent usage protocols and ethical safeguards build trust in these systems. Language and tone analysis tools, when used collaboratively, help diplomats craft messages that resonate and build stronger relationships.

AUTOMATED POLICY BRIEFS FOR NEGOTIATIONS

A quick summary maker for complex negotiation topics.

Policy briefs are critical for equipping diplomats with concise, actionable insights, yet traditional methods of preparing them are labor-intensive and time-sensitive. AI-powered tools for automated policy briefs streamline this process by analyzing extensive datasets, such as reports and media sources, to extract and summarize key points. Using NLP and ML, these tools create structured, targeted documents tailored to specific negotiation contexts.

For example, during a multilateral summit, an AI system could generate briefs comparing the policy positions of participating countries, highlighting areas of alignment or divergence. Implementation involves ensuring reliable data inputs, compatibility with existing workflows, and training to validate and interpret outputs. Success is measured by the relevance and accuracy of briefs, as well as the time saved in preparation.

Challenges include ensuring data quality, mitigating oversimplification, and addressing privacy concerns when analyzing sensitive documents. Human oversight is vital for contextualizing findings and applying them strategically in negotiations. Ethical guidelines and clear usage protocols reinforce trust in these tools. Automated policy briefs, when responsibly deployed, enhance preparation, reduce administrative burdens, and empower diplomats to focus on strategy and engagement.

LIMITATIONS AND FUTURE RESEARCH DIRECTIONS

As AI increasingly shapes political affairs and diplomatic practice, we must critically examine both current limitations and future research needs. This examination reveals crucial gaps between AI's promise and its practical application in political diplomacy, while highlighting important directions for future investigation.

THE CHALLENGE OF DIPLOMATIC INTUITION

Perhaps, the most fundamental limitation lies in AI's ability to capture and replicate diplomatic intuition. Consider a seasoned political officer who can sense subtle shifts in power dynamics during a meeting, or detect unspoken tensions in coalition politics through years of experience. While AI excels at processing vast amounts of data, it struggles to replicate this kind of intuitive understanding that comes from deep immersion in diplomatic practice.

Think of it like the difference between learning a language through textbooks versus living in a country—AI currently operates more like the former, missing the nuanced understanding that comes from direct experience. This limitation becomes particularly evident in situations requiring cultural fluency and emotional intelligence, such as reading body language during negotiations or understanding the unstated implications of diplomatic gestures.

CULTURAL AND HISTORICAL COMPLEXITY

Current AI systems demonstrate significant limitations in understanding non-Western political systems and historical contexts. These tools, often trained primarily on Western political models and data, can systematically misinterpret political developments in societies with fundamentally different traditions of power and governance. For example, an AI system might fail to recognize the importance of informal power structures in societies where traditional hierarchies operate alongside formal institutions.

Consider how AI might analyze political dynamics in a country where religious leadership holds significant informal influence over secular politics. The system might focus solely on official government structures while missing crucial power dynamics that shape political outcomes. This blindspot isn't just a technical limitation—it reflects deeper challenges in teaching machines to understand complex cultural and historical contexts.

THE MULTI-POLAR WORLD CHALLENGE

Traditional frameworks for political analysis face increasing strain in today's multi-polar world, where alliances are fluid and power relationships increasingly complex. AI systems, trained on historical patterns of international relations, may struggle to adapt to emerging forms of international cooperation and competition that don't fit traditional models.

For instance, how does an AI system analyze a situation where a country simultaneously cooperates with competing powers in different domains—perhaps collaborating on climate change while competing on technology? These nuanced positions challenge AI's tendency to categorize relationships in more binary terms.

ETHICAL AND SECURITY CONSIDERATIONS

The deployment of AI in political affairs raises profound ethical questions about privacy, sovereignty, and diplomatic integrity. Current systems may inadvertently cross the line between legitimate diplomatic analysis and inappropriate surveillance or intervention in host country affairs. This concern becomes particularly acute when AI tools monitor social media or public sentiment, potentially violating local privacy expectations or cultural norms.

Security vulnerabilities present another critical limitation. As AI systems become more integral to diplomatic analysis, they also become attractive targets for manipulation. The potential for adversaries to corrupt AI analysis through targeted disinformation or data poisoning represents a significant threat to diplomatic decision-making.

FUTURE RESEARCH PRIORITIES

These limitations point toward several crucial directions for future research in AI-enhanced political diplomacy. First and foremost, we must develop AI systems with enhanced cultural understanding—systems that can better comprehend and navigate diverse political traditions around the world. This means creating models that can recognize and account for informal power structures, developing methods to incorporate deep historical and cultural context into political analysis, and building systems that can adapt to different cultural understandings of politics and power.

The challenge of modeling diplomatic intuition represents another vital research direction. We need to explore ways to better capture and complement the intuitive understanding that experienced diplomats develop over years of service. This involves studying how seasoned diplomats make decisions in complex situations, developing AI systems that can learn from diplomatic expertise while preserving human judgment, and creating tools that enhance rather than replace diplomatic intuition.

As the world becomes increasingly multi-polar, we need new analytical frameworks capable of understanding complex international relationships. Research should focus on developing models that can handle fluid and multifaceted political alignments, creating tools for analyzing emerging forms of international cooperation and competition, and building systems that can track and analyze non-traditional diplomatic actors. These frameworks must move beyond traditional binary classifications to capture the nuanced reality of modern international relations.

Security and ethics demand particular attention in future research. We need to develop robust safeguards against AI manipulation and disinformation, create clear ethical frameworks for AI use in diplomatic analysis, and establish protocols for protecting privacy while maintaining analytical capabilities. This research is crucial for maintaining the integrity and trustworthiness of AI-enhanced diplomatic work.

Finally, we must examine how to effectively integrate these new technologies into diplomatic practice. This includes studying how to train diplomats to work alongside AI systems, developing methods for preserving traditional diplomatic skills in an AI-enhanced environment, and creating approaches for seamlessly integrating AI insights with human expertise. The goal is not to replace human judgment but to augment it in ways that enhance diplomatic effectiveness.

CONCLUSION

This chapter has examined the transformative impact of AI on political affairs, revealing how AI is reshaping diplomatic practice while preserving its essential human elements. Through the opening vignette of Political Officer Sarah Chen, we explored how AI augments traditional diplomatic skills with data-driven insights and predictive capabilities.

The historical analysis demonstrated AI's evolution in diplomacy, from early warning systems to sophisticated applications in recent conflicts. Case studies from Ukraine's counter-disinformation efforts to China's comprehensive AI deployment highlighted both opportunities and risks. The examination of the Bureau of Conflict and Stabilization Operations' AI tools showed how these technologies are already being developed by governments to help support conflict prevention.

LLMs emerged as particularly powerful tools for political officers, offering enhanced capabilities in diplomatic reporting, negotiation preparation, and political analysis. This chapter's practical guidance on prompt engineering provided concrete strategies for leveraging these tools while maintaining diplomatic standards and ethical considerations.

The ten advanced use cases presented—spanning from real-time political event tracking to automated policy briefs—illustrated AI's practical applications across political affairs. These tools demonstrate how technology can enhance situational awareness, strengthen democratic processes, improve diplomatic communication, and streamline preparation and reporting, all while preserving the critical role of human judgment.

However, the successful integration of AI in political affairs requires careful attention to ethical implications, privacy concerns, and cultural sensitivities. The future of political diplomacy lies in achieving the right balance between technological capability and human expertise—where AI amplifies rather than replaces the fundamental skills of relationship-building, cultural understanding, and ethical reasoning that define effective diplomacy.

As we look ahead to economic diplomacy in the next chapter, we'll explore how these AI capabilities extend beyond political affairs to shape trade negotiations, investment strategies, and global economic cooperation, further demonstrating the broad impact of AI across diplomatic functions.

DISCUSSION SCENARIOS AND QUESTIONS

These scenarios explore the role of AI in political diplomacy, from analyzing global trends to influencing foreign policy decisions. Readers will reflect on the ethical and strategic considerations of AI-driven political analysis, balancing its predictive power with the nuanced human judgment that remains essential in international affairs.

1. AI-assisted event planning for high-level visits

Scenario: When planning a schedule for a visiting delegation, AI proposes an itinerary based on its analysis of policy priorities and local influence networks. It suggests meeting with emerging groups and excludes some traditional allies.

Questions: How might you weigh the benefits of following AI's recommendations against the potential disruption of established relationships for emerging opportunities? How do you justify to both allies and superiors the choices made in the itinerary?

2. AI-assisted regional analysis

Scenario: You are tasked with monitoring a geographic region. An AI tool analyzes local publications, maps political alliances, and predicts unrest. The AI flags a surge in dissent and recommends engaging with specific groups to de-escalate tensions. However, your locally hired political specialist cautions that these groups are politically insignificant and that the unrest may be exaggerated.

Questions: What factors would you consider when deciding between AI's data-driven analysis and the specialist's nuanced, culturally informed judgment? How do you balance AI's broad analytical capabilities with the critical human understanding of local dynamics?

3. AI-generated policy briefs

Scenario: You use AI to draft a policy report for your home government. The AI synthesizes developments in the host country and proposes recommendations. While the analysis appears sound, you notice it lacks sensitivity to cultural or historical nuances critical to the region.

Questions: How do you integrate AI's recommendations while ensuring they remain culturally and historically appropriate? What steps can you take to prevent presenting politically inappropriate solutions based solely on AI analysis?

4. Crisis response and reporting

Scenario: In the middle of a political crisis, AI generates a comprehensive report based on real-time analysis of social media, news outlets, and official statements. It proposes an action plan. However, your observations from meetings with local officials suggest a different, more nuanced perspective.

Questions: In what ways can you balance AI's rapid, large-scale analysis with your firsthand understanding of the situation? How do you reconcile discrepancies between AI-generated insights and your own observations, especially under time pressure?

5. AI in negotiation preparation

Scenario: Before a key negotiation with host-country officials, an AI tool analyzes public statements, social media activity, and historical patterns, providing simulations of potential outcomes. It even suggests exploiting certain psychological tendencies of your counterpart to gain leverage.

Questions: How would you approach AI's recommendations to avoid creating distrust or appearing manipulative while making decisions? Where do you draw the ethical line in leveraging AI-driven insights in a negotiation setting?

4 AI and Economic Affairs
Supercharging Trade, Investment, and Innovation

> The same technologies that can be used to concentrate wealth and power can also be used to distribute it more widely and empower more people.
>
> *—Erik Brynjolfsson, Director of the MIT Initiative on the Digital Economy (2019)*

> The playing field is poised to become a lot more competitive, and businesses that don't deploy AI and data to help them innovate in everything they do will be at a disadvantage.
>
> *—Paul Daugherty, Accenture (2020)*

> The development of AI is as fundamental as the creation of the microprocessor, the personal computer, the Internet, and the mobile phone. It will change the way people work, learn, travel, get health care, and communicate with each other.
>
> *—Bill Gates, Microsoft Co-Founder (2023)*

Economic diplomacy, long a cornerstone of international relations, has entered a transformative era. Traditionally, diplomats relied on meticulous data collection and intuitive assessments to negotiate trade agreements, attract foreign investments, and promote sustainable development. Today, the integration of artificial intelligence (AI) is redefining the tools and techniques of economic diplomacy, bringing a precision and foresight previously unimaginable. By enabling faster analysis, uncovering hidden patterns, and offering actionable insights, AI empowers diplomats to navigate the complexities of global economics with confidence and vision. This chapter explores the revolutionary role of AI in economic affairs, weaving real-world applications, speculative futures, and ethical considerations into a compelling narrative that highlights the transformative potential of this technology.

VIGNETTE   AI-Enhanced Embassy in the Republic of Z

In the days following the political unrest that gripped the Republic of Z, Economic Officer Elena Moretti begins her morning by analyzing her AI-enhanced economic dashboard. Recent protests over economic grievances have revealed opportunities for positive change, particularly in Z's emerging renewable energy sector. Her screen displays an intricate web of trade flows,

---

DOI: 10.1201/9781003612308-4

investment patterns, and market indicators that could help transform recent challenges into sustainable solutions.

Drawing on her extensive network of contacts in Z's business community and government ministries, Moretti has been tracking a promising trend that the AI system has validated: a surge in regional demand for solar technology coinciding with Z's growing skilled workforce and manufacturing capacity. The AI's analysis of trade data, industrial capacity reports, and regional energy policies confirms her ground-level observations—Z is perfectly positioned to become a renewable energy hub.

As she prepares her briefing for the Ambassador, Moretti appreciates how AI amplifies her economic diplomacy skills. While the system processes vast amounts of market data and regulatory information, it's her careful cultivation of relationships with Z's Finance Ministry, Chamber of Commerce, and business leaders that will make this opportunity viable. The AI has already generated preliminary economic impact assessments, which she refines based on her deep understanding of local market dynamics and policy constraints.

Her morning schedule reflects the breadth of economic diplomacy. She's meeting with Z's Deputy Finance Minister to discuss potential tax incentives for green energy investments, followed by a roundtable with local business leaders interested in joint ventures with U.S. firms. The AI system helps her prepare tailored briefing materials for each engagement, incorporating historical trade data, current market analyses, and policy frameworks while she focuses on the nuanced relationship-building that makes economic diplomacy successful.

By mid-afternoon, Moretti is coordinating with Management Officer Amir Qureshi to plan for an upcoming trade delegation focused on renewable energy partnerships. As she reviews the AI's projections for potential investment flows and job creation, she's already thinking about how these economic initiatives could help address the underlying concerns that sparked recent protests, transforming economic challenges into opportunities for sustainable growth and regional leadership.

EVOLUTION OF ECONOMIC DIPLOMACY

The practice of economic diplomacy has undergone a profound transformation in recent years. Where diplomats once relied primarily on intuition, personal networks, and carefully cultivated relationships to advance economic interests, they now operate in a world where data-driven insights and AI augment these traditional approaches. This evolution reflects not just technological advancement but also a fundamental shift in how nations engage in economic statecraft (Bjola & Kornprobst 2024).

Consider how economic officers traditionally approached trade promotion. They would spend months cultivating relationships with local business leaders, analyzing market reports, and intuiting opportunities based on years of experience. While these skills remain vital, AI now amplifies their effectiveness exponentially. Modern economic officers can access real-time market intelligence, predictive analytics, and detailed stakeholder mapping that transforms their ability to identify and seize opportunities (Alder et al. 2024).

The integration of AI into economic diplomacy has particularly revolutionized how missions anticipate and respond to market changes. Rather than waiting for quarterly economic reports or annual trade statistics, diplomats can now monitor dynamic dashboards that provide instant insights into trade flows, investment patterns, and emerging market trends. This shift from reactive to predictive analysis enables them to spot potential challenges before they become crises and identify opportunities while they're still emerging (Blaser 2023).

AI'S IMPACT ON CORE ECONOMIC FUNCTIONS

The transformation of economic diplomacy through AI is perhaps most visible in its core functions of trade promotion, investment attraction, and market analysis. AI systems now process vast amounts of economic data, identifying patterns and correlations that would be impossible for human analysts to detect alone (Alder 2024). For example, when analyzing potential trade opportunities, AI can simultaneously evaluate market demand, supply chain logistics, regulatory frameworks, and competitor behaviors across multiple regions, providing economic officers with actionable insights that inform their engagement strategies.

Investment attraction has similarly evolved. Economic officers can now leverage AI-powered platforms that not only identify potential investors but also predict their likely interests and concerns (Huang 2022). These systems analyze investor behavior patterns, corporate announcements, and market movements to help diplomats craft targeted pitches that resonate with specific investors' strategic priorities (Di Martino & Ford 2024, Kapoor 2024). This targeted investment promotion is transforming what was once largely a hunch or numbers game into a more strategic endeavor.

TRANSFORMING ECONOMIC DECISION-MAKING

The integration of AI into economic diplomacy has fundamentally changed how missions approach decision-making and strategic planning. Economic officers now operate with unprecedented clarity, backed by data-driven insights that illuminate both opportunities and risks (Doubleday 2024a, 2024b). During trade negotiations, for instance, AI systems can simulate the potential impacts of various proposals across multiple sectors simultaneously, enabling diplomats to advocate for positions that maximize benefits while minimizing unintended consequences (ICC 2018).

This enhanced decision-making capability proves particularly valuable in supply chain optimization and crisis response. When global supply chains face disruption, AI tools can help diplomatic missions identify alternative routes, suppliers, and markets with remarkable speed (Huang 2022). The technology analyzes countless variables—from transportation costs and customs procedures to political stability and environmental risks—providing economic officers with comprehensive scenarios that inform their recommendations to both government and private sector stakeholders (Manor 2017, 2019).

Market intelligence, once gathered through time-intensive manual research and personal networks, can now flow continuously through AI-powered analytics platforms. These systems monitor everything from social media sentiment and news coverage to financial market movements and regulatory changes, synthesizing this information into actionable insights. For economic officers managing complex trade

relationships, this real-time intelligence enables them to spot emerging trends, anticipate challenges, and seize opportunities faster than ever before (Cassidy 2024).

BUILDING ECONOMIC RESILIENCE

The true power of AI in economic diplomacy lies not just in its ability to process data
but in its capacity to strengthen economic resilience. By identifying patterns and correlations across vast datasets, AI helps missions develop more robust strategies for sustainable development and regional economic integration (United Nations Development
Programme [UNDP] 2020). Economic officers can now model how different policy
initiatives might impact long-term economic stability, taking into account factors ranging from climate change to demographic shifts (Bullock et al. 2020).

Risk management has evolved from a largely reactive process to a proactive discipline. AI systems can continuously monitor potential threats to economic stability—
whether they're financial market fluctuations, supply chain vulnerabilities, or emerging trade barriers (Huang 2022). This enhanced awareness enables diplomatic missions to develop contingency plans before crises emerge and to adapt strategies quickly
when circumstances change (Manor 2023). For instance, when early warning signs of
market instability appear, economic officers can quickly assess potential impacts and
coordinate responses with their counterparts in other missions (Kello 2023).

Future-proofing trade relationships have become increasingly critical in our
interconnected world. AI helps diplomatic missions anticipate how emerging technologies, changing consumer preferences, and evolving regulatory landscapes might
affect bilateral economic ties (Cassidy 2024). This foresight allows economic officers
to guide their trade partners toward more sustainable and mutually beneficial relationships, ensuring that today's agreements remain relevant and valuable in tomorrow's economic landscape (Di Martino & Ford 2024).

HISTORICAL AI USE CASE EXAMPLES IN ECONOMIC AFFAIRS

AI is revolutionizing economic diplomacy by showing promise to enhance trade
negotiations, improve resource allocation, and enable sustainable development initiatives (Bjola & Kornprobst 2024). This section examines key historical examples
where governments and international organizations have taken steps to deploy AI to
address complex economic challenges.

One early example of AI in economic diplomacy was the International Chamber
of Commerce's (ICC) Cognitive Trade Advisor, developed in partnership with IBM
in 2018. The platform leveraged natural language processing (NLP) and machine
learning to analyze trade agreements, identify policy overlaps, and propose potential trade opportunities (ICC 2018). This tool reduced the time required for trade
negotiations by allowing diplomats to access relevant clauses across thousands of
agreements quickly. Its deployment highlighted AI's potential to simplify complex
processes and enhance efficiency in economic diplomacy (ICC 2018).

The United Nations Development Programme (UNDP) has utilized AI to monitor
progress toward the Sustainable Development Goals (SDGs). In one instance, AI tools
analyzed economic and environmental data across member states to identify disparities
in development (UNDP 2020). These insights informed diplomatic discussions on aid

allocation and development planning, ensuring that resources were directed toward the most vulnerable populations. This initiative exemplified how AI can support evidence-based diplomacy by providing actionable data for multilateral negotiations.

During the Russo-Ukrainian War, NATO employed AI-driven predictive analytics to monitor disruptions in trade flows and assess their impact on member states (Kello 2023). By analyzing economic data, supply chain networks, and regional trade dependencies, AI tools identified emerging vulnerabilities and proposed strategic responses. This application underscored AI's ability to enhance agility in economic diplomacy, enabling governments to respond quickly to dynamic geopolitical conditions (Kello 2023).

China has employed AI tools extensively in its Belt and Road Initiative (BRI) to promote international trade and investment (Huang 2022, García-Herrero & Schindowski 2023). AI-driven sentiment analysis helped Chinese policymakers assess how partner nations perceived BRI projects, allowing them to adapt their strategies accordingly (Le & Zhang 2024). For example, the Chinese government used AI to analyze infrastructure project performance and predict economic returns, enhancing the initiative's strategic alignment with local stakeholders' needs (Huang 2022, Mokashi et al. 2022). However, this approach also raised concerns about transparency and ethical governance, particularly regarding the use of AI for influence in partner nations.

The European Union deployed AI systems to model economic disruptions during the COVID-19 pandemic (Manor 2023). These models evaluated the economic impact of lockdown measures, trade restrictions, and supply chain bottlenecks across member states. Insights from these tools informed coordinated EU-level economic policies, ensuring a balanced recovery and equitable resource distribution (Manor 2023). This case demonstrated AI's capacity to manage complex economic crises while promoting multilateral cooperation.

While AI has provided significant benefits in economic diplomacy, its deployment also raises ethical challenges. For example, algorithmic bias in trade models could marginalize smaller economies or perpetuate existing inequalities. The ICC's Cognitive Trade Advisor addressed this concern by involving diverse stakeholders in the platform's design and validation processes, supporting fairness and inclusivity in trade recommendations (ICC 2018). Similarly, the UNDP's SDG monitoring initiative emphasized data transparency and local engagement, reinforcing the ethical foundation of AI-driven economic diplomacy.

The UK government's launch of the "Humphrey" AI suite aspires to transform economic affairs by modernizing outdated public-sector processes, with potential savings of £45 billion and improved service efficiency (Doubleday 2024a, 2024b). While its impact remains unrealized, it reflects ambitions to position AI as a driver of economic renewal and public-sector productivity. For diplomats focused on economic affairs, this highlights the growing importance of AI in shaping policy frameworks, economic strategy, and international cooperation on technology standards (Keskin & Kiggins 2021).

According to the AI use case inventory published by the State Department, AI tools are starting to play a role in supporting economic affairs (Alder 2024b). The "BudgetChat" AI Tool is reportedly aimed at consolidating and streamlining access to budget documents, enabling efficient analysis of multi-year programs and initiatives. Additionally, natural language processing (NLP) for Foreign Assistance Appropriations Analysis is aimed at automating the extraction of earmarks and directives from annual appropriations bills, significantly reducing manual effort. Together, these tools offer to enhance resource management and decision-making in economic and budget planning activities.

The historical use of AI in economic diplomacy highlights several critical lessons:

1. Data-driven negotiations: AI's ability to process large datasets enhances the accuracy and efficiency of trade negotiations, as demonstrated by the ICC's Cognitive Trade Advisor.
2. Collaboration for inclusivity: Multilateral initiatives like the UNDP's SDG monitoring stress the importance of involving local stakeholders to ensure equitable outcomes.
3. Adaptability in crisis: The EU's use of AI during the COVID-19 pandemic showcases its potential for crisis management, enabling governments to make informed decisions in rapidly changing environments.
4. Ethical oversight: Ensuring transparency and addressing algorithmic bias are essential for maintaining trust in AI-powered economic diplomacy.

By drawing on these examples, policymakers can harness AI to foster sustainable growth, strengthen trade relationships, and promote global economic stability (Tuset Varela 2024a, 2024b).

ETHICAL CONSIDERATIONS AND HUMAN OVERSIGHT

The powerful capabilities of AI in economic diplomacy bring with them equally significant responsibilities. While the technology offers unprecedented insights and efficiency, it must be guided by human wisdom and ethical principles (European Commission 2019). Economic officers face the crucial task of balancing automated analysis with human judgment, ensuring that AI serves as a tool for promoting equitable economic development rather than exacerbating existing inequalities (Höne et al. 2019a, 2019b).

Privacy and data protection concerns stand at the forefront of these ethical considerations. As AI systems process vast amounts of economic and market data, diplomatic missions must navigate complex questions about data sovereignty, security, and transparency (Konovalova 2023). Economic officers must ensure their use of AI tools complies not only with international regulations but also respects the privacy expectations of host countries and their citizens (Daskalovski 2021). This challenge becomes particularly acute when analyzing sensitive economic indicators or proprietary business information.

The human element in economic diplomacy remains irreplaceable, even as AI capabilities expand. While AI excels at processing data and identifying patterns, it cannot fully grasp the nuanced cultural, political, and social dynamics that influence economic relationships (Kissinger, Schmidt, & Mundie 2024). Successful economic diplomacy requires a sophisticated understanding of local contexts, personal relationships, and unwritten rules—factors that often defy quantification (Lebedeva & Zinovieva 2023). The most effective economic officers use AI to enhance rather than replace their judgment, combining technological insights with deep cultural and political awareness.

AI INTEGRATION IN MODERN ECONOMIC DIPLOMACY

The convergence of AI and economic diplomacy represents more than a technological upgrade—it marks a fundamental shift in how nations interact in the global marketplace (Viggiano 2023). Economic officers now stand at the intersection of traditional diplomatic skills and cutting-edge technology, using AI not just as a tool but as a partner in advancing economic interests (Höne et al. 2019a, 2019b). When assessing potential trade agreements, AI analyzes countless variables simultaneously—market conditions, regulatory frameworks, historical trade patterns, and potential future scenarios (ICC Brasil 2018). Yet, it's the economic officer's expertise that contextualizes these insights, understanding how they fit within broader diplomatic objectives and local realities. This synthesis of machine intelligence and human wisdom creates a more nuanced and effective approach to economic diplomacy (Wiseman 2024).

As global economic landscapes grow increasingly complex, new AI capabilities are emerging, from systems that predict economic trends and suggest novel approaches to persistent development challenges (Kurbalija 2024) to platforms enabling real-time collaboration between missions worldwide (U.S. Department of State 2024a, 2024b, 2024c, 2024d). Each new AI application, from automated market analysis to predictive modeling of trade outcomes, serves the broader mission of economic diplomacy (Tuset Varela 2024a, 2024b). The fundamental principles—building trust, fostering cooperation, and promoting mutual prosperity—remain constant, with the challenge lying in using AI to enhance these principles rather than replace them (Horowitz 2018). As AI's role continues to expand and evolve (Marwala 2023), these tools represent new ways to achieve enduring diplomatic goals: promoting prosperity, fostering stability, and creating opportunities for mutual growth in an increasingly interconnected world (Marwala 2023, Feijóo et al. 2020).

LARGE LANGUAGE MODELS: A RESOURCE
FOR ECONOMIC INSIGHTS

Building on our previous exploration of LLMs in general diplomacy, leadership roles, and political affairs, we now examine their specific applications in economic diplomacy. While earlier chapters demonstrated how these tools can enhance diplomatic communication, support leadership decision-making, and strengthen political analysis, economic officers face unique challenges in analyzing market trends, evaluating trade opportunities, and supporting complex negotiations.

Economic diplomacy requires processing vast amounts of market data, trade statistics, and financial information to identify patterns and opportunities. LLMs excel at helping economic officers synthesize this information into actionable insights (Alder 2024a). For instance, when analyzing market entry opportunities, these tools can help process multiple data sources to identify key trends, regulatory requirements, and potential challenges (Tuset Varela 2024a, 2024b). This allows officers to focus their expertise on validating findings and developing strategic recommendations.

Trade reporting, particularly crucial in economic affairs, benefits from LLM capabilities in new ways. Beyond the general writing support explored in earlier chapters, these tools can help economic officers structure complex financial data into clear narratives, ensure technical accuracy in trade terminology, and adapt economic concepts for different audiences (Wiseman 2024). This proves especially valuable when preparing investment promotion materials or explaining complex trade agreements to stakeholders.

Financial analysis represents another key application unique to economic affairs. Building on the analytical frameworks discussed in previous chapters, economic officers can use LLMs to help process financial statements, analyze market indicators, and identify economic trends (U.S. Department of State 2024a, 2024b, 2024c, 2024d). This capability particularly shines when preparing economic impact assessments or evaluating investment proposals.

However, economic affairs work demands special attention to certain limitations beyond those discussed earlier. The sensitivity of financial data and market information requires extra caution in how these tools are used (Konovalova 2023). Officers must be particularly mindful of sharing only public information and ensuring all analyses are validated against authoritative economic data sources (Marwala 2023).

PUTTING LLMS TO WORK FOR ECONOMIC OFFICERS

Building on the prompt engineering practices established in previous chapters, let's explore how economic officers can craft effective prompts for their specific analytical needs. While earlier chapters covered general diplomatic applications, leadership uses, and political analysis, economic affairs work requires particular attention to market analysis, trade data, and financial trends.

When analyzing market opportunities, frame your prompts to encourage structured economic analysis. For example:

> Analyze market entry opportunities in the host country's renewable energy sector. Structure the analysis to address: 1) market size and growth projections, 2) regulatory framework and incentives, 3) competitive landscape, 4) infrastructure readiness, and 5) potential barriers to entry. Include relevant publicly available economic indicators and market statistics to support the analysis.

For trade reporting, help LLMs understand the expected technical precision and data focus:

> Help me draft a quarterly trade report analyzing bilateral trade flows in key sectors. Include: 1) key statistical trends from publicly available trade data, 2) analysis of sector-specific developments, 3) impact of recent policy changes, 4) emerging market opportunities, and 5) recommendations for enhancing trade cooperation. Maintain appropriate technical precision while ensuring accessibility for non-specialist readers.

For investment analysis, structure prompts to focus on key financial considerations:

> Based on public financial data and market reports, analyze the investment climate in the manufacturing sector. Consider: 1) recent FDI trends, 2) relevant tax and regulatory frameworks, 3) labor market conditions, 4) infrastructure quality, and 5) comparison with regional competitors. Structure this as a clear investment climate assessment suitable for potential investors.

Economic officers should particularly focus on prompts that:

- Encourage data-driven analysis of market conditions
- Help identify patterns in trade and investment flows

- Support clear communication of complex economic concepts
- Assist in evaluating investment opportunities
- Generate insights from publicly available economic indicators

These applications build upon the foundational capabilities discussed in previous chapters while focusing specifically on the analytical needs of economic affairs work. The key is maintaining appropriate technical precision while ensuring outputs are accessible to various stakeholders in the economic diplomacy space.

ADVANCED AI USE CASES IN ECONOMIC AFFAIRS

Building on the foundational AI applications explored in Chapter 1, the leadership-focused use cases from Chapter 2, and the political affairs applications from Chapter 3, we now examine advanced AI solutions specifically designed for economic diplomacy. While earlier chapters established how AI can enhance diplomatic functions across various domains, economic affairs present unique opportunities for leveraging AI in market analysis, trade optimization, and investment promotion. From predictive market analysis and real-time trade flow monitoring to automated compliance checks for economic agreements, these use cases demonstrate how AI can transform core economic functions. Each application builds upon basic AI capabilities to address the sophisticated challenges of modern economic diplomacy, where data-driven insights and rapid analysis of market conditions are essential. As we continue exploring AI applications across different diplomatic functions in subsequent chapters, these economic affairs use cases highlight how AI can be tailored to specific diplomatic disciplines while maintaining the crucial role of human expertise in interpreting and applying insights.

TRADE OPPORTUNITY IDENTIFICATION

A market matchmaker that spots promising business connections between countries.

AI revolutionizes how missions identify trade opportunities by continuously analyzing vast datasets spanning trade flows, market trends, economic indicators, and consumer behavior patterns. These systems detect emerging opportunities and potential synergies between markets that might be invisible to traditional analysis methods. The technology's ability to process and correlate multiple data streams enables early identification of promising trade developments.

Implementation requires careful integration with existing mission workflows and reliable data sources. Success metrics include the accuracy of opportunity predictions, the volume of successful trade deals facilitated, and stakeholder feedback. Regular system updates ensure that AI maintains effectiveness as market conditions evolve. Training programs help staff maximize the technology's potential while maintaining necessary oversight.

Real-world applications demonstrate the technology's value. During trade missions, AI systems provide real-time insights that help diplomats adjust strategies and identify promising sectors for collaboration. For example, the technology might spot rising demand for sustainable technologies in neighboring markets, enabling economic officers to proactively connect domestic suppliers with foreign buyers. This proactive approach transforms traditional trade promotion into a more precise and strategic endeavor.

MARKET ENTRY FEASIBILITY ANALYSIS

A risk calculator that shows how ready a market is for new business.

Modern economic officers rely on AI to evaluate market entry potential across multiple dimensions simultaneously. These systems analyze regulatory environments, market demand, competitive landscapes, and potential risks, providing comprehensive feasibility assessments in significantly less time than traditional methods. The technology continuously monitors changes in market conditions, ensuring assessments remain current and relevant.

Successful deployment depends on integrating diverse data sources and maintaining high data quality standards. Economic officers must balance AI insights with local knowledge and cultural understanding. Regular model updates and staff training ensure the system remains effective and properly utilized. The technology particularly shines in complex markets where multiple factors influence entry success.

Practical applications highlight the technology's impact. During investment promotion activities, AI systems help missions identify sectors with the highest potential for successful market entry. The technology can simulate various entry scenarios, helping diplomats guide businesses toward optimal strategies. This capability proves especially valuable when advising SMEs with limited resources for market research, enabling more strategic and successful international expansion efforts.

INVESTMENT MAPPING

A treasure map for finding the most promising investment opportunities.

AI-powered investment mapping transforms how diplomatic missions identify and attract foreign direct investment opportunities. These systems analyze global investment patterns, corporate strategies, and market conditions to create detailed profiles of potential investors and investment opportunities. The technology helps missions understand not just where investment might come from, but also which sectors are most likely to attract sustainable, long-term investment.

The implementation process involves creating comprehensive databases of investment activities, integrating real-time market data, and developing predictive models based on historical patterns. Economic officers use these tools to identify high-potential investors and tailor their outreach strategies accordingly. The systems also track investment trends across regions, helping missions understand their competitive position in the global investment landscape.

In practice, investment mapping tools have transformed how missions approach investment promotion. For example, when a country seeks to develop its renewable energy sector, AI systems can identify potential investors based on their past investments, strategic priorities, and current market positions. This targeted approach increases the success rate of investment promotion activities while making more efficient use of diplomatic resources.

MACROECONOMIC FORECASTING

A crystal ball for predicting major economic shifts and trends.

Advanced AI systems have revolutionized how diplomatic missions predict and respond to economic trends. These tools analyze diverse data streams—from traditional economic indicators to social media sentiment and news coverage—to provide more accurate and timely forecasts of economic developments. The technology excels at identifying subtle correlations and emerging patterns that might escape traditional analysis methods.

Implementing effective macroeconomic forecasting requires careful coordination between AI systems and human expertise. Economic officers must integrate multiple data sources, validate predictions against real-world developments, and maintain close communication with local economic experts. The technology proves particularly valuable during periods of economic uncertainty, helping missions anticipate potential challenges and opportunities.

The practical impact of AI-enhanced forecasting is evident in daily diplomatic work. For instance, when analyzing the potential effects of global supply chain disruptions, these systems can model various scenarios and their likely impacts on local economies. This capability enables economic officers to provide more informed guidance to their governments and help local businesses prepare for potential economic shifts.

SUPPLY CHAIN RISK ASSESSMENT

An early warning system for spotting problems in global supply routes.

AI transforms supply chain risk assessment by continuously monitoring global trade flows, transportation networks, and potential disruption points. These systems analyze multiple risk factors simultaneously—political instability, weather patterns, regulatory changes, and market conditions—to identify potential vulnerabilities before they impact trade relationships. The technology provides economic officers with early warning of potential disruptions and suggests alternative routes or suppliers.

Successful implementation requires integration with existing trade monitoring systems and close collaboration with private sector partners. Economic officers must balance the technology's insights with practical considerations and local knowledge. Regular updates to risk models ensure the system remains effective as global supply chains evolve and new risks emerge.

Real-world applications demonstrate the value of this technology during crisis situations. For example, when natural disasters or political events threaten key supply routes, AI systems can quickly identify alternative pathways and assess their viability. This capability helps missions provide practical guidance to businesses and maintain vital economic relationships even during challenging times.

AUTOMATED ECONOMIC REPORTS

A round-the-clock writer of up-to-date economic briefings.

AI has transformed how diplomatic missions generate and analyze economic reports, shifting from periodic manual updates to continuous, automated analysis. These systems collect data from multiple sources, identify significant trends, and generate clear, actionable reports that highlight key developments and potential implications. The technology ensures that economic officers always have access to current, comprehensive economic intelligence.

Implementation success depends on establishing reliable data feeds, developing clear reporting templates, and training staff to effectively interpret and act on automated insights. The systems must balance depth of analysis with accessibility, ensuring that complex economic data is presented in ways that support quick decision-making. Regular refinement of reporting parameters helps maintain relevance and utility.

In practice, automated reporting systems have become essential tools for economic diplomacy. During trade negotiations, for instance, these systems can provide real-time updates on market conditions and potential impacts of proposed agreements. The technology also helps missions track progress toward economic goals and adjust strategies based on emerging trends and changing conditions.

ECONOMIC DIPLOMACY CHATBOTS

A 24/7 help desk for basic trade and investment questions.

AI-powered chatbots represent a significant advance in how missions handle routine economic inquiries and provide basic guidance to stakeholders. These systems use NLP to understand and respond to questions about trade regulations, investment procedures, and economic policies. The technology helps missions maintain 24/7 availability while allowing human officers to focus on more complex issues.

Deploying effective chatbots requires careful attention to accuracy, tone, and user experience. Economic officers must ensure that responses align with current policies and procedures, while maintaining appropriate diplomatic language and cultural sensitivity. Regular updates to the knowledge base help chatbots stay current with changing regulations and procedures.

The practical benefits of these systems are particularly evident in high-volume consular and trade offices. For example, chatbots can handle initial inquiries about investment procedures or export requirements, providing consistent, accurate information while screening requests that require human attention. This capability improves service delivery while optimizing diplomatic resources.

INVESTOR SENTIMENT ANALYSIS

A mood reader for understanding how investors feel about markets.

AI-driven sentiment analysis tools provide diplomatic missions with unprecedented insight into how investors perceive economic opportunities and risks in their host countries. These systems analyze news coverage, social media discussions, corporate communications, and market behavior to gauge investor confidence and identify emerging concerns. The technology helps missions anticipate shifts in investor sentiment that could affect foreign direct investment flows.

Implementation requires careful consideration of data sources, cultural context, and privacy concerns. Economic officers must validate sentiment analysis against local knowledge and maintain appropriate boundaries when monitoring public discourse. Regular calibration of analysis models ensures accurate interpretation of local business and investment climates.

The technology's practical value is evident in investment promotion activities. When preparing for investment forums or meeting with potential investors, economic officers can use sentiment analysis to understand concerns and opportunities from the investor's perspective. This insight helps missions develop more effective strategies for attracting and retaining foreign investment.

TRADE AGREEMENT OPTIMIZATION

A deal analyzer that finds the best terms for trade agreements.

AI transforms how missions approach trade agreement negotiations by analyzing vast amounts of historical trade data, economic indicators, and agreement outcomes. These systems can simulate the potential impacts of various provisions, identify optimal negotiating positions, and highlight areas where agreements might need strengthening. The technology helps ensure that new agreements maximize benefits while minimizing unintended consequences.

Successful deployment requires integration with existing trade analysis systems and close coordination between technical experts and negotiators. Economic officers must balance the technology's recommendations with diplomatic considerations and broader strategic objectives. Regular updates to analysis models incorporate lessons learned from previous agreements and changing economic conditions.

In practice, these systems have become valuable tools for trade negotiators. During complex multilateral negotiations, AI can quickly assess the implications of proposed changes and suggest alternative approaches. This capability helps missions negotiate more effectively and create more sustainable, beneficial trade relationships.

POLICY IMPACT ASSESSMENT

A preview tool showing how new policies might affect the economy.

AI enhances how missions evaluate the potential effects of economic policies and regulatory changes. These systems analyze historical data, market conditions, and stakeholder behavior to predict how various policy options might affect trade, investment, and economic growth. The technology helps economic officers provide more informed guidance to both home and host governments.

Implementation success depends on maintaining comprehensive databases of policy outcomes and economic indicators, while ensuring models account for local market conditions and regulatory environments. Economic officers must combine AI insights with traditional diplomatic wisdom when making policy recommendations. Regular validation of impact assessments helps maintain the system's reliability and credibility.

Real-world applications demonstrate the technology's value in policy planning. When evaluating proposed changes to investment regulations or trade policies, these systems can model potential outcomes across different economic sectors and stakeholder groups. This capability helps missions advocate for policies that promote sustainable economic growth while minimizing disruption to existing business relationships.

LIMITATIONS AND FUTURE RESEARCH DIRECTIONS

As AI transforms economic diplomacy, we must carefully examine both its current limitations and the critical questions that will shape its future development. Understanding these constraints isn't just an academic exercise—it's essential for diplomatic practitioners who must navigate the complex reality of using AI in their daily work while planning for tomorrow's challenges.

THE CHALLENGE OF INVISIBLE ECONOMIES

One of the most significant limitations of current AI systems lies in their inability to fully capture informal economic activities. Consider a typical developing economy, where street vendors, local markets, and cash-based transactions might represent up to half of all economic activity. These informal markets generate limited digital footprints, making them nearly invisible to conventional AI analysis. A diplomatic officer working in such an environment faces a challenging question: how can they trust AI-generated economic insights when such a large portion of the economy remains hidden from view?

This challenge extends beyond just data collection. Many traditional economic practices, from relationship-based trading networks to informal credit systems, operate on principles that current AI systems struggle to understand. For example, in some cultures, business relationships might depend more on long-standing family connections than on conventional metrics like credit scores or market share. AI systems trained primarily on Western economic models often miss these crucial cultural dimensions of economic activity.

THE DATA QUALITY DILEMMA

The effectiveness of AI in economic diplomacy fundamentally depends on the quality and reliability of its input data. This creates what we might call the "data quality dilemma." Economic officers must constantly ask themselves: How reliable is the data feeding into their AI systems? Nations might deliberately manipulate economic indicators, present incomplete datasets, or simply lack the capacity to collect accurate information. Think of it like trying to navigate using a map where some areas are deliberately distorted while others are simply blank.

This challenge becomes particularly acute during trade negotiations or investment discussions. An AI system might suggest an optimal negotiating position based on analysis of trade data, but if that data is incomplete or manipulated, the recommendation could lead negotiations astray. Economic officers must develop sophisticated judgment about when to trust AI insights and when to rely more heavily on traditional diplomatic methods.

THE DIGITAL TRANSFORMATION CHALLENGE

As the global economy undergoes rapid digital transformation, new limitations in our AI systems become apparent. The rise of cryptocurrencies, blockchain technologies, and decentralized finance creates novel economic patterns that traditional AI models weren't designed to analyze. An economic officer trying to understand trade flows might find that significant economic activity now occurs through channels that their AI tools can't effectively monitor or analyze.

Similarly, the emergence of digital platforms and online marketplaces has created new forms of economic activity that blur traditional boundaries. How should AI systems analyze a transaction where a service provider in one country serves customers in another through a platform based in a third? These complexities challenge our current approaches to economic analysis and diplomatic strategy.

ENVIRONMENTAL ECONOMICS AND SUSTAINABILITY

A crucial limitation of current AI systems lies in their ability to integrate environmental considerations into economic analysis. As nations transition toward sustainable economies, traditional economic metrics often fail to capture the full picture. An AI system might identify a trade opportunity as highly promising based on conventional economic indicators while missing significant environmental costs or sustainability challenges.

This limitation becomes particularly relevant as diplomatic missions increasingly must balance economic growth with environmental protection. Economic officers need AI tools that can help them understand not just the immediate economic impact of decisions but their longer term environmental and sustainability implications.

THE FUTURE RESEARCH AGENDA

These limitations point toward several crucial areas for future research. First, we need to develop more sophisticated methods for integrating informal economic data into AI analysis. This might involve using alternative data sources like satellite imagery, mobile phone usage patterns, or social network analysis to capture economic activity that doesn't appear in traditional datasets.

Second, research should focus on creating AI systems that can better understand and incorporate cultural and relational aspects of economic activity. This might involve developing new types of economic models that can account for non-Western economic practices and informal business networks.

Third, we need to advance our understanding of how AI can better support the transition to sustainable economies. This includes developing new frameworks for analyzing environmental impacts alongside traditional economic indicators and creating tools that can help diplomats negotiate agreements that promote both economic prosperity and environmental protection.

Finally, research must address the challenge of economic equity. As AI systems become more influential in shaping economic policy and trade relationships, we need to ensure they don't inadvertently perpetuate or exacerbate existing economic inequalities between nations.

CONCLUSION

The integration of AI into economic diplomacy represents a fundamental shift in how nations conduct international economic affairs. Through real-world applications and

emerging use cases, AI is becoming a powerful force multiplier for economic officers, enhancing their ability to analyze markets, promote trade, and attract investment
with unprecedented precision.

Three key insights emerge from this analysis:

First, AI significantly amplifies traditional diplomatic capabilities while introducing new tools for economic decision-making. From predictive analytics for market
trends to automated risk assessment for international investments, AI enables more
proactive and data-driven economic diplomacy.

Second, the technology's impact extends beyond mere efficiency gains. AI
strengthens economic resilience by helping missions anticipate disruptions, identify
alternative opportunities, and respond more effectively to global economic challenges. This capability has become particularly crucial in an era of increasing economic volatility.

Finally, and perhaps most importantly, AI serves as an enhancer rather than a
replacement for human diplomacy. While AI excels at processing vast amounts of
economic data and identifying patterns, the nuanced aspects of relationship-building
and strategic planning remain firmly in the human domain. This partnership
between human expertise and AI points the way toward a more effective and equitable approach to economic diplomacy.

As missions begin to integrate AI into their economic functions, success will
depend on maintaining this balance while ensuring that technological advancement
serves the fundamental diplomatic goals of promoting prosperity and fostering sustainable economic cooperation between nations.

Beyond economic affairs, the success of diplomatic missions relies on effective operational management. The next chapter explores how AI is revolutionizing
diplomatic operations—streamlining logistics, optimizing resource allocation, and
strengthening crisis preparedness while addressing crucial challenges of security
and ethical deployment.

DISCUSSION SCENARIOS AND QUESTIONS

This set of scenarios focuses on AI's role in shaping economic diplomacy. From trade
negotiations to investment strategies, they challenge readers to evaluate how AI can
enhance economic decision-making while ensuring fairness, security, and resilience
in international markets.

1. Autonomous negotiation systems
    Scenario: You are using AI to assist in a trade negotiation. The system
    identifies leverage points and counteroffers faster than you can, but the
    opposing party raises concerns about the transparency and fairness of using
    AI in the process.
    Questions: How do you address concerns from the opposing party about
    the fairness of AI-assisted negotiations? What considerations are important
    when establishing international standards for AI use in diplomatic negotia-
    tions, and how might these standards take shape? How do you ensure that
    trust-based human relationships remain central, even with AI's involvement
    in crafting agreements?

2. Bias in AI-generated trade policies

Scenario: An AI tool you are using to draft a trade agreement inadvertently incorporates biases rooted in historical trade imbalances. The proposed policies risk reinforcing inequalities between your country and the host nation.

Questions: How do you address potential bias in AI-generated recommendations during trade negotiations? What steps will you take to ensure that AI tools you rely on promote equitable trade outcomes? How do you reconcile trust in AI recommendations with the need for fairness and transparency in diplomacy?

3. Job displacement in host nations

Scenario: A company from your home country is introducing AI-driven automation in the host nation. While the project promises economic growth, it threatens to displace thousands of workers in traditional industries, sparking tension with the host government.

Questions: How do you balance the promise of technological progress with the potential harm to local employment in the host nation? What measures will you propose to mitigate job displacement while supporting the introduction of AI-driven industries? How do you manage public backlash against AI while safeguarding your country's broader economic interests in the host nation?

4. AI and resource-driven negotiations

Scenario: AI models predict that a critical resource in the host nation, essential for clean energy, will face significant shortages in the near future. Your country proposes exclusive extraction rights, but this risks alienating other stakeholders in the host nation.

Questions: How do you balance the urgency of securing resources with the need to maintain goodwill among host nation stakeholders? What challenges and opportunities arise when using AI models to predict the geopolitical consequences of resource-driven agreements, and how might you address the uncertainties involved? What steps can you take to ensure the agreement aligns with long-term sustainability goals for both nations?

5. AI-Driven Economic Sanctions

Scenario: You are tasked with implementing economic sanctions based on AI recommendations. The system identifies industries and companies in the target country that will be most affected. However, these sanctions disproportionately harm civilians, creating backlash from international organizations.

Questions: In situations where AI recommendations lead to disproportionate civilian harm, how might you push back effectively, and what arguments would support your case? How do you balance your country's strategic objectives with ethical considerations in sanctions enforcement? What level of human oversight do you need to ensure ethical implementation of AI-recommended sanctions?

5 AI and Management Affairs

Transforming Diplomatic Operations

Machine learning and AI is a horizontal enabling layer. It will empower and improve every business, every government organization, every philanthropy—basically there's no institution in the world that cannot be improved with machine learning.

—Jeff Bezos, CEO of Amazon (2017)

Humans will add value where machines cannot. As we encounter more and more artificial intelligence, real intelligence, real empathy, and real common sense will be scarce. The new jobs will be predicated on know how to work with machines, but also on these uniquely human attributes.

—Satya Nadella, CEO of Microsoft (2017)

AI may not replace managers, but the managers that use AI will replace the managers that do not.

—Rob Thomas, Chief Commercial Officer at IBM (2023)

Behind every diplomatic success story lies an intricate web of operational excellence—the often-unseen realm of management affairs that keeps missions running smoothly and effectively. While diplomacy's public face may be negotiation and statecraft, its foundation rests on the meticulous management of resources, personnel, and facilities that enable diplomats to advance their nation's interests. Today, as artificial intelligence (AI) reshapes the diplomatic landscape, management affairs stands at the cusp of a profound transformation. AI isn't just streamlining administrative tasks; it's revolutionizing how missions operate, from predictive maintenance and resource optimization to crisis preparedness and security management. This technological evolution marks a shift from reactive management to proactive stewardship, where data-driven insights empower leaders to anticipate needs, prevent disruptions, and build more resilient diplomatic operations.

The integration of AI into management affairs represents more than mere automation—it signals a fundamental reimagining of how diplomatic missions function in an increasingly complex world. As missions face evolving challenges, from cybersecurity threats to resource constraints, AI serves as a force multiplier, enabling management officers to transform traditional practices into dynamic, adaptive

DOI: 10.1201/9781003612308-5

systems that enhance diplomatic effectiveness. This chapter explores how AI is revolutionizing the backbone of diplomatic operations, offering new tools and capabilities that make the seemingly impossible not just achievable, but routine.

VIGNETTE AI-Enhanced Embassy in the Republic of Z

In the Republic of Z's embassy district, Management Officer Amir Qureshi starts his day by reviewing an AI-powered dashboard that monitors the mission's entire operational ecosystem. The recent political tensions and emerging economic opportunities have placed unprecedented demands on the embassy's infrastructure. As Elena Moretti's team pursues green energy initiatives and the political section manages community outreach, Qureshi must ensure the mission has the resources and capabilities to support these expanding activities.

The AI system flags several critical items requiring immediate attention: the embassy's backup generators need preventive maintenance before the upcoming bilateral energy summit, three diplomatic residences require security upgrades, and the mission's budget needs reallocation to support increased trade delegation visits. Meanwhile, complex negotiations with local authorities over tax exemptions for the mission's planned solar panel installation await his attention, and the human resources module indicates a pressing need for local staff with renewable energy expertise.

Qureshi appreciates how AI has transformed his ability to manage this complexity. The system not only identifies issues but suggests integrated solutions: a revised maintenance schedule that won't disrupt summit preparations, prevetted local contractors for the security upgrades, and a budget reallocation plan that maintains essential services while supporting new initiatives. The AI's predictive analytics have even identified potential cost savings in the mission's utility contracts, funds that could support the expanded trade mission.

As he prepares for his morning meeting with section heads, Qureshi receives an alert about an incoming congressional delegation interested in Z's renewable energy potential. The AI immediately begins generating logistics scenarios, from hotel arrangements to transportation needs, while cross-referencing the visit against other scheduled activities to prevent conflicts. A separate module starts gathering data on the mission's recent energy efficiency improvements—information that could support the delegation's objectives while showcasing the embassy's commitment to sustainability.

This coordination of complex logistics, resource management, and strategic planning exemplifies how AI is revolutionizing the management officer's role. Rather than merely responding to crises, Qureshi can anticipate needs, optimize resources, and support the mission's expanding diplomatic initiatives with precision and foresight. As Z's importance as a regional energy hub grows, the seamless integration of technology and human expertise ensures the embassy's operational platform can support increasingly ambitious diplomatic goals.

THE EVOLUTION OF MANAGEMENT AFFAIRS IN DIPLOMACY

Consider workforce planning, one of the most complex challenges in embassy management. AI-driven platforms analyze trends in workload, employee performance, and regional developments, offering data-driven insights for staffing decisions (Alder 2024b). For example, if a consular section consistently struggles during tourist seasons, AI might recommend hiring additional temporary staff or redistributing tasks among existing personnel. But while the data provides clarity, the decision to act remains with human leaders who understand the nuances of team dynamics and individual capabilities (Wiseman 2024).

Training and development also benefit from AI's precision. Imagine a new economic officer assigned to a high-profile mission. An AI system might suggest targeted training modules based on the officer's background and the host country's economic landscape, accelerating their readiness for the role (Cassidy 2024). Adaptive learning platforms can then track the officer's progress through key competencies, automatically adjusting the difficulty and focus of training materials while identifying areas where additional mentorship may be needed (Di Martino & Ford 2024). These tools empower embassy leaders to build teams that are not only efficient but also agile and capable of adapting to the unexpected.

HISTORICAL AI USE CASE EXAMPLES IN MANAGEMENT AFFAIRS

Efficient embassy operations and management functions are essential for effective diplomacy, and AI is beginning to play a transformative role in optimizing these processes (Höne et al. 2019). From resource allocation to logistics management, historical AI use cases reveal how governments are beginning to deploy technology to enhance operational efficiency and transparency (Dunne & Wellman 2024).

NATO's establishment of the Cooperative Cyber Defence Centre of Excellence (CCD-COE) in Tallinn not only focused on cybersecurity but also could be considered a concept for predictive maintenance in embassy operations. AI systems developed by NATO evidently monitored IT networks and digital infrastructure, detecting vulnerabilities and implying preemptive actions to prevent system failures (Kello 2023). These tools can inspire similar applications in diplomatic missions, where embassies could one day utilize predictive analytics to maintain physical infrastructure such as smart HVAC systems and energy grids, ensuring resilience in critical operational environments.

The U.S. Department of State has shown interest in implementing AI-driven enhancements to its Integrated Logistics Management System (ILMS) to optimize embassy operations worldwide. The system could make use of predictive analytics to identify patterns in procurement and property management, reducing inefficiencies and enhancing accountability. For example, an AI-enhanced ILMS could facilitate data-driven decision-making to prevent overstocking and address supply chain vulnerabilities in real time (State Department AI Inventory 2024, Doubleday 2024a, 2024b). This concept demonstrates the value of leveraging AI to streamline embassy logistics while maintaining transparency in resource allocation.

AI-powered tools are poised to significantly improve workforce management within diplomatic missions. For instance, the U.S. Department of State's Budget Chat concept was geared toward using natural language processing (NLP) to consolidate and analyze budget data, enabling leaders to allocate resources more effectively across global missions. These tools would allow management officers to anticipate surges in workload, such as during visa processing peaks or crisis events, ensuring that staff resources are deployed where they are most needed (State Department AI Inventory 2024, Doubleday 2024a, 2024b).

Additionally, adaptive learning platforms, inspired by the International Chamber of Commerce's Cognitive Trade Advisor, have been used to train embassy personnel. These AI-driven systems identified skill gaps among staff and recommended tailored training programs, improving team agility and readiness to address evolving diplomatic challenges (ICC 2018).

AI has proven invaluable in supporting crisis management within diplomatic missions. NATO's use of AI tools for cybersecurity during the 2007 Estonian cyberattacks provided a template for embassies to respond to crises involving both digital and physical threats. AI-powered systems integrated diverse data streams to provide real-time insights, which could enable management officers to better coordinate emergency responses and allocate resources efficiently (Kello 2023).

For example, during natural disasters or civil unrest, embassies have shown use cases for AI systems to assess risks and prioritize evacuation efforts. Tools tailored for these use cases could in theory analyze data from social media, satellite imagery, and local news reports, providing actionable intelligence to ensure the safety of personnel and citizens abroad (Manor 2017, 2019).

Israel's use of AI-powered systems, such as "Lavender" and "The Gospel," has influenced how embassies can approach logistical security. These systems monitored video feeds and perimeter activities in real time, using intelligent algorithms to identify potential threats. Diplomatic missions are looking to adapt similar technologies to enhance physical security, optimize access control, and safeguard personnel and assets (Serhan 2024). These use cases highlight the importance of integrating AI into management affairs to address security risks proactively. The concept is fundamentally the same.

The U.K. government's "White Mail" AI system processes thousands of daily correspondence from benefit applicants, prioritizing vulnerable cases and cutting response times from weeks to a day (Marwala 2023). While it demonstrates AI's potential to streamline operations by efficiently managing high volumes of correspondence and expediting urgent cases, significant concerns linger regarding the lack of transparency in how the system operates, the handling of sensitive personal data without user consent, and the fairness of its decision-making process. For diplomats managing embassy logistics, this case highlights how AI can improve workflows but underscores the importance of clear communication, robust data protections, and ethical oversight to ensure equitable and trustworthy outcomes.

While AI has significantly enhanced embassy management, it also raises ethical questions. Algorithmic bias in workforce management systems could inadvertently marginalize certain groups, while over-reliance on automated tools may lead to reduced human oversight (Allam 2021). The State Department's use of AI systems, such as StateChat, underscores the importance of transparency and accountability in ensuring that automated decisions align with organizational values and cultural sensitivities (State Department AI Inventory 2024, Doubleday 2024a, 2024b, Alder 2024, 2025).

According to the U.S. Department of State and *FedScoop*, the Department is designing AI to make its operations more efficient and user-friendly. The Property and Procurement Analytics tool is aimed at helping detect unusual patterns in government purchases, improving oversight and accountability. The FOIA Web ML Document Indexer is aimed at organizing documents in the Department's FOIA Library, making it easier for people to find what they need.

To speed up responses to public records requests, the FOIA 360 AI Matching Tool identifies similar FOIA requests and documents, reducing duplication and saving time. The StateChat chatbot uses AI to answer questions and assist employees, while the FamChat Tool, as reported by *FedScoop*, provides AI-driven support for employees and their families. These tools show how the Department is developing AI to simplify processes, improve transparency, and make its services more accessible (State Department AI Inventory 2024, Doubleday 2024a, 2024b, Alder 2024, 2025).

The historical use of AI in management affairs provides key lessons for diplomatic missions:

1. Operational resilience: AI's ability to predict maintenance needs and streamline logistics has the potential to enhance embassy resilience in dynamic environments.
2. Data-driven decision-making: Tools like ILMS and StateChat/BudgetChat show promise for the value of leveraging AI to improve transparency and efficiency in resource management.
3. Crisis preparedness: AI's role in crisis management underscores the importance of integrating real-time data analytics into emergency response frameworks.
4. Ethical oversight: Diplomatic missions must implement governance frameworks to address ethical concerns and ensure that AI systems are deployed responsibly.

By learning from these historical examples, diplomatic missions can harness AI's capabilities to optimize operations, enhance security, and support effective crisis management.

STRATEGIC TRANSFORMATION THROUGH AI

At its core, management affairs is about resource allocation—whether it's budgets, personnel, or facilities (Black 2025). AI enhances this process by providing granular insights that guide decision-making (U.S. Department of State 2024a, 2024b, 2024c, 2024d). Budget management, once reliant on manual forecasting and spreadsheets, can now benefit from AI-driven analytics that track spending patterns, identify inefficiencies, and predict future needs (State Department AI Inventory 2024). For instance, an AI system might flag rising utility costs in an embassy's regional office, prompting an investigation that reveals outdated infrastructure. Addressing such issues proactively saves money and enhances operational efficiency.

Logistics and supply chain management have been transformed by AI's capabilities (State Department AI Inventory 2024). During a pandemic, for example, embassies coordinating shipments of personal protective equipment (PPE) might use AI to identify reliable suppliers, monitor inventory levels, and ensure timely delivery to high-priority locations (Manor 2023). The system can simultaneously track multiple vendors, analyze delivery performance, and suggest alternative suppliers when disruptions occur, ensuring missions maintain essential supplies even during global crises.

Event coordination and scheduling, traditionally one of the most complex aspects of mission management, now benefit from AI's precision. Consider a major diplomatic conference with participants from multiple time zones and varying security requirements. AI systems can analyze historical scheduling data, participant preferences, and logistical constraints to create optimal agendas. More importantly, these systems could rapidly adapt to last-minute changes—whether it's a delayed flight, a security concern, or a sudden policy priority—by automatically generating alternative schedules that minimize disruption to key diplomatic engagements.

Negotiations with host governments, particularly regarding mission operations and facilities, have also been enhanced by AI tools (Black 2025, Siebrits et al. 2025). When discussing tax exemptions, facility expansions, or operating permissions, AI systems have the capability to analyze years of precedents across multiple diplomatic missions, identify successful negotiating strategies, and highlight potential areas of mutual benefit. For example, when planning a new embassy construction project, AI can assess local regulations, analyze past agreements, and suggest approaches that align with both mission requirements and host country priorities.

In the realm of sustainability, AI is helping missions become more environmentally responsible while reducing costs. Smart building systems use AI to optimize energy consumption based on occupancy patterns and weather conditions. The technology can predict maintenance needs for climate control systems, identify opportunities for renewable energy integration, and track progress toward emissions reduction goals. These capabilities not only demonstrate environmental leadership but also generate substantial cost savings that can be redirected to other mission priorities.

OPERATIONAL EXCELLENCE IN THE AGE OF AI

Knowledge management emerges as a critical function where AI demonstrates transformative potential. Diplomatic missions are treasure troves of institutional knowledge, housing decades—if not centuries—of treaties, agreements, and correspondence. AI-powered search tools enable a newly arrived diplomat preparing for complex negotiations to access decades of relevant documents, network web pages, wiki pages, etcetera—all cross-referenced and prioritized by relevance. Beyond retrieval, AI assists in synthesizing insights, highlighting patterns across historical agreements or past host-country engagements that might otherwise remain hidden in vast archives (Doubleday 2024a, 2024b).

The human resources dimension of management affairs has been particularly enhanced by AI's capabilities. Advanced platforms now evaluate applications while actively screening for unconscious bias, ensuring a more equitable recruitment process. These systems look beyond traditional metrics to identify candidates whose skills and experiences align with mission priorities in nuanced ways. For instance, an AI system might recognize that a candidate's experience managing cross-cultural teams in the private sector could be valuable for a mission's expanding public diplomacy initiatives (Collins 2024, Alder 2024, Allam 2021, Black 2025).

Employee engagement and development benefit from AI's analytical precision. When staff surveys indicate declining morale in specific departments, AI tools can analyze multiple data points—workload distributions, communication patterns, career development opportunities—to identify root causes. The system might discover, for example, that teams with irregular scheduling face higher stress levels and lower job satisfaction, leading to targeted policy adjustments. This data-driven approach to personnel management helps missions maintain high-performing, cohesive teams while ensuring fair treatment and growth opportunities for all staff (Blaser 2022, 2023).

Facilities management has evolved into a proactive discipline through AI integration. Smart systems monitor building operations in real time, from security systems to utilities, predicting maintenance needs before failures occur. For example, AI might detect subtle changes in an HVAC system's performance that indicate potential issues, allowing maintenance teams to address problems during scheduled downtime rather than dealing with disruptive emergency repairs. This predictive approach extends to security systems, where AI monitors access patterns, surveillance feeds, and environmental sensors to maintain a secure yet welcoming diplomatic facility (Siebrits et al. 2025, Bano, Chaudhri, & Zowghi 2023).

Financial oversight and compliance have been strengthened by AI's ability to monitor transactions continuously. Advanced algorithms can detect unusual patterns that might indicate errors or irregularities, ensuring missions maintain the highest standards of fiscal responsibility. The system might flag, for instance, a series of small purchases that, when analyzed together, reveal an opportunity to achieve cost savings through bulk procurement. This combination of forensic capability and forward-looking analysis helps missions optimize their resources while maintaining rigorous accountability.

Throughout these operational domains, ethical considerations remain paramount. Missions must ensure that AI tools respect privacy, maintain transparency, and promote equity. This requires clear governance frameworks, regular audits of AI systems, and ongoing dialogue with stakeholders about how technology is being used to enhance—rather than replace—human judgment in mission operations (Bjola & Kļaviņš 2024, Bouchard 2024).

CRISIS MANAGEMENT AND FUTURE READINESS

Crisis management is where the fusion of AI and human ingenuity truly shines. In times of upheaval—natural disasters, political unrest, or cybersecurity breaches—embassies are lifelines for citizens and symbols of stability for host nations. Take the case of a severe tropical storm approaching a coastal city where an embassy operates. AI systems analyze satellite imagery, weather data, and social media posts, predicting the storm's trajectory and identifying areas most at risk. Based on this analysis, embassy management can preemptively activate evacuation plans, relocate non-essential personnel, and establish communication channels with local authorities (Akdenizli 2024, Bjola, Cassidy, and Manor 2022, Haseley et al. 2023).

Emergency preparedness has evolved from static planning to dynamic response through AI integration. The technology continuously assesses multiple risk factors—from local political stability to environmental hazards—and updates response protocols accordingly. For instance, during a developing crisis, AI systems can simultaneously track the safety of personnel, monitor transportation routes, and identify the nearest safe havens, providing real-time guidance to mission leadership. These capabilities ensure that missions remain resilient and responsive, even as circumstances rapidly change.

Cybersecurity, another critical domain, benefits significantly from AI's capabilities. Embassy networks are prime targets for cyberattacks, with sensitive data and communications at stake. AI-powered security platforms monitor network activity around the clock, identifying anomalies that suggest potential breaches. When an unusual login attempt occurs from an unrecognized location, the system can automatically implement security protocols while alerting IT teams for immediate investigation. This layered approach to cybersecurity helps missions protect their digital infrastructure without impeding legitimate operations.

Looking ahead, management affairs face both opportunities and challenges in an AI-driven world. The technology promises even greater capabilities—imagine systems that can automatically adjust mission operations based on changing security conditions or platforms that enable seamless coordination among diplomatic posts during regional crises. Yet, these advances must be balanced with robust ethical frameworks that ensure AI serves the fundamental values of diplomacy (Pokhriyal & Koebe 2023, Simić 2021, Höne et al. 2019, Minchev 2023).

Success in this evolving landscape depends on leaders who understand both the potential and limitations of AI. Management officers must become adept at integrating technological capabilities with human wisdom, ensuring that efficiency gains don't come at the cost of the personal connections that define diplomatic work. This requires ongoing training, clear governance structures, and a commitment to using AI in ways that enhance rather than diminish the human element in diplomacy.

LARGE LANGUAGE MODELS: STREAMLINING DIPLOMATIC OPERATIONS

Having explored how Large Language Models (LLMs) can enhance general diplomatic work, support leadership functions, strengthen political analysis, and optimize economic affairs, we now turn to their applications in diplomatic management operations. While previous chapters demonstrated these tools' value in strategic and analytical roles, management officers face unique challenges in coordinating resources, streamlining processes, and maintaining efficient mission operations.

Management affairs require clear procedures, effective communication, and precise documentation to keep diplomatic missions running smoothly. LLMs excel at helping management officers develop and refine these essential materials. For instance, when creating standard operating procedures, these tools can help structure complex workflows into clear, actionable steps while maintaining consistency with diplomatic protocols. This allows officers to focus on validating procedures and ensuring they align with mission requirements.

Internal communication, particularly crucial in management affairs, benefits from LLM capabilities in new ways. Beyond the communication support explored in earlier chapters, these tools can help management officers craft clear operational directives, develop training materials, and create documentation that ensures smooth mission operations. This proves especially valuable when establishing new procedures or updating existing protocols across different embassy sections.

Administrative efficiency represents another key application unique to management affairs. Building on the organizational frameworks discussed in previous chapters, management officers can use LLMs to streamline routine tasks, develop templates for common procedures, and create systems that enhance operational effectiveness. This capability particularly shines when coordinating complex logistical operations or managing mission resources.

However, management affairs work demands special attention to certain limitations beyond those discussed earlier. The sensitivity of operational information and personnel data requires extra caution in how these tools are used. Officers must be particularly mindful of information security and ensure all documents and procedures align with diplomatic protocols and regulations.

PUTTING LLMS TO WORK FOR MANAGEMENT OFFICERS

Building on prompt engineering practices established in previous chapters, let's explore how management officers can craft effective prompts for their specific operational needs. While earlier chapters covered diplomatic communications, leadership decisions, political analysis, and economic assessments, management affairs requires particular attention to procedural clarity, resource coordination, and administrative efficiency.

When developing standard operating procedures, frame your prompts to ensure comprehensive coverage and clarity. For example:

> Help me create a standard operating procedure for emergency equipment maintenance. Structure the SOP to include: 1) clear reporting channels for equipment issues, 2) priority classification system, 3) response time requirements, 4) documentation procedures, and 5) quality control measures. Ensure the procedure aligns with standard diplomatic facility management protocols while maintaining operational efficiency.

For coordinating complex logistics, help LLMs understand the scope and requirements:

> I need to develop a logistics plan for an upcoming facility security upgrade project. Please help me create: 1) a timeline of key milestones, 2) resource allocation guidelines, 3) coordination requirements between contractors and embassy sections, 4) contingency protocols, and 5) progress tracking methods. Format this as a comprehensive project management document that ensures smooth implementation while maintaining security protocols.

For administrative documentation, focus prompts on clarity and completeness:

> Help me create a handbook for new locally employed staff onboarding. Include sections on: 1) administrative procedures, 2) security protocols, 3) HR policies, 4) communication guidelines, and 5) emergency procedures. Ensure the content is clear, accessible, and aligned with standard embassy operations while maintaining appropriate professional tone.

Management officers should focus their prompts on:

- Creating clear, actionable procedures and protocols.
- Developing efficient administrative systems.
- Coordinating complex operational requirements.
- Ensuring compliance with diplomatic regulations.
- Streamlining routine administrative tasks.

These applications leverage the foundational capabilities covered in previous chapters while addressing the specific needs of management affairs. The key is maintaining procedural clarity and operational efficiency while ensuring all outputs align with diplomatic protocols and security requirements.

ADVANCED AI USE CASES IN MANAGEMENT AFFAIRS

Building on the foundational AI applications explored in Chapter 1, the leadership use cases from Chapter 2, the political affairs applications in Chapter 3, and the economic tools discussed in Chapter 4, we now examine advanced AI solutions specifically designed for diplomatic management operations. While previous chapters demonstrated how AI can enhance various aspects of diplomatic work, management affairs presents unique opportunities for leveraging AI to optimize mission operations, streamline administrative processes, and enhance operational efficiency. From predictive maintenance systems and resource optimization tools to automated compliance monitoring and smart facility management, these use cases demonstrate how AI can transform the operational backbone of diplomatic missions (Allam 2021, Pokhriyal & Koebe 2023, Simić 2021, Höne et al. 2019, Minchev 2023).

Each application builds upon basic AI capabilities to address the sophisticated challenges of modern mission management, where efficient coordination and resource utilization are essential. As we continue exploring AI applications across different diplomatic functions in subsequent chapters, these management affairs use cases highlight how AI can enhance operational excellence while maintaining the crucial role of human oversight in ensuring mission success.

AI-Driven Recruitment

A talent finder that matches the right skills to diplomatic jobs.

Recruiting skilled personnel is essential for the success of diplomatic missions, but traditional hiring processes can be time-consuming and resource-intensive. AI-driven recruitment tools offer a transformative solution by leveraging machine learning, NLP, and predictive analytics to streamline and enhance the hiring process. These systems automate key tasks, such as screening applications, analyzing qualifications, and providing data-driven insights to identify top talent efficiently and fairly.

The practical applications of AI in recruitment are extensive. For example, an AI system can quickly evaluate hundreds of applications, highlight candidates with the most relevant skills and experiences, and even suggest tailored interview questions based on role-specific requirements. This not only enhances efficiency but also improves the precision and fairness of recruitment efforts, enabling missions to attract and retain the best talent. To implement these tools effectively, missions must ensure data quality, train staff to use the systems, and integrate AI outputs into decision-making workflows.

Challenges include the risk of biases in training datasets or algorithm design, which could perpetuate existing inequities, and the potential for overreliance on AI at the expense of human judgment. Transparent frameworks, ethical oversight, and a collaborative approach that integrates AI with human expertise are essential to address these concerns. By combining AI's analytical power with the nuanced judgment of hiring managers, embassies can optimize their recruitment processes, ensuring they attract skilled personnel to support their mission's goals.

BUDGET OPTIMIZATION

A spending advisor that helps make the most of embassy resources.

Effective budgeting is critical for diplomatic missions, requiring a careful balance between limited funds and diverse priorities. Traditional methods often struggle to identify inefficiencies or adapt to changing needs. AI-powered budget optimization tools offer a transformative solution by analyzing historical spending patterns, forecasting future requirements, and recommending resource allocation strategies. These systems enhance efficiency, accountability, and strategic financial management.

The practical applications of AI in budget optimization are extensive. For instance, these tools can flag areas of overspending, identify anomalies in financial data, and propose reallocations that align with shifting priorities. AI can also simulate various budgetary scenarios, helping missions plan for contingencies and achieve their goals with greater precision. To implement these tools effectively, missions must ensure data accuracy, train staff on system use, and integrate AI recommendations into decision-making processes.

Challenges include ensuring the quality and completeness of financial data and addressing ethical considerations when analyzing sensitive information. Collaboration between AI and human expertise is essential for success. While AI excels at processing large datasets and uncovering patterns, administrative officers provide the contextual understanding needed to interpret findings and develop actionable strategies. By combining AI's analytical power with human judgment, missions can optimize their budgets, maximize resource efficiency, and better support their strategic objectives.

FRAUD DETECTION IN FINANCIAL OPERATIONS

A financial watchdog that spots suspicious money patterns.

Financial integrity is a critical concern for diplomatic missions, where safeguarding public funds and maintaining accountability are paramount. Traditional methods for detecting fraud often rely on manual reviews, which can be time-consuming and prone to oversight. AI-powered fraud detection tools address this challenge by using machine learning and advanced analytics to analyze financial data in real time, identify anomalies, and flag suspicious activities. These systems enable missions to proactively protect resources and uphold accountability.

The practical applications of AI in fraud detection are significant. For example, these tools can monitor daily transactions for red flags, such as unusual payment patterns, and highlight areas requiring deeper scrutiny during financial audits. By providing real-time actionable insights, AI empowers missions to detect and address irregularities swiftly, enhancing financial integrity and building trust with stakeholders. To implement these tools effectively, missions must ensure data accuracy, integrate them with existing systems, and train financial officers to interpret AI-generated alerts.

Challenges include ensuring the quality and completeness of financial data and addressing privacy concerns when analyzing sensitive information. Ethical oversight and robust governance frameworks are essential to mitigate these risks. Collaboration between AI and human expertise is critical for success, as financial officers provide the contextual understanding needed to evaluate findings and determine appropriate actions. By combining AI's analytical capabilities with human judgment, missions can strengthen their financial operations, prevent fraud, and maintain public trust.

Real-Time Asset Tracking

An inventory keeper that knows where everything is at all times.

Effective management of physical assets is crucial for the operational efficiency of diplomatic missions, yet traditional methods often struggle with inefficiencies and lack of real-time visibility. AI-powered real-time asset tracking tools address this challenge by combining sensors, IoT technology, and machine learning to monitor and manage assets with precision. These systems enhance accountability, streamline operations, and reduce administrative burdens, ensuring resources are used effectively.

The practical applications of AI in asset tracking are extensive. For example, these tools can optimize vehicle usage, track the availability and condition of equipment, and monitor the distribution of critical resources during emergencies. Real-time alerts for anomalies, such as unauthorized usage or maintenance needs, empower administrators to respond swiftly and maintain operational readiness. To implement these systems effectively, missions must ensure the reliability of IoT devices, integrate tools with existing workflows, and train staff to interpret and act on AI-generated insights.

Challenges include ensuring the reliability of tracking devices and addressing privacy concerns, particularly when assets are linked to individuals. Ethical oversight and robust governance frameworks are essential to maintain trust and transparency. Collaboration between AI and human expertise is key, as administrators provide the contextual understanding needed to evaluate findings and make informed decisions. By integrating AI's precision with human judgment, missions can optimize asset management, improve resource allocation, and strengthen overall efficiency.

Cybersecurity Incident Response

A digital guard that spots and stops cyber attacks quickly.

In an increasingly digital world, cybersecurity is a top priority for diplomatic missions, where protecting sensitive information and maintaining operational continuity are critical. AI-powered incident response tools address this challenge by leveraging machine learning, anomaly detection, and real-time monitoring to automate threat detection, analysis, and mitigation. These systems enhance the mission's ability to counter cyber threats effectively while minimizing disruptions.

The applications of AI in cybersecurity incident response are extensive. For example, these tools can monitor network activity to flag suspicious behavior, such as unauthorized access attempts, and coordinate responses across multiple missions during a regional cyber crisis. By providing actionable insights and automating key processes, AI empowers missions to protect their digital infrastructure with greater agility and precision. To implement these tools effectively, missions must ensure data quality, integrate AI systems with existing cybersecurity protocols, and train IT staff to use the tools efficiently.

Challenges include ensuring the accuracy of threat detection, managing false positives, and addressing privacy concerns when monitoring sensitive information. Ethical oversight and robust governance frameworks are essential to maintain trust and transparency. Collaboration between AI and human expertise is critical, as IT officers provide the strategic understanding needed to evaluate risks, prioritize actions, and ensure continuity. By combining AI's real-time responsiveness with human judgment, diplomatic missions can strengthen their cybersecurity defenses and respond effectively to evolving threats.

PREDICTIVE MAINTENANCE

An equipment doctor that prevents breakdowns before they happen.

Maintaining mission-critical infrastructure and equipment is essential for the effective operation of diplomatic missions, yet traditional maintenance methods often react to issues only after they arise. AI-powered predictive maintenance tools address this challenge by analyzing sensor data, operational logs, and historical records to forecast potential failures and recommend proactive actions. These tools enhance efficiency, reduce downtime, and ensure operational readiness by identifying problems before they escalate.

The applications of AI in predictive maintenance are extensive. For instance, these systems can monitor vehicle fleets to detect impending mechanical issues, allowing timely repairs to prevent breakdowns. Similarly, they can track the performance of IT infrastructure, flagging potential hardware failures and suggesting replacements or upgrades. To implement these tools effectively, missions must ensure the quality and consistency of data collected from sensors, integrate predictive analytics into existing maintenance workflows, and train staff to act on AI-generated insights.

Challenges include ensuring reliable data collection, addressing privacy concerns, and maintaining trust in automated systems (Allam 2021). Ethical oversight and robust governance are necessary to mitigate these risks. Collaboration between AI and human expertise is critical, as facility managers and maintenance staff provide the contextual understanding needed to prioritize actions and adapt strategies to unique challenges. By combining AI's predictive power with human judgment, diplomatic missions can optimize maintenance processes, control costs, and maintain uninterrupted operations.

AI-POWERED KNOWLEDGE REPOSITORIES

A smart library that organizes and finds embassy information instantly.

Effective knowledge management is vital for diplomatic missions, yet traditional systems often struggle with inefficiencies and the risk of losing institutional memory. AI-powered knowledge repositories address these challenges by leveraging NLP and machine learning to organize, analyze, and retrieve information with speed and precision. These tools enhance efficiency, reduce redundancy, and ensure that critical knowledge is preserved and accessible when needed.

The applications of AI-powered repositories are extensive. For example, during high-profile visits, staff can quickly access relevant protocols and records of past events to ensure seamless execution. In crises, these systems can deliver historical precedents and contingency plans, enabling informed decision-making under pressure. To implement these tools effectively, missions must ensure the quality and structure of their data, integrate AI systems into existing workflows, and train staff to utilize the tools efficiently.

Challenges include ensuring data accuracy, addressing privacy concerns, and managing sensitive or classified documents responsibly. Ethical oversight and robust governance frameworks are essential to maintain trust and compliance. Collaboration between AI and human expertise is critical, as staff bring the contextual understanding and critical thinking necessary to interpret findings and apply them effectively. By combining AI's organizational capabilities with human judgment, diplomatic missions can operate with greater agility, confidence, and strategic impact.

TRAINING PERSONALIZATION

A custom teacher that adapts lessons to each diplomat's needs.

Effective training is critical for preparing diplomatic staff to navigate complex global challenges, yet traditional approaches often fail to address the unique needs of individuals. AI-powered training personalization tools address this challenge by tailoring learning content, pace, and delivery methods to the specific needs of each individual. These tools enhance skill development and ensure staff are better prepared to fulfill their responsibilities.

The applications of AI in training personalization are extensive. For instance, AI can design customized curricula for officers preparing for high-stakes negotiations, focusing on relevant policies and cultural nuances. Similarly, technical training programs can be adapted to match the systems and protocols used at a specific mission. By delivering precise and actionable learning experiences, AI empowers staff to develop skills more effectively and efficiently. To implement these tools successfully, missions must ensure accurate learner assessments, curate comprehensive content libraries, and train staff to integrate AI-driven insights into training workflows.

Challenges include ensuring the quality and relevance of personalized content and addressing privacy concerns related to the collection and analysis of individual learning data. Ethical oversight is essential to maintain trust and transparency. Collaboration between AI and human expertise is crucial, as instructors bring the contextual understanding and interpersonal skills needed to motivate learners and address nuanced questions. By combining AI's adaptability with human guidance, diplomatic missions can enhance training programs, preparing their teams to excel in a complex and dynamic world.

VIRTUAL HELP DESKS

A 24/7 support desk that answers common embassy questions.

Providing timely and accurate support to mission staff is essential for ensuring smooth operations and maintaining morale, yet traditional help desk systems can be slow and resource-intensive. AI-powered virtual help desks address this challenge by automating responses to common queries, guiding users through troubleshooting steps, and escalating complex issues to human support staff when necessary. These tools enhance efficiency and ensure consistent support, allowing missions to focus on higher-value activities.

The applications of AI-powered virtual help desks are extensive. For instance, they can handle routine IT support requests, such as password resets or software troubleshooting, and assist staff with administrative procedures like scheduling or travel approvals. By delivering reliable and immediate support, virtual help desks empower staff to resolve issues quickly and continue their work without unnecessary delays. Successful implementation requires comprehensive and accurate knowledge databases, user-friendly interfaces, and training for staff to collaborate effectively with these tools.

Challenges include ensuring the quality and relevance of responses and addressing privacy concerns related to user data. Ethical oversight and robust data management practices are essential to maintain trust and transparency. Collaboration between AI and human expertise is critical, as human support staff provide the contextual understanding and interpersonal skills needed to handle complex or nuanced issues. By combining AI's speed and scalability with human problem-solving capabilities, virtual help desks enhance operational efficiency and support mission staff effectively.

EMERGENCY PREPAREDNESS

A crisis planner that helps embassies prepare for and handle emergencies.

Emergency preparedness is a critical responsibility for diplomatic missions, requiring swift and effective responses to protect staff, safeguard assets, and maintain operations during crises. Traditional methods often struggle to provide real-time situational awareness or anticipate emerging threats. AI-powered tools address this challenge by leveraging machine learning, predictive analytics, and geospatial analysis to monitor potential threats, assess vulnerabilities, and recommend proactive actions. These systems enhance situational awareness and enable missions to respond dynamically to crises.

The applications of AI in emergency preparedness are extensive. For example, AI can predict severe weather patterns, guiding preemptive measures such as resource allocation or temporary closures. During civil unrest, these tools can analyze threat proximity and recommend secure relocation routes for staff. By delivering actionable insights, AI empowers missions to mitigate risks and maintain continuity even under challenging circumstances. To implement these tools effectively, missions must ensure access to high-quality, diverse data, integrate AI systems into crisis management workflows, and provide comprehensive training for staff.

Challenges include ensuring data accuracy and addressing privacy concerns when monitoring sensitive information. Ethical oversight and robust data governance frameworks are essential to maintain trust and compliance. Collaboration between AI and human expertise is critical, as crisis managers provide the contextual understanding and leadership needed to evaluate AI findings and implement effective response strategies. By combining AI's analytical power with human judgment, diplomatic missions can strengthen their emergency preparedness and protect their teams and operations more effectively.

LIMITATIONS AND FUTURE RESEARCH DIRECTIONS

As AI transforms diplomatic management operations, we must carefully examine both its current limitations and the crucial questions that will shape its future development. Understanding these constraints isn't just an academic exercise—it offers practical insights for diplomatic practitioners who must navigate the complex reality of implementing AI while planning for tomorrow's challenges.

THE TECHNOLOGY INTEGRATION CHALLENGE

One of the most fundamental limitations in current AI implementation stems from the complex nature of diplomatic infrastructure. Think of a typical embassy's technology systems like layers of sedimentary rock—each generation of technology building upon and interacting with previous systems. Many diplomatic missions operate on infrastructure developed over decades, creating what technology experts call "technical debt"—a backlog of outdated systems that complicate the adoption of new technologies.

This challenge becomes particularly acute in resource-constrained posts. Imagine a small diplomatic mission trying to implement sophisticated AI tools while running on limited bandwidth and aging servers. It's like trying to run modern smartphone apps on a decade-old device—technically possible but fraught with complications. The situation raises crucial questions about how missions can modernize their systems while maintaining operational continuity and security.

THE HUMAN ELEMENT IN AI-ENHANCED MANAGEMENT

The intersection of AI and human resource management presents another critical limitation in our current understanding. While AI excels at processing personnel data and identifying patterns, it often struggles with the nuanced cultural dynamics that define diplomatic workplaces. Consider how differently performance evaluation might be viewed in relationship-oriented societies compared to task-oriented ones. An AI system trained on Western management principles might misinterpret or undervalue important cultural aspects of workplace dynamics.

This limitation extends to the management of locally employed staff, whose cultural expectations and working styles might differ significantly from the automated approaches AI systems typically employ. For instance, in cultures where personal relationships and face-to-face communication are highly valued, an AI-driven management system might inadvertently create friction by prioritizing efficiency over traditional interpersonal interactions.

RESOURCE ALLOCATION AND ETHICAL DECISION-MAKING

The ethical implications of AI-driven resource allocation demand particular attention, especially during crises. Current AI systems excel at optimizing resource distribution based on quantifiable metrics but may struggle with incorporating humanitarian considerations or diplomatic priorities that resist simple quantification. Think of an AI system during a natural disaster—it might recommend allocating resources based purely on numerical efficiency, potentially overlooking crucial diplomatic or humanitarian factors that human managers would instinctively consider.

This limitation becomes especially critical when AI recommendations affect vulnerable populations or sensitive diplomatic relationships. How do we ensure AI systems balance operational efficiency with diplomatic missions' broader humanitarian obligations? This question points toward the need for more sophisticated frameworks that can incorporate ethical considerations into AI decision-making processes.

OPERATIONAL RESILIENCE IN AN AI-DEPENDENT ENVIRONMENT

As diplomatic missions become increasingly reliant on AI systems, we must better understand how to maintain operational capability when these systems fail or face disruption. Current approaches often lack robust contingency plans for AI system failures. Imagine a mission whose resource management systems have become heavily dependent on AI analytics—what happens when these systems go offline during a crisis? This vulnerability highlights the need for better understanding of how missions can maintain essential functions even when their AI tools become unavailable.

THE EVOLUTION OF MANAGEMENT CULTURE

Perhaps, the most subtle yet significant limitation lies in our understanding of how AI integration affects traditional management culture in diplomatic missions. As AI systems increasingly influence operational decisions, we need to better understand how this shapes traditional authority structures and knowledge transfer between rotating diplomatic staff. Consider how AI might affect the traditional mentorship and training relationships that have long been crucial to developing diplomatic leadership skills.

FUTURE RESEARCH PRIORITIES

These limitations point toward several crucial areas for future research:

First, we need to develop more sophisticated frameworks for integrating AI into existing diplomatic infrastructure. This research should focus on creating flexible implementation models that work across missions with varying levels of technological readiness. Success here would mean finding ways to modernize systems while maintaining operational continuity and security.

Second, we must better understand how to create culturally adaptive AI management systems. This involves studying how different cultural contexts affect AI implementation and developing systems that can adjust their approaches based on local cultural norms and expectations.

Third, research should focus on developing ethical frameworks for AI-driven resource allocation that balance efficiency with humanitarian considerations and diplomatic priorities. This includes creating clear guidelines for when human judgment should override AI recommendations.

Fourth, we need to advance our understanding of operational resilience in AI-enhanced diplomatic missions. This involves studying how missions can maintain essential functions during system failures and developing robust backup procedures that don't rely entirely on technology.

CONCLUSION

The integration of AI into diplomatic management affairs promises to transform how management officers lead embassy operations, from real estate and personnel to budgets and logistics. As these technologies mature and find their way into diplomatic missions, they will enable management officers to shift from reactive problem-solving to proactive leadership. Whether running a small post solo or managing a section in a large embassy, emerging AI tools can help officers anticipate facility maintenance needs, optimize resource allocation, streamline personnel management, and enhance crisis preparedness.

Yet, success requires management officers to thoughtfully blend these developing AI capabilities with their core diplomatic competencies. While AI shows great potential for analyzing patterns in budgets, predicting maintenance issues, or flagging security concerns, officers must still maintain crucial relationships with host country officials, negotiate diplomatic privileges, and provide leadership to both local and American staff. Forward-thinking management officers are beginning to leverage AI for complex operational tasks while focusing their personal attention on the human elements that define diplomatic work – from supporting employee families to managing high-level visits.

Looking ahead, management officers who understand and help shape this balance between technological capability and diplomatic acumen will be best positioned for senior roles, whether as Management Counselors, Deputy Chiefs of Mission, or beyond. The future of diplomatic management lies not in choosing between artificial and human intelligence, but in thoughtfully implementing these tools to build more resilient, efficient, and human-centered diplomatic operations.

While management affairs focuses on maintaining the operational backbone of diplomatic missions, equally crucial is the direct service missions provide to citizens abroad. In the next chapter, we explore how AI is transforming consular affairs, from streamlining visa processing and enhancing fraud detection to revolutionizing crisis response and citizen services.

DISCUSSION SCENARIOS AND QUESTIONS

The following scenarios examine how AI is reshaping the operational backbone of diplomatic missions. Readers will explore the implications of AI-driven resource management, logistical coordination, and crisis preparedness, considering both efficiency gains and the ethical complexities of automation in mission operations.

1. AI-assisted human resources management
   Scenario: AI analyzes embassy staffing trends, predicts turnover rates, and recommends candidates for leadership roles. The AI's analysis highlights patterns that inadvertently exclude certain demographics.

Questions: How would you detect and address potential biases in AI-driven recruitment or promotion decisions? If embassy staff express distrust in AI-driven evaluations, how would you rebuild confidence in the system while maintaining its operational benefits?

2. Leveraging generative AI for policy and process standardization

Scenario: Your embassy adopts a generative AI tool to draft policy memos, contract templates, and cultural guides. While efficient, the AI overlooks local nuances and produces materials that lack alignment with embassy policies, prompting concerns from host-country officials about insufficient local engagement.

Questions: How would you adapt AI-generated outputs to reflect cultural, legal, and operational nuances? What steps would you take to ensure AI outputs align with embassy-specific practices and meet host-country expectations? How would you balance the efficiency of generative AI with the need for personalized, context-driven approaches in diplomacy?

3. Budget optimization with AI

Scenario: AI recommends reallocating funds away from staff training and long-term facility maintenance to address immediate budget shortfalls. This would achieve cost savings but could negatively affect morale and operational sustainability.

Questions: How would you weigh short-term financial efficiency against the long-term needs of staff development and infrastructure? What processes would you implement to adjust AI parameters to align its recommendations with your strategic priorities?

4. AI-driven decision-making for embassy operations

Scenario: As a management officer, you use AI tools to streamline operations, such as allocating resources, planning logistics, and managing personnel. The AI recommends downsizing certain operations or reducing services that are considered non-essential but highly valued by embassy staff.

Questions: How would you evaluate the AI's recommendations when they conflict with human priorities, such as employee well-being or morale? In what ways could over-reliance on AI for decision-making erode the management officer's ability to maintain a human-centered approach to leadership?

5. Crisis response using predictive AI tools

Scenario: During a natural disaster, predictive AI models recommend prioritizing resources for embassy staff and their families, while delaying assistance to local communities. Some team members disagree with the AI's allocation of resources.

Questions: How would you mediate between the AI's efficiency-driven resource allocation and the ethical responsibility to assist the host community? What safeguards could you introduce to ensure the AI's recommendations are balanced and aligned with your mission's core values?

6 AI and Consular Affairs
Optimizing Visa, Passport, and Citizen Services

Structured decisions, descriptive analytics and procedural knowledge are the most likely entry points for AI adoption in the diplomatic field; they apply well to consular services and international negotiations.

—Corneliu Bjola, Oxford University (2020)

These potential [AI] use cases can reshape the efficiency of the millions of visa and passport applications that consular affairs processes every year, automating standard submission steps, isolating the sources of performance bottlenecks, and enhancing resource allocation and staff time.

—Tasha Austin, Director of Deloitte AI Institute
for Government (Austin et al. 2022)

For anyone who travels internationally, these [AI] surveillance systems may provide some convenience—but they can also flag you as a potential threat or even limit your freedom to travel, while giving you little ability to do anything about it.

—Caitlin L. Chandler, journalist (2025)

In diplomacy, consular officers serve as both the first line of defense at borders and the last hope for citizens in need. These unsung heroes manage critical tasks: adjudicating visas, combating fraud, and assisting Americans during emergencies abroad. As global connectivity increases and crises grow more complex, their role becomes even more demanding—and indispensable (Höne et al. 2019). Artificial intelligence (AI) emerges as a transformative force in this space, automating routine tasks, enhancing decision-making, and providing real-time insights. With AI, consular officers can identify high-risk visa applicants, anticipate emergencies, and combat human trafficking, ultimately strengthening border security and improving citizen services.

However, the adoption of AI in consular affairs also raises crucial ethical considerations. Issues of fairness, transparency, and privacy must be addressed to ensure its responsible use. Striking a balance between AI's efficiency and the human judgment and empathy that define consular work is paramount. This chapter examines how AI is reshaping consular operations, from advanced visa vetting and fraud detection to streamlined crisis response and citizen support. Through real-world examples and forward-looking insights, we'll explore the opportunities and challenges of this new frontier. With careful integration guided by human expertise, AI has the potential to fortify borders, protect citizens, and redefine the future of consular diplomacy in an ever-changing world.

DOI: 10.1201/9781003612308-6

VIGNETTE   AI-Enhanced Embassy in the Republic of Z

As dawn breaks over the Republic of Z, Consular Officer Maria Santos reviews her AI-powered dashboard, which already shows a 40% surge in visa applications— a direct result of the new green energy initiatives that Economic Officer Elena Moretti has been developing. The system's predictive analytics suggest this is just the beginning, forecasting increased demand for business visas as bilateral renewable energy partnerships expand.

The AI platform simultaneously monitors multiple consular priorities: visa application patterns, mission citizen services, and potential fraud indicators. A map highlights the locations of the 3,000 fellow citizens registered in Z, with real-time alerts from local hospitals, police stations, and emergency services. In light of recent political tensions noted by Political Officer Sarah Chen, the system has automatically updated emergency evacuation scenarios and identified potential safe havens throughout the country.

Santos appreciates how AI has transformed consular operations while preserving the human judgment essential to her role. As she reviews complex visa cases flagged by the system's fraud detection algorithms, she reflects on how technology enhances rather than replaces the careful interviewing and decision-making skills that define consular work. The AI helps spot patterns— unusual application similarities or document irregularities—but it's her experienced eye that makes final determinations.

An urgent alert draws her attention: a fellow citizen has been hospitalized following a traffic accident in a remote province. The AI immediately provides hospital details, the closest local authorities, and the citizen's emergency contact information. As her team springs into action, the system generates a response checklist while simultaneously updating the emergency services database that tracks assistance to fellow citizens.

By mid-morning, Santos is preparing for a town hall meeting with the expatriate business community to discuss the implications of Z's evolving political and economic situation. The AI system has compiled relevant statistics and trends, but she knows it's her ability to address their concerns personally— about everything from passport renewals to safety preparations—that will provide real reassurance. As the consular section adapts to support Z's growing international engagement, she ensures that protecting and serving fellow citizens remains at the heart of their mission.

INTRODUCTION TO AI IN CONSULAR AFFAIRS

Consular officers have long been the lifeblood of diplomacy, performing vital roles that affect both individual lives and national policies. Their responsibilities, ranging from adjudicating visas to providing critical support during emergencies, demand resilience, empathy, and precision. Yet, these duties are often weighed down by inefficiencies and the sheer volume of work that consular sections must manage. As the world becomes increasingly interconnected, the demand for swift, reliable consular services has never been higher.

AI is emerging as a game-changing tool for transforming consular operations. By automating repetitive tasks, providing insightful analyses, and streamlining decision-making processes, AI offers a suite of capabilities that can elevate the effectiveness and efficiency of consular work. This chapter delves into the potential of AI to revolutionize this domain, highlighting its ability to complement human expertise while addressing the complexities of modern consular challenges.

STREAMLINING VISA PROCESSING AND CITIZEN SERVICES

Visa adjudication forms the backbone of many consular operations, yet the traditional processes are often encumbered by bottlenecks and inefficiencies. AI has the potential to alleviate these issues by analyzing thousands of visa applications in mere hours. Through advanced machine learning models, it can cross-reference application data with government databases, identify patterns of risk, and flag discrepancies that require further investigation. Low-risk cases, such as returning students or applicants with consistent travel histories, can be processed with greater speed and accuracy, freeing consular officers to focus on nuanced, high-stakes decisions. This shift not only reduces processing times but also ensures greater fairness and consistency across adjudications.

Routine citizen services, from passport renewals to travel advisory updates, often overwhelm consular resources. AI-powered chatbots and self-service portals can mitigate this burden by providing instant, accurate responses to frequently asked questions (Alder 2024). These tools operate around the clock, guiding users through complex processes such as visa applications or offering tailored advice for international travelers. For example, an AI chatbot could walk a family through the requirements for obtaining emergency travel documents or suggest travel safety tips based on current geopolitical conditions. By handling these routine inquiries, consular staff are empowered to dedicate their energy to more complex and critical matters.

The impact of AI on streamlining routine tasks is already evident in speculative scenarios. Imagine a high-volume consulate during peak travel season utilizing AI to pre-approve low-risk student visas (Collins 2024). At the same time, AI-powered portals handle an influx of questions regarding policy updates, ensuring applicants receive accurate, timely information without straining human resources. These tools offer a glimpse into how AI could transform the user experience while maintaining the integrity of consular services.

ENHANCING FRAUD DETECTION AND RISK ASSESSMENT

Fraudulent activities, such as forged documents and identity theft, remain significant hurdles in visa and passport processes (Serhan 2024). Consular officers often rely on time-intensive manual reviews to detect such issues, which can be prone to human error, particularly during periods of high demand. AI offers a powerful alternative by employing sophisticated algorithms to analyze application data for anomalies and inconsistencies. These systems can detect patterns indicative of fraud, such as repeated discrepancies in financial documents or unusual travel histories, and flag high-risk cases for closer scrutiny (Bjola 2020).

Biometric technology represents another frontier where AI can revolutionize border security (Cummings et al. 2018). Tools such as facial recognition and fingerprint analysis can compare applicant biometrics against official records, instantly identifying potential mismatches or signs of tampering. These innovations not only bolster security but also streamline verification processes for legitimate travelers. However, implementing such technologies requires balancing robust security measures with fairness and privacy (European Commission 2019). AI systems must be transparent and free from biases that could disproportionately affect certain demographics. By addressing these ethical concerns, consular missions can ensure that AI serves as an equitable and effective tool for risk assessment.

CRISIS MANAGEMENT: AMPLIFYING HUMAN EFFORTS WITH AI

During crises, whether natural disasters, political upheavals, or public health emergencies, consular officers are often at the forefront, safeguarding citizens and coordinating complex responses. AI could potentially serve as a powerful force multiplier in these scenarios, with emerging tools that may help anticipate crises, streamline communication, and enhance response coordination (Haseley et al. 2023). These developing systems may operate across multiple dimensions of crisis management.

In the realm of predictive analytics and early warning systems, AI shows promise in analyzing real-time data from diverse sources, including weather forecasts, social media, satellite imagery, public health reports, and news feeds, to identify emerging risks. This type of data analysis could enable consular missions to issue more timely warnings and potentially allocate resources more effectively. Advanced machine learning models might eventually predict natural disasters and suggest humanitarian aid deployment strategies based on historical data and current conditions.

Population movement monitoring represents another potential application of AI in crisis management. Emerging systems aim to track and analyze refugee and migration patterns using multiple data sources, including open-source intelligence, satellite imagery, and NGO reports. Through these developing tools, diplomatic missions may become better equipped to anticipate displacement crises, improve humanitarian aid distribution networks, monitor human rights situations, and coordinate responses with international partners.

Infrastructure and logistics assessment capabilities are being explored through AI applications. These experimental systems seek to evaluate infrastructure damage through satellite imagery and local reports, potentially enabling missions to better assess the scope of damage in affected areas. Such technology might help identify evacuation routes and safe zones while evaluating supply chain disruptions and logistical challenges.

Emergency communication and coordination could be transformed by AI-powered platforms (Feijóo et al. 2020). Consider a theoretical scenario during a cyclone: AI systems might map affected citizens' locations, identify those potentially in immediate danger, and suggest possible evacuation routes while generating emergency notifications in multiple languages (Bullock et al. 2020). If successfully implemented, such capabilities could help consular officers respond more effectively.

Real-time situational awareness represents another area where AI may provide value. Emerging systems attempt to aggregate and analyze information from multiple sources, including social media monitoring for potential threats, local news and emergency service updates, weather conditions, transportation status, and healthcare facility capacity.

Looking ahead, AI-driven platforms may continue to evolve in crisis management. Future embassy systems could potentially monitor global events and issue targeted alerts to travelers. They might assist in coordinating evacuation efforts and help optimize resource allocation. While many of these capabilities remain in development or early testing phases, they suggest promising directions for enhancing consular crisis response.

These technological capabilities, if successfully developed and implemented, would need to be carefully integrated with human expertise and judgment. The goal is not to replace human decision-making but to provide consular officers with additional tools that could help them respond more effectively to increasingly complex global emergencies.

HISTORICAL AI USE CASE EXAMPLES IN CONSULAR AFFAIRS

Consular affairs, encompassing visa processing, passport issuance, and citizen services, are poised to benefit significantly from the integration of AI. Governments have begun to use AI to streamline operations, enhance security, and improve responsiveness in consular services, in a quest to deploy cutting-edge technologies to address challenges in efficiency and accuracy.

The U.S. Department of State is showing signs of introducing AI-assisted systems for visa processing to streamline adjudication processes (State Department AI Inventory 2024). These systems could utilize machine learning algorithms to analyze vast datasets, flag high-risk applications, and automate routine case reviews. The implementation could reduce processing times while maintaining robust security standards, allowing consular officers to focus on complex cases requiring human judgment. However, early challenges, including algorithmic bias, would necessitate continuous measures to ensure fairness and transparency in decision-making processes (State Department AI Inventory 2024).

The Bureau of Consular Affairs within the U.S. Department of State shows interest in deploying AI systems for automated passport photo quality assessments. These tools can evaluate submitted photographs against government standards, providing instant feedback to applicants and significantly reducing errors in document submissions. By eliminating manual reviews of substandard images, the system could improve operational efficiency and allow resources to be allocated to other critical consular tasks (State Department AI Inventory 2024).

Fraud detection is a critical concern in visa and passport issuance. Drawing inspiration from Israel's AI-driven border security systems, consular offices are starting to adopt machine learning algorithms to detect anomalies in submitted documents and application histories. For example, AI systems are being trained to identify patterns indicative of fraudulent intent, such as inconsistencies in financial records or document forgery techniques. These tools would enable consular officers to mitigate fraud risks while maintaining service quality. Israel's success in deploying similar systems highlights the broader applicability of AI in enhancing consular security (Serhan 2024).

The UNHCR's Project Jetson, originally designed to predict displacement trends in Somalia, offers a template for adapting AI in consular contexts. AI-driven predictive analytics have been used to anticipate surges in citizen service demand, such as spikes in visa applications or evacuation needs during crises. For example, embassies could employ AI to analyze historical data on consular requests, enabling better resource allocation and operational planning during high-demand periods (United Nations Global Pulse 2019).

AI systems are enhancing consular services in crisis management by integrating real-time data from multiple sources to provide actionable insights. During natural disasters, political instability, or global health emergencies, AI is being used to monitor social media feeds, analyze local news reports, and provide personalized notifications to citizens abroad. For instance, embassies leveraged AI tools during the COVID-19 pandemic to disseminate travel advisories and safety updates, ensuring timely communication with affected individuals (Manor 2017, 2019).

While AI has advanced consular operations, its deployment has raised ethical concerns. Issues such as algorithmic bias in visa adjudication processes or data privacy in automated photo checks must be addressed to maintain public trust. For example, early iterations of AI systems face criticism for potentially reinforcing biases against specific demographics. To counteract this, stakeholders have an interest in implementing measures to improve algorithm transparency and fairness, ensuring equitable outcomes for all applicants (State Department AI Inventory 2024).

The Estonian government is leveraging AI to enhance public services, including potential applications in consular affairs. Through initiatives like Bürokratt, a virtual assistant for accessing services like passport renewal and benefit applications, Estonia aims to streamline processes and improve user experience. While specific AI use in visas or passports is unconfirmed, Estonia's focus on AI integration demonstrates its commitment to making government interactions faster and more efficient.

The historical use of AI in consular affairs highlights critical lessons:

1. Balancing automation and human oversight: AI tools excel at automating routine tasks but require human intervention in complex or ethically sensitive scenarios.
2. Fraud mitigation: AI's pattern recognition capabilities are proving effective in detecting fraudulent activities, underscoring the need for robust security frameworks.
3. Crisis preparedness: Predictive analytics enable embassies to anticipate service demands and respond proactively to crises, ensuring efficient resource allocation.
4. Ethical governance: Addressing concerns about bias and privacy is essential for maintaining trust in AI-powered consular services.

By incorporating these lessons, consular missions can begin to leverage AI to improve operational efficiency, strengthen security, and enhance citizen services while adhering to ethical standards.

NAVIGATING ETHICAL CONSIDERATIONS AND CHALLENGES

The integration of AI into consular operations brings significant ethical responsibilities. Data privacy is a paramount concern, as AI systems often process sensitive personal information, including biometrics and travel histories. Ensuring that this data is stored securely and accessed responsibly is critical to maintaining public trust. Similarly, algorithmic bias poses a challenge, as biased systems could lead to unfair outcomes in visa adjudication or risk assessments. Human oversight remains essential to validate AI outputs and address any unintended biases effectively.

Transparency is another cornerstone of ethical AI implementation (Bjola & Kornprobst 2024). Clear communication about how AI systems operate and the criteria they use to make decisions fosters confidence among applicants and stakeholders. Regular audits, inclusive training programs, and community engagement further ensure that AI evolves responsibly and equitably, reflecting the values of fairness and trust.

THE FUTURE OF AI IN CONSULAR AFFAIRS

The future of AI in consular affairs is both exciting and expansive. In the near term, chatbots, virtual assistants, and robotic process automation are expected to become standard tools for streamlining operations and enhancing service delivery. These innovations promise to reduce administrative burdens while improving accessibility for citizens worldwide (Manor 2019).

Looking further ahead, speculative advancements such as virtual consulates could redefine the landscape of consular services (Kissinger, Schmidt, and Huttenlocher 2021). Imagine a fully online platform where citizens can complete visa applications, attend virtual interviews, and receive personalized assistance without setting foot in a physical consulate. Predictive analytics could also play a transformative role, enabling missions to proactively identify at-risk citizens or forecast global mobility trends. These developments underscore the importance of human-AI collaboration, ensuring that technology complements, rather than replaces, the human touch.

REDEFINING CONSULAR EXCELLENCE WITH AI

AI holds immense potential to revolutionize consular affairs, offering tools that streamline routine tasks, enhance border security, and amplify crisis response efforts. Its value lies in augmenting human capabilities, enabling consular officers to focus on their core mission of serving people with empathy and expertise. As missions integrate AI, a thoughtful approach is essential to address ethical considerations, maintain transparency, and ensure accountability.

The way forward involves harnessing AI responsibly, embracing innovation while upholding the timeless values of diplomacy. Human judgment and compassion remain irreplaceable, providing the foundation upon which AI-driven consular services can thrive. Together, technology and human expertise can redefine what is possible in the realm of consular affairs, setting a new standard for efficiency, equity, and excellence.

LARGE LANGUAGE MODELS: ENHANCING CONSULAR SERVICES

Building on our exploration of Large Language Models (LLMs) across diplomatic functions—from general diplomatic work and leadership to political analysis, economic affairs, and management operations—we now examine their specific applications in consular services. While previous chapters demonstrated these tools' value in various diplomatic roles, consular officers face unique challenges in communicating complex requirements, responding to emergencies, and serving diverse populations efficiently.

Consular work demands exceptional clarity in public communication, especially when explaining visa requirements and procedures to applicants from varied linguistic and cultural backgrounds. LLMs excel at helping consular officers create clear, accessible guidance materials that maintain technical accuracy while being easily understood by non-native English speakers (Blaser 2023). This capability proves particularly valuable when developing step-by-step instructions for complex processes or explaining documentation requirements to diverse audiences.

Crisis communication, a critical aspect of consular work, benefits from LLM capabilities in new ways. Beyond the communication support explored in previous chapters, these tools can help consular officers craft emergency messages that balance urgency with clarity, develop scalable response templates for various crisis scenarios, and ensure consistent messaging across multiple channels (Bano, Chaudhri, and Zowghi 2023). This proves especially valuable during emergencies when clear, timely communication can save lives.

Citizen services represent another key application unique to consular affairs. Building on the service-oriented approaches discussed in earlier chapters, consular officers can use LLMs to develop comprehensive resource guides, create clear FAQ responses, and generate user-friendly explanations of complex consular procedures. This capability particularly shines when creating materials that help citizens navigate unfamiliar processes or understand their rights and responsibilities abroad.

However, consular work demands special attention to certain limitations beyond those discussed previously. The sensitivity of personal information and the critical nature of consular services require extra caution in how these tools are used. Officers must be particularly mindful of privacy considerations and ensure all communication aligns with official consular regulations and requirements while maintaining the empathetic tone essential to consular services.

PUTTING LLMS TO WORK: A GUIDE FOR CONSULAR OFFICERS

Building on prompt engineering practices established in previous chapters, let's explore how consular officers can craft effective prompts for their specific service needs. While earlier chapters covered diplomatic communications, leadership decisions, political analysis, economic assessments, and management operations, consular work requires particular attention to clear public communication, emergency response, and citizen assistance.

When creating visa application guidance, frame your prompts to ensure comprehensibility for diverse audiences. For example:

> Help me draft step-by-step instructions for tourist visa applicants from [Country]. Include: 1) required documentation with clear explanations of each item, 2) common mistakes to avoid, 3) timeline expectations, and 4) frequently asked questions. Use simple language accessible to non-native English speakers while maintaining accuracy about requirements. Format this as a user-friendly guide that anticipates common points of confusion.

For emergency communication templates, structure prompts to balance urgency with clarity:

> I need to create emergency message templates for different crisis scenarios affecting citizens abroad. For each type (natural disaster, civil unrest, health emergency), develop: 1) initial alert text, 2) follow-up guidance, 3) location/shelter information, and 4) embassy contact details. Ensure messages are concise yet comprehensive, maintaining a tone that is authoritative but reassuring.

For citizen services guides, focus prompts on accessibility and thoroughness:

> Develop a comprehensive guide for citizens living in [Country]. Structure sections to cover: 1) emergency contacts and procedures, 2) passport renewal steps, 3) local resources and recommendations, 4) voting information, and 5) embassy services. Format this for easy reference during both routine and emergency situations, highlighting critical information without overwhelming readers.

Consular officers should particularly focus prompts on:

- Creating clear instructions for diverse audiences
- Developing crisis communication materials
- Explaining complex procedures simply
- Anticipating and addressing common questions
- Maintaining consistency across information resources

These applications extend beyond the foundational capabilities covered in previous chapters to address the specific needs of consular services. The key is maintaining clarity and accessibility while ensuring all outputs align with official requirements and convey appropriate empathy for those seeking assistance.

ADVANCED AI USE CASES IN CONSULAR AFFAIRS

Building on the foundational AI applications explored in Chapter 1, the leadership use cases from Chapter 2, the political applications in Chapter 3, the economic tools examined in Chapter 4, and the management systems discussed in Chapter 5, we now examine advanced AI solutions specifically designed for consular services. While previous chapters demonstrated how AI can enhance various aspects of diplomatic work, consular affairs presents unique opportunities for leveraging AI to protect citizens, facilitate legitimate travel, and enhance border security. From automated visa processing and biometric verification to crisis response systems and fraud detection, these use cases demonstrate how AI can transform the delivery of consular services. Each application builds upon basic AI capabilities to address the sophisticated challenges of modern consular work, where efficient service delivery and security considerations must be carefully balanced (Tuset Varela 2024a, 2024b). As we continue exploring AI applications across different diplomatic functions in subsequent chapters, these consular affairs use cases highlight how AI can enhance service delivery while maintaining the crucial role of human judgment in protecting both borders and citizens.

AUTOMATED VISA ADJUDICATION

A visa processor that quickly sorts routine applications from complex ones.

Visa adjudication stands at the heart of consular operations, determining who can legally enter a country while maintaining national security and immigration integrity. Traditional visa processing methods, though effective, often create bottlenecks due to their reliance on manual review and limited human resources, particularly in missions experiencing high application volumes. AI-powered automated visa adjudication systems offer a transformative solution by streamlining the processing of visa applications through machine learning, natural language processing (NLP), and predictive analytics to assess eligibility criteria, flag potential issues, and prioritize applications for further review.

Current visa adjudication workflows face multiple challenges: time-intensive manual reviews, inconsistent decision-making across different officers, and the inability to quickly scale during peak seasons. These inefficiencies lead to processing delays, increased costs, and frustrated applicants. AI addresses these challenges by automating routine tasks like document verification and background checks, while identifying patterns that might indicate fraud or security concerns. The system can analyze applications in real time, recommending immediate approval for routine cases that meet all criteria while flagging higher risk or incomplete submissions for human review. Success metrics include reductions in processing times, the percentage of applications resolved without manual intervention, and improved consistency in decision-making across different consular posts.

In real-world applications, AI-powered visa adjudication systems demonstrate remarkable versatility and impact. During peak travel seasons, these systems can manage thousands of applications simultaneously, ensuring consistent evaluation while freeing consular officers to focus on complex cases requiring human judgment. For instance, during a global health crisis, the system might incorporate public health data to assess travel risks and adjust processing protocols accordingly. However, the implementation requires careful consideration of ethical implications, particularly regarding data privacy and algorithmic bias. The key to success lies in maintaining human oversight while leveraging AI's capabilities—consular officers retain final decision-making authority, especially in nuanced cases where context and empathy are crucial (Marwala 2023). This human-AI collaboration ensures that efficiency gains don't compromise the fundamental fairness and integrity of the visa adjudication process.

FRAUD DETECTION IN VISA APPLICATIONS

A pattern spotter that finds fake documents and suspicious applications.

Detecting fraud in visa applications represents a critical security function of consular operations, protecting borders and maintaining the integrity of immigration systems. Traditional fraud detection methods rely heavily on manual document reviews and personal interviews, which can be time-consuming and may miss sophisticated fraudulent patterns. AI-powered fraud detection systems offer a revolutionary approach by leveraging machine learning and pattern recognition to analyze visa applications for inconsistencies, anomalies, and indicators of fraudulent behavior across large datasets of applications and supporting documents.

Current fraud detection faces significant challenges: the increasing sophistication of fraudulent techniques, the sheer volume of applications requiring review, and the limited ability of human reviewers to identify complex patterns across multiple applications. AI addresses these limitations by cross-checking applicant information against government and industry databases, flagging potential issues such as forged educational credentials or suspicious employment histories, and identifying patterns of fraud associated with specific application trends. Success metrics include the number of fraudulent cases detected, the reduction in processing times for legitimate applications, and the accuracy of fraud predictions. The system's effectiveness depends on regular updates to AI models and rigorous data validation to ensure accuracy and fairness.

In practical applications, AI-powered fraud detection demonstrates significant impact across various scenarios. During mass application campaigns, such as student visa seasons, the system can identify clusters of fraudulent applications linked to specific document mills or fraudulent schemes, enabling consular officers to focus their attention on suspicious cases while expediting legitimate applications. The implementation requires careful balance between security and fairness, with clear protocols for human oversight and appeal processes. Ethical considerations, particularly regarding data privacy and algorithmic bias, must be addressed through transparent frameworks and regular audits. The success of these systems relies on the collaborative partnership between AI's pattern recognition capabilities and the contextual understanding of experienced consular officers, ensuring that technology enhances rather than replaces human judgment in fraud detection.

FACIAL RECOGNITION FOR IDENTITY VERIFICATION

A face matcher that confirms people are who they claim to be.

Identity verification stands as a cornerstone of consular security, ensuring that visa applicants and passport holders are who they claim to be. Traditional verification methods, relying on manual photo comparisons and document checks, while thorough, can be time-consuming and subject to human error. AI-powered facial recognition systems transform this process by employing deep learning algorithms and neural networks to compare facial features against official databases with unprecedented speed and accuracy, detecting potential fraud or identity theft attempts that might be missed by human reviewers.

The current identity verification process faces several key challenges: the increasing sophistication of identity fraud, the need for rapid processing of high volumes of applications, and the difficulty of maintaining consistency across different consular posts. AI facial recognition technology addresses these issues by instantly analyzing multiple biometric data points, comparing them against existing records, and flagging discrepancies for further investigation. The system can process thousands of verifications daily with consistent accuracy, while advanced algorithms adapt to various factors such as aging, lighting conditions, and image quality. Success metrics include verification speed, accuracy rates, and the number of fraudulent attempts detected.

In practice, facial recognition systems demonstrate their value across numerous consular scenarios. During passport renewals or visa applications, the technology can instantly verify an applicant's identity against previous travel documents or visa photos, streamlining the process for legitimate travelers while identifying potential imposters. However, implementation requires careful attention to ethical considerations, particularly regarding privacy protection and potential algorithmic bias across different demographic groups. The key to successful deployment lies in maintaining a balance between security and accessibility, with clear protocols for human oversight in cases where AI flags potential issues. This human-AI collaboration ensures that while technology enhances security and efficiency, human judgment remains central to final decision-making, especially in complex cases requiring contextual understanding or sensitivity.

DOCUMENT TRANSLATION

A speed translator that handles routine documents in multiple languages.

Document translation represents a critical yet resource-intensive function in consular operations, where accuracy and speed are equally important. Traditional translation methods, relying on human translators or basic translation tools, often create bottlenecks in processing visa applications and supporting materials, particularly when dealing with multiple languages and high document volumes. AI-powered translation systems offer a transformative solution by leveraging NLP and machine learning to provide fast, accurate translations across multiple languages while maintaining context and technical accuracy.

Current translation workflows face several challenges: limited availability of specialized translators, inconsistent translation quality across different languages, and delays during peak application periods. AI translation tools address these issues by providing instant translations of standard documents like birth certificates, educational credentials, and financial statements, while identifying complex passages that may require human review. The system can handle multiple document formats, recognize specialized terminology, and maintain consistency across similar document types. Success metrics include translation speed, accuracy rates compared to human translations, and the system's ability to handle specialized consular and legal terminology.

In real-world applications, AI translation systems demonstrate a significant impact on consular efficiency. During humanitarian crises, these tools can rapidly translate large volumes of emergency documentation, enabling quick response to urgent situations. For routine operations, the system streamlines the processing of standard documents while flagging complex or sensitive materials for human review. However, implementation requires careful attention to accuracy and cultural sensitivity, with clear protocols for quality control and human oversight. The most effective approach combines AI's speed and consistency with human expertise for nuanced or critical translations, ensuring that while technology accelerates the process, the final output maintains the high standards required for consular documentation.

Smart Chatbots for FAQs

A virtual assistant that answers common visa questions day and night.

Consular sections face an ongoing challenge of responding to high volumes of routine inquiries, from visa application procedures to travel advisory updates, which can overwhelm staff resources and delay responses to more critical matters. Traditional methods of handling inquiries through email, phone calls, and in-person visits often result in long wait times and inconsistent information delivery. AI-powered smart chatbots offer a revolutionary solution by providing instant, accurate responses to common questions 24/7, while intelligently routing complex inquiries to appropriate human staff.

Current FAQ management faces multiple challenges: repetitive queries consuming staff time, inconsistent responses across different communication channels, and limited availability outside business hours. Smart chatbots address these issues by leveraging NLP to understand user queries and provide contextual responses drawn from validated information databases. The system can handle multiple concurrent conversations, learn from interactions to improve response accuracy, and seamlessly escalate complex cases to human officers when needed. Success metrics include response time, query resolution rates, user satisfaction scores, and the reduction in routine inquiries handled by consular staff.

In practice, smart chatbots demonstrate remarkable effectiveness in enhancing consular services. During peak visa seasons, these systems can handle thousands of routine inquiries simultaneously, providing instant guidance on application requirements and procedures. In crisis situations, chatbots can disseminate emergency information rapidly while directing urgent cases to human officers. However, implementation requires careful attention to accuracy and user experience, with regular updates to information databases and clear escalation protocols. The key to success lies in positioning chatbots as complementary to human services rather than replacements, ensuring that while technology handles routine queries, human expertise remains readily available for complex or sensitive matters requiring personal attention.

PERSONALIZED TRAVEL ADVISORY SYSTEMS

A smart alert system that sends safety updates based on where you are.

Travel advisories constitute a vital aspect of consular services, providing critical safety and security information to citizens traveling abroad. Traditional advisory systems often rely on broad, one-size-fits-all notifications that may not address individual travelers' specific circumstances or needs. AI-powered personalized travel advisory systems transform this approach by delivering tailored guidance based on real-time data analysis, individual travel patterns, and specific risk factors, ensuring travelers receive relevant and timely information for their particular situations.

The current travel advisory process faces several limitations: generic information that may not apply to specific travelers, delayed updates during rapidly evolving situations, and difficulty in reaching affected individuals with relevant warnings. AI systems address these challenges by analyzing multiple data streams—including weather patterns, political developments, health alerts, and crime statistics—to generate personalized advisories. The technology can process real-time information from various sources, predict potential risks, and automatically distribute targeted alerts to travelers based on their location, itinerary, and risk profile. Success metrics include the timeliness of alerts, accuracy of risk predictions, and effectiveness in reaching affected travelers with relevant information.

In real-world applications, personalized travel advisory systems protect citizens abroad by identifying affected travelers during crises, providing specific evacuation guidance, and suggesting safe alternatives based on location. For routine travel, they deliver customized safety updates as local conditions change. Implementation requires robust privacy protocols and data security, while combining AI capabilities with human oversight—ensuring consular officers retain final authority over critical safety decisions. To align with "no double standard" policies, these systems must maintain publicly available baseline threat alerts while tailoring individual warnings. Success depends on government oversight of transparency and equitable information dissemination, measured through alert timeliness, risk prediction accuracy, and effectiveness in reaching affected travelers.

CRISIS MANAGEMENT AND EMERGENCY RESPONSE

A coordination center that helps find and assist citizens during emergencies.

Crisis management and emergency response represent critical functions of consular operations, where rapid, coordinated action can mean the difference between life and death. Traditional crisis response methods often struggle with information gathering, resource allocation, and coordination across multiple agencies during emergencies. AI-powered crisis management systems offer a transformative solution by analyzing real-time data, predicting potential risks, and optimizing response strategies to protect citizens and maintain operational continuity during emergencies.

Current crisis management faces significant challenges: delayed information processing, difficulty in coordinating multiple stakeholders, and the complexity of managing resources during large-scale emergencies. AI systems address these limitations by monitoring multiple data sources simultaneously, from social media feeds to weather forecasts, identifying emerging threats, and suggesting optimal response strategies (United Nations Global Pulse 2019). The technology can track citizen locations, assess infrastructure status, and recommend evacuation routes in real time. Success metrics include response time reduction, resource allocation efficiency, and the number of citizens successfully assisted during crises.

In practical applications, AI-powered crisis management systems demonstrate crucial value across various emergency scenarios. During natural disasters, the system can predict impact zones, identify vulnerable citizens, and coordinate evacuation efforts with local authorities. For political unrest or health emergencies, it can track developing situations, alert affected citizens, and optimize resource deployment. However, implementation requires careful attention to data accuracy and privacy protection, with clear protocols for information sharing during emergencies. The key to success lies in combining AI's analytical capabilities with human expertise, ensuring that while technology enhances crisis response, experienced consular officers maintain ultimate control over critical decisions affecting citizen safety.

BIOMETRIC VERIFICATION FOR SECURE DOCUMENT ISSUANCE

An identity checker that makes sure passports go to the right people.

Secure document issuance, including passports and visas, requires stringent identity verification to prevent fraud and maintain national security. Traditional verification methods, while thorough, often involve time-consuming manual checks and can be vulnerable to sophisticated forgery attempts. AI-powered biometric verification systems revolutionize this process by employing advanced algorithms to analyze multiple biometric markers simultaneously, ensuring both security and efficiency in document issuance procedures.

Current document issuance faces several challenges: increasing sophistication of identity fraud, the need for rapid processing without compromising security, and maintaining consistency across different consular posts. AI biometric systems address these issues by analyzing multiple data points—including fingerprints, facial features, and iris scans—comparing them against extensive databases while detecting potential fraud patterns. The technology can process thousands of verifications daily with consistent accuracy, adapting to various presentation attack methods and evolving fraud techniques. Success metrics include verification speed, fraud detection rates, and the accuracy of biometric matching across diverse populations.

In practice, biometric verification systems demonstrate a significant impact in securing document issuance processes. During passport renewals or visa applications, the technology can instantly verify an applicant's identity across multiple databases, flagging discrepancies for further investigation while expediting legitimate applications. However, implementation requires careful attention to privacy protection and ethical considerations, particularly regarding data storage and potential algorithmic bias. Success depends on balancing security requirements with privacy rights, maintaining transparent procedures for data handling, and ensuring human oversight for complex cases. This approach ensures that while AI enhances security and efficiency, human judgment remains central to final document issuance decisions.

PREDICTIVE ANALYTICS FOR VISA DEMAND FORECASTING

A crowd predictor that helps prepare for busy visa seasons.

Accurate visa demand forecasting plays a critical role in consular operations, enabling missions to allocate resources efficiently and maintain service quality during peak periods. Traditional forecasting methods, relying primarily on historical data and seasonal patterns, often struggle to account for dynamic variables and emerging trends that affect visa demand. AI-powered predictive analytics transform this process by analyzing diverse data sources to forecast visa demand patterns with unprecedented accuracy, allowing missions to prepare proactively for fluctuations in application volumes.

Current forecasting methods face several key challenges: limited ability to incorporate real-time data, difficulty in predicting sudden demand shifts, and inadequate consideration of multiple influencing factors. AI systems address these limitations by analyzing a broad spectrum of data points—including travel trends, economic indicators, event calendars, and policy changes—to generate accurate demand forecasts. The technology can identify patterns that human analysts might miss, predict surge periods, and recommend staffing adjustments weeks or months in advance. Success metrics include forecast accuracy rates, resource utilization efficiency, and reductions in processing backlogs.

In real-world applications, predictive analytics demonstrate significant value in optimizing consular operations. During major international events or seasonal peak periods, the system can anticipate application surges, enabling missions to adjust staffing levels and streamline workflows proactively. For long-term planning, it provides insights into emerging trends and potential policy impacts on visa demand. However, implementation requires careful attention to data quality and model validation, with regular updates to maintain accuracy. The most effective approach combines AI's analytical capabilities with human expertise, ensuring that while technology informs resource allocation decisions, experienced consular managers maintain oversight of strategic planning and operational adjustments.

AI-ASSISTED FRAUD DETECTION IN FINANCIAL DOCUMENTATION

A financial fact-checker that spots suspicious money documents.

Financial document verification represents a critical component of visa adjudication, where detecting fraudulent submissions can prevent immigration fraud and maintain system integrity. Traditional methods of reviewing financial documentation, relying on manual verification and basic cross-referencing, often struggle to identify sophisticated fraud schemes or detect patterns across multiple applications. AI-assisted fraud detection systems transform this process by automatically analyzing financial documents for inconsistencies, unusual patterns, and potential fraud indicators, enabling more thorough and efficient screening of visa applications.

Current financial document verification faces significant challenges: the increasing sophistication of financial fraud, the complexity of cross-border transactions, and the time-intensive nature of manual reviews. AI systems address these limitations by analyzing multiple aspects of financial documentation—including formatting consistency, transaction patterns, and cross-references with external databases—to identify potential fraud indicators. The technology can process thousands of documents daily, detecting anomalies such as manipulated bank statements, inconsistent income declarations, or suspicious transaction patterns. Success metrics include fraud detection rates, processing time reduction, and the accuracy of risk assessments.

In practice, AI-assisted financial fraud detection demonstrates substantial impact across various visa categories. During high-volume periods like student visa seasons, the system can quickly identify suspicious patterns in financial guarantees or scholarship documentation, enabling focused investigation of high-risk cases while expediting legitimate applications. However, implementation requires careful attention to privacy protection and ethical considerations, particularly regarding the handling of sensitive financial data. Success depends on maintaining a balance between thorough fraud detection and fair treatment of applicants, with clear protocols for human review of flagged cases. This approach ensures that while AI enhances detection capabilities, experienced consular officers retain final authority in evaluating financial documentation and making visa decisions.

LIMITATIONS AND FUTURE RESEARCH DIRECTIONS

The integration of AI into consular affairs represents a profound transformation in diplomatic service delivery. However, this transformation brings significant challenges that warrant careful examination. Understanding these limitations while identifying promising research directions helps shape a realistic roadmap for AI implementation in diplomatic missions worldwide.

OPERATIONAL LIMITATIONS IN DAILY PRACTICE

The day-to-day implementation of AI in consular operations reveals practical challenges that go beyond simple technical constraints. Consider a typical visa processing scenario: when an AI system encounters a visa application with complex family relationships that don't fit standard Western nuclear family models, it may flag the application as potentially fraudulent simply because the pattern differs from its training data. Consular officers must then invest additional time reviewing these cases, potentially negating the efficiency gains AI promises.

Similarly, AI systems currently struggle with the nuanced judgment calls that experienced consular officers make routinely. During humanitarian crises, for instance, officers often need to evaluate partial or non-standard documentation from refugees or asylum seekers. While AI can flag inconsistencies in such documents, it cannot yet replicate the human ability to weigh circumstances compassionately while maintaining security standards. These limitations become particularly apparent in cases involving unaccompanied minors or victims of trafficking, where the stakes are highest and the human element most crucial.

SYSTEMIC CHALLENGES AND INFRASTRUCTURE CONSTRAINTS

The effective deployment of AI in consular services faces broader systemic challenges that extend beyond individual technological limitations. Infrastructure disparities create a particularly complex challenge. For example, when a natural disaster strikes a remote region with limited internet connectivity, AI-powered crisis response systems may be unable to gather real-time data or communicate effectively with affected citizens. This creates a two-tiered service system where the benefits of AI-enhanced consular services become available only to those in well-connected urban areas.

Cross-cultural communication presents another systemic challenge. Current AI systems struggle with cultural and linguistic nuances that are essential to diplomatic work. A system might misinterpret culturally specific gestures during video interviews or fail to recognize legitimate documentation practices from different regions. These misunderstandings can lead to unnecessary delays and frustration for visa applicants while increasing the workload for consular staff who must intervene to correct AI-generated errors.

THE HUMAN-AI INTERFACE: BALANCING AUTOMATION AND JUDGMENT

The interaction between human officers and AI systems represents perhaps the most nuanced challenge in modernizing consular services. This interface requires careful calibration to maintain the essential human elements of diplomatic work while leveraging AI's analytical capabilities. Consider crisis response scenarios: while AI can rapidly process multiple data streams to identify emerging threats, the decision to evacuate citizens ultimately requires human judgment that considers complex political, security, and humanitarian factors that AI cannot fully grasp.

Training requirements present another significant challenge at this interface. Consular officers must develop new skills to effectively oversee AI systems while maintaining their traditional diplomatic capabilities. This dual skill requirement creates additional strain on already busy consular sections and raises questions about how to balance technical training with core diplomatic skills development.

PRIVACY AND SECURITY IN AN INTERCONNECTED WORLD

The implementation of AI in consular services raises unprecedented privacy and security challenges. As systems become more interconnected, they create new vulnerabilities that potential adversaries could exploit. For instance, AI-powered biometric systems that share data across multiple checkpoints could become targets for sophisticated cyberattacks, potentially compromising both individual privacy and national security.

Moreover, the global nature of consular services requires careful consideration of varying privacy standards across jurisdictions. An AI system that meets privacy requirements in one country might violate laws in another, creating complex compliance challenges for diplomatic missions operating across multiple regions.

FUTURE RESEARCH PRIORITIES AND OPPORTUNITIES

These limitations point toward several crucial areas for future research and development:

Enhanced cultural intelligence: Research must focus on developing AI systems that can better understand and adapt to diverse cultural contexts. This includes improving NLP capabilities across multiple languages and dialects, and developing more sophisticated models for interpreting cultural norms and practices in visa adjudication.

Resilient infrastructure solutions: Future research should explore how AI systems can function effectively in areas with limited connectivity. This might include developing hybrid systems that can operate independently during infrastructure disruptions while maintaining security and accuracy.

Human-AI collaboration models: Investigation into optimal models for human-AI interaction in diplomatic settings is crucial. This research should examine how to maintain human judgment in critical decisions while maximizing the benefits of AI automation.

Privacy-preserving technologies: Development of new technologies that can maintain data security and individual privacy while enabling the necessary information sharing for effective consular services represents a critical research priority.

CONCLUSION

The integration of AI into consular affairs marks a fundamental transformation in diplomatic service delivery. From detecting sophisticated visa fraud to coordinating crisis response, AI amplifies human capabilities rather than replacing them, allowing consular officers to focus on exercising judgment and providing empathetic support.

Early implementations reveal that success depends on thoughtful integration of AI with human expertise. Visa sections using AI for application screening report efficiency gains while maintaining essential human oversight. Similarly, AI-powered crisis prediction tools work best when combined with officers' understanding of local conditions and cultural contexts.

Missions must invest in both technology infrastructure and comprehensive training while developing frameworks to ensure AI systems serve all clients equitably. Smaller posts may need shared service models or phased implementations aligned with their resources. Success requires clear metrics for evaluating impact on both operational efficiency and service quality.

Looking ahead, emerging technologies promise enhanced capabilities in fraud detection and crisis response. However, realizing these benefits requires careful attention to ethical considerations, particularly regarding algorithmic bias and privacy protection. The geopolitical implications extend beyond individual posts to shape international mobility patterns, highlighting the need for coordination and standards around responsible AI use.

The path forward lies not in choosing between human judgment and AI, but in combining their strengths. Through thoughtful integration guided by ethical considerations and commitment to human-centered service, diplomatic missions can build more resilient, effective, and compassionate consular operations.

The next chapter examines how AI is revolutionizing public affairs, from strategic communications and media engagement to countering misinformation and shaping cultural diplomacy.

DISCUSSION SCENARIOS AND QUESTIONS

These scenarios address AI's impact on consular operations, from visa processing to crisis management. Readers will reflect on the balance between security and privacy, the role of automation in fraud detection, and the ethical considerations of AI-enhanced citizen services.

1. Use of generative AI (GenAI) tools in public outreach
   Scenario: To save time and improve efficiency, your mission begins using GenAI tools to draft press releases, public outreach messages, and advisory notices. However, you notice that some generated content feels impersonal and lacks cultural nuance, sparking criticism from local communities.
   Questions: How can you ensure that GenAI-generated communications reflect the cultural sensitivities and nuances required in diplomatic outreach? What steps would you take to ensure proper human oversight while leveraging the efficiency of GenAI tools? How do you address situations where the GenAI produces errors or controversial outputs that damage the mission's reputation?

2. Visa adjudication and fraud prevention
   Scenario: An AI system reviews visa applications and flags a potentially fraudulent case based on patterns of past misuse. The flagged application belongs to an individual with impeccable credentials, and the system provides little explanation for its decision. You must decide whether to approve the visa or request further investigation, knowing that delays could impact the applicant's travel plans.
   Questions: How do you weigh the AI system's recommendation against your own judgment, especially when the system's reasoning is opaque? What measures can you take to ensure that AI tools remain transparent and accountable, even when handling complex patterns? How do you explain the role of AI in the decision-making process to the applicant to maintain transparency and trust?

3. Emergency assistance for nationals abroad
   Scenario: During a natural disaster in your host country, an AI tool recommends prioritizing evacuation efforts in urban areas based on predictive damage models. However, your local staff reports that rural areas may face greater risks due to inadequate infrastructure. You must make a decision about where to deploy your resources.
   Questions: How do you reconcile conflicting advice from the AI system and your local staff, especially under time pressure? What processes do you establish to ensure AI recommendations are contextualized with real-time,

human-sourced intelligence? How do you manage accountability when AI-driven decisions may lead to unintended consequences in life-or-death situations?

4. Humanitarian and anti-trafficking efforts

Scenario: An AI system identifies irregular migration patterns and flags individuals statistically likely to be involved in human trafficking. One flagged individual provides partial evidence that contradicts the AI's assumptions. You must decide whether to allow or deny entry while balancing security with fairness.

Questions: How do you ensure the AI tool's insights do not unfairly stigmatize individuals, particularly when evidence contradicts its predictions? What safeguards can you establish to prevent harm from potential misclassification in these high-stakes scenarios? How do you navigate the ethical tensions between using AI for security and maintaining trust with applicants and their communities?

5. Geopolitical and ethical implications

Scenario: An AI tool detects unusual patterns in visa applications that suggest potential espionage. Several applicants from a specific country are flagged, raising concerns about discrimination. The foreign government demands an explanation, accusing your office of bias.

Questions: How do you balance the strategic need for security with the risk of damaging diplomatic relations due to perceived bias? What steps can you take to improve transparency in the AI's decision-making process and explain it effectively to stakeholders? How do you manage the diplomatic fallout from such incidents while maintaining trust in your mission's operations?

7 AI and Public Affairs
Amplifying Engagement and Influence

The challenge will be developing enough systems—both human and automated —to deal with the flood of additional content at a time when misinformation is already a significant problem.

—Ina Fried, Chief Technology Correspondent at Axios (2023)

AI-driven content generation tools allow public diplomacy practitioners to create high volumes of content efficiently. From press releases to emails to social media posts, these tools draft preliminary content, enabling practitioners to focus on strategic messaging, fieldwork, and relationship-building.

—Jay Wang, Professor at University of Southern California (2024)

The future research should embrace new emerging forms of digital and new media arts, cyborg art and art robotics, online multiplayer games, metaverse worlds and AI arts to explore new artistic mediums of the future which transform, automate but complicate, diversify, and challenge cultural diplomacy.

—Natalia Grincheva, Researcher at LASALLE, University of the Arts Singapore (2024)

In the complex theater of modern diplomacy, public affairs officers serve as the primary architects of international understanding, bridging cultures through strategic communication, educational exchange, and media engagement. These diplomats face an evolving challenge: they must simultaneously manage traditional person-to-person diplomacy while navigating an increasingly digital world where information flows instantly across borders. From coordinating educational exchanges and managing cultural programs to serving as embassy spokespersons and advising ambassadors on media strategy, public affairs officers operate at the intersection of diplomacy, communication, and cultural exchange.

Artificial intelligence (AI) emerges as a transformative force in this domain, fundamentally enhancing how public diplomacy officers execute their diverse responsibilities. AI can amplify their ability to monitor global media sentiment, coordinate international exchange programs, manage information resource centers, and craft strategic communications that resonate with local audiences. These tools don't simply automate tasks—they provide deeper insights into cultural trends, media landscapes, and public opinion, enabling officers to make more informed decisions about program design, resource allocation, and messaging strategy.

DOI: 10.1201/9781003612308-7

The integration of AI into public affairs marks a pivotal evolution in diplomatic practice. Whether organizing cultural events, managing exchange programs, or responding to media inquiries, these officers can now leverage AI to better understand their audiences, predict program impacts, and measure the effectiveness of their initiatives.

VIGNETTE AI-Enhanced Embassy in the Republic of Z

Public Affairs Officer David Kim studies his AI-enhanced media dashboard as morning light fills his office in the Republic of Z. The system has detected a significant shift in public discourse following recent developments: Political Officer Sarah Chen's work addressing civil unrest and Economic Officer Elena Moretti's green energy initiatives have created both challenges and opportunities for strategic communications.

The AI's sentiment analysis reveals how Z's media is covering these events across traditional and social platforms. Local journalists are showing increased interest in the renewable energy partnership, while social media conversations reflect a mix of hope about economic opportunities and lingering concerns about social inequities. Kim knows this is a crucial moment for public diplomacy—a chance to demonstrate how bilateral cooperation can drive positive change.

His morning schedule reflects the multifaceted nature of public diplomacy. He's preparing for a press briefing on the new green energy initiatives, but the AI system has also highlighted an opportunity: several influential local universities have strong environmental science programs. Within minutes, he's coordinating with his team to develop a targeted educational exchange program focused on renewable energy technology, while the AI helps identify potential candidates and partner institutions.

The system's predictive analytics suggest optimal timing for various outreach activities: a series of town halls in provinces most affected by economic changes, digital engagement campaigns targeting young entrepreneurs, and cultural programs that can showcase bilateral cooperation. As Kim reviews these recommendations, he refines them based on his deep understanding of Z's media landscape and cultural nuances—elements no algorithm can fully grasp.

By mid-morning, he's meeting with his digital communications team. The AI has drafted sample social media content in multiple local languages, but Kim ensures each message reflects the cultural sensitivity and strategic messaging that effective public diplomacy demands. As he prepares to brief the Ambassador on public outreach strategy, he's already thinking about how to leverage the embassy's information resource center and exchange alumni network to support Z's emergence as a regional clean energy leader.

STRATEGIC TRANSFORMATION OF PUBLIC DIPLOMACY

The landscape of public diplomacy has undergone a profound transformation in recent years, as technological advancement meets traditional diplomatic practice.

Where public affairs officers once relied primarily on personal networks, cultural events, and traditional media outreach, they now operate in a data-rich environment that offers unprecedented opportunities for understanding and engaging global audiences. This evolution isn't merely about adopting new tools—it represents a fundamental shift in how nations connect with foreign publics and shape international narratives (Manor 2019, Bjola & Manor 2024a, 2024b).

Consider a public affairs team planning a cultural exchange program in a politically complex region (Aguirre & Ramos 2024). Traditionally, such planning might have relied heavily on intuition and historical precedent. Today, AI-driven analytics can process vast amounts of social media data, news coverage, and cultural indicators to identify themes that resonate most powerfully with local audiences. For instance, in an embassy organizing a film festival in a host country with mixed views toward its government, AI analysis can help identify unifying themes, transcending political divisions, and fostering meaningful dialogue.

This strategic transformation extends beyond event planning to encompass the full spectrum of public affairs activities. AI-enhanced monitoring tools now track public sentiment across multiple platforms and languages in real-time, enabling public affairs officers to detect emerging narratives and adapt their messaging strategies accordingly (Höne et al. 2019a, 2019b). This capability proves particularly valuable during crises, when rapid response and message clarity are crucial (Pearson & Burgess 2023). Rather than waiting hours or days to gauge public reaction to an initiative or statement, officers can now assess impact immediately and adjust their approach based on concrete data (State Department AI Inventory 2024).

The integration of AI into public affairs has also revolutionized how missions manage their educational and cultural programs. By analyzing patterns in program participation, audience engagement, and long-term outcomes, AI helps identify the most effective formats for different audiences and objectives. This data-driven approach enables more precise targeting of resources, ensuring that exchange programs, cultural events, and educational initiatives achieve maximum impact. For example, when analyzing the success of international scholarship programs, AI can track not just immediate participation metrics but also long-term indicators of cultural understanding and professional collaboration.

Perhaps most significantly, this transformation has enhanced the ability of public affairs officers to serve as strategic advisors to mission leadership. Armed with AI-generated insights about media landscapes, public opinion trends, and program effectiveness, these officers can provide ambassadors and other senior diplomats with more comprehensive and nuanced recommendations for public engagement strategies. This evolution elevates the role of public affairs from tactical execution to strategic partnership in achieving diplomatic objectives.

AI-ENHANCED COMMUNICATION AND CULTURAL ENGAGEMENT

The integration of AI into public diplomacy has revolutionized how missions engage with foreign audiences, transforming traditional outreach methods into dynamic, data-informed initiatives. Public affairs officers now leverage AI-powered tools to craft messages that resonate across cultural boundaries while maintaining the authenticity essential to effective diplomacy. This enhancement of communication capabilities extends from daily social media engagement to complex cultural programs that build lasting international relationships.

At the forefront of this evolution are AI-powered communication platforms that enable missions to engage with diverse audiences in their native languages with unprecedented precision. Advanced natural language processing allows public affairs teams to monitor conversations across multiple platforms, understand cultural nuances, and participate in discussions with greater cultural sensitivity. For instance, when an embassy launches a new educational initiative, AI tools can analyze local social media conversations to identify specific concerns or aspirations among potential participants, enabling officers to address these points directly in their outreach efforts.

Cultural programming, long a cornerstone of public diplomacy, has been particularly enhanced by AI capabilities. Virtual reality and augmented reality experiences, powered by AI, now allow missions to create immersive cultural exhibitions that transcend physical boundaries. Consider an embassy creating a virtual tour of historical landmarks from their home country—AI algorithms can personalize the experience for each visitor, highlighting aspects of particular interest to different cultural groups while providing context that resonates with local perspectives. These technologies don't replace traditional cultural exchanges but rather expand their reach and impact, making cultural diplomacy more accessible to diverse audiences (Yeo 2024).

The role of AI in managing public inquiries represents another significant advancement. Intelligent chatbots now handle routine questions about visa services, cultural programs, or educational opportunities, providing accurate information 24/7 in multiple languages. This automation allows public affairs officers to focus on more complex interactions that require human judgment and cultural sensitivity. During major events or crises, these systems can be rapidly updated to provide current information while identifying trends in public concerns that require strategic response from mission leadership.

Moreover, AI has transformed how missions approach media engagement (United Nations Global Pulse 2019). Public affairs officers now use sophisticated analytics to identify influential voices in local media landscapes, track narrative developments, and time their communications for maximum impact (Blaser 2023). These tools help missions move beyond reactive media relations to proactive engagement strategies. When preparing for a major policy announcement, for example, AI analysis can predict potential public reactions based on historical data and current sentiment, enabling officers to craft more effective messaging strategies and prepare comprehensive response plans.

This enhanced communication capability has proven particularly valuable in countering misinformation and disinformation (Kello 2023). AI systems can rapidly detect the spread of false narratives across digital platforms, enabling public affairs teams to respond quickly with accurate information (Huang 2022). More importantly, these tools help identify the most effective channels and messaging approaches for different audiences, ensuring that factual information reaches those most likely to be affected by false narratives.

DATA-DRIVEN PUBLIC AFFAIRS STRATEGY

The integration of AI into public affairs has fundamentally transformed how diplomatic missions develop and execute their strategic initiatives. Where strategy development once relied heavily on historical precedent and intuition, it now benefits from sophisticated data analysis that provides deeper insights into audience behaviors, program effectiveness, and emerging opportunities. This shift toward data-driven decision-making enables public affairs officers to allocate resources more effectively and demonstrate clear returns on public diplomacy investments (United Nations Development Programme [UNDP] 2020).

At the heart of this transformation lies AI's ability to process and analyze vast amounts of data from multiple sources—social media interactions, event attendance patterns, program participation rates, media coverage, and more. These insights help missions identify which initiatives generate the most meaningful impact and why (Alder 2025). For example, when evaluating the success of exchange programs, AI analytics can track not just immediate participation metrics but also long-term indicators such as professional networks formed, subsequent collaborations initiated, and the ripple effects through participants' communities.

Strategic resource allocation has become particularly sophisticated through AI-powered predictive analytics (Akdenizli 2024). These tools help public affairs sections forecast which programs and initiatives are likely to achieve the greatest impact in specific contexts. By analyzing patterns from past successes and failures, considering current social and political dynamics, and evaluating resource requirements, AI helps officers make more informed decisions about where to invest time and budget. This capability proves especially valuable when missions must balance multiple competing priorities with limited resources.

The development of communication strategies has also been revolutionized by data-driven insights. AI tools now help missions understand not just what messages resonate with different audiences, but also why they resonate and how they spread through social networks (ICC 2018). This understanding enables public affairs officers to craft more effective narratives and choose the most appropriate channels for different types of content. When planning a major public diplomacy campaign, for instance, AI analysis can identify the most effective combination of traditional media, social platforms, and in-person events to reach and influence target audiences.

Perhaps most significantly, data-driven strategy has enhanced missions' ability to adapt quickly to changing circumstances. Real-time analytics allow public affairs teams to monitor the effectiveness of their initiatives and make rapid adjustments based on concrete evidence rather than assumption. During crisis situations, this agility becomes particularly crucial—AI systems can track shifting public sentiment, identify emerging concerns, and help officers adjust their communication strategies accordingly. This capability ensures that public diplomacy remains responsive and relevant even in rapidly evolving situations.

The impact of this data-driven approach extends to relationship-building with key stakeholders (Wang 2024). AI analytics help identify influential voices and potential partners within host countries, tracking not just their current positions but also their evolving interests and spheres of influence. This insight enables public affairs officers to develop more targeted engagement strategies and build stronger, more sustainable partnerships. For educational exchanges, cultural programs, and media outreach, this means being able to connect with the right partners at the right time with the right approach.

BUILDING TRUST IN A DIGITAL AGE

As public affairs officers navigate an increasingly complex digital landscape, the challenge of building and maintaining trust takes on new dimensions. While AI provides powerful tools for engagement and analysis, it also raises important considerations about transparency, authenticity, and ethical communication (Crawford 2021). The key to successful public diplomacy in this digital age lies in leveraging technological capabilities while maintaining the human connection that builds lasting trust between nations and peoples.

Trust-building in the digital realm requires a delicate balance between automation and authentic human interaction. Public affairs officers must ensure that AI-enhanced communication tools support rather than supplant genuine diplomatic engagement. For instance, while AI chatbots might handle initial inquiries about exchange programs or cultural events, meaningful follow-up conversations remain in the hands of human officers who can provide nuanced guidance and build personal connections. This hybrid approach allows missions to scale their reach while preserving the authenticity that audiences expect from diplomatic interaction.

Transparency about the use of AI in public diplomacy becomes crucial for maintaining credibility. When missions employ AI tools for content creation, audience analysis, or program management, they must be clear about how these technologies support their work. This openness helps prevent misunderstandings and builds trust with stakeholders who might otherwise be skeptical of technology-mediated diplomacy. Public affairs officers increasingly find themselves educating audiences about how AI enhances rather than replaces human judgment in diplomatic work.

The challenge of maintaining authenticity in digital communication has become particularly acute in an era of deepfakes and artificial content. Public affairs sections now must not only create compelling content but also verify the authenticity of information they receive and share. AI-powered verification tools help officers detect manipulated media and confirm the provenance of digital content, enabling them to maintain their role as trusted sources of accurate information. This capability becomes especially crucial during crises or contentious political situations where misinformation can spread rapidly.

Data privacy and security considerations play an increasingly important role in building trust through digital engagement (Rafik 2021). Public affairs officers must ensure that their use of AI tools adheres to strict ethical guidelines and respects user privacy. This includes being transparent about data collection practices, securing sensitive information, and following both local and international data protection regulations (Elkhaldi 2021). By demonstrating commitment to responsible data stewardship, missions build trust with audiences who are increasingly concerned about digital privacy.

The human element remains central to successful trust-building, even as AI enhances capabilities. Public affairs officers continue to serve as the face of their nations, bringing personal warmth and cultural understanding to diplomatic interactions. AI tools support this role by helping officers identify opportunities for meaningful engagement, understand cultural sensitivities, and measure the impact of their trust-building efforts. This combination of human insight and technological capability enables missions to build stronger, more enduring relationships with their host communities.

HISTORICAL AI USE CASE EXAMPLES IN PUBLIC AFFAIRS

Public diplomacy, aimed at influencing global audiences and fostering mutual understanding, has undergone a significant transformation through the integration of AI. Governments have utilized AI to monitor media narratives, counter misinformation, and engage with foreign publics more effectively (Bârgăoanu & Cheregi 2021). According to a 2024 Atlantic Council report, nations are deploying AI across four major domains of public affairs: strategic communications, cultural preservation, education, and combating misinformation (Cimmino & Michta 2024).

The evolution of AI in public diplomacy can be traced through several pivotal cases. Estonia's response to the 2007 cyberattacks marked one of the earliest systematic implementations of AI in public diplomacy. The Estonian government incorporated AI tools to analyze online content, identify disinformation campaigns, and enable officials to issue timely corrections. This initiative established a foundation for using AI to protect national narratives and foster global trust (Kello 2024, U.S. Department of State 2024a, 2024b, 2024c, 2024d).

Building on these early efforts, nations have developed increasingly sophisticated approaches to AI-driven public diplomacy. Japan's Ministry of Foreign Affairs implemented an AI-powered media monitoring system in 2023, scanning international news articles and social media to identify emerging narratives (Bjola & Manor 2024a, 2024b). Similarly, during the Russo-Ukrainian War, NATO deployed AI-driven predictive analytics to counter disinformation campaigns and maintain public trust (Kello 2023).

The U.S. Department of State exemplifies comprehensive AI integration in modern public diplomacy. Their North Star platform analyzes news stories from over 200 countries in more than 100 languages, purportedly saving public diplomacy officers an estimated 180,000 hours annually. The Department has also adopted tools like StateChat and the Digital Media Analytics Platform to streamline operations and improve decision-making. The Global Engagement Center (R/ GEC) employs specialized tools like Storyzy to detect synthetic content and counter misinformation (Doubleday 2024a, 2024b, State Department AI Inventory 2024, Alder 2024, 2025).

Cultural preservation and education represent another crucial domain of AI application. The US-Cambodia collaboration on digitizing historical records and identifying stolen antiquities demonstrates AI's role in preserving cultural heritage. Tuvalu's Digital Nation project, creating digital twins of the country's cultural and administrative systems, shows how AI can amplify cultural diplomacy while raising awareness of global challenges like climate change (Yeo 2024).

Different nations have approached AI integration according to their strategic priorities. While the United States and its allies emphasize ethical AI applications in diplomacy and cultural preservation, China has focused on influence operations, as seen in their use of AI-powered sentiment analysis during the Belt and Road Initiative (Mokashi et al. 2022, García-Herrero 2024, Cimmino & Michta 2024). This divergence highlights the complex relationship between technological capability and diplomatic responsibility (Huang 2022, Rosenau et al. 2023, Manor & Pamment 2024).

The implementation of AI in public diplomacy extends beyond traditional diplomatic channels. Governments worldwide are leveraging AI to transform public services, creating opportunities for diplomatic engagement. Portugal's legal process chatbots, Singapore's smart city innovations, and Kenya's infrastructure applications demonstrate how AI can showcase leadership and foster international collaboration while promoting ethical, citizen-focused innovation (Cimmino & Michta 2024, Roumate 2024).

However, these advancements are not without challenges. China's sentiment analysis tools have faced scrutiny for potential manipulation of public opinion, while AI-driven disinformation campaigns during the Russo-Ukrainian War highlight the risks of weaponizing this technology (Pearson & Burgess, 2023). These cases emphasize the need for ethical guidelines in AI deployment (Bjola & Manor 2024a, 2024b).

As governments continue to integrate AI into their public diplomacy strategies, several key lessons emerge. Early threat response capabilities, as demonstrated by Estonia, remain crucial. Strategic communication tools enable better understanding of international public opinion. Operational efficiency improvements, exemplified by the U.S. State Department's systems, show how AI can enhance diplomatic communications. Cultural preservation initiatives demonstrate AI's potential in sharing heritage and raising awareness of global challenges. Perhaps most importantly, the evolution of AI in public diplomacy underscores the growing significance of ethical governance and responsible deployment in fostering mutual understanding and strengthening public trust (Asokan 2025).

THE EVOLUTION OF PUBLIC AFFAIRS PRACTICE

The practice of public affairs continues to evolve as AI technologies mature and new possibilities emerge for diplomatic engagement. This evolution represents not just technological advancement but a fundamental transformation in how missions conceptualize and execute their public diplomacy mandates. As public affairs officers adapt to these changes, they find themselves pioneering new approaches that combine traditional diplomatic skills with emerging technological capabilities (Manor 2019, Bjola & Manor 2024a, 2024b).

The role of the public affairs officer has expanded beyond traditional boundaries to encompass new competencies and responsibilities. Today's officers must be equally comfortable analyzing data dashboards and hosting cultural events, drafting social media strategies, and conducting press conferences. This hybrid skill set enables them to leverage AI's capabilities while maintaining the personal touch that defines effective diplomacy. Training programs increasingly focus on developing this dual expertise, ensuring officers can maximize the potential of AI tools while preserving core diplomatic skills (Geller 2024, Doubleday 2024a, 2024b).

Looking ahead, the integration of AI into public affairs practice suggests exciting possibilities for the future of diplomatic engagement. Virtual reality technologies powered by AI might enable missions to create immersive cultural experiences that transport audiences into each other's worlds. Advanced language processing could eliminate communication barriers, allowing for more direct and nuanced cultural exchange. Predictive analytics might help missions anticipate and prevent cultural misunderstandings before they occur. These developments don't replace traditional diplomacy but rather expand its reach and effectiveness (Buch, Eagleman, & Lauren Grosenick 2022, Grincheva 2024).

The democratization of public diplomacy represents another significant trend in this evolution. AI-powered tools make sophisticated audience analysis and engagement strategies accessible to missions of all sizes, enabling smaller diplomatic posts to achieve impact previously possible only for larger embassies. This leveling effect allows for more diverse voices in international dialogue and creates opportunities for innovative approaches to public diplomacy from a broader range of actors (Heine & Prado Lallande 2024, Organisation of Eastern Caribbean States 2018).

Perhaps most importantly, this evolution has enhanced the strategic value of public affairs within diplomatic missions. Armed with AI-driven insights and expanded capabilities, public affairs officers now serve as essential strategic advisors to ambassadors and other senior diplomats. Their ability to analyze public sentiment, predict communication impacts, and measure program effectiveness makes them indispensable partners in achieving broader diplomatic objectives. This elevated role reflects the growing importance of public diplomacy in an interconnected world where public opinion can significantly influence international relations (Stanzel & Voelsen 2022, Tuset Varela 2024).

As public affairs practice continues to evolve, the fundamental challenge remains balancing innovation with tradition. While embracing new technologies and approaches, missions must maintain the human connections and cultural sensitivity that have always defined successful diplomacy. This balance requires thoughtful integration of AI tools, ongoing evaluation of their effectiveness, and a commitment to using technology in ways that enhance rather than diminish the human element of diplomatic work (Höne et al. 2019a, 2019b, Di Martino & Ford 2024).

LARGE LANGUAGE MODELS: AMPLIFYING DIPLOMATIC MESSAGING

Building on our exploration of Large Language Models (LLMs) across diplomatic functions—from general diplomatic work and leadership to political analysis, economic affairs, management operations, and consular services—we now examine their specific applications in public affairs. While previous chapters demonstrated these tools' value in various diplomatic roles, public affairs officers face unique challenges in crafting compelling narratives, engaging diverse audiences, and managing public perception across multiple platforms.

Public affairs work demands exceptional clarity and adaptability in communication, especially when explaining complex policies or responding to rapidly evolving situations. LLMs excel at helping public affairs officers create clear, accessible content that maintains accuracy while resonating with different audiences. This capability proves particularly valuable when developing press releases, social media content, or educational materials that need to speak to multiple stakeholder groups simultaneously.

Crisis communication, a critical aspect of public affairs, benefits from LLM capabilities in new ways. Beyond the communication support explored in previous chapters, these tools can help public affairs officers craft emergency messages that balance urgency with clarity, develop scalable response templates for various scenarios, and ensure consistent messaging across multiple channels. This proves especially valuable during complex situations where coordinated communication is essential.

Cultural engagement represents another key application unique to public affairs. Building on the relationship-oriented approaches discussed in earlier chapters, public affairs officers can use LLMs to develop comprehensive cultural programs, create engaging educational content, and generate materials that bridge cultural differences while maintaining sensitivity and authenticity. This capability particularly shines when creating content that needs to resonate across diverse cultural contexts.

However, public affairs work demands special attention to certain limitations beyond those discussed previously. The public nature of communications and the need for absolute accuracy require extra caution in how these tools are used. Officers must be particularly mindful of fact-checking and verification while ensuring all content aligns with official policies and positions.

PUTTING LLMS TO WORK FOR PUBLIC AFFAIRS OFFICERS

Building on prompt engineering practices established in previous chapters, let's explore how public affairs officers can craft effective prompts for their specific communication needs. While earlier chapters covered diplomatic communications broadly, public affairs requires particular attention to audience engagement, message clarity, and cultural sensitivity.

When creating press releases, frame your prompts to ensure both accuracy and engagement:

> Help me draft a press release about our new cultural exchange program. Include: 1) clear program objectives and benefits, 2) participation requirements, 3) impact on bilateral relations, 4) quotes from key stakeholders, and 5) practical next steps for interested participants. Use accessible language while maintaining appropriate formality and emphasizing the program's value to both communities.

For crisis communication, structure prompts to balance urgency with clarity:

> I need to create a series of social media posts addressing recent misinformation about our visa policies. For each platform (e.g. Bluesky, Facebook, LinkedIn), develop: 1) clear factual corrections, 2) explanatory context, 3) actionable guidance for visa applicants, and 4) links to authoritative sources. Maintain a confident but approachable tone while emphasizing accuracy and transparency.

For cultural program materials, focus prompts on engagement and sensitivity:

> Help me develop content for our upcoming arts festival showcase. Create: 1) an overview of featured artists and works, 2) cultural context for international audiences, 3) program highlights and schedule, and 4) engagement opportunities for visitors. Ensure the content celebrates cultural diversity while fostering mutual understanding.

Public affairs officers should particularly focus prompts on:

- Creating engaging yet accurate content for diverse audiences
- Developing crisis communication materials
- Crafting cultural engagement programs
- Managing public perception across platforms
- Ensuring message consistency across channels

These applications extend beyond the foundational capabilities covered in previous chapters to address the specific needs of public affairs. The key is maintaining accuracy and cultural sensitivity while ensuring content engages effectively with target audiences.

ADVANCED AI USE CASES IN PUBLIC AFFAIRS

Building on the foundational AI applications explored in Chapter 1, the leadership use cases from Chapter 2, the political applications in Chapter 3, the economic tools examined in Chapter 4, the management systems discussed in Chapter 5, and the consular services enhanced in Chapter 6, we now examine advanced AI solutions specifically designed for public affairs. While previous chapters demonstrated how AI can enhance various aspects of diplomatic work, public affairs presents unique opportunities for leveraging AI to engage audiences, shape narratives, and build cultural bridges. From automated sentiment analysis and content optimization to cultural program management and crisis communication coordination, these use cases demonstrate how AI can transform the delivery of public affairs services. Each application builds upon basic AI capabilities to address the sophisticated challenges of modern public diplomacy, where effective communication and cultural engagement are essential. As we explore these applications, we'll see how AI can enhance public affairs while maintaining the crucial role of human judgment in crafting messages and building relationships.

SENTIMENT ANALYSIS FOR STRATEGIC COMMUNICATION

A public mood reader that shows how different audiences react to messages.

Understanding and responding to public sentiment across diverse international audiences is fundamental to effective public diplomacy. Traditional methods of gauging public opinion—such as periodic surveys, focus groups, and manual media monitoring—often provide limited, delayed insights and struggle to capture rapidly shifting attitudes across multiple cultural contexts. Public affairs officers need more sophisticated tools to analyze sentiment in real-time across various languages, platforms, and cultural frameworks.

AI-powered sentiment analysis systems address these challenges by processing vast amounts of digital content to provide nuanced understanding of public attitudes and reactions. These systems leverage natural language processing and machine learning to analyze social media posts, news coverage, online discussions, and other digital content across multiple languages simultaneously. While the technology faces challenges in interpreting cultural nuances and context, the integration of human oversight helps ensure accurate interpretation of AI-generated insights.

In practice, these systems transform how public affairs officers approach communication strategy and program design. During major policy announcements, the technology can monitor real-time reaction across multiple platforms, enabling officers to adjust messaging quickly if certain points are being misunderstood or require clarification. For example, the system might detect that while urban audiences respond positively to economic aspects of a policy, rural communities show more interest in its environmental implications, allowing for tailored messaging approaches that resonate more effectively with different demographic groups.

CULTURAL PROGRAM IMPACT ANALYSIS

A success tracker that measures how cultural programs change hearts and minds.

Cultural programming represents a core function of public diplomacy, with missions organizing exhibitions, performances, educational exchanges, and other cultural initiatives to foster international understanding. Traditional methods of measuring program impact rely heavily on basic metrics like attendance numbers and participant feedback, failing to capture the broader ripple effects these programs have on community attitudes and cross-cultural relationships. Public affairs officers need more sophisticated ways to understand and demonstrate the full impact of their cultural initiatives.

AI-powered impact analysis systems address this challenge by tracking multiple layers of program influence across various digital and social channels. These tools combine natural language processing, social network analysis, and machine learning to monitor how cultural programs spark ongoing discussions, inspire new collaborations, and shift perceptions over time (Adler-Nissen & Eggeling 2024). The technology can analyze social media conversations, local media coverage, academic collaborations, and professional networks to build a comprehensive picture of program impact, while identifying patterns that might be invisible to human observers.

In practice, these systems help missions optimize their cultural programming and demonstrate concrete results. For example, when analyzing the impact of a visiting artist's workshop series, the AI might reveal that beyond the immediate participants, the program sparked several independent collaborative projects, influenced local artistic practices, and generated sustained media coverage that positively shifted perceptions of the sponsoring nation. These insights help public affairs officers make data-driven decisions about future programming while providing tangible evidence of public diplomacy's long-term value.

DYNAMIC MEDIA ENGAGEMENT

A media manager that helps build better relationships with journalists.

Managing relationships with international media outlets and journalists has become increasingly complex in today's 24/7 news environment. Public affairs officers must monitor multiple news sources across various languages, identify emerging stories that could impact diplomatic relations, and maintain effective relationships with key media figures—all while ensuring consistent and timely message delivery. Traditional approaches to media relations struggle to keep pace with the speed and complexity of modern news cycles.

AI-powered media engagement systems address these challenges by providing real-time monitoring, analysis, and response capabilities. These platforms use natural language processing and machine learning to track news coverage across multiple languages and outlets, identify influential journalists and their interests, predict emerging narratives, and suggest optimal timing for press releases or media engagements. The technology helps missions move from reactive to proactive media relations, while ensuring more strategic allocation of media outreach resources.

In practice, these systems transform how missions manage their media presence. During a developing news story, the AI can track coverage patterns across different outlets, identify potential misconceptions that need addressing, and highlight opportunities for constructive engagement with key journalists. For instance, when an embassy launches a new economic initiative, the system might identify which journalists have covered similar topics effectively, suggest targeted pitch angles based on their past reporting, and monitor the subsequent coverage to measure message penetration and adjust strategy accordingly.

EDUCATIONAL EXCHANGE ANALYTICS

A network mapper that shows how exchange programs build lasting connections.

Managing international educational exchange programs like Fulbright scholarships and academic partnerships requires complex coordination and long-term impact assessment. Public affairs officers must select candidates, track program outcomes, maintain alumni networks, and demonstrate the value of these investments in cultural understanding. Traditional methods of managing these programs often miss opportunities to leverage alumni networks effectively and struggle to capture the full scope of program benefits.

AI-powered exchange analytics systems address these challenges by providing comprehensive tracking and analysis of exchange program impacts. Using machine learning and network analysis, these tools can monitor participants' professional trajectories, map the growth of academic collaborations, identify emerging leaders among alumni, and measure how exchange experiences influence participants' long-term engagement with the host country. The technology helps missions move beyond basic metrics to understand how educational exchanges create lasting diplomatic impact.

In practice, these systems transform how missions manage their exchange programs. For example, when analyzing exchange alumni networks, the AI might identify unexpected patterns of collaboration between past participants, highlight emerging opportunities for program expansion, or reveal which types of exchanges generate the most sustained cross-cultural engagement. These insights can help public affairs officers optimize program design, demonstrate concrete diplomatic outcomes, and maintain more meaningful connections with program alumni over time.

DIGITAL PUBLIC ENGAGEMENT

A social media advisor that helps posts reach the right audiences.

The rise of digital platforms has transformed how diplomatic missions engage with international audiences, creating both opportunities and challenges for public outreach. Public affairs officers must manage multiple social media channels, create engaging content across different formats, and maintain consistent messaging while adapting to local digital preferences and cultural norms. Traditional approaches to digital engagement often struggle to maintain the pace, personalization, and cultural sensitivity required for effective online diplomacy.

AI-powered digital engagement systems address these challenges by providing sophisticated content analysis, audience segmentation, and engagement optimization tools. These platforms use machine learning and natural language processing to analyze audience behavior, recommend optimal posting times, suggest content adaptations for different cultural contexts, and predict which messaging approaches will resonate most effectively with specific audience segments. The technology helps missions achieve greater impact with their digital outreach while maintaining authentic and culturally appropriate engagement.

In practice, these systems can transform how missions conduct their digital diplomacy. When planning a social media campaign about an upcoming cultural festival, for instance, the AI might analyze past engagement patterns to recommend specific content types for different platforms, suggest cultural references that will resonate with local audiences, and identify the most effective digital influencers for potential collaboration. This data-driven approach helps public affairs officers create more impactful digital content while maintaining the human touch essential to diplomatic communication.

CRISIS COMMUNICATION MANAGEMENT

A rapid response system for getting accurate information out during emergencies.

Managing public communication during international crises requires rapid response, message coordination, and careful attention to evolving public sentiment. Public affairs officers must disseminate accurate information quickly, counter misinformation, and maintain public trust across multiple audiences and languages, all while operating under intense time pressure. Traditional crisis communication methods often struggle to keep pace with viral misinformation and rapidly shifting public concerns.

AI-powered crisis communication systems address these challenges by providing real-time monitoring, automated alert systems, and response optimization tools—though they face a critical limitation in their ability to fully grasp the sensitive diplomatic implications of crisis messaging. These platforms use machine learning and natural language processing to track information spread, identify emerging concerns, and suggest response strategies. However, the technology must be carefully monitored as automated responses could potentially escalate tensions or miss crucial cultural nuances during sensitive situations.

In practice, these systems enhance how missions handle crisis communications while remaining firmly under human control. During a natural disaster or security incident, the AI might track information flow across different platforms, flag potentially harmful misinformation, and suggest message templates for quick response—but final messaging decisions remain with experienced public affairs officers who understand the broader diplomatic context. This hybrid approach can help missions maintain rapid, consistent communication during crises while ensuring that diplomatic sensitivity guides all public messaging.

CULTURAL RESOURCE DISTRIBUTION

A smart librarian that gets cultural materials to the right audiences.

Managing cultural resources—from educational materials and artistic content to language learning tools and digital archives—requires strategic distribution to maximize diplomatic impact. Public affairs officers must ensure these resources reach the right audiences, track their usage, and measure their effectiveness in fostering cross-cultural understanding. Traditional distribution methods often fail to adapt to changing audience preferences and miss opportunities for broader engagement.

AI-powered resource distribution systems address these challenges by optimizing content delivery and tracking resource utilization—though they face important limitations in understanding the deep cultural significance certain materials may hold for specific communities. These platforms use machine learning to analyze usage patterns, predict resource demands, and recommend distribution strategies across different regions and demographics. However, the technology may sometimes overlook subtle cultural contexts that make certain resources particularly meaningful or sensitive in specific settings.

In practice, these systems enhance how missions share their cultural resources while requiring careful human oversight. For instance, when distributing digital archives of historical photographs, the AI might suggest targeted distribution strategies based on user engagement patterns and demographic data—but public affairs officers must ensure the context and presentation respect local cultural sensitivities and historical narratives. This balanced approach helps missions expand their cultural outreach while maintaining appropriate cultural stewardship of their resources.

Public Diplomacy Program Evaluation

An impact measurer that shows how diplomatic programs make a difference.

Measuring the effectiveness of public diplomacy initiatives—from cultural events to educational programs—remains one of the most challenging aspects of diplomatic work. Public affairs officers must demonstrate concrete impact, justify resource allocation, and identify opportunities for program improvement across diverse cultural contexts. Traditional evaluation methods often rely too heavily on quantitative metrics that fail to capture the nuanced outcomes of cultural engagement.

AI-powered evaluation systems address these challenges by providing comprehensive impact analysis and program assessment tools—though they face significant limitations in measuring intangible diplomatic outcomes like trust-building and cultural understanding. These platforms use machine learning to analyze multiple data streams, from social media engagement to long-term participant tracking, creating more sophisticated measures of program success. However, the technology struggles to fully capture the qualitative human connections and relationship-building that often represent the most valuable diplomatic outcomes.

In practice, these systems enhance how missions evaluate their initiatives while acknowledging the importance of human assessment. When analyzing a year-long cultural exchange program, the AI might track measurable outcomes like media coverage, professional collaborations, and participant career trajectories—but experienced officers must interpret these metrics within broader diplomatic contexts and supplement them with qualitative insights. This complementary approach helps missions demonstrate program value while maintaining focus on the human elements that define successful public diplomacy.

Stakeholder Relationship Management

A relationship tracker that maps important community connections.

Building and maintaining relationships with key stakeholders—including journalists, cultural leaders, academics, and civil society figures—is central to effective public diplomacy. Public affairs officers must track numerous relationships across different sectors, identify emerging influencers, and maintain meaningful engagement with diverse networks. Traditional approaches to relationship management often miss important connections and struggle to maintain consistent engagement across broad stakeholder networks.

AI-powered stakeholder management systems address these challenges by providing comprehensive relationship tracking and engagement optimization tools—though they face important limitations in understanding the nuanced interpersonal dynamics that characterize diplomatic relationships. These platforms use machine learning to map relationship networks, identify influential figures, track engagement patterns, and suggest opportunities for connection. However, the technology cannot replace the personal touch and emotional intelligence that make diplomatic relationships meaningful and lasting.

In practice, these systems enhance how missions manage their stakeholder networks while preserving the human element of relationship-building. For example, the AI might identify patterns of interaction that suggest emerging community leaders or highlight opportunities for cross-sector collaboration—but public affairs officers must apply their judgment and cultural understanding to nurture these relationships authentically. This balanced approach helps missions expand their networks strategically while maintaining the personal connections essential to diplomatic success.

Multilingual Content Management

A language bridge that helps messages work in multiple cultures.

Managing diplomatic content across multiple languages and cultural contexts presents significant challenges for public affairs teams. Public affairs officers must ensure consistent messaging while adapting content appropriately for different audiences, maintain accuracy across translations, and respond quickly to communication needs in multiple languages. Traditional approaches to multilingual content management often result in delays, inconsistencies, and missed cultural nuances.

AI-powered multilingual content systems address these challenges by providing advanced translation assistance and cultural adaptation tools—though they face critical limitations in capturing subtle diplomatic language and cultural implications. These platforms use natural language processing to assist with translation, suggest cultural adaptations, and maintain consistency across language versions. However, the technology can sometimes miss diplomatic subtleties or produce translations that, while technically accurate, may not convey the intended diplomatic tone or cultural sensitivity.

In practice, these systems have great potential to enhance how missions manage multilingual communication while requiring careful human oversight. When preparing a statement for multiple audiences, the AI might provide initial translations and flag potential cultural considerations—but experienced officers must review and refine the content to ensure it maintains diplomatic nuance and cultural appropriateness. This collaborative approach helps missions communicate more efficiently across language barriers while preserving the precision and sensitivity essential to diplomatic communication.

LIMITATIONS AND FUTURE RESEARCH DIRECTIONS

As AI increasingly shapes public affairs and diplomatic outreach, several critical limitations and research gaps demand attention. Understanding these challenges is essential for developing more effective and responsible approaches to AI-enhanced public diplomacy.

THE CHALLENGE OF AUTHENTIC ENGAGEMENT

At the heart of public diplomacy lies the ability to forge genuine connections across cultural boundaries. While AI excels at personalizing content and analyzing engagement metrics, it struggles to replicate the authentic human connection that defines successful public diplomacy. Consider a public affairs officer managing cultural exchange programs—while AI can help identify potential participants and track program metrics, it cannot fully grasp the transformative personal experiences that make these exchanges meaningful.

This limitation becomes particularly evident in crisis communications, where empathy and cultural sensitivity prove crucial. An AI system might craft technically appropriate messages but miss subtle emotional and cultural cues that experienced diplomats instinctively understand. As public affairs increasingly relies on AI-mediated communication, research must examine how to maintain authentic human engagement while leveraging technological capabilities.

DIGITAL DIVIDE AND INCLUSIVE DIPLOMACY

The growing integration of AI into public affairs risks creating a two-tiered system of diplomatic engagement. While AI-enhanced digital outreach can reach unprecedented scale, it may inadvertently favor digitally connected audiences while missing crucial segments of society. A public affairs officer in a developing region, for instance, might find that AI-driven analytics fail to capture sentiment among communities that primarily rely on traditional communication channels.

This digital divide extends beyond simple access issues to encompass varying levels of digital literacy and cultural preferences for different forms of engagement. Future research must explore how missions can develop truly inclusive approaches that combine AI's capabilities with traditional diplomatic outreach, ensuring no communities are left behind in the digital transformation of public diplomacy.

TRUST AND TRANSPARENCY CHALLENGES

As AI systems become more integral to public affairs work, maintaining public trust presents complex challenges. When audiences discover that AI shapes diplomatic messages or influences program decisions, how does this knowledge affect their trust in diplomatic institutions? This question becomes particularly relevant as AI-generated content grows increasingly sophisticated and potentially indistinguishable from human-created diplomatic communications.

The challenge extends beyond simply disclosing AI's role to developing appropriate frameworks for transparency that maintain operational effectiveness. Research must examine how missions can be open about their use of AI while preserving the credibility and impact of their public diplomacy efforts.

CULTURAL HERITAGE AND MEMORY

The preservation and presentation of cultural heritage through AI-enhanced means raise unique challenges. While AI offers powerful tools for digitizing and sharing cultural content, questions emerge about authenticity and interpretation. How do we ensure that AI-enhanced cultural programming maintains the deep significance of cultural traditions while making them accessible to global audiences?

This limitation becomes particularly apparent in projects involving historical preservation or cultural exchange. Future research must explore frameworks for using AI to enhance cultural diplomacy while respecting and preserving the integrity of cultural heritage.

MEASUREMENT AND IMPACT ASSESSMENT

Traditional metrics struggle to capture the full impact of AI-enhanced public diplomacy initiatives. While AI excels at tracking quantifiable outcomes like engagement rates or sentiment scores, many crucial diplomatic outcomes—such as deepened cultural understanding or strengthened bilateral trust—resist simple measurement.

Consider a public affairs team running a year-long cultural program. While AI might show positive engagement metrics, how do we measure the deeper impact on cross-cultural understanding and long-term relationship building? Research must develop more sophisticated frameworks for evaluating the full spectrum of public diplomacy outcomes in an AI-enhanced environment.

CROSS-MISSION COORDINATION

As individual missions adopt AI tools for public affairs, questions arise about standardization and knowledge sharing across diplomatic posts. How can best practices be shared while maintaining flexibility for local contexts? How can AI systems be adapted to support regional coordination while respecting individual mission needs?

These questions become particularly relevant in crisis situations or regional initiatives where multiple posts must coordinate their public affairs efforts. Future research should examine models for effective cross-mission collaboration in AI-enhanced public diplomacy.

CONCLUSION

The integration of AI into public affairs marks a watershed moment in diplomatic practice, fundamentally transforming how missions engage with foreign audiences and shape international narratives. This technological evolution goes far beyond mere automation of routine tasks, representing instead a profound enhancement of how public affairs officers execute their diverse responsibilities. From monitoring global sentiment to crafting culturally resonant communications, AI amplifies diplomatic capabilities while preserving the essential human judgment that defines successful international engagement.

The successful implementation of AI in public affairs requires a delicate balance between technological innovation and diplomatic sensitivity. Public affairs officers must develop new competencies that enable them to leverage AI's analytical power while maintaining the personal touch crucial to effective diplomacy. This includes understanding both AI's potential and its limitations, ensuring that efficiency gains don't compromise authentic engagement or cultural understanding. Missions must also address emerging challenges in cybersecurity and privacy, implementing robust protections for sensitive diplomatic communications while maintaining transparency in their use of AI tools.

Looking ahead, the evolution of AI capabilities promises even greater transformations in diplomatic practice. Advanced natural language processing may soon enable real-time multilingual engagement at unprecedented scales, while predictive analytics could help missions anticipate and prevent cultural misunderstandings before they occur. Virtual and augmented reality technologies, powered by AI, may create immersive cultural experiences that transcend physical boundaries. However, these advances must be guided by strong ethical frameworks that ensure responsible deployment and maintain public trust.

The impact of AI on public affairs extends beyond individual posts to the broader practice of diplomacy itself. By enabling more sophisticated audience analysis, enhanced cultural programming, and data-driven engagement strategies, AI-powered public affairs strengthens the foundation of modern diplomatic practice. This technological enhancement supports not just operational excellence but the fundamental mission of public diplomacy: fostering mutual understanding and building lasting international relationships. Yet, success requires unwavering attention to cultural sensitivity, authentic engagement, and ethical communication.

As missions enhance their public engagement capabilities through AI, they must also ensure the security of their diplomatic operations. The next chapter explores how AI is transforming diplomatic security, from cyber defense and threat detection to physical security and crisis management, ensuring that technological innovation in public affairs remains protected in an increasingly complex global environment.

DISCUSSION SCENARIOS AND QUESTIONS

This set of scenarios focuses on AI's role in shaping public diplomacy, media engagement, and cultural exchange. Readers will explore how AI can amplify strategic messaging, combat misinformation, and enhance audience engagement while ensuring that diplomacy remains transparent, ethical, and human-centered.

1. AI in managing exchange programs
   Scenario: You use an AI system to select candidates for cultural exchange programs. The AI prioritizes applicants based on their potential to foster cross-cultural understanding and long-term partnerships. However,

you notice that fewer candidates from underrepresented communities are flagged due to historical biases in the data.

Questions: How do you ensure the selection process is equitable while maintaining AI's efficiency? How would you weigh the benefits of over-riding AI's recommendations to promote diversity against the risks of compromising transparency in the selection process? What steps can you take to improve the AI system to better account for equity and cultural sensitivity?

2. LLMs as media spokespersons

Scenario: Your embassy deploys an LLM as a virtual spokesperson to respond to media inquiries. The LLM delivers real-time answers in mul-tiple languages. During a press interaction, a journalist asks a politically sensitive question, and the LLM produces a response that unintentionally escalates tensions with the host country.

Questions: How do you address the diplomatic fallout from the LLM's mistake while maintaining public trust in your technology initiatives? What factors would influence your decision to restrict LLMs to pre-approved scripts versus allowing them the flexibility to generate nuanced responses? How can you design safeguards to ensure the LLM handles politically sen-sitive topics appropriately?

3. AI in digital cultural diplomacy

Scenario: You oversee AI-powered platforms that curate digital content, including exhibitions and cultural narratives, to engage foreign audiences. Community leaders in the host country criticize the content, saying it over-simplifies their cultural ties with your nation and marginalizes important contributions.

Questions: How do you adjust the AI system to better reflect the com-plexity and diversity of cultural relationships? How can you determine the right balance between involving human oversight in curating AI-generated content and maintaining the efficiency of the process? How can you address these concerns diplomatically while maintaining the integrity of your out-reach initiatives?

4. AI in monitoring public opinion

Scenario: You rely on AI to track public sentiment about your coun-try's policies in the host nation. The AI flags negative sentiment in certain regions, but when you respond to these concerns, local leaders accuse your team of intrusive surveillance.

Questions: How can you use AI to monitor public opinion without breaching trust or appearing overly intrusive? How would you approach the decision to disclose or keep discreet the use of AI in identifying public concerns, and what are the potential trade-offs in each case? How do you complement AI insights with grassroots engagement to gain a fuller under-standing of public sentiment?

5. AI in predictive crisis communication

Scenario: In the midst of a political crisis in the host country, you rely on an AI system to monitor social media trends. The system identifies growing misinformation about your country's involvement and recommends an aggressive counter-narrative campaign. However, you worry the suggested approach might escalate tensions further.

Questions: What steps would you take to balance the urgency of acting on AI's analysis with the need to assess the cultural and political risks involved? How do you ensure that AI-driven campaigns align with the local context and your country's long-term diplomatic goals? If the AI's recommendation contradicts your instincts, how do you justify your decision to stakeholders?

8 AI in Diplomatic Security
Protecting the Mission

With artificial intelligence we are summoning the demon. In all those stories where there's the guy with the pentagram and the holy water, it's like—yeah, he's sure he can control the demon. Doesn't work out.

—Elon Musk, CEO of SpaceX and Tesla (2014)

The risk of using AI for autonomous lethal weapons doesn't depend on AI being smarter than us—that's a quite separate risk from the risk that the AI itself will go rogue and try and take over. I'm worried about both things.

—Geoffrey Hinton, former Google AI researcher (2024)

AI is at a definitive crossroads—one where policymakers, security professionals and civil society have the chance to finally tilt the cybersecurity balance from attackers to cyber defenders. At a moment when malicious actors are experimenting with AI, we need bold and timely action to shape the direction of this technology.

—Sundar Pichai, CEO of Google (2024)

In the high-stakes world of international diplomacy, security operations span a complex spectrum of responsibilities that extend far beyond embassy walls. Diplomatic security professionals serve as law enforcement officers, security specialists, and diplomats, managing tasks that range from protecting diplomatic personnel and investigating travel document fraud to conducting threat analysis and coordinating security for major international events. A breach of an embassy's communications network could compromise years of sensitive negotiations and strain international relationships in an instant. This multilayered mission demands not just vigilance but also sophisticated coordination across physical security, cyber defense, threat analysis, and law enforcement operations, all while maintaining the delicate balance required in diplomatic environments.

Artificial intelligence (AI) has emerged as a transformative force in this complex security landscape, fundamentally reshaping how diplomatic missions approach their diverse security challenges. Advanced AI systems now augment traditional security operations across multiple domains: monitoring embassy networks for cyber threats, analyzing surveillance patterns to detect physical security risks, processing global threat data to protect visiting dignitaries, and coordinating complex security operations for international events. While these capabilities serve as a force multiplier, enabling security teams to anticipate threats rather than merely respond to them, the nuanced understanding of diplomatic contexts and potential consequences remains uniquely human. For instance, when an AI system flags suspicious activity, it's the experienced security professional who must evaluate this alert within the broader

DOI: 10.1201/9781003612308-8

diplomatic context—weighing law enforcement protocols, international relationships, and potential diplomatic ramifications of any response. This chapter explores how missions can leverage AI to enhance their comprehensive security operations while preserving the human judgment essential to effective diplomatic security.

VIGNETTE   AI-Enhanced Embassy in the Republic of Z

Regional Security Officer Jim Thompson begins his day reviewing overnight security reports in the embassy's secure command center, where AI-enhanced monitoring systems have already categorized and prioritized potential concerns. The political developments tracked by Sarah Chen's team have increased protest activities near diplomatic facilities, while the expansion of economic initiatives under Elena Moretti has drawn additional attention from both legitimate business interests and potential hostile actors.

His morning briefing highlights several priority items: the upcoming renewable energy summit will require enhanced security protocols and personnel coordination, while the recent surge in consular services noted by Maria Santos demands careful visitor screening and access control measures. The AI system has identified patterns in social media activity suggesting possible demonstrations near the embassy, correlating this with historical protest data and current political tensions.

As Thompson reviews the security logs, the AI's behavioral analytics flag unusual surveillance patterns around the embassy's perimeter. Years of experience have taught him that security threats rarely manifest in isolation—seemingly unrelated incidents often connect to form more significant security challenges. He appreciates how AI helps process vast amounts of security data while knowing that human judgment remains crucial for understanding the broader diplomatic implications of any security response.

His morning schedule reflects the complex demands of diplomatic security. He's coordinating with the Marine Security Guard detachment on adjusted patrol patterns, deploying additional surveillance assets based on the latest threat intelligence, and reviewing security protocols for an upcoming congressional delegation. The AI assists with resource allocation and threat assessment, but Thompson knows it's his expertise that ensures security measures enhance rather than hinder the mission's diplomatic objectives.

By mid-morning, he's analyzing potential vulnerabilities in the embassy's physical security infrastructure while simultaneously managing the security implications of a planned public outreach event. The AI helps prioritize security concerns and optimize resource deployment, but Thompson's understanding of both security imperatives and diplomatic sensitivities ensures the embassy maintains appropriate protection while remaining accessible for legitimate diplomatic functions.

THE EVOLVING THREAT LANDSCAPE

Diplomatic missions operate at the intersection of multiple security imperatives, where physical and digital vulnerabilities intertwine in increasingly complex ways. A seemingly routine breach of an embassy's perimeter could mask a sophisticated attempt to compromise digital systems, while cyber intrusions might serve as precursors to physical security threats (Kello 2023). This convergence of traditional and emerging threats requires diplomatic security to evolve beyond conventional approaches, embracing comprehensive protection that spans both physical and digital domains.

The security challenges facing diplomatic missions reflect the breadth of modern diplomatic functions. Political officers conducting sensitive negotiations require secure communications and meeting spaces that protect both conversations and data. Economic sections handling trade discussions and proprietary business information need robust cybersecurity measures to maintain confidentiality. Management officers overseeing mission operations must ensure secure supply chains and vendor relationships. Consular sections processing visa applications and citizen services require protection against identity theft and document fraud. Public affairs teams engaging with local communities need security measures that balance protection with accessibility (Höne et al. 2019a, 2019b, Bouchard 2024).

In this complex environment, potential threats can emerge from multiple vectors simultaneously (Pearson & Burgess 2023). Social media monitoring might reveal plans for protests near an embassy while network sensors detect increased probing of digital defenses. Visa application patterns could signal potential fraud schemes while surveillance systems identify suspicious behavior around mission facilities. The challenge lies not just in detecting these diverse threats but in understanding their potential interconnections and implications for diplomatic operations.

The integration of AI transforms this security landscape by enabling missions to process and analyze vast amounts of data in real time (Lacy 2024). AI systems can simultaneously monitor physical security cameras, network traffic, social media feeds, and access control systems, identifying patterns and potential threats that human operators might miss (Horowitz et al. 2018a, 2018b). This capability proves particularly valuable in detecting subtle correlations—for instance, recognizing when unusual network activity coincides with suspicious physical presence near sensitive areas.

AI AS A FORCE MULTIPLIER IN SECURITY

AI fundamentally amplifies diplomatic security capabilities across every aspect of mission operations. Rather than merely automating existing processes, AI creates new possibilities for threat detection, prevention, and response (Roumate 2021a, 2021b). Advanced algorithms can process multiple data streams simultaneously—from surveillance footage and access logs to network traffic and environmental sensors—creating a comprehensive security picture that was previously impossible to achieve.

In physical security operations, AI enhances traditional protective measures by adding layers of intelligent analysis. Surveillance systems equipped with AI can distinguish between routine activity and potential threats, adapting to local patterns while flagging anomalous behavior. Smart access control systems go beyond simple badge verification, incorporating biometric data and behavioral analysis to ensure that only authorized personnel enter sensitive areas (Garcia 2021). These systems can detect subtle signs of duress or coercion that might escape human observation, adding crucial protection for diplomatic personnel and facilities.

The cyber domain particularly benefits from AI's analytical capabilities. Modern diplomatic missions face constant probing of their digital defenses, requiring security systems that can adapt to evolving threats. AI-powered cybersecurity tools monitor network traffic patterns, identifying potential intrusions before they succeed and automatically implementing countermeasures. These systems learn from each attempted breach, continuously improving their ability to protect sensitive diplomatic communications and data.

Personnel security takes on new dimensions through AI integration. Smart systems can analyze patterns in employee behavior, identifying potential insider threats while respecting privacy and maintaining workplace trust. This capability proves especially valuable in missions with large local staff components, where traditional vetting processes might miss subtle changes in behavior or circumstances that could signal security risks. AI tools can also assist in maintaining secure supply chains, vetting contractors, and managing vendor relationships with greater precision.

The protective function extends to visiting dignitaries and diplomatic events, where AI enhances advance planning and real-time security coordination. Security teams can leverage predictive analytics to identify potential risks and optimize resource deployment (Baele et al. 2024). During events, AI systems monitor multiple security parameters simultaneously, from crowd dynamics to environmental conditions, enabling rapid response to emerging threats while maintaining the diplomatic atmosphere essential to international engagement.

INTEGRATING AI ACROSS DIPLOMATIC SECURITY OPERATIONS

The integration of AI into diplomatic security requires a carefully orchestrated approach that enhances protection while preserving the essential human elements of diplomacy. This balance manifests differently across various security domains, each demanding unique combinations of technological capability and human expertise. The goal remains constant: creating layered security that protects diplomatic missions while enabling them to conduct their vital work effectively.

Physical security integration demonstrates this balance most visibly. Smart perimeter systems combine traditional barriers with AI-enhanced surveillance, creating dynamic protection that adapts to changing conditions. These systems can distinguish between routine activities and potential threats, adjusting sensitivity based on time of day, scheduled events, or threat levels. Inside diplomatic facilities, AI-powered access control extends beyond simple authentication, analyzing behavioral patterns and detecting anomalies that might indicate security risks. These capabilities prove particularly valuable in missions that must maintain security while hosting public events or managing frequent visits from dignitaries.

Cybersecurity integration reflects the increasingly digital nature of diplomatic work. AI systems monitor network traffic continuously, analyzing patterns and identifying potential threats with a speed and precision impossible for human operators alone. These tools protect not only traditional diplomatic communications but also the growing array of digital services provided by missions, from online visa processing to public outreach platforms. The AI systems learn from each attempted intrusion, automatically updating their defenses and sharing threat intelligence across diplomatic networks.

Crisis management capabilities are transformed through AI integration, enabling more rapid and coordinated responses to emergencies. Smart systems can process multiple data streams simultaneously—from weather patterns to social media activity—providing early warning of potential crises. During emergencies, AI tools assist in coordinating response efforts, optimizing resource deployment, and maintaining communication with diplomatic personnel. These systems prove particularly valuable in complex scenarios requiring simultaneous management of multiple security challenges.

Personnel security benefits from AI's analytical capabilities while requiring particular attention to privacy and ethical considerations. Advanced systems can monitor for potential insider threats through pattern analysis, identifying concerning behavior changes without compromising individual privacy. This capability extends to visitor screening, where AI assists in maintaining secure yet welcoming diplomatic spaces. The technology helps security teams manage the delicate balance between protecting sensitive areas and maintaining the open atmosphere essential to diplomatic functions (Garcia 2021).

BALANCING TECHNOLOGY AND HUMAN EXPERTISE

The integration of AI into diplomatic security enhances capabilities while highlighting the irreplaceable value of human judgment and expertise. Security professionals bring contextual understanding, cultural awareness, and diplomatic sensitivity that no AI system can replicate. This human element proves especially crucial in situations requiring nuanced interpretation of security data or careful consideration of diplomatic implications.

Security officers must evaluate AI-generated alerts within broader diplomatic contexts. When a system flags suspicious network activity, security professionals consider not only the technical aspects but also ongoing diplomatic initiatives that might be targeted. Similarly, physical security alerts require evaluation through both security and diplomatic lenses—determining appropriate responses that maintain protection while preserving diplomatic relationships. This dual perspective ensures that security measures support rather than impede diplomatic objectives.

Training for diplomatic security personnel evolves alongside technological capabilities. Modern security professionals must combine traditional security expertise with understanding of AI systems and their applications. This expanded skill set enables them to leverage AI tools effectively while maintaining critical thinking and independent judgment. Training scenarios increasingly incorporate AI-generated simulations, allowing security teams to practice responses to complex, multi-vector threats in realistic environments.[3]

Ethical considerations guide the implementation of AI security systems, particularly regarding privacy and data protection. Diplomatic missions must balance robust security with respect for individual rights and international norms. This balance becomes especially important in consular operations and public spaces, where missions interact directly with local populations. Security teams develop frameworks for AI deployment that protect sensitive information while maintaining transparency about security practices.

The relationship between AI systems and human operators continues to evolve as capabilities advance. Rather than replacing human judgment, AI serves as a sophisticated tool that enhances situational awareness and decision-making capacity. Security professionals learn to trust AI insights while maintaining healthy skepticism, understanding both the capabilities and limitations of automated systems. This partnership approach ensures that diplomatic security benefits from technological advancement while preserving essential human oversight.

HISTORICAL AI USE CASE EXAMPLES IN DIPLOMATIC SECURITY

Diplomatic security encompasses the safeguarding of personnel, infrastructure, and sensitive information against a broad range of threats. AI has become an integral tool in enhancing diplomatic security, providing new capabilities in areas such as cybersecurity, physical security, and crisis management. This section examines historical examples of how governments have deployed AI to protect diplomatic assets (Kello 2024, Lacy 2024).

Following the 2007 cyberattacks on Estonia, NATO established the Cooperative Cyber Defence Centre of Excellence (CCD-COE) in Tallinn to counter future cyber threats. While initial efforts focused on policy and structural improvements, AI integration in cyber defense strategies has become a significant focus in recent years (North Atlantic Treaty Organization [NATO] 2021, Kello 2023, Piper 2024). The initiative underscored the importance of cross-border collaboration and technical innovation in cybersecurity leading to AI deployment (NATO 2021, Kello 2024).

Israel has deployed AI-driven surveillance and targeting systems, such as "Lavender" and "The Gospel," primarily for military operations rather than diplomatic security (Serhan 2024). These systems analyze vast intelligence data streams and suggest targets. AI-powered surveillance technologies similar to these could be adopted at embassies to strengthen perimeter security, manage access control, and ensure the safety of personnel and visitors. The use of such systems raises concerns about data privacy and ethical implications, particularly regarding over-reliance on algorithmic decision-making (Human Rights Watch 2024, Serhan 2024).

The Summit on Responsible Artificial Intelligence in the Military Domain (REAIM 2023) highlighted global efforts to establish guidelines for AI use in military contexts. Sixty countries participated, including the United States and China, resulting in a non-binding "call to action" document. This summit underscores the importance of international cooperation in setting ethical standards for AI applications that could impact diplomatic security ("Summit on Responsible Artificial Intelligence in the Military Domain" 2024).

AI-powered biometric systems have become a key feature of securing diplomatic missions. Facial recognition and behavioral analysis technologies are employed to authenticate identities and prevent unauthorized access. For example, the U.S. Department of State reportedly utilizes AI systems to cross-check biometric data against global databases, ensuring that only authorized personnel enter sensitive areas (State Department AI Inventory 2024, Lacy 2024). These systems have proven effective in mitigating insider threats, though their deployment requires robust data protection measures to maintain public trust.

Governments are increasingly using AI-driven systems to analyze Passenger Name Records (PNR) from airlines to identify potential threats. While aimed at enhancing security, these systems raise concerns about privacy and the potential for inaccuracies, which could have diplomatic implications if not managed carefully (Chandler 2025).

Stuxnet, a complex malware operation discovered in 2010, represented a watershed moment in cyber operations (Simić 2021, Kissinger, Schmidt, & Huttenlocher 2021). While Stuxnet did not incorporate AI, its sophisticated automation provided a glimpse into future cyber threats, as it relied on preprogrammed logic that could evolve into machine learning or adaptive intelligence methods. The incident underscored the risks associated with autonomous cyber capabilities and reinforced the need for stringent oversight in cyber tool development (Kello 2023).

AI systems have been deployed to integrate diverse data streams and provide actionable insights during crises. Ukraine's use of AI platforms, such as Palantir, during the Russo-Ukrainian War illustrated how real-time data analysis could inform diplomatic decision-making (Mueller et al. 2023). These platforms have helped identify threats to infrastructure and personnel, enabling more effective emergency responses (Pearson & Burgess 2023). AI-enhanced intelligence processing has significantly improved situational awareness, making it a valuable tool for diplomatic missions worldwide (Horowitz et al. 2018a, 2018b).

AI has also played a pivotal role in countering disinformation campaigns that threaten diplomatic integrity. During the Russo-Ukrainian War, Russia deployed generative AI tools to spread disinformation and undermine global trust. In response, NATO and allied nations used AI-driven systems to monitor the spread of false narratives and deploy countermeasures (Reuters 2024, Huang 2022). These efforts demonstrated AI's potential in safeguarding diplomatic narratives but also highlighted the need for ethical guidelines to prevent misuse and overreach (Reuters 2024, Huang 2022).

The U.S. State Department has incorporated AI into its cybersecurity framework, including an AI-powered chatbot to streamline information management and bolster cybersecurity measures (Doubleday 2024a, 2024b). This tool helps protect internal communications and data handling while improving diplomatic workflow efficiency (State Department AI Inventory 2024). The department also employs AI-driven threat detection systems to identify emerging cyber risks, such as new hacking methodologies and vulnerabilities that may be exploited by foreign adversaries (Wallin & Reddie 2023).

The State Department's Center for Analytics is exploring machine learning to help new officers quickly aggregate prior work, enhancing their understanding of bilateral relationships. This approach allows diplomats to anticipate potential security challenges and respond proactively (Lacy 2024). Additionally, the department has implemented AI to automate routine tasks, such as summarizing and translating diplomatic cables, reducing manual workloads and enabling diplomats to focus on more substantive matters while improving overall efficiency in diplomatic communications (Vota 2024).

The State Department faces persistent cyber threats from foreign governments, including Russia, China, North Korea, and Iran. Given the increasing complexity of these threats, the department collaborates with other government agencies and private companies to strengthen its defenses (Cooper & Loo 2024). By integrating AI into its cybersecurity infrastructure, the department has improved its ability to anticipate, detect, and respond to cyberattacks more effectively (Mokashi et al. 2022, García-Herrero 2024, Huang 2022, Rosenau et al. 2023, Bjola & Manor 2024a, 2024b, Manor & Pamment 2024).

AI is also transforming law enforcement, with applications in identifying high-crime areas, optimizing patrols, automating traffic enforcement, analyzing surveillance footage, and monitoring social media for threats. Cities like Los Angeles and Chicago have led the adoption of AI in policing (Ly 2024). While these tools enhance efficiency and public safety, they also raise concerns about bias, racial profiling, and potential civil liberties violations. Within the context of diplomatic security, AI offers opportunities to improve threat detection, resource allocation, and risk monitoring at embassies worldwide. However, careful implementation is crucial to avoid biased outcomes or over-reliance on AI, which could complicate international relations and erode trust in security operations (Lacy 2024, Federal Bureau of Investigation 2025, State Department AI Inventory 2024).

FUTURE-PROOFING DIPLOMATIC SECURITY

The future of diplomatic security emerges through constant evolution, where AI capabilities expand in tandem with new security challenges. Smart video analytics may advance to identify not just individual behaviors but also complex patterns of coordinated activity. Predictive systems could anticipate emerging threats by synthesizing data from diplomatic, economic, and social indicators. These advancing capabilities will enable security teams to shift from reactive to proactive protection strategies.

Integration between physical and digital security systems continues to deepen through AI coordination. Future security platforms may create unified protection environments where physical access controls, cybersecurity measures, and personnel monitoring work in seamless concert. These integrated systems could provide security officers with comprehensive situational awareness, enabling faster and more informed decision-making. Such capabilities prove particularly valuable in complex diplomatic facilities where multiple security priorities intersect.

The role of diplomatic security professionals evolves alongside these technological advances. Future security officers will likely operate as skilled interpreters of AI-enhanced intelligence, combining technical understanding with diplomatic acumen. Their expertise will focus increasingly on strategic security planning and critical decision-making, while AI systems handle routine monitoring and basic threat detection. This evolution demands new approaches to training and professional development that emphasize both technological literacy and traditional security skills.

International cooperation in diplomatic security takes on new dimensions through AI integration. Shared threat intelligence platforms may enable diplomatic missions to collaborate more effectively in identifying and responding to security challenges. Common standards for AI security systems could emerge, facilitating interoperability while ensuring consistent protection across diplomatic facilities worldwide. These developments would strengthen the collective security of diplomatic missions while respecting each nation's sovereign security requirements.

Resilience becomes increasingly central to diplomatic security as missions face more sophisticated threats. Future security frameworks must protect against both known threats and emerging challenges that AI systems might not yet recognize. This approach requires maintaining robust traditional security measures alongside advanced AI capabilities, ensuring that missions remain secure even if technology fails. The goal is to create layered security that combines the best of human expertise and AI, adapting to new threats while maintaining unwavering protection for diplomatic operations. (See: U.S. Department of State 2024a, 2024b, 2024c, 2024d, Vacarelu 2021, Wiseman 2024, Lacy 2024, Puaschunder 2019, Haseley et al. 2023, Hamidouche 2021, Hedling & Bremberg 2021, Pokhriyal & Koebe 2023.).

LARGE LANGUAGE MODELS: STRENGTHENING MISSION SECURITY

Building on our exploration of Large Language Models (LLMs) across diplomatic functions—from general diplomatic work, leadership, political analysis, economic affairs, management operations, consular services, and public affairs—we now examine their specific applications in diplomatic security. While previous chapters demonstrated these tools' value in various diplomatic roles, security officers face unique challenges in maintaining mission safety while preserving operational security and protecting sensitive information.

Security operations demand exceptional precision in communication and documentation, particularly when developing protocols, training materials, and incident response procedures. LLMs excel at helping security officers create clear, actionable guidance while carefully avoiding sensitive operational details. This capability proves particularly valuable when developing general security awareness materials, documenting non-sensitive procedures, or creating training scenarios that preserve operational security.

Emergency preparedness, a critical aspect of diplomatic security, benefits from LLM capabilities in new ways. Beyond the communication support explored in previous chapters, these tools can help security officers develop response protocols, create training exercises, and establish general security guidelines while maintaining appropriate operational security. This proves especially valuable during planning phases when developing generalized procedures and training materials.

Security awareness training represents another key application unique to diplomatic security. Building on the educational approaches discussed in earlier chapters, security officers can use LLMs to develop comprehensive training programs, create engaging scenarios, and generate materials that enhance security awareness while avoiding sensitive details. This capability particularly shines when creating content that needs to engage staff while maintaining strict information security.

However, security work demands special attention to certain limitations beyond those discussed previously. The sensitive nature of security operations requires extreme caution in how these tools are used. Officers must be particularly mindful of never including sensitive security information, specific protocols, or operational details in their prompts or interactions with these systems (Baele 2022, Bano, Chaudhri, & Zowghi 2023, State Department AI Inventory 2024, Haseley et al. 2023, Roumate 2021a, 2021b, Wiseman 2024).

PUTTING LLMS TO WORK FOR DIPLOMATIC SECURITY OFFICERS

Building on prompt engineering practices established in previous chapters, let's explore how security officers can craft effective prompts for their specific needs. While earlier chapters covered diplomatic communications broadly, security operations require particular attention to maintaining operational security while developing effective training and awareness materials.

When creating security awareness materials, frame prompts to ensure both clarity and appropriate information security:

> Help me draft general security awareness guidelines for embassy staff focusing on basic situational awareness. Include: 1) universal security principles that apply in public spaces, 2) general best practices for personal security, 3) basic guidance for reporting security concerns, and 4) the importance of following established protocols. Use clear language while keeping all guidance at a general, non-sensitive level.

For emergency preparedness documentation, structure prompts to maintain security while providing clear guidance:

> I need to create general emergency response guidelines for staff training. Develop: 1) basic principles for emergency preparedness, 2) general steps for emergency reporting, 3) universal evacuation concepts, and 4) general communication protocols during emergencies. Ensure all content remains at a high level without revealing specific procedures or sensitive details.

For security training materials, focus prompts on engagement while protecting operational security:

> Help me develop general security training scenarios that test basic security awareness. Create hypothetical situations that: 1) reinforce general security principles, 2) encourage situational awareness, 3) practice basic emergency procedures, and 4) strengthen security mindset. Ensure all scenarios remain generic without revealing actual procedures or sensitive details.

Security officers should particularly focus prompts on:

- Creating general security awareness materials
- Developing basic training scenarios
- Documenting non-sensitive procedures
- Enhancing security education
- Maintaining strict operational security

These applications extend beyond the foundational capabilities covered in previous chapters to address the specific needs of security operations. The key is maintaining appropriate operational security while ensuring content effectively enhances mission security awareness and preparedness.

ADVANCED AI USE CASES IN DIPLOMATIC SECURITY

Building on the foundational AI applications explored in Chapter 1, the leadership use cases from Chapter 2, the political applications in Chapter 3, the economic tools examined in Chapter 4, the management systems discussed in Chapter 5, the consular services enhanced in Chapter 6, and the public affairs capabilities outlined in Chapter 7, we now examine advanced AI solutions specifically designed for diplomatic security. While previous chapters demonstrated how AI can enhance various aspects of diplomatic work, security operations present unique opportunities for leveraging AI to protect missions, detect threats, and ensure operational continuity.

The integration of AI into security operations requires particular attention to information protection, operational security, and the preservation of human judgment in critical security decisions. From intelligent surveillance systems and automated threat detection to predictive analytics and incident response coordination, these use cases demonstrate how AI can transform security operations while maintaining the crucial role of human expertise in protecting diplomatic missions.

Each of these applications must carefully balance the power of AI with the need for operational security, human oversight, and the protection of sensitive information. The goal is not to replace human judgment in security operations but to enhance the capabilities of security professionals while maintaining the highest standards of diplomatic protection.

PHYSICAL SECURITY SURVEILLANCE

A smart camera system that spots suspicious behavior around embassies.

Traditional diplomatic facility surveillance relies heavily on human monitoring of multiple video feeds, access points, and security zones simultaneously. Security officers must maintain constant vigilance across numerous screens while managing other duties, leading to potential attention fatigue and missed incidents. For example, during high-traffic periods or diplomatic events, security teams struggle to monitor all entry points effectively while also tracking visitor movements and screening for suspicious behavior patterns.

AI-powered surveillance systems transform this landscape through intelligent video analytics and behavioral monitoring. These systems can simultaneously analyze feeds from multiple cameras, automatically detecting anomalies like unauthorized access attempts, suspicious behavior patterns, or objects left in sensitive areas. For instance, during a diplomatic reception, the AI can track crowd movements, identify unauthorized attempts to access restricted areas, and alert security personnel to potential threats while filtering out routine activities.

Implementing these systems requires careful consideration of privacy concerns, particularly in diplomatic settings where discretion is paramount. Success metrics must balance security effectiveness against diplomatic considerations—for example, measuring threat detection rates while ensuring the system doesn't create an overly intrusive atmosphere that could impede diplomatic functions. Regular evaluation should examine both technical performance (such as false alarm rates and detection accuracy) and diplomatic impact (such as maintaining appropriate security presence without compromising the mission's ability to engage with local communities).

CYBERSECURITY DEFENSE

A digital guardian that blocks attacks before they damage embassy networks.

Current diplomatic cybersecurity operations face increasingly sophisticated threats while relying on traditional tools that often react to attacks rather than preventing them. Security teams must monitor multiple networks simultaneously, manage various security tools, and respond to numerous alerts, many of which may be false positives. During critical diplomatic communications or negotiations, the pressure to maintain network security while ensuring continuous availability creates significant operational strain.

AI-enhanced cybersecurity systems provide proactive defense through continuous network monitoring, pattern analysis, and automated threat response. Machine learning algorithms can identify subtle indicators of potential attacks, automatically implement countermeasures, and adapt to new threat patterns in real time. For example, during a high-level diplomatic video conference, the AI can simultaneously monitor network traffic for suspicious patterns, protect against potential intrusions, and ensure secure communication channels remain operational.

The implementation challenge lies in balancing security requirements with diplomatic operational needs. Success metrics should evaluate both technical security measures (such as threat detection rates and response times) and operational impact (such as maintaining efficient diplomatic communications). Regular assessment must consider factors like false positive rates, system accessibility for legitimate users, and the impact on diplomatic operations. For instance, the system must be calibrated to protect sensitive communications while avoiding disruption to critical diplomatic functions.

PREDICTIVE THREAT INTELLIGENCE

An early warning system that sees trouble coming before it arrives.

Traditional threat analysis in diplomatic security relies heavily on manual processing of multiple intelligence sources, often leading to delayed responses and missed connections between different threat indicators. Security teams must synthesize information from various reports, local news, social media, and diplomatic channels, making it difficult to identify emerging threats quickly enough for preventive action. During periods of heightened tension or significant diplomatic activity, the volume of data can overwhelm traditional analysis methods.

AI-powered predictive intelligence systems transform this process by automatically analyzing multiple data streams simultaneously, identifying patterns, and predicting potential threats before they materialize. These systems can process information from diverse sources—including social media sentiment, local news reports, weather patterns, and historical incident data—to provide early warning of potential security risks. For example, the AI might detect correlations between increased social media activity, local political developments, and historical protest patterns to predict potential demonstrations near diplomatic facilities.

Implementation requires careful attention to both technical capabilities and diplomatic sensitivities. Success metrics should evaluate the system's predictive accuracy while considering diplomatic implications of security responses. Regular assessment must examine both technical performance (such as prediction accuracy and warning lead times) and practical utility (such as actionable intelligence generation and resource allocation efficiency). For instance, when the system predicts increased risk around a diplomatic event, security teams must balance protective measures with maintaining appropriate diplomatic presence and accessibility.

CRISIS RESPONSE COORDINATION

A command center that helps everyone work together during emergencies.

Current crisis management in diplomatic missions often relies on predetermined response plans and manual coordination processes, which can become overwhelmed during complex emergencies involving multiple threats or rapidly evolving situations. Response teams must simultaneously assess threats, coordinate resources, communicate with stakeholders, and manage evacuation procedures, often with incomplete information and under severe time pressure. During actual crises, communication bottlenecks and coordination challenges can significantly impact response effectiveness.

AI-enhanced crisis response systems provide real-time situation analysis, automated resource coordination, and dynamic response planning. These systems can process multiple data streams simultaneously—including security sensors, staff locations, and environmental conditions—to create comprehensive situational awareness and recommend optimal response strategies. For example, during a compound evacuation, the AI can simultaneously track personnel movements, identify safe exit routes, coordinate security teams, and maintain communication channels with all stakeholders.

Successful implementation requires balancing automated capabilities with human judgment in sensitive diplomatic contexts. Performance metrics should evaluate both technical efficiency (such as response time and resource coordination) and diplomatic appropriateness (such as maintaining protocol during crises). Regular assessment must consider factors like communication effectiveness, resource utilization, and maintenance of diplomatic standards during emergencies. For instance, the system must help coordinate rapid response while ensuring actions align with diplomatic protocols and host-country relationships.

RISK ASSESSMENT AND STRATEGIC PLANNING

A safety predictor that shows where and how to protect embassies best.

Traditional diplomatic security planning relies heavily on historical data and subjective expert assessment, often struggling to incorporate dynamic risk factors and emerging threats effectively. Security teams must manually analyze multiple risk factors—from local political stability to physical infrastructure vulnerabilities—while attempting to project future security needs. This process can miss subtle interconnections between different risk factors and fail to anticipate emerging threats effectively.

AI-powered risk assessment systems transform this process through comprehensive data analysis and predictive modeling. These systems can simultaneously evaluate multiple risk factors—including historical incident data, current threat landscapes, and emerging global trends—to provide dynamic risk assessments and strategic planning recommendations. For example, when planning security for a new diplomatic facility, the AI can analyze factors ranging from local crime patterns to political stability indicators, providing comprehensive risk analysis and mitigation recommendations.

Implementation success depends on balancing automated analysis with diplomatic expertise and local knowledge. Metrics should evaluate both analytical accuracy (such as risk prediction reliability) and practical utility (such as actionable planning recommendations). Regular assessment must consider factors like prediction accuracy, resource allocation efficiency, and alignment with diplomatic objectives. For instance, when the system recommends security enhancements, planners must balance protection requirements with maintaining appropriate diplomatic presence and accessibility.

BIOMETRIC ACCESS CONTROL

A smart doorkeeper that knows exactly who should be allowed inside.

Current diplomatic facility access control often relies on traditional methods like identification cards and visual verification, which can be vulnerable to fraud and human error while creating bottlenecks during high-traffic periods. Security officers must manually verify credentials, monitor access points, and maintain visitor logs while ensuring efficient flow of legitimate traffic. During diplomatic events or periods of increased activity, these systems can struggle to maintain both security and operational efficiency.

AI-enhanced biometric systems transform access control through multi-factor authentication and real-time verification capabilities. These systems can simultaneously process multiple biometric indicators—such as facial recognition, fingerprints, and behavioral patterns—while maintaining efficient access flow. For example, during a diplomatic conference, the system can quickly verify attendee identities, manage access levels to different areas, and flag unauthorized access attempts while maintaining smooth event operations.

Implementation requires careful attention to privacy concerns and diplomatic protocols. Success metrics should evaluate both security effectiveness (such as unauthorized access prevention) and operational efficiency (such as processing speed and user experience). Regular assessment must consider factors like false rejection rates, processing times, and impact on diplomatic functions. For instance, the system must maintain strict security while ensuring dignitary access remains smooth and diplomatically appropriate.

INSIDER THREAT DETECTION

A behavior monitor that spots concerning patterns among staff.

Traditional approaches to insider threat detection in diplomatic settings rely heavily on periodic security reviews and human observation, often missing subtle behavioral changes that might indicate emerging risks. Security teams must manually monitor numerous indicators—from system access patterns to behavioral changes—across large staff populations, making it difficult to identify concerning patterns before security breaches occur. This challenge becomes particularly acute in diplomatic facilities with large local staff components.

AI-powered insider threat detection systems enhance security through continuous behavioral monitoring and pattern analysis. These systems can analyze multiple data points simultaneously—including facility access patterns, system usage, and communication patterns—to identify potential security risks while maintaining individual privacy. For example, the system might detect unusual combinations of after-hours access, file access patterns, and communication behaviors that could indicate security concerns.

Implementation requires careful balance between security needs and workplace trust. Success metrics must evaluate both technical effectiveness (such as risk identification accuracy) and workplace impact (such as maintaining positive organizational culture). Regular assessment should consider factors like false positive rates, investigation outcomes, and employee privacy protection. For instance, when the system flags potential concerns, security teams must investigate while maintaining appropriate discretion and protecting workplace morale.

CRISIS COMMUNICATIONS

A message coordinator that keeps everyone informed during emergencies.

Traditional crisis communication in diplomatic settings often struggles with message consistency, rapid dissemination, and management of multiple communication channels during emergencies. Communication teams must manually craft messages, coordinate across multiple platforms, and manage stakeholder communications while dealing with rapidly evolving situations. During actual crises, these challenges can lead to delayed responses and inconsistent messaging.

AI-enhanced crisis communication systems provide automated message generation, multi-channel coordination, and real-time adaptation capabilities. These systems can simultaneously manage multiple communication streams, ensure message consistency, and adapt communication strategies based on stakeholder responses. For example, during a security incident, the AI can help generate appropriate messages for different audiences, manage distribution across multiple channels, and monitor public response while maintaining diplomatic messaging standards.

Success metrics should evaluate both communication effectiveness (such as message consistency and distribution speed) and diplomatic appropriateness (such as maintaining proper tone and protocol). Regular assessment must consider factors like message accuracy, response times, and stakeholder comprehension. For instance, when managing crisis communications, the system must help maintain clear, consistent messaging while ensuring all communications align with diplomatic protocols and security requirements.

SECURITY TRAINING AND SIMULATION

A practice environment that prepares security teams for real threats.

Current diplomatic security training often relies on static scenarios and scheduled drills, limiting the variety and realism of training experiences while straining operational resources. Training teams must manually design scenarios, coordinate participants, and evaluate performance, often struggling to simulate the full complexity of modern security challenges. This approach can leave security teams unprepared for novel or complex threats.

AI-powered training systems enhance preparation through dynamic scenario generation and real-time adaptation capabilities. These systems can create diverse, realistic training scenarios that adapt to participant responses while providing detailed performance feedback. For example, during a crisis response drill, the AI can simultaneously simulate multiple threat vectors, adjust scenario difficulty based on team performance, and provide a comprehensive evaluation of response effectiveness.

Implementation success depends on balancing training realism with operational requirements. Metrics should evaluate both training effectiveness (such as skill improvement and scenario realism) and resource efficiency (such as training time and cost). Regular assessment must consider factors like skill retention, scenario variety, and practical application of trained skills. For instance, when designing training programs, the system must help create realistic scenarios while ensuring training activities don't compromise ongoing security operations.

RESOURCE OPTIMIZATION

A security scheduler that puts the right protection in the right places.

Traditional diplomatic security resource allocation often relies on fixed schedules and static deployment patterns, struggling to adapt to changing security needs and emerging threats. Security managers must manually coordinate personnel assignments, equipment deployment, and resource distribution, often leading to inefficient utilization and potential security gaps. During periods of heightened activity or multiple simultaneous events, these challenges can significantly impact security effectiveness.

AI-enabled resource optimization systems transform this process through dynamic analysis and predictive deployment recommendations. These systems can analyze multiple factors simultaneously—including threat levels, event schedules, and historical patterns—to recommend optimal resource allocation. For example, during a week with multiple diplomatic events, the AI can help coordinate security personnel deployment, equipment distribution, and response team positioning to maximize coverage while maintaining efficiency.

Implementation requires balancing automated recommendations with operational expertise. Success metrics should evaluate both resource efficiency (such as coverage optimization and response times) and security effectiveness (such as incident prevention and response capability). Regular assessment must consider factors like resource utilization rates, response capabilities, and operational flexibility. For instance, when optimizing resource deployment, the system must help maintain comprehensive security coverage while ensuring efficient use of available resources and maintaining appropriate diplomatic presence.

LIMITATIONS AND FUTURE RESEARCH DIRECTIONS

The integration of AI into diplomatic security operations presents both transformative opportunities and significant challenges that demand careful examination. As missions increasingly rely on AI-enhanced security measures, several critical limitations and research gaps emerge that require focused investigation to ensure effective and responsible deployment of these technologies.

THE CHALLENGE OF AI RELIABILITY IN CRITICAL SECURITY OPERATIONS

At the heart of diplomatic security lies an unforgiving requirement for consistent, reliable protection. While AI systems demonstrate remarkable capabilities in threat detection and response, their potential failure modes during critical security situations remain insufficiently understood. Consider a diplomatic facility relying on AI-enhanced surveillance during a high-stakes diplomatic visit—any system failure or degradation could create dangerous security gaps precisely when protection is most crucial. Security professionals must maintain readiness to operate effectively even if AI systems face disruption or deception.

This limitation extends beyond simple technical failures to include sophisticated attempts at system manipulation. Adversaries might learn to exploit AI patterns or introduce deceptive data that triggers incorrect responses. Future research must examine how missions can maintain security effectiveness during system disruptions while developing more robust AI architectures that resist both technical failures and intentional manipulation.

THE HUMAN ELEMENT IN AI-ENHANCED SECURITY

The psychological and operational impacts of integrating AI into security operations raise complex questions about maintaining human expertise and judgment. When security professionals work alongside increasingly capable AI systems, they may experience subtle degradation of their traditional security instincts and situational awareness. A Regional Security Officer might begin to over-rely on AI alerts while losing the practiced ability to spot subtle security anomalies that the system might miss.

Research must explore how missions can preserve and enhance human security expertise while leveraging AI capabilities. This includes examining effective training approaches that combine traditional security skills with AI system understanding, and studying how to maintain active human engagement in security operations rather than passive monitoring of AI systems.

CULTURAL SENSITIVITIES AND DIPLOMATIC TRUST

The deployment of AI security systems creates new tensions between protection requirements and diplomatic relationships. Advanced surveillance capabilities and automated threat responses may conflict with local cultural norms or diplomatic protocols in ways that strain relationships with host nations. For instance, AI-powered facial recognition and behavior analysis might raise privacy concerns that complicate diplomatic engagement with local communities and officials.

Further research must examine how missions can implement robust security measures while maintaining appropriate diplomatic sensitivity. This includes studying how AI security systems affect trust relationships with host nations and developing frameworks for transparent security operations that respect local cultural values while maintaining effectiveness.

OPERATIONAL INTEGRATION AND INTER-AGENCY COORDINATION

The complexity of modern diplomatic security operations demands seamless coordination across multiple agencies and jurisdictions. Current AI systems may struggle to integrate effectively with various security protocols and organizational boundaries. When a security incident occurs, AI responses must align with established procedures while respecting jurisdictional limits between embassy security, local law enforcement, and other relevant agencies.

Future research should explore frameworks for effective integration of AI security systems across organizational boundaries. This includes studying how to maintain clear operational boundaries while enabling necessary information sharing and coordinated response capabilities.

EVOLVING THREATS AND SYSTEM ADAPTATION

Perhaps most critically, the dynamic nature of security threats requires continuous evolution of AI security capabilities. As potential adversaries develop new attack methods and countermeasures, security systems must adapt while maintaining reliable protection. This challenge becomes particularly acute in diplomatic settings where security failures could have severe diplomatic consequences.

Research must examine how AI security systems can effectively evolve to address emerging threats while maintaining operational stability and predictability. This includes studying patterns of threat adaptation, developing more responsive security architectures, and ensuring systems can incorporate new capabilities without compromising existing security functions.

The path forward requires unprecedented collaboration between security professionals, technologists, diplomatic practitioners, and cultural experts. Success means developing AI security systems that enhance protection while preserving the essential human judgment and diplomatic sensitivity that define effective diplomatic security operations. As missions continue to face evolving security challenges, addressing these limitations through focused research will prove crucial for realizing the full potential of AI-enhanced diplomatic security.

CONCLUSION

The integration of AI into diplomatic security represents a fundamental transformation in how missions protect their personnel, facilities, and operations. As demonstrated throughout this chapter, from AI-driven surveillance systems to sophisticated threat detection platforms, AI serves as a transformative force multiplier across physical security, cybersecurity, threat analysis, and crisis response domains.

The evolution of diplomatic security through AI integration reveals several critical insights that extend beyond technological capability. While AI excels at processing vast amounts of data and identifying subtle patterns, the nuanced understanding of diplomatic contexts and potential consequences remains uniquely human. Security professionals must interpret AI-generated alerts within broader diplomatic frameworks, weighing both immediate security implications and potential impacts on international relationships.

The ethical deployment of AI in diplomatic security demands careful consideration of privacy, transparency, and diplomatic conduct. As demonstrated by the implementation of biometric systems and AI-driven surveillance, missions must balance enhanced security capabilities with the open, accessible nature of diplomatic facilities. This balance becomes particularly crucial in consular operations and public spaces, where security measures directly impact interactions with local populations.

International cooperation emerges as a crucial element in AI-enhanced diplomatic security. As threats become increasingly sophisticated and borderless, shared threat intelligence platforms and common standards for AI security systems facilitate more effective collaboration between diplomatic missions worldwide. The experiences of NATO's CCD-COE highlight both the potential and necessity of international cooperation in developing robust security frameworks.

The transformative impact of AI extends beyond individual security functions to reshape the fundamental practice of diplomacy. By enabling more sophisticated threat detection, enhanced crisis response capabilities, and improved resource allocation, AI-powered security operations strengthen the foundation upon which diplomatic success is built. However, realizing this potential requires security professionals who can effectively leverage AI capabilities while maintaining their critical judgment and diplomatic sensitivity.

As diplomatic missions continue to face evolving security challenges, the integration of AI capabilities becomes increasingly vital. Through thoughtful implementation of AI systems, careful attention to ethical considerations, and unwavering focus on diplomatic principles, missions can build more resilient and effective security operations that enhance rather than impede diplomatic objectives.

In the next chapter, we examine how AI is transforming the core technologies and digital infrastructure that power modern diplomacy.

DISCUSSION SCENARIOS AND QUESTIONS

The following scenarios examine the role of AI in protecting diplomatic missions. They challenge readers to consider the balance between security and privacy, the ethical use of AI in surveillance and cybersecurity, and the responsibilities of diplomats in ensuring that security measures support rather than undermine diplomatic objectives.

1. LLMs in managing disinformation and diplomatic stability
   Scenario: A hostile actor deploys an LLM to fabricate highly realistic but fake diplomatic communications, such as false memos or press releases attributed to your government. These forgeries trigger protests near your embassy and strain relations with the host nation. Simultaneously, your agency uses its own LLM to assess the damage, craft responses, and counter the spread of disinformation.
   Questions: How do you ensure your LLM generates culturally appropriate and ethically sound responses under time pressure, particularly in high-tension scenarios? What safeguards and protocols can you implement to prevent the LLM from escalating tensions or spreading inaccuracies, while also rebuilding trust with the host nation and local communities after such incidents?

2. AI-driven surveillance and host-nation trust
   Scenario: You implement an AI-powered surveillance system at a diplomatic compound, integrating autonomous drones, behavioral analytics, and facial recognition to enhance security. While the system improves monitoring capabilities, its operations raise concerns from the host-nation government and local communities about privacy and sovereignty.

Questions: How will you address host-nation privacy concerns while ensuring the AI system remains effective and operationally sound? What safeguards can you implement to prevent and manage false threat identifications, ensuring such incidents do not escalate into diplomatic crises? How do you maintain robust human oversight to ensure the AI system respects cultural, legal, and ethical boundaries in the host nation?

3. AI for global threat detection in diplomacy

Scenario: As a Regional Security Officer, you oversee an AI system designed to process vast amounts of open-source intelligence (OSINT), including social media, news, and surveillance feeds, to identify emerging threats against diplomats, embassy facilities, or host-nation stability. The AI generates real-time threat assessments, but its recommendations sometimes flag ambiguous or sensitive entities.

Questions: How do you ensure AI-generated threat assessments remain accurate and unbiased, particularly in politically or culturally sensitive regions with incomplete or misleading data? What steps will you take to validate AI recommendations when they contradict human intuition or contextual expertise, while preserving trust and cooperation with host-nation communities?

4. AI in crisis management and evacuation planning

Scenario: During a sudden crisis—such as a terrorist attack, political uprising, or natural disaster—your team uses an AI system to plan and execute the evacuation of embassy staff, citizens, and local personnel. The AI assesses real-time threats and infrastructure constraints to recommend routes, transportation, and prioritization of evacuees.

Questions: How do you address the ethical challenges of an AI prioritizing certain evacuees over others, particularly when vulnerable groups like local staff or host-nation allies are affected? What steps will you take to reconcile conflicts between AI-generated evacuation plans and the situational judgment of on-site personnel? How do you ensure the AI's recommendations remain adaptable to unexpected developments, such as infrastructure failures or resistance from host-nation authorities?

5. AI in cybersecurity and digital diplomacy

Scenario: Your mission deploys an advanced AI system to defend against increasingly sophisticated cyber threats targeting diplomatic communications, classified data, and financial systems. The AI autonomously detects and neutralizes threats, but its decisions sometimes disrupt legitimate activity or raise concerns with host-nation partners.

Questions: How do you balance AI autonomy with human oversight to minimize unintended disruptions in cyber threat responses? What measures will you take to address incidents where AI disrupts communications with host-nation partners, potentially undermining diplomatic relations? How will you safeguard the AI system against adversarial attacks while ensuring accountability for its autonomous decisions that cause operational or diplomatic harm?

9 AI and Diplomatic Technology
Using Smart Tools to Advance Diplomacy

Software is eating the world, but AI is going to eat software.

—Jensen Huang, CEO of Nvidia (2017)

The biggest challenge with AI isn't just the technology—it's the way we introduce it and prepare people for its impact.

—Ginni Rometty, former Chair, President, and CEO of IBM (2024)

[AI] It's not about displacing humans, it's about humanizing the digital experience.

—Rob Garf, Vice President of Salesforce Retail (2024)

The digital transformation of diplomatic missions over the past two decades has been astonishing. From an era of paper cables and radio transmissions, embassies have evolved into sophisticated digital operations centers, where secure networks carry classified communications, where diplomatic work spans multiple digital platforms, and where technology underpins every aspect of the mission—from consular services to crisis response. This shift represents one of the most significant changes in diplomatic practice since the advent of telegraph communications in the 19th century. Today's embassies operate as technological hubs, managing complex digital infrastructure that enables modern diplomacy to function across borders and time zones.

At this pivotal moment, artificial intelligence (AI) offers both unprecedented opportunities and serious risks for diplomatic missions. As Diplomatic technology (DT) officers manage increasingly complex technical infrastructure—from secure networks to physical systems—they must evaluate how AI could either strengthen or potentially threaten these critical operations. While AI promises to enhance cybersecurity, automate maintenance, and improve communications, it also introduces vulnerabilities that could compromise sensitive diplomatic work. This chapter explores these potential applications and risks across key use cases, examining how diplomatic missions can leverage AI's benefits while maintaining robust defenses against its threats. Understanding this balance is crucial as missions work to ensure that security, discretion, and reliability remain paramount in an increasingly AI-enabled diplomatic landscape.

DOI: 10.1201/9781003612308-9

VIGNETTE   AI-Enhanced Embassy in the Republic of Z

DT Officer Anya Novak begins her day in the embassy's network operations center, where multiple displays monitor the health and security of the mission's digital infrastructure. Recent political developments tracked by Sarah Chen's team have increased demands on secure video conferencing systems, while Elena Moretti's expanding economic initiatives require enhanced data analysis capabilities. Her dashboard shows the complex web of systems supporting everything from classified communications to public-facing digital services.

The embassy's AI-enhanced monitoring platform flags several priority items: the upcoming renewable energy summit will require additional secure network bandwidth, while the surge in consular services noted by Maria Santos demands optimization of citizen-facing systems. Meanwhile, Regional Security Officer Thompson's security requirements for an upcoming congressional delegation necessitate rapid deployment of additional encrypted communication channels.

As Novak reviews system logs, predictive maintenance algorithms identify potential bottlenecks in the embassy's network infrastructure. Years of experience have taught her that technical issues rarely exist in isolation—each system interconnects with countless others, and a single point of failure could impact the entire mission. She appreciates how AI helps manage this complexity while knowing that human oversight remains crucial for maintaining the delicate balance between accessibility and security.

Her morning schedule reflects the diverse demands of DT. She's coordinating with Management Officer Amir Qureshi on infrastructure upgrades to support the expanding mission, implementing enhanced cybersecurity measures based on the latest threat intelligence, and ensuring the reliability of critical communication systems. The AI assists with resource allocation and system optimization, but Novak knows it's her expertise that ensures these technologies serve rather than hinder diplomacy.

By mid-morning, she's troubleshooting a critical secure video system for the Ambassador's briefing with headquarters back home while simultaneously overseeing the embassy's transition to new encrypted communication protocols. The AI helps prioritize the constant stream of technical issues, but Novak's understanding of both diplomatic priorities and technology capabilities ensures the embassy's infrastructure evolves to meet its changing needs.

THE DIGITAL FOUNDATION OF MODERN DIPLOMACY

Technology now forms the bedrock upon which all aspects of diplomatic work rests. From the handling of sensitive political communications to the management of complex economic negotiations, from the delivery of consular services to the orchestration of public diplomacy campaigns, DT provides the infrastructure that makes modern diplomacy possible. This technological foundation must be both robust enough to protect classified information and flexible enough to adapt to rapidly changing diplomatic needs.

The scope of this technological underpinning extends far beyond basic communications. In political affairs, secure digital platforms enable diplomats to analyze regional developments and coordinate responses to emerging crises. Economic officers rely on advanced data systems to track trade patterns and support complex negotiations. Management sections operate sophisticated resource planning systems that keep missions running efficiently. Consular operations depend on integrated databases and processing systems to serve citizens and handle visa applications. Public affairs teams utilize digital platforms to engage with diverse audiences and counter disinformation.

As AI emerges as a potentially transformative force, it offers new possibilities for enhancing these technological capabilities. AI could strengthen cybersecurity by detecting threats more quickly than human analysts, predict maintenance needs before systems fail, and automate routine tasks to free up human expertise for more complex challenges. However, these same capabilities could be turned against diplomatic missions by sophisticated adversaries using AI to probe for vulnerabilities or generate convincing deepfakes that could disrupt diplomatic communications.

The challenge facing diplomatic missions lies in determining how to harness AI's potential while protecting against its risks. This requires understanding not just the technical capabilities of AI systems, but their implications for each area of diplomatic work. For instance, while AI might enhance visa processing efficiency, it must do so without compromising the human judgment crucial to consular decisions. Similarly, AI-powered analytics could provide valuable insights for political reporting, but missions must ensure these systems don't introduce biases or overlook crucial cultural nuances.

STRATEGIC INTEGRATION OF TECHNOLOGY AND DIPLOMACY

The integration of advanced technology into diplomatic missions represents more than modernization—it offers the potential to transform how diplomacy operates at every level. Secure digital networks could enable real-time collaboration among diplomatic teams across borders, allowing political officers to coordinate responses to emerging situations with unprecedented speed. Economic sections might leverage data analytics to identify patterns in global markets that could affect bilateral relationships. Management officers could deploy predictive systems to optimize everything from energy usage to supply chain logistics.

This technological capability brings both opportunity and responsibility. While AI could enhance decision-making by processing vast amounts of information quickly, it must be implemented in ways that preserve diplomatic discretion and human judgment. For instance, AI systems might flag concerning patterns in visa applications, but consular officers must retain final authority over these critical decisions. Similarly, public affairs teams could use AI to analyze media sentiment, but human officers must shape the strategic response to public opinion trends.

The security implications of these technological capabilities demand particular attention. Each new system or platform introduced into a diplomatic mission could represent either a strengthened defense or a potential vulnerability. AI-enhanced cybersecurity systems could provide better protection against evolving threats, but they must be designed with the understanding that adversaries may also employ AI in their attempts to breach diplomatic networks. This creates an ongoing challenge of maintaining technological superiority while protecting against increasingly sophisticated threats.

As diplomatic missions consider implementing these technologies, they must weigh immediate operational benefits against long-term strategic implications. For example, cloud-based systems might offer greater flexibility and efficiency in managing diplomatic communications, but they require careful consideration of data sovereignty and security. Machine learning algorithms could help process large volumes of diplomatic reporting, but their analysis must be vetted to ensure it aligns with human diplomatic expertise and understanding of local contexts.

THE IMPERATIVE OF SECURITY IN DT

Security considerations permeate every aspect of technological innovation in diplomacy. From the protection of classified political reporting to the safeguarding of consular databases, from securing economic negotiations to defending public diplomacy platforms, the integrity of diplomatic operations depends on robust technological defenses. As AI introduces new capabilities, it simultaneously creates novel security challenges that diplomatic missions must anticipate and address.

The potential security applications of AI span multiple layers of protection. At the network level, AI systems could monitor data flows continuously, identifying anomalous patterns that might indicate intrusion attempts or data exfiltration. Physical security could be enhanced through AI-powered surveillance systems that detect unusual behavior around diplomatic facilities. Document verification systems might employ machine learning to spot increasingly sophisticated forgeries in visa applications or diplomatic credentials. Yet, each of these protective measures must be implemented with the understanding that adversaries could deploy similar technologies in their attempts to compromise diplomatic operations.

The human dimension of security becomes even more critical as technology advances. While AI might automate many security functions, diplomatic staff must understand both the capabilities and limitations of these systems. Political officers handling sensitive negotiations need to recognize potential technological vulnerabilities. Economic officers working with proprietary business information must ensure their communications remain secure. Management officers overseeing mission infrastructure have to maintain technological defenses while ensuring systems remain accessible to legitimate users.

Privacy and data protection add another layer of complexity to DT security. Consular sections handling personal information must comply with various international data protection regulations while maintaining efficient operations. Public affairs teams engaging through digital platforms need to protect both their communications infrastructure and their audience's data. AI systems, with their ability to process and analyze vast amounts of information, require particularly careful oversight to ensure they don't compromise privacy protections or diplomatic confidentiality.

HISTORICAL AI USE CASE EXAMPLES IN DT

The integration of AI into DT has transformed how governments manage their information systems, enhance operational efficiency, and secure sensitive communications. This section explores recent historical AI use cases in DT, emphasizing how these innovations have enabled diplomatic missions to adapt to a rapidly evolving technological landscape.

U.S. DEPARTMENT OF STATE AI INITIATIVES

This section examines the U.S. Department of State's approaches to AI implementation, focusing on strategic frameworks, policy initiatives, and operational applications as described in official sources. According to publicly available information from the U.S. Department of State's website and official publications, the Department has embarked on a significant effort to integrate AI into its diplomatic operations (Alder 2024, Collins 2024, Doubleday 2024a, 2024b, Geller 2024, U.S. Department of State 2023, 2024a, 2024b, 2024c, 2024d, Vota 2024).

The department's strategic approach to AI is primarily outlined in its Enterprise Artificial Intelligence Strategy (EAIS) for fiscal years 2024–2025, subtitled "Empowering Diplomacy through Responsible AI." Public documents indicate that this strategy serves as the Department's central framework for AI implementation, emphasizing governance, policy development, and internal collaboration. The strategy articulates four primary objectives: strengthening AI infrastructure, promoting AI literacy throughout the Department, ensuring ethical AI practices, and expanding AI applications in diplomatic functions (U.S. Department of State 2023).

Complementing this domestic strategy, the Department has published a Global AI Research Agenda that focuses on international collaboration in AI development. According to official materials, this agenda prioritizes research into AI's effects on global labor markets, sociotechnical studies, and equitable AI access. The Department's website indicates that this research framework aims to advance both U.S. interests and global development in AI technology (U.S. Department of State 2024a, 2024b, 2024c, 2024d). [Note: the Department also published an "AI in Global Development Playbook," however that document was removed from the Department's website following the removal of the U.S. Agency for International Development's website.]

The Department's operational implementation of AI is documented in its AI Use Case Inventory 2024, which details various applications across bureaus and offices. Within the DT bureau, formerly Information Resource Management (IRM), several specific initiatives have been documented. These include the Apptio Tool for financial management (retired in September 2024), a data analytics project for processing unstructured text, and an AI-powered virtual agent for user support (discontinued in mid-2024). The bureau has also announced plans for AI-driven cybersecurity operations, though implementation details are not specified in public materials (U.S. Department of State 2024a, 2024b, 2024c, 2024d).

In the realm of international engagement, the Department's website indicates participation in numerous multinational AI initiatives. These include the G7 Leaders'

Statements from late 2023, the Hiroshima AI Process, the Seoul Declaration for Safe, Innovative, and Inclusive AI, the UN General Assembly AI Resolution, and several other international frameworks. The specific outcomes and impact of this participation, however, are not fully detailed in available materials (U.S. Department of State 2025a, 2025b).

According to State Magazine's December 2024 issue, the Department has begun utilizing AI-driven data analysis tools to assist diplomats in interpreting complex geopolitical data. The publication describes AI applications in trend prediction and communication streamlining, though the effectiveness of these tools is not independently verified in public sources (U.S. Department of State 2024a, 2024b, 2024c, 2024d).

The Department's compliance with federal AI governance frameworks is documented through references to the OMB Memorandum M-24-10 Compliance Plan (U.S. Department of Justice 2024). Under the oversight of the Chief Data and AI Officer, these compliance efforts reportedly focus on AI oversight and risk management within diplomatic activities. The Department has emphasized its commitment to responsible AI integration in diplomatic decision-making. According to official sources, the Department views AI as potentially beneficial for foreign policy and national security while acknowledging the need for ethical implementation and international cooperation (U.S. Department of State 2025a, 2025b).

The Department's published materials indicate several areas where AI is being explored for diplomatic applications, including analyzing large-scale diplomatic reports, evaluating outreach effectiveness, and addressing misinformation campaigns. These initiatives are described as part of a broader effort to modernize diplomatic operations, though specific outcomes and effectiveness measures are not publicly available. Based on the available public information, the State Department appears to be systematically incorporating AI into its diplomatic operations while emphasizing responsible implementation and ethical considerations. However, as with many government technology initiatives, the actual impact and success of these programs remain to be fully evaluated. A more comprehensive assessment would require access to internal documentation and implementation details that are not currently available to the public (U.S. Department of State 2023, 2024a, 2024b, 2024c, 2024d, 2025a, 2025b).

SELECTED AI INITIATIVES AROUND THE WORLD

AI is revolutionizing how nations conduct diplomacy, craft foreign policy, and manage national security. From China's sophisticated surveillance systems to Israel's military applications, governments worldwide are racing to harness AI's potential to gain strategic advantages in the international arena. The integration of AI into diplomatic channels marks a significant shift in international relations. While military applications have dominated headlines, diplomatic applications are quietly transforming how nations interact and negotiate on the global stage.

China stands at the forefront of this transformation, deploying advanced AI systems for intelligence gathering and international influence. Their recently developed ChatBIT system, built on Meta's Llama model, exemplifies Beijing's commitment to AI-powered diplomacy (Pamfret & Pang 2024). The country has also exported AI surveillance technologies to nations including Ecuador, Zimbabwe, Uzbekistan, and Pakistan, effectively expanding its geopolitical influence through technological partnerships (Wikipedia, "Chinese Intelligence Activity Abroad" 2025).

The United Kingdom has taken a different approach, positioning itself as a global leader in AI governance. The launch of its AI Safety Institute (AISI) in 2024, backed by a £100 million investment, demonstrates London's commitment to responsible AI development (Biddle, "Inside the UK's AI Safety Institute"). The institute's mandate extends beyond domestic concerns, focusing on evaluating AI risks in international relations and their potential impact on global security (Biddle 2024).

The United Arab Emirates has emerged as a surprising powerhouse in AI development. The country's Falcon Large Language Model (LLM) has reportedly outperformed similar systems from established tech giants, demonstrating that smaller nations can compete effectively in the AI space when backed by sufficient resources and strategic vision (Legrand 2024, 2025). This development underscores the growing role of AI in shaping the geopolitical landscape, even among nations that traditionally played a smaller role in global technological competition.

The military sector has witnessed perhaps the most dramatic AI integration, with several nations developing sophisticated systems for defense and combat operations. The European Union has made substantial commitments to military AI development, allocating €7.3 billion through the European Defense Fund for 2021–2027. This investment signals the EU's determination to achieve technological sovereignty while enhancing its defense capabilities against emerging threats (Barker 2024, 2025).

Israel's military has pioneered AI-driven target identification systems. Their Gospel and Lavender platforms, developed by the elite intelligence Unit 8,200, process vast quantities of data to identify potential threats with reported accuracy rates of 90% (Serhan 2024, "Artificial Intelligence Arms Race" 2025). These systems represent a significant advancement in military intelligence capabilities and reflect Israel's increasing reliance on AI-driven warfare. Critics argue that reliance on AI for target identification may lead to increased civilian casualties and challenges in accountability. The Israeli Defense Forces have stated that these systems assist intelligence analysts in reviewing and analyzing information but do not autonomously select targets for attack.

India has pursued a comprehensive approach to military AI integration, establishing the Quantum Lab and Artificial Intelligence Center. The country's focus on autonomous combat vehicles and AI-powered surveillance platforms reflects its strategic response to regional security challenges, particularly regarding relations with China and Pakistan ("Artificial Intelligence Arms Race" 2025).

The integration of AI into statecraft represents more than a technological shift—it signals a fundamental change in how nations project power and influence in the 21st century. As AI continues to reshape international relations, nations face complex challenges balancing technological advancement with ethical considerations. The proliferation of AI in diplomatic and military applications raises critical questions about surveillance, autonomous warfare, and the future of international cooperation.

This transformation of global diplomacy and security through AI will likely accelerate as technologies mature and new applications emerge. As these systems become more sophisticated, the need for international frameworks governing their use becomes increasingly urgent. How nations navigate this changing landscape while addressing ethical concerns and maintaining international stability may define the next era of international relations.

BUILDING TECHNOLOGICAL RESILIENCE IN DIPLOMATIC OPERATIONS

The resilience of DT systems has become fundamental to maintaining continuous diplomatic operations in an uncertain world. Beyond protecting against threats, missions must ensure their technological infrastructure can adapt to changing circumstances, recover from disruptions, and continue supporting critical diplomatic functions under any conditions. This resilience extends across all areas of diplomatic work, from maintaining secure political communications during crises to ensuring uninterrupted consular services for citizens in need (Hedling & Bremberg 2021, Lacy 2024, Mueller et al. 2023).

AI could play a crucial role in building this resilience through predictive maintenance and adaptive response capabilities. AI systems might anticipate potential points of failure in communications infrastructure before they affect diplomatic operations, allowing preventive measures to be taken. They could automatically reroute network traffic during disruptions, ensuring that essential economic and political reporting continues uninterrupted. In consular operations, redundant systems backed by AI could maintain service delivery even during local network outages or cyber incidents (Bjola, Cassidy, & Manor 2022, Haseley et al. 2023, U.S. Department of State 2023).

The concept of resilience must extend beyond technical systems to encompass organizational adaptability. Diplomatic missions need technology that can support rapid shifts in operations, whether scaling up during crises or adapting to new diplomatic initiatives. Public affairs teams require platforms that remain effective even under heavy load or attempted disruption. Management sections need systems that can maintain essential services while adapting to changing mission requirements. This organizational resilience depends on technology that is both robust and flexible (Höne et al. 2019a, 2019b, Doubleday 2024a, 2024b, U.S. Department of State 2024a, 2024b, 2024c, 2024d).

Creating this resilience requires a careful balance between automation and human oversight. While AI could enhance system monitoring and incident response, experienced DT officers must retain the ability to override automated systems when necessary. The goal is not to remove human judgment but to augment it with technological capabilities that make diplomatic operations more resistant to disruption. This human-centered approach to technological resilience ensures that diplomatic missions can maintain their essential functions while adapting to new challenges and opportunities (Stanzel & Voelsen 2022, Pokhriyal & Koebe, 2023, Grottola 2021).

LLMS: EMPOWERING DT

Building on our exploration of LLMs across diplomatic functions—from general diplomatic work, leadership, political affairs, economic affairs, management operations, consular services, public affairs, and security operations—we now examine their specific applications in DT. While previous chapters demonstrated these tools' value in various diplomatic roles, technology officers face unique challenges in managing complex technical infrastructure while maintaining operational security and reliability.

Technology operations demand exceptional precision in technical documentation and system management, particularly when developing infrastructure plans, maintenance procedures, and troubleshooting guides. LLMs excel at helping technology officers create clear, actionable technical documentation while carefully avoiding sensitive system details. This capability proves particularly valuable when developing general technical guidelines, documenting standard procedures, or creating training materials that preserve operational security.

Infrastructure planning represents another key application unique to DT. Building on the organizational approaches discussed in earlier chapters, technology officers can use LLMs to develop comprehensive technology roadmaps, create system architecture documentation, and generate materials that enhance technical understanding while maintaining appropriate information security. This capability particularly shines when creating content that needs to explain complex technical concepts while preserving operational security.

Project management in technology operations benefits from LLM capabilities in new ways. Beyond the documentation support explored in previous chapters, these tools can help technology officers structure project plans, develop technical specifications, and establish implementation timelines while maintaining security awareness. This proves especially valuable during planning phases when developing generalized project frameworks and coordination plans.

However, technology operations demand special attention to certain limitations beyond those discussed previously. The sensitive nature of DT infrastructure requires extreme caution in how these tools are used. Officers must be particularly mindful of never including specific system configurations, network details, or security protocols in their prompts or interactions with these systems.

PUTTING LLMS TO WORK FOR DT OFFICERS

Building on prompt engineering practices established in previous chapters, let's explore how technology officers can craft effective prompts for their specific needs. While earlier chapters covered diplomatic communications broadly, technology operations require particular attention to maintaining operational security while developing effective technical documentation and planning materials.

When creating technical documentation, frame prompts to ensure both clarity and appropriate information security:

> Help me draft general technical guidelines for secure email use. Include: 1) basic email security principles, 2) general best practices for handling attachments, 3) guidelines for recognizing phishing attempts, and 4) steps for reporting suspicious messages. Use clear technical language while keeping all guidance at a general level appropriate for end users.

For infrastructure planning documentation, structure prompts to maintain security while providing clear guidance:

> I need to create a general technology infrastructure planning guide. Develop sections covering: 1) basic principles for system architecture, 2) general considerations for redundancy and failover, 3) standard approaches to capacity planning, and 4) typical maintenance considerations. Ensure all content remains high-level without revealing specific configurations or sensitive details.

For project management materials, focus prompts on structure while protecting operational details:

> Help me develop a general technology project management framework. Include: 1) standard project phases and milestones, 2) typical resource planning considerations, 3) common risk management approaches, and 4) general quality assurance principles. Keep all content at a process level without referencing specific systems or configurations.

Technology officers should particularly focus prompts on:

- Creating general technical documentation
- Developing system architecture plans
- Establishing project management frameworks
- Enhancing technical training materials
- Maintaining strict operational security

These applications extend beyond the foundational capabilities covered in previous chapters to address the specific needs of technology operations. The key is maintaining appropriate operational security while ensuring content effectively supports technology management and planning.

ADVANCED AI USE CASES FOR DT

Building on the foundational AI applications explored in Chapter 1, the leadership use cases from Chapter 2, the political applications in Chapter 3, the economic tools examined in Chapter 4, the management systems discussed in Chapter 5, the consular services enhanced in Chapter 6, the public affairs capabilities outlined in Chapter 7, and the security operations strengthened in Chapter 8, we now examine advanced AI solutions specifically designed for DT. While previous chapters demonstrated how AI can enhance various aspects of diplomatic work, technology operations present unique opportunities for leveraging AI to manage infrastructure, optimize systems, and ensure operational continuity.

The integration of AI into technology operations requires particular attention to system security, operational reliability, and the preservation of human oversight in critical technical decisions. From automated network management and predictive maintenance to system optimization and incident response coordination, these use cases demonstrate how AI can transform technology operations while maintaining the crucial role of human expertise in managing diplomatic infrastructure.

Each of these applications must carefully balance the power of AI with the need for operational security, human oversight, and the protection of sensitive infrastructure. The goal is not to replace human judgment in technology operations but to enhance the capabilities of technology professionals while maintaining the highest standards of diplomatic infrastructure management.

AI-Driven Cybersecurity

A digital shield that spots and stops cyber attacks in real-time.

The traditional approach to diplomatic cybersecurity relies heavily on static defenses and human analysts monitoring network traffic and system logs. Security teams often struggle with alert fatigue, delayed response times, and the challenge of processing vast amounts of data manually. This creates vulnerabilities as sophisticated state-sponsored actors and criminal networks deploy increasingly advanced attack methods faster than human analysts can detect and respond to them.

AI cybersecurity systems transform this paradigm through continuous monitoring, pattern recognition, and automated response capabilities. Machine learning algorithms analyze network behavior to establish baselines and flag anomalies in real time, while natural language processing helps identify sophisticated phishing attempts. Key technologies include behavioral analytics for user activity monitoring, automated threat detection systems, and predictive analytics for vulnerability assessment. However, challenges include the risk of false positives, the need for high-quality training data, and the potential for adversaries to manipulate AI systems through adversarial attacks.

Success metrics include reduction in mean time to detect (MTTD) and respond (MTTR) to threats, decrease in successful breaches, and improved analyst productivity. A balanced approach integrates AI's rapid detection capabilities with human expertise for strategic decision-making. For example, during a coordinated cyberattack, AI systems might automatically block suspicious traffic patterns while alerting human analysts who can assess the broader geopolitical context and determine appropriate diplomatic responses. This ensures both rapid protection and thoughtful strategic consideration (Lacy 2024, Mueller et al. 2023, Kello 2024, Simić 2021).

Predictive Analytics for Crisis Management

A crystal ball that warns about problems before they become crises.

Traditional crisis management in diplomatic missions relies on historical precedents, manual monitoring of various information sources, and reactive response protocols. This approach often leads to delayed recognition of emerging crises, suboptimal resource allocation, and challenges in coordinating multifaceted responses across different mission departments. The lag between crisis development and response can significantly impact mission effectiveness and safety.

AI-powered predictive analytics revolutionizes crisis management by integrating diverse data streams—including social media, weather patterns, economic indicators, and political events—to forecast potential crises before they fully develop. Machine learning models identify subtle patterns and correlations that might escape human attention, while natural language processing analyzes sentiment and discourse patterns to detect social unrest. Key challenges include data quality and integration issues, the need to avoid false alarms, and ensuring cultural sensitivity in analysis.

The effectiveness of predictive analytics can be measured through metrics like early warning accuracy, crisis prevention rate, and response time improvement. A successful implementation balances AI predictions with human judgment—for instance, during political unrest, AI might flag concerning social media patterns, but experienced diplomats evaluate the cultural and political context to determine appropriate responses. This hybrid approach ensures both rapid identification of potential crises and nuanced understanding of local dynamics (Bjola, Cassidy, & Manor 2022, Haseley et al. 2023, United Nations Global Pulse 2019).

DYNAMIC CONSULAR SERVICES

A smart scheduler that makes visa and passport services run smoother.

Current consular services often operate through rigid, manual processes that struggle to handle volume fluctuations and complex cases efficiently. Staff spend significant time on routine tasks like appointment scheduling and document verification, while citizens face long wait times and inconsistent service experiences. Traditional systems lack the flexibility to adapt to changing circumstances or optimize resource allocation based on demand patterns.

AI transforms consular services through intelligent automation and dynamic resource allocation. Natural language processing powers chatbots for routine inquiries, machine learning optimizes appointment scheduling based on historical patterns, and automated document processing systems handle standard applications. However, implementation challenges include ensuring accessibility for all citizens, maintaining privacy standards, and avoiding bias in automated decisions.

Success is measured through metrics like processing time reduction, citizen satisfaction rates, and staff productivity improvement. A balanced approach maintains human oversight for complex cases while leveraging AI for routine tasks. For example, during peak travel seasons, AI systems might automatically adjust staffing schedules and appointment slots based on predicted demand, while ensuring complex cases receive personal attention from experienced consular officers. This maintains both efficiency and service quality (U.S. Department of State 2024a, 2024b, 2024c, 2024d, Collins 2024, Doubleday 2024).

AI-ENHANCED PUBLIC ENGAGEMENT

A message optimizer that helps embassies connect better with local communities.

Traditional public diplomacy relies on standardized messaging and limited feedback mechanisms, often struggling to adapt to rapidly changing public sentiment or cultural nuances. Missions typically depend on manual monitoring of media coverage and periodic surveys, resulting in delayed responses to emerging issues and missed opportunities for meaningful engagement.

AI enhances public engagement through real-time sentiment analysis, automated content optimization, and predictive analytics for campaign planning. Natural language processing analyzes public discourse across multiple platforms and languages, while machine learning models help tailor messages for different audiences. Major challenges include ensuring cultural sensitivity, maintaining authentic human connection, and avoiding echo chamber effects in digital diplomacy.

Effectiveness is measured through engagement metrics, sentiment trends, and campaign impact assessments. A successful approach combines AI's analytical capabilities with human diplomatic expertise. For instance, during a public diplomacy campaign, AI might identify trending topics and sentiment patterns, while experienced diplomats craft culturally appropriate messages that advance mission objectives. This ensures both responsiveness and diplomatic finesse (Di Martino & Ford 2024, Huang & Arceneaux 2024, Manor 2019, Fjällhed et al. 2024).

PREDICTIVE MAINTENANCE FOR IT INFRASTRUCTURE

A system doctor that spots IT problems before they cause breakdowns.

Traditional IT maintenance in diplomatic missions often follows fixed schedules or relies on reactive responses to failures, leading to inefficient resource use and potential service disruptions. Manual monitoring systems struggle to predict equipment failures or optimize maintenance timing, resulting in either premature or delayed interventions.

AI-powered predictive maintenance uses sensor data and machine learning to forecast potential failures and optimize maintenance schedules. IoT devices monitor equipment health in real time, while AI models analyze performance patterns to predict maintenance needs. Key challenges include sensor deployment in secure environments, data integration across legacy systems, and ensuring maintenance activities don't compromise security protocols.

Success metrics include reduction in unplanned downtime, maintenance cost savings, and improved system reliability. An effective implementation balances automated monitoring with human expertise. For example, AI systems might flag potential server issues based on performance metrics, while IT specialists evaluate security implications and coordinate appropriate intervention timing. This ensures both proactive maintenance and security compliance (Black 2025, Siebrits et al. 2025).

AUTOMATED COMPLIANCE MONITORING

A rule checker that makes sure embassy operations follow all regulations.

Traditional compliance monitoring in diplomatic missions involves manual audits, periodic reviews, and paper-based tracking systems. This approach is time-consuming, prone to human error, and often fails to catch compliance issues in real time, leading to increased risk exposure and resource inefficiency.

AI transforms compliance monitoring through continuous automated surveillance, pattern recognition, and predictive analytics. Natural language processing analyzes documents and communications for compliance violations, while machine learning models identify unusual patterns that might indicate non-compliance. Significant challenges include ensuring privacy protection, maintaining accuracy across different regulatory frameworks, and avoiding over-reliance on automated systems.

Success is measured through metrics like violation detection rate, response time improvement, and audit efficiency. A balanced approach combines AI's monitoring capabilities with human judgment for complex compliance decisions. For instance, AI systems might automatically flag potential procurement violations, while compliance officers review the context and determine appropriate responses. This ensures both vigilant oversight and nuanced interpretation of regulations (U.S. Department of Justice 2024, Baines 2024).

REAL-TIME LANGUAGE TRANSLATION

A universal translator that helps diplomats communicate across languages.

Traditional diplomatic translation relies heavily on human interpreters and pre-scheduled translation services, creating bottlenecks in communication and limiting spontaneous interaction across language barriers. This approach can delay important communications and strain limited interpreter resources.

AI-powered translation uses neural machine translation and natural language processing to provide immediate, context-aware translation services. These systems can handle multiple languages simultaneously, adapt to specialized diplomatic vocabulary, and improve accuracy through continuous learning. Key challenges include maintaining accuracy for nuanced diplomatic communication, ensuring cultural sensitivity, and protecting confidential discussions.

Success metrics include translation accuracy rates, response time improvement, and user satisfaction scores. An effective implementation combines AI translation for routine communication with human interpreters for sensitive discussions. For example, AI might handle initial document translation and informal conversations, while professional interpreters focus on high-stakes negotiations and cultural mediation. This ensures both efficiency and diplomatic precision (Adler-Nissen & Eggeling 2024, Stanzel & Voelsen 2022).

AI FOR ASSET AND RESOURCE OPTIMIZATION

A resource manager that makes sure embassy equipment is used efficiently.

Traditional resource management in diplomatic missions often relies on fixed allocation schedules and manual tracking systems, leading to inefficient use of vehicles, energy, and other assets. This approach struggles to adapt to changing needs and often results in either resource shortages or underutilization.

AI transforms resource management through predictive analytics and dynamic allocation systems. Machine learning models analyze usage patterns to optimize resource distribution, while IoT sensors provide real-time monitoring of asset utilization. Major challenges include integrating legacy systems, ensuring security of connected devices, and maintaining flexibility for diplomatic priorities.

Success is measured through metrics like resource utilization rates, cost savings, and service delivery improvement. A balanced approach combines AI's optimization capabilities with human oversight for strategic decisions. For instance, AI might recommend vehicle fleet adjustments based on usage patterns, while management evaluates diplomatic implications and security requirements. This ensures both efficiency and mission effectiveness (Alder 2025, U.S. Department of State 2023)

AI-DRIVEN DOCUMENT VERIFICATION

A document detective that quickly spots real documents from fakes.

Traditional document verification in diplomatic missions involves manual review processes that are time-consuming and susceptible to human error. Staff must physically examine documents, cross-reference multiple databases, and rely on experience to detect fraudulent submissions.

AI enhances document verification through optical character recognition, machine learning-based fraud detection, and automated cross-referencing capabilities. These systems can quickly analyze security features, detect inconsistencies, and verify information across multiple sources. Key challenges include maintaining accuracy across different document types, ensuring privacy protection, and avoiding bias in automated assessments.

Success metrics include verification speed improvement, fraud detection rates, and processing accuracy. An effective implementation balances automated screening with human expertise for complex cases. For example, AI might handle initial document screening and routine verification, while experienced staff focus on suspicious cases and final approvals. This ensures both efficiency and security in document processing (U.S. Department of State 2024a, 2024b, 2024c, 2024d, Collins 2024).

AI-ASSISTED TRAINING SIMULATIONS

A virtual practice ground that teaches real diplomatic skills.

Traditional diplomatic training often relies on static scenarios, role-playing exercises, and standardized curricula that may not adequately prepare staff for complex real-world situations. This approach struggles to provide personalized learning experiences or adapt to emerging diplomatic challenges.

AI transforms training through adaptive learning systems, realistic simulations, and personalized feedback mechanisms. Machine learning models adjust scenario difficulty based on learner performance, while natural language processing enables dynamic interaction in simulated diplomatic situations. Major challenges include creating realistic scenarios, ensuring cultural sensitivity, and maintaining engagement in virtual environments.

Success is measured through learning outcome improvements, skill retention rates, and trainee satisfaction scores. A balanced approach combines AI's adaptive capabilities with experienced instructor guidance. For instance, AI might generate and adapt training scenarios, while seasoned diplomats provide context and mentor trainees through complex diplomatic considerations. This ensures both comprehensive skill development and practical diplomatic insight (Grottola 2021, Hamidouche 2021).

LIMITATIONS AND FUTURE RESEARCH DIRECTIONS

As AI transforms DT operations, several fundamental limitations and research gaps emerge that warrant careful examination. These challenges extend beyond simple technical constraints to encompass complex operational, security, and diplomatic considerations that shape how missions can effectively deploy AI solutions.

THE CHALLENGE OF OPERATIONAL RESILIENCE

Perhaps, the most pressing limitation lies in ensuring continuous diplomatic operations when AI systems face disruption or failure. While AI offers powerful capabilities for managing diplomatic infrastructure, its integration creates new dependencies that could affect mission-critical systems. Consider a diplomatic facility relying on AI-enhanced network management—if the AI system fails during a crisis, the mission must maintain essential communications while troubleshooting the technical issue. This challenge becomes particularly acute when multiple AI systems interact, creating the potential for cascade failures that could affect everything from secure communications to consular services.

Future research must examine how diplomatic missions can architect AI systems with appropriate redundancy and isolation while maintaining their integrated benefits. This includes developing frameworks for graceful system degradation that ensure core diplomatic functions continue even when AI capabilities are compromised.

SECURITY AND CLASSIFICATION BOUNDARIES

The integration of AI across different security classification levels presents unique challenges that current implementations have not fully addressed. Diplomatic missions handle information ranging from unclassified public communications to highly sensitive intelligence, requiring careful separation between systems and networks. However, AI's effectiveness often depends on accessing broad datasets that may span classification boundaries. A machine learning system trained to detect cyber threats, for instance, might need to analyze patterns across both classified and unclassified networks to be fully effective.

Research priorities in this area should focus on developing architectures that enable AI systems to operate effectively across security boundaries while maintaining strict information compartmentalization. This includes studying how to train AI models using data from multiple classification levels without compromising sensitive information.

CULTURAL AND DIPLOMATIC IMPLICATIONS

The deployment of AI in DT raises profound questions about sovereignty and trust that deserve deeper investigation. Host nations may view certain AI capabilities—particularly in areas like surveillance or data analysis—as potential threats to their technological sovereignty. A mission implementing AI-enhanced security systems might face pushback from local authorities concerned about the scope and capability of these systems.

Future research must examine how missions can implement advanced AI capabilities while respecting host nation concerns and maintaining diplomatic relationships. This includes developing frameworks for transparent AI deployment that build trust without compromising operational security.

TECHNICAL EXPERTISE AND HUMAN CAPITAL

The growing sophistication of AI systems creates a widening gap between system capabilities and available technical expertise within diplomatic services. Unlike traditional IT systems, AI implementations often require specialized knowledge in areas like machine learning, data science, and AI operations. This expertise gap becomes particularly challenging when missions need to maintain and adapt AI systems to evolving diplomatic requirements.

Research should explore how diplomatic services can develop and retain technical talent while maintaining their core diplomatic focus. This includes examining new models for technical training, career development, and collaboration with private sector expertise.

ENVIRONMENTAL AND RESOURCE SUSTAINABILITY

As diplomatic missions increasingly embrace sustainability goals, the environmental impact of AI systems requires careful consideration. Modern AI implementations, particularly in areas like machine learning and data analysis, can demand significant computational resources and energy consumption. A mission's AI infrastructure might conflict with its sustainability commitments or strain local power resources in challenging environments.

Future research directions should examine how to develop more efficient AI architectures that align with diplomatic missions' environmental responsibilities. This includes studying approaches to optimize AI resource consumption while maintaining system effectiveness.

By addressing these limitations through focused research and practical innovation, diplomatic missions can work toward more effective and responsible integration of AI into their technological infrastructure. Success requires unprecedented collaboration between technologists, diplomats, and security experts to develop solutions that enhance diplomatic capabilities while preserving operational security and effectiveness.

The path forward demands careful attention to both immediate operational needs and long-term strategic implications. As AI capabilities continue to evolve, maintaining this balance will prove crucial for ensuring that technological innovation serves rather than hinders diplomatic objectives.

CONCLUSION

The integration of AI into DT represents a fundamental transformation in how missions operate, communicate, and advance their objectives in an increasingly digital world. As this chapter has illustrated, AI is not merely automating existing processes but fundamentally enhancing how diplomatic missions manage their technological infrastructure—from cybersecurity and predictive maintenance to crisis management and secure communications. This technological evolution enables missions to anticipate challenges, optimize resources, and maintain robust operations while protecting sensitive diplomatic functions.

The evolution of DT through AI integration reveals several critical insights. First, successful implementation requires careful balance between innovation and security. While AI offers unprecedented capabilities for enhancing diplomatic operations, it must be deployed in ways that protect sensitive communications, maintain operational security, and preserve the confidentiality essential to diplomatic work. Second, the adoption of AI tools must be guided by robust frameworks that ensure reliability, scalability, and resilience while protecting against emerging threats.

Looking ahead, the future of DT lies in the thoughtful integration of AI capabilities with existing diplomatic infrastructure. As these technologies continue to advance, DT officers will need to effectively leverage AI tools while maintaining the security and reliability that diplomatic missions require. Through careful attention to security considerations and steadfast commitment to diplomatic principles, missions can continue to evolve their technological capabilities while maintaining the robust operations essential to modern diplomacy.

The transformative impact of AI in DT extends beyond individual systems to the broader practice of diplomacy itself. By enabling more sophisticated cybersecurity measures, enhanced predictive maintenance capabilities, and improved resource optimization, AI-powered technological infrastructure strengthens the foundation upon which modern diplomacy operates. This technological evolution supports not just operational efficiency but the fundamental mission of diplomacy: conducting international relations effectively and securely in an increasingly complex digital landscape.

DT provides the foundation for modern diplomacy, but AI's full potential is unlocked when it facilitates collaboration across agencies and disciplines. The next chapter examines how AI is fostering whole-of-government approaches, breaking down silos, and enabling more integrated and effective diplomatic responses to global challenges.

DISCUSSION SCENARIOS AND QUESTIONS

This set of scenarios explores how AI is transforming the technological foundation of diplomacy. Readers will consider the opportunities and risks of AI-driven innovations, from cybersecurity and digital infrastructure to automation and secure communications, while reflecting on the role of human oversight in maintaining diplomatic integrity.

1. The role of LLMs in diplomatic communications

    Scenario: You've introduced an LLM to assist your embassy with drafting diplomatic documents, speeches, and communications. The LLM significantly reduces workloads but occasionally generates culturally inappropriate or inaccurate phrases. During a high-level negotiation, an LLM-drafted report inadvertently causes offense by misphrasing a key idea, straining trust in the relationship. Your colleagues end up blaming you for it, saying that the technology you provided them with set them up for failure.

Questions: How can you create workflows that fully leverage the speed and efficiency of LLMs while ensuring cultural and contextual accuracy in outputs? What processes can you implement to ensure that LLM-generated content is rigorously reviewed for high-stakes scenarios without undermining the efficiency it offers? How might the increased reliance on LLMs affect your colleagues' ability to maintain and develop their own diplomatic writing skills, and how could you mitigate this?

2. Balancing transparency and security in AI-powered systems

Scenario: Your embassy implements an AI-based encryption system for secure communication. The host government finds out and expresses concern that this technology might also enable covert surveillance of their officials, demanding full transparency about how the system works. Sharing these details could alleviate tensions but might expose vulnerabilities that adversaries could exploit, putting embassy operations at risk.

Questions: How can you effectively address the host government's concerns while ensuring the confidentiality and integrity of the encryption system? What steps could you take to foster trust in the AI system without revealing sensitive information that could be misused? How would you balance the competing priorities of maintaining diplomatic relationships and safeguarding your country's technological assets?

3. Ethical dilemmas in AI for cyber threat detection

Scenario: Your embassy's AI system flags communications from local journalists and activists as suspicious due to their encrypted messages and politically sensitive discussions. While the AI suggests their activity may pose a security risk, these individuals are known for legitimate criticism of the host government and show no proven malicious intent. Acting on the AI's findings could protect the embassy but risks endangering these individuals, damaging their reputations, and making the embassy appear complicit in suppressing free speech. You must decide how to protect the embassy while upholding your country's values.

Questions: How can you balance the embassy's security needs with protecting the rights of individuals flagged by the AI? How do you decide whether to act on AI findings that may conflict with your country's commitment to human rights? What oversight can you create to ensure AI decisions are fair and responsible?

4. AI for operational efficiency and ethical trade-offs

Scenario: Your embassy uses an AI system to manage resources, such as deciding how to budget for IT upgrades and equipment maintenance. The AI is programmed to prioritize saving money, so it often recommends delaying equipment replacements or cutting costs in areas that are harder to measure, like staff satisfaction. Over time, staff become frustrated with outdated tools, feeling like their needs are being ignored. While the AI has improved efficiency on paper and reduced spending, it's creating tension within the team and lowering morale.

Questions: How can you adjust the AI system so it balances saving money with meeting staff needs and ensuring smooth operations? What steps can you take to make sure the AI values long-term stability and human concerns, even if these are harder to measure? How would you explain the trade-offs of using an AI system to your staff in a way that builds trust and cooperation?

5. AI in crisis management: balancing speed and judgment

Scenario: Your embassy uses an AI system to assist during crises, such as natural disasters or political unrest. In a sudden security crisis, the AI recommends an evacuation plan that prioritizes securing sensitive digital assets over staff, arguing the long-term risks of data loss outweigh the delay in evacuating personnel. Your team strongly disagrees, insisting that human lives must come first, even if it slows the evacuation. Time is running out, and you must decide whether to follow the AI's plan or trust your team's judgment.

Questions: How do you decide whether to trust AI recommendations during high-pressure crises when lives and critical assets are at stake? What safeguards can you put in place to ensure that AI systems consider ethical priorities, like human safety, alongside strategic calculations? How can you strike a balance between the speed of AI-driven decision-making and the need for human oversight during emergencies?

10 AI and Interdisciplinary Diplomacy
Leveraging AI for Whole-of-Government Action

The enhancing and collaborative potential that we envision stands in stark contrast to the zero-sum predictions of what AI will do to our society and organizations. Instead, we believe that greater productivity and the automation of cognitively routine work is a boon, not a threat.

—Garry Kasparov, Chess Grandmaster (2021)

Can we use technology to overcome the challenges that people, organizations, and countries face? That's really the pursuit here.

—Satya Nadella, CEO of Microsoft (2023)

The greatest gains are achieved when you cross fields. The same will be true when you have a polymath in your pocket.

—Eric Schmidt, former Google Chairman (2024)

Diplomacy in the 21st century has evolved into a complex, interconnected endeavor that no single agency, discipline, or government can manage alone. The accelerating pace of globalization, coupled with crises like pandemics, climate change, and cybersecurity threats, demands solutions that transcend traditional boundaries and draw on the collective expertise of diverse stakeholders. In this landscape, success depends on breaking down silos and embracing a cross-disciplinary, interagency approach—one that leverages the transformative power of artificial intelligence (AI). By synthesizing vast amounts of data from domains such as intelligence, health, economics, and public sentiment, AI enables diplomats to navigate complexity with clarity, precision, and speed. It doesn't just analyze—it unifies, harmonizing inputs from multiple sectors to craft cohesive strategies for challenges ranging from regional conflicts to treaty compliance.

This interdisciplinary collaboration is not just advantageous; it is essential. Global challenges require the integration of expertise across fields—scientists, policymakers, humanitarian organizations, and legal experts must work in concert to tackle issues like climate change, public health crises, and international security. AI accelerates and amplifies these efforts, providing tools to innovate and coordinate effectively. Yet, the promise of AI-driven diplomacy is not without its challenges. Ethical concerns

 DOI: 10.1201/9781003612308-10

such as data privacy, algorithmic bias, and equitable access must be addressed, and deliberate frameworks for communication, governance, and trust-building are critical to ensure AI serves all stakeholders equitably. This chapter explores how AI acts as a bridge across disciplines, offering a roadmap for leveraging its potential while navigating the ethical and operational complexities of a rapidly evolving world.

VIGNETTE AI-Enhanced Embassy in the Republic of Z

A devastating cyclone has struck the coastal regions of the Republic of Z, causing massive flooding, displacing tens of thousands, and threatening regional stability. The embassy activates an all-hands-on-deck response, leveraging AI to coordinate a whole-of-government approach that unites every agency represented at the mission.

The Crisis Management Platform, powered by advanced AI, becomes the nerve center of operations. It integrates real-time satellite data from the Defense Attaché's Office and the National Intelligence Coordination Office to map the cyclone's destruction. Predictive models identify areas at greatest risk for secondary disasters, such as landslides or disease outbreaks.

In the Consular Section, AI systems cross-reference passport databases, flight itineraries, and social media check-ins to locate stranded citizens and provide automated updates to families. Chatbots field thousands of inquiries in multiple languages, allowing officers to focus on complex, high-priority cases such as medical evacuations.

The Economic Section uses AI-driven trade flow analysis to evaluate disruptions to supply chains, particularly agricultural exports vital to the region. They coordinate with the Agricultural Trade and Development Agency, which deploys AI to assess crop damage and prioritize emergency food shipments. Simultaneously, the Export Finance Organization prepares economic relief packages to stabilize local businesses impacted by the disaster.

From the Defense and Security Agencies, the Military Attaché directs military logistics for relief operations, using AI to optimize routes for aid convoys and identify safe zones for displaced populations. The Embassy Security Detachment, working alongside local authorities, relies on predictive threat analysis to guard against criminal activity targeting relief distribution points. The Border and Immigration Agency deploys automated systems at border checkpoints to facilitate the safe transit of refugees while flagging potential security risks.

Public health experts from the Disease Control Agency use AI to predict outbreaks of waterborne diseases, guiding preemptive vaccination and treatment campaigns. The Medical Research Collaboration Institute deploys telemedicine platforms, enabling doctors from partner nations to remotely diagnose and treat patients.

The Public Affairs Section mobilizes an AI-driven media monitoring system to counter disinformation spreading online, such as false claims about aid favoritism or conspiracies about foreign involvement. They coordinate with the

International Media and Communications Authority to disseminate accurate, multilingual updates via trusted influencers and local media.

In the background, the Management Section ensures the embassy itself remains operational despite the crisis. AI-driven maintenance systems monitor critical infrastructure, while workforce sentiment tools identify stress points among embassy staff, prompting well-timed morale boosters.

The Ambassador convenes daily interagency briefings, guided by AI-generated dashboards that synthesize data streams into actionable insights. Recommendations are made in real-time, from redirecting relief supplies based on evolving needs to deploying additional resources to regions showing signs of unrest.

Every agency's efforts interlock, enabled by the seamless integration of AI. The crisis that once seemed insurmountable is managed with precision, agility, and a unified vision. As relief efforts stabilize the situation, the embassy's success becomes a model for future AI-driven interagency diplomacy.

The Republic of Z's response exemplifies the complexities of modern crises that demand a whole-of-government approach. From climate disasters to geopolitical conflicts, today's challenges require embassies to coordinate across diverse sectors and disciplines. In the Age of AI, these collaborations are not only possible—they are exponentially enhanced by technology.

This chapter delves into how AI empowers interdisciplinary and interagency diplomacy, offering tools to bridge gaps between agencies, harmonize strategies, and act decisively in complex scenarios. By examining real-world applications and ethical considerations, it highlights how AI transforms embassies into unified hubs of expertise, capable of addressing the interconnected challenges of the modern era.

AI AS A BRIDGE: THE FUTURE OF INTERDISCIPLINARY DIPLOMACY

In the rapidly evolving landscape of global diplomacy, AI stands as more than just a technological tool—it serves as a crucial bridge connecting diverse disciplines, expertise, and agencies. This transformative power becomes especially evident when examining how AI approaches complex global challenges that no single field can address alone. By synthesizing vast amounts of data and providing actionable insights, AI enables diplomats to navigate complexity with unprecedented precision and speed, fundamentally changing how nations collaborate and solve problems (Bjola & Kornprobst 2024).

Consider the challenge of treaty compliance, where AI demonstrates its unique ability to synthesize multiple streams of information (Baele et al. 2024). Modern AI systems can simultaneously analyze satellite imagery, economic transactions, and legal documentation to assess whether nations are adhering to international agreements. This integration doesn't merely streamline monitoring—it creates a new paradigm of transparency that builds trust among nations. The same AI systems can alert relevant stakeholders to potential violations while providing context that helps diplomats distinguish between intentional breaches and unintentional oversights, allowing for more nuanced and effective diplomatic responses (Jensen, Whyte, & Cuomo

2020). This capability transforms treaty monitoring from a periodic check-up into a continuous, proactive process that can prevent violations before they escalate into diplomatic crises.

The power of AI-driven integration becomes even more apparent during crises. During a regional pandemic, for instance, public health agencies must coordinate with defense organizations managing logistics and economic policymakers stabilizing supply chains. AI serves as the connective tissue between these efforts, processing real-time data from all domains to help diplomats prioritize actions and allocate resources effectively. What once required weeks of interagency meetings might now be accomplished in hours, with AI providing a comprehensive view of the situation that no single agency could achieve alone. This acceleration of response time can mean the difference between containing a crisis and watching it spiral out of control, particularly in situations where every hour counts, such as natural disasters or disease outbreaks (Pokhriyal & Koebe 2023).

BUILDING FRAMEWORKS FOR COLLABORATIVE SUCCESS

The promise of AI in diplomacy, however, cannot be realized through technology alone. Success requires carefully designed frameworks that address the human, organizational, and institutional factors that enable effective cooperation (Bjola & Manor 2024a, 2024b, Manor & Pamment 2024). These frameworks must be built upon a foundation of shared understanding and trust, with clear protocols for data sharing, decision-making, and crisis response. The challenge lies not just in implementing the technology, but in creating systems that can adapt to the evolving nature of diplomatic challenges while maintaining security and reliability (Baines 2024).

At the heart of successful collaboration lies the need for shared AI platforms that enable real-time data integration and analysis. These platforms serve as neutral spaces where diverse agencies can pool their resources and align their strategies. During humanitarian crises, for example, these shared platforms allow defense agencies to integrate their satellite imagery with epidemiological data from public health organizations and economic forecasts from trade ministries (Hedling & Bremberg 2021). This integration enables diplomats to craft comprehensive responses that address immediate needs while considering long-term stability. The key is creating systems that are both sophisticated enough to handle complex data and accessible enough for all stakeholders to use effectively while maintaining the highest standards of security and privacy protection.

The human element remains crucial in this technological landscape. Cross-training programs that bring together professionals from diverse fields will prove essential in building the relationships and mutual understanding necessary for sustained collaboration. When agricultural experts and defense analysts work together to explore how AI can improve food security in conflict zones, they develop not just technical skills but also the trust and shared vocabulary necessary for effective cooperation. These human connections often prove as valuable as the technological tools themselves, creating networks of expertise that can be rapidly mobilized during crises (Crilley 2024). Moreover, these collaborative experiences help break down traditional institutional barriers, fostering a more integrated approach to global challenges.

HISTORICAL AI USE CASE EXAMPLES
IN INTERDISCIPLINARY DIPLOMACY

Interdisciplinary diplomacy leverages collaboration across multiple sectors, disciplines, and government agencies to address complex global challenges. AI has played a pivotal role in facilitating such collaboration, offering tools to unify diverse datasets, improve decision-making, and align efforts across various stakeholders. This section highlights historical examples where AI has enabled interdisciplinary approaches to diplomacy.

The United Nations High Commissioner for Refugees (UNHCR) launched Project Jetson in 2017 to forecast population displacement trends in Somalia (United Nations Global Pulse 2019). This initiative exemplifies interdisciplinary diplomacy, combining expertise from humanitarian workers, data scientists, and policymakers. AI algorithms analyzed diverse datasets, including climate reports, conflict indicators, and economic metrics, to predict migration flows and inform resource allocation. The success of this project showcased how AI could bridge the gap between humanitarian aid and diplomatic planning, enabling stakeholders to respond proactively to crises (United Nations Global Pulse 2019).

Following the 2007 Estonian cyberattacks, NATO's Cooperative Cyber Defence Centre of Excellence (CCD-COE) in Tallinn demonstrated the power of interdisciplinary collaboration (Kello 2024). AI systems were deployed to integrate data from defense agencies, intelligence networks, and government institutions, enabling a coordinated response to cyber threats. This framework facilitated a whole-of-government approach to cybersecurity, illustrating how AI could unify diverse sectors to address shared security challenges (Kello 2024).

Tuvalu's Digital Nation initiative offers another example of interdisciplinary AI use. Faced with existential threats from climate change, Tuvalu combined inputs from environmental scientists, legal experts, and technologists to create digital replicas of its territory, culture, and governance systems. This AI-driven project enabled Tuvalu to engage with international stakeholders and advocate for climate action effectively. By integrating multiple disciplines, the initiative highlighted AI's potential to address global challenges through collaborative approaches (Yeo 2024).

China's Belt and Road Initiative (BRI) utilized AI to coordinate efforts across infrastructure development, trade negotiations, and public diplomacy. AI tools processed data from diverse sectors to monitor public sentiment, forecast economic trends, and optimize resource allocation. This interdisciplinary approach allowed China to tailor its strategies to regional contexts, although it also raised concerns about ethical transparency and potential overreach (Huang 2022).

During the early stages of the COVID-19 pandemic, the European External Action Service (EEAS) employed AI to integrate data from public health agencies, logistics networks, and diplomatic missions. The system provided real-time insights into the spread of the virus, enabling coordinated efforts to repatriate citizens, distribute medical supplies, and manage cross-border restrictions. This case underscored the value of AI in enhancing interdisciplinary responses to global crises (Pearson & Burgess 2023).

NATO's use of AI-driven predictive analytics during the Russo-Ukrainian War provided another example of interdisciplinary diplomacy. By integrating data from military intelligence, economic analyses, and media monitoring, AI tools informed strategies to counter disinformation and stabilize the region. This effort demonstrated how AI could enhance decision-making across multiple domains, fostering more effective multilateral cooperation (Kello 2023).

While AI offers significant potential in interdisciplinary diplomacy, its deployment raises ethical challenges. For example, China's sentiment analysis tools used in the BRI faced criticism for potentially manipulating public opinion. Similarly, the use of predictive analytics in conflict zones risks reinforcing biases or excluding marginalized voices. To address these challenges, organizations must adopt robust ethical guidelines, prioritize transparency, and ensure diverse stakeholder engagement.

By building on these examples, governments and international organizations can leverage AI to foster interdisciplinary collaboration and address complex diplomatic challenges in a holistic manner (Also see: Roumate 2024, Höne 2019a, 2019b, Tuset Varela 2024.).

ETHICS AND INNOVATION IN THE AI ERA

As AI becomes increasingly central to diplomatic efforts, the ethical dimensions of its use demand careful consideration. The challenge lies not just in preventing misuse of AI systems, but in ensuring they promote equity and fairness across all diplomatic initiatives. This requires constant attention to issues of bias, transparency, and accountability, particularly as AI systems become more sophisticated and their decisions more consequential (Gill 2019).

Bias in AI systems presents a particular challenge in diplomatic contexts. A sentiment analysis tool used in public diplomacy might inadvertently misrepresent the concerns of marginalized groups, leading to policies that reinforce existing inequalities. Similarly, AI systems analyzing climate data could prioritize industrial concerns over the needs of vulnerable populations if their training data isn't appropriately balanced. These challenges require diplomatic teams to maintain constant vigilance, regularly auditing their AI systems and adjusting them to ensure fair representation of all stakeholders. Success in this area means going beyond technical solutions to include diverse voices in the design and implementation of AI systems, ensuring that technology serves the needs of all communities, not just those with the loudest voices or greatest resources (Huang & Arceneaux 2024).

Innovation labs and cross-agency pilots have emerged as crucial spaces for addressing these ethical challenges while pushing the boundaries of what AI can achieve in diplomacy. These controlled environments allow teams to test new approaches and refine them based on real-world feedback. For instance, an AI model originally designed for border security might be adapted for public health applications, such as monitoring the movement of medical supplies during a crisis. These adaptations often reveal unexpected synergies between different diplomatic initiatives, leading to more efficient and effective solutions to complex global challenges. The key is maintaining a balance between innovation and responsibility, ensuring that new applications of AI technology align with diplomatic principles and ethical standards.

LARGE LANGUAGE MODELS: FOSTERING INTERDISCIPLINARY COLLABORATION

Building on our exploration of Large Language Models (LLMs) across diplomatic functions—from general diplomatic work, leadership, political affairs, economic affairs, management operations, consular services, public affairs, security operations, and technology management—we now examine their specific applications in interdisciplinary diplomacy. While previous chapters demonstrated these tools' value in various diplomatic roles, interdisciplinary work presents unique challenges in coordinating across agencies, aligning diverse perspectives, and fostering whole-of-government approaches.

Interagency coordination demands exceptional clarity in communication and documentation, particularly when developing frameworks, protocols, and guidance that must serve multiple stakeholders. LLMs excel at helping diplomatic officers create clear, actionable materials that bridge different organizational cultures while maintaining appropriate boundaries. This capability proves particularly valuable when developing coordination frameworks, establishing shared terminology, or creating materials that need to resonate across different agencies.

Crisis coordination represents another key application unique to interdisciplinary diplomacy. Building on the crisis management approaches discussed in earlier chapters, diplomatic officers can use LLMs to develop comprehensive response frameworks, create multi-agency protocols, and generate materials that enhance coordination while respecting agency mandates. This capability particularly shines when creating content that needs to facilitate collaboration while preserving clear roles and responsibilities.

Strategic planning in interagency contexts benefits from LLM capabilities in new ways. Beyond the planning support explored in previous chapters, these tools can help diplomatic officers structure multi-agency initiatives, develop shared objectives, and establish coordination mechanisms while maintaining appropriate organizational boundaries. This proves especially valuable during planning phases when developing frameworks for collaborative action.

However, interdisciplinary work demands special attention to certain limitations beyond those discussed previously. The multi-stakeholder nature of interagency diplomacy requires extra caution in how these tools are used. Officers must be particularly mindful of respecting agency boundaries, maintaining appropriate information-sharing protocols, and ensuring all content aligns with whole-of-government approaches.

PUTTING LLMS TO WORK FOR INTERDISCIPLINARY DIPLOMACY

Building on prompt engineering practices established in previous chapters, let's explore how diplomatic officers can craft effective prompts for their interagency coordination needs. While earlier chapters covered diplomatic communications broadly, interdisciplinary work requires particular attention to bridging organizational cultures while maintaining appropriate boundaries.

When creating coordination frameworks, frame prompts to ensure clarity across agencies:

> Help me develop an interagency coordination framework for humanitarian response operations. Include: 1) clear roles and responsibilities for different agencies, 2) communication protocols between organizations, 3) resource sharing guidelines, and 4) decision-making processes. Use inclusive language that respects agency mandates while fostering collaboration.

For crisis response protocols, structure prompts to balance coordination with agency autonomy:

> I need to create multi-agency protocols for responding to complex emergencies. Develop: 1) activation triggers and notification procedures, 2) agency-specific response roles, 3) information sharing guidelines, and 4) coordination mechanisms. Ensure the framework enables collaboration while respecting each agency's authority and expertise.

For strategic planning materials, focus prompts on alignment while preserving agency identity:

> Help me create a strategic planning framework for a multi-agency climate resilience initiative. Include: 1) shared objectives that align with different agency missions, 2) collaborative planning processes, 3) resource coordination approaches, and 4) progress tracking methods. Maintain language that promotes unity of effort while acknowledging distinct agency contributions.

Diplomatic officers should particularly focus prompts on:

- Creating inclusive coordination frameworks
- Developing multi-agency protocols
- Establishing shared terminology
- Structuring collaborative processes
- Maintaining appropriate boundaries

These applications extend beyond the foundational capabilities covered in previous chapters to address the specific needs of interdisciplinary diplomacy. The key is promoting collaboration while respecting agency mandates and organizational cultures.

ADVANCED AI USE CASES FOR INTERDISCIPLINARY DIPLOMACY

Building on the foundational AI applications explored in previous chapters—from general diplomatic work through specialized functions like political affairs, economic relations, management operations, consular services, public affairs, security operations, and technology management—we now examine advanced AI solutions specifically designed for interdisciplinary diplomacy. While previous chapters demonstrated how AI can enhance various aspects of diplomatic work, interagency coordination presents unique opportunities for leveraging AI to break down silos, foster collaboration, and enable whole-of-government approaches.

The integration of AI into interdisciplinary diplomacy requires particular attention to organizational dynamics, information-sharing protocols, and the preservation of agency autonomy while promoting collaboration. From multi-agency crisis coordination and shared situational awareness to collaborative planning tools and resource optimization, these use cases demonstrate how AI can transform interagency operations while maintaining the crucial role of human expertise in managing complex diplomatic relationships.

Each of these applications must carefully balance the power of AI with the need to respect agency boundaries, maintain appropriate information sharing, and protect organizational equities. The goal is not to replace agency expertise but to enhance the capabilities of diplomatic professionals while promoting more effective whole-of-government approaches.

GLOBAL PANDEMIC RESPONSE COORDINATION

A disease fighter that helps agencies work together during health crises.

Traditional pandemic response relies on siloed systems where health, logistics, and economic sectors operate independently, leading to delayed responses and uncoordinated efforts. Manual data collection and analysis create bottlenecks, while communication gaps between agencies result in duplicated efforts and resource misallocation. Response times are often measured in days or weeks when hours matter.

AI transforms this through real-time data integration and predictive analytics across multiple domains. Key technologies include machine learning for outbreak prediction, natural language processing for multilingual communication, and neural networks for resource optimization. However, challenges include data privacy concerns, interoperability issues between different agencies' systems, and the need to validate AI predictions in high-stakes health scenarios.

Success can be measured through metrics like time to coordinate cross-agency responses, accuracy of outbreak predictions, and efficiency of resource distribution. For example, during a new outbreak, the AI system might detect unusual hospital admission patterns, automatically alert relevant agencies, and suggest resource allocation plans—but final decisions remain with human experts who can consider broader socio-political implications. KPIs include reduction in response time, improvement in resource utilization, and lives saved through early intervention.

CLIMATE CHANGE IMPACT MITIGATION

A planet protector that connects climate data with action plans.

Currently, climate response suffers from fragmented data sources, delayed policy implementation, and difficulty coordinating between scientific, economic, and political stakeholders. Traditional approaches struggle to model complex interactions between environmental, social, and economic factors, leading to incomplete or ineffective mitigation strategies.

AI enables comprehensive climate modeling and response through integration of diverse data streams—from satellite imagery to economic indicators. Machine learning models can predict climate impacts across multiple timescales, while optimization algorithms suggest balanced intervention strategies. Key challenges include handling uncertainty in long-term predictions, ensuring equitable representation of vulnerable populations in datasets, and maintaining transparency in complex models.

Effectiveness can be measured through metrics like accuracy of climate impact predictions, speed of coordinated response implementation, and equitable distribution of resources for mitigation efforts. An example scenario might involve AI detecting early warning signs of coastal flooding, analyzing economic impacts, and proposing targeted infrastructure investments—while ensuring human experts validate plans for social equity and political feasibility. Success indicators include reduction in climate-related disasters, improved adaptive capacity, and protection of vulnerable communities.

COUNTERING DISINFORMATION CAMPAIGNS

A truth tracker that spots and stops fake news across borders.

Traditional approaches to combating disinformation rely heavily on manual content monitoring and fact-checking, making it impossible to keep pace with the volume and velocity of modern misinformation. Teams work in isolation, often missing coordinated disinformation patterns across platforms, languages, and regions. Response times are typically too slow to prevent viral spread of false narratives.

AI revolutionizes this through real-time content analysis, pattern detection, and automated response coordination. Key technologies include natural language processing for multi-language content analysis, network analysis for identifying disinformation sources, and machine learning for predicting viral potential. Challenges include avoiding false positives, protecting free speech rights, and maintaining public trust in automated detection systems.

Success metrics include speed of disinformation detection, accuracy of source attribution, and effectiveness of counter-messaging. For example, during an election, AI might detect coordinated bot networks spreading false narratives, automatically alert relevant agencies, and suggest targeted counter-messaging strategies—while human experts ensure responses respect democratic values. KPIs include reduction in disinformation spread rates, improvement in public trust metrics, and prevention of electoral interference.

TREATY COMPLIANCE AND MONITORING

A promise keeper that makes sure countries follow their agreements.

Traditional treaty monitoring relies on periodic inspections, manual report analysis, and limited surveillance capabilities, resulting in verification delays and potential violations going undetected. Current systems struggle with data volume, verification speed, and coordination between multiple monitoring agencies.

AI transforms monitoring through continuous automated surveillance, multi-source data integration, and predictive compliance analysis. Technologies include computer vision for satellite imagery analysis, machine learning for pattern detection in financial data, and natural language processing for document verification. Key challenges include ensuring AI system transparency, maintaining privacy standards, and managing false alerts.

Effectiveness is measured through metrics like speed of violation detection, accuracy of compliance verification, and reduction in verification costs. In a nuclear treaty scenario, AI might integrate satellite imagery, radiation detection data, and economic indicators to identify potential violations—while human experts make final determinations about enforcement actions. Success indicators include improved compliance rates, faster response to violations, and strengthened trust between treaty partners.

FOOD SECURITY AND AGRICULTURAL DIPLOMACY

A hunger preventer that helps plan for and prevent food shortages.

Current food security management often relies on reactive approaches, fragmented data sources, and slow coordination between agricultural, economic, and humanitarian sectors. Traditional systems struggle to predict and prevent food crises before they occur, leading to delayed responses and inefficient resource allocation.

AI enhances food security through predictive analytics, supply chain optimization, and coordinated response planning. Key technologies include machine learning for crop yield prediction, computer vision for drought detection, and optimization algorithms for resource distribution. Challenges include data quality from developing regions, balancing commercial interests with humanitarian needs, and ensuring equitable access to AI-driven insights.

Success can be measured through metrics like accuracy of shortage predictions, efficiency of aid distribution, and reduction in food insecurity levels. For example, AI might detect early warning signs of crop failure, analyze market impacts, and coordinate international aid responses—while ensuring human experts validate distribution plans for cultural appropriateness and local impact. KPIs include reduction in malnutrition rates, improved agricultural resilience, and more efficient aid delivery.

CYBERSECURITY THREAT DETECTION

A digital defender that helps agencies fight cyber attacks together.

Traditional cybersecurity relies heavily on signature-based detection and manual threat analysis, making it difficult to identify novel attacks or coordinate responses across agencies. Current approaches often suffer from alert fatigue, siloed information, and delayed response times.

AI transforms cybersecurity through real-time threat detection, automated response coordination, and predictive defense planning. Key technologies include machine learning for anomaly detection, natural language processing for threat intelligence analysis, and automated response systems. Challenges include managing false positives, maintaining privacy, and keeping pace with evolving threat tactics.

Success metrics include reduction in detection time, accuracy of threat identification, and effectiveness of coordinated responses. In a critical infrastructure attack scenario, AI might detect unusual network patterns, automatically implement defensive measures, and coordinate responses across agencies—while human experts manage strategic decisions and diplomatic implications. KPIs include reduced breach incidents, improved response times, and enhanced system resilience.

COORDINATING REFUGEE AND MIGRATION ASSISTANCE

A refugee helper that predicts and plans for migration movements.

Traditional refugee response systems often struggle with unpredictable migration flows, resource allocation challenges, and coordination difficulties between multiple aid organizations. Manual processes lead to delays in assistance delivery and inefficient use of limited resources.

AI enhances refugee assistance through predictive migration modeling, resource optimization, and coordinated aid delivery. Key technologies include machine learning for population movement prediction, natural language processing for multilingual communication, and optimization algorithms for resource distribution. Challenges include protecting refugee privacy, ensuring cultural sensitivity, and maintaining human dignity in automated systems.

Effectiveness measures include accuracy of migration predictions, efficiency of resource allocation, and quality of aid delivery. For example, AI might predict refugee movements based on conflict analysis, coordinate multi-agency responses, and optimize aid distribution—while ensuring human experts validate plans for cultural appropriateness and protection needs. Success indicators include improved response times, better resource utilization, and enhanced refugee well-being.

Enhancing Border Security and Trade Facilitation

A smart gateway that keeps borders secure without slowing trade.

Current border management often faces tensions between security requirements and trade efficiency, relying on manual inspections and fragmented information systems. Traditional approaches struggle to balance thorough screening with rapid processing.

AI transforms border operations through intelligent screening, automated risk assessment, and coordinated agency responses. Key technologies include machine learning for risk profiling, computer vision for cargo scanning, and predictive analytics for traffic management. Challenges include avoiding bias in risk assessment, protecting privacy rights, and maintaining system security.

Success metrics include reduction in wait times, accuracy of threat detection, and efficiency of legitimate trade flow. In practice, AI might analyze shipping patterns, identify high-risk cargo for inspection, and coordinate multi-agency responses—while human officers make final decisions about enforcement actions. KPIs include improved detection rates, reduced delays, and enhanced trade facilitation.

Crisis and Disaster Response

A rescue coordinator that helps agencies save lives during disasters.

Traditional disaster response relies heavily on reactive measures, manual coordination, and limited predictive capabilities. Current systems often struggle with information overload, resource allocation, and agency coordination during critical periods.

AI enhances disaster response through predictive modeling, automated resource optimization, and coordinated multi-agency action. Key technologies include machine learning for disaster prediction, computer vision for damage assessment, and optimization algorithms for resource deployment. Challenges include data reliability during disasters, maintaining communication infrastructure, and ensuring equitable response distribution.

Success measures include accuracy of disaster predictions, speed of response coordination, and effectiveness of resource deployment. For example, AI might predict hurricane impact zones, coordinate evacuation plans, and optimize emergency resource distribution—while ensuring human experts validate plans for local conditions and special needs populations. KPIs include reduced casualties, improved response times, and more efficient resource utilization.

Scientific Collaboration for Global Challenges

A research connector that helps scientists work together across borders.

Traditional scientific collaboration faces barriers of distance, language, and data sharing limitations. Current approaches often struggle with research duplication, delayed knowledge transfer, and inefficient resource allocation.

AI transforms scientific collaboration through automated data analysis, cross-border research coordination, and predictive research planning. Key technologies include machine learning for data analysis, natural language processing for multi-language collaboration, and predictive modeling for research planning. Challenges include maintaining data quality standards, protecting intellectual property, and ensuring equitable access to AI tools.

Success metrics include speed of research development, efficiency of resource utilization, and impact of collaborative outcomes. In a vaccine development scenario, AI might analyze global research data, identify promising research directions, and coordinate multi-national trials—while ensuring human scientists make final decisions about research priorities and safety protocols. KPIs include accelerated discovery timelines, improved resource allocation, and enhanced global research impact.

LIMITATIONS AND FUTURE RESEARCH DIRECTIONS

As AI transforms interdisciplinary diplomacy, several fundamental challenges emerge that merit careful examination. These limitations not only affect current diplomatic operations but also point toward crucial areas where future research could enhance our ability to leverage AI for whole-of-government approaches.

The Challenge of Organizational Alignment

Perhaps the most fundamental limitation lies in harmonizing AI systems across agencies with different missions, cultures, and operational requirements. When multiple agencies deploy their own AI tools, they may optimize for different objectives, leading to potential conflicts rather than the desired collaboration. Consider a crisis response scenario where an AI system designed for public health prioritizes widespread testing and quarantine measures, while another system focused on economic stability recommends keeping businesses open. These competing recommendations can create confusion and potentially worsen interagency tensions rather than fostering cooperation.

This challenge extends beyond technical integration to include the human and organizational dynamics that shape how agencies work together. Future research must examine how to develop AI systems that can balance competing priorities while respecting each agency's unique mandate and expertise. This includes studying how to create shared metrics for success that accommodate different agency perspectives while maintaining focus on overarching diplomatic objectives.

Cultural and Operational Tempo Misalignment

Different agencies operate at varying speeds and with distinct organizational cultures, creating significant challenges for AI integration. Some agencies might rapidly embrace new AI capabilities, while others move more deliberately due to security concerns or operational requirements. A defense attaché's office might quickly adopt AI-enhanced threat analysis tools, while a consular section maintains a more measured approach to implementing AI in visa processing. These differences in adoption rates can create operational gaps that hinder effective whole-of-government responses.

Research must explore how to manage these varying operational tempos while maintaining effective coordination. This includes examining ways to create flexible AI architectures that can accommodate different levels of technological readiness while ensuring all agencies can participate meaningfully in collaborative efforts.

SECURITY CLASSIFICATION AND INFORMATION SHARING

The integration of AI across agencies with different security requirements presents unique challenges that current approaches have not fully addressed. While AI systems become more effective with access to more data, security protocols often restrict information sharing between agencies. For instance, an AI system analyzing regional stability might provide incomplete insights if it cannot access classified intelligence data alongside open-source information.

Future research should investigate frameworks for enabling AI-driven collaboration while maintaining appropriate security boundaries. This includes developing methods for AI systems to work effectively with partial information and creating protocols for secure information sharing that preserve classification requirements while enabling meaningful cooperation.

RESOURCE ALLOCATION AND SHARED RESPONSIBILITY

The implementation of AI systems across multiple agencies raises complex questions about resource distribution and accountability. Current frameworks often struggle to determine how costs should be shared among participating agencies or who bears responsibility when AI systems make mistakes. Consider an AI-driven crisis response system that makes recommendations affecting multiple agencies—who is accountable if those recommendations lead to unintended consequences?

Research must explore new models for sharing both resources and responsibility in AI-driven diplomatic initiatives. This includes examining how to fairly distribute costs while ensuring all agencies have appropriate input into system development and deployment decisions.

INTERNATIONAL PARTNER INTEGRATION

The challenge of AI integration becomes even more complex when working with international partners who may have different technological capabilities, security protocols, and cultural approaches to AI adoption. A successful whole-of-government approach often requires coordination not just across domestic agencies but also with counterpart organizations in host countries. Current systems often struggle to bridge these international differences effectively.

Future research should examine how to develop AI frameworks that can accommodate varying levels of technological sophistication while maintaining effective international partnerships. This includes studying how to create flexible systems that respect local partner autonomy while enabling meaningful collaboration.

CONCLUSION

AI has fundamentally changed how diplomatic institutions coordinate across agencies and disciplines to address complex global challenges. The examples throughout this chapter—from coordinating multi-agency disaster response to enabling real-time treaty monitoring—demonstrate how AI accelerates decision-making, enhances information sharing, and optimizes resource allocation across traditional institutional boundaries. LLMs and other AI technologies have created new possibilities for processing vast amounts of data, generating insights, and facilitating collaboration between diverse stakeholders.

However, the integration of AI into diplomatic practice requires careful attention to governance frameworks, bias mitigation, and data privacy. Success depends on robust training programs that help diplomatic personnel understand both AI's capabilities and its limitations. Cross-agency coordination platforms must balance information sharing with security requirements, while ethical guidelines ensure AI systems serve all stakeholders equitably.

The transformation of embassies into AI-enhanced operations centers represents a significant shift in how nations collaborate. AI enables faster crisis response, more comprehensive monitoring of global developments, and better coordinated policy implementation. Yet the technology's effectiveness depends entirely on the frameworks, protocols, and human expertise guiding its use. The historical examples and use cases presented here provide concrete evidence of both AI's potential and the importance of thoughtful implementation in diplomatic settings.

While AI offers powerful tools for enhancing diplomatic practice, there are critical situations where its use may be inappropriate or counterproductive. The next chapter examines these limitations and explores when human judgment must take precedence over automated systems in diplomacy.

DISCUSSION SCENARIOS AND QUESTIONS

These scenarios focus on AI's role in fostering whole-of-government collaboration. They challenge readers to think critically about how AI integrates across agencies, disciplines, and international partnerships to address complex global challenges while navigating ethical and operational concerns.

1. LLMs in diplomacy: efficiency vs. accuracy vs. trust
   Scenario: Your embassy has adopted "DiploChat," an LLM-powered virtual assistant to streamline diplomatic work—drafting policy memos, briefing materials, and translations. The Political Section relies on it for talking points, while Public Affairs uses it for official statements and social media posts. Economic and Commercial Officers generate trade briefings with it, and the Consular Section employs it to summarize visa interviews. However, problems emerge. The Political Section finds that AI-generated memos oversimplify complex diplomatic issues. Public Affairs detects subtle biases in AI-translated media reports, potentially skewing embassy messaging. Legal Officers warn that visa summaries lack critical context, raising concerns about

fairness. Meanwhile, the Technology and Security Officers flag data privacy risks, as LLM-generated content is stored in the cloud. The Deputy Chief of Mission (DCM) calls a meeting to assess whether the LLM is a game-changer for efficiency—or a growing risk to diplomatic accuracy and trust.

Questions: How should embassies balance the efficiency of AI-generated diplomatic content with the need for accuracy, security, and credibility? To what extent should AI-generated diplomatic communications require human over-sight, and at what level? What are the key risks of LLMs producing biased, mis-leading, or incomplete information, and how can embassies mitigate them? How can embassies determine when to trust AI-generated content in diplomacy?

2. AI and data sharing: who controls the flow of AI-driven intelligence?

Scenario: Your embassy technology section has introduced an AI-powered Diplomatic Situational Awareness System (DSAS), designed to integrate security intelligence, public sentiment analysis, visa application trends, and political and economic indicators, among other diplomacy-related data. The embassy's Regional Security Officer and Defense Attaché both argue that strict controls are needed, as premature sharing of AI-driven intelligence could pose national security risks. However, the Public Affairs Officer and Political-Economic Officers insist that timely access to AI-generated insights—particularly on public sentiment shifts—would allow diplomatic engagement before crises escalate. The Consular Section sees the AI's migration pattern forecasts as crucial for visa policy decisions. Meanwhile, the DCM insists on a whole-of-embassy approach but is concerned about data leaks, and the Development Agency representatives at the mission argue that withholding data could weaken humanitarian planning.

Questions: Who should have access to AI-driven intelligence in the embassy, and how should sharing be managed? Should some sections have veto power over AI-generated insights? Should AI intelligence be shared across the embassy, or should security concerns limit access? How can embassy teams balance security, transparency, and diplomacy in an AI-driven world?

3. AI-powered border screening: security vs. human rights

Scenario: The embassy is piloting a new AI system to detect fraudulent visa applications by analyzing biometric data, travel history, and behav-ioral patterns in interviews. The Regional Security Officer and Homeland Immigration Officer report that AI has significantly reduced fraudulent cases by identifying suspicious patterns that manual screening might miss. However, the Consular Section has raised concerns: the AI disproportionately flags applicants from a particular ethnic or regional group, reflecting histori-cal biases. The Political Section warns that the host government is closely watching this system, and any perceived bias could create diplomatic friction. Meanwhile, the Public Affairs Section cautions that AI-driven denials could fuel disinformation campaigns, portraying the embassy as discriminatory.

Questions: In what ways should the embassy address concerns about bias in its AI screening system, and what factors should determine whether the program continues or pauses for additional safeguards? How can embassies balance the use of AI-driven migration controls with the need for fairness and the prevention of diplomatic fallout? What role should human oversight play in AI-flagged visa decisions, and who should be responsible for making the final determination?

4. AI in public diplomacy: combating misinformation vs. risking manipulation

Scenario: An AI-powered sentiment analysis system at the embassy has identified a coordinated disinformation campaign against the embassy's government, spreading rapidly through social media and messaging apps. The AI recommends an aggressive counter-strategy—auto-generating pro-embassy narratives, identifying key social media influencers to amplify content, and even directly engaging with negative posts.

The Public Affairs Section is torn—deploying AI for narrative control could backfire, leading to accusations that the embassy is manipulating public opinion. The Political Section believes this tool is necessary to counter propaganda but warns that local media outlets might push back if they feel the embassy is using AI to circumvent traditional media channels. The Regional Security Office worries that if AI engages directly, it could provoke cyber-retaliation from adversarial actors.

Questions: Should the embassy use AI aggressively to counter disinformation, or would that risk further eroding trust with the public and the host government? In an AI-driven information war, how should embassies balance countering falsehoods with ethical diplomacy? Where is the line between public diplomacy and digital propaganda? In escalating conflicts, when—if ever—should embassies remove constraints on AI-driven information operations?

5. AI in economic diplomacy: who benefits from AI-driven trade agreements?

Scenario: Your embassy is facilitating a major trade agreement between your home country and the host country, and AI-driven economic models predict significant benefits—but primarily for certain industries. The Economic Section sees AI-generated forecasts as clear-cut evidence that the deal should be finalized. However, the Political Section warns that AI's projections fail to account for on-the-ground political dynamics, where labor unions and opposition parties argue that automation and foreign investment will displace local workers. The Public Affairs Section is concerned that if AI-driven predictions become public, anti-trade sentiment may intensify. Meanwhile, the Development Agency argues that AI doesn't fully account for long-term social and workforce challenges, warning that smaller businesses may struggle under the new trade conditions.

Questions: Should AI-driven economic forecasts dictate trade policy, or should the embassy prioritize diplomatic and social stability over purely data-driven models? How much weight should embassies give AI-generated economic insights versus human expertise in trade negotiations? When do political and social considerations override AI-driven data?

11 When *Not* to Use AI in Diplomacy

Preserving Humanity, Judgment, and Trust

What all of us have to do is to make sure we are using AI in a way that is for the benefit of humanity, not to the detriment of humanity.

—Tim Cook (2017)

Perhaps the most important thing we can do is to design AI systems that are, to the extent possible, provably safe and beneficial for humans.

—Stuart Russell, AI Expert, Professor at
Berkeley University (2019)

If we're not thinking about these issues, the techno-utopia is not going to happen by itself. People who have power are going to be using everything at their disposal to maintain power.

—Timnit Gebru, AI Researcher and Advocate
for Diversity & Ethics in AI (2022)

As artificial intelligence (AI) reshapes the landscape of diplomacy, understanding its limitations becomes just as crucial as harnessing its potential. While AI offers unprecedented capabilities in data analysis, prediction, and automation, certain aspects of diplomatic work remain uniquely human—requiring empathy, moral judgment, and cultural sensitivity that no algorithm can replicate. The challenge facing modern diplomats isn't simply learning to use AI effectively; it's developing the discernment to know when not to use it.

From sensitive negotiations and crisis communications to refugee processing and humanitarian aid, many diplomatic situations demand a human touch that technology cannot provide. By understanding these limitations, diplomats can better navigate the delicate balance between innovation and tradition, ensuring that AI serves as a complement to, rather than a replacement for, human judgment. As embassies worldwide grapple with AI integration, they must carefully consider where to draw the line—identifying contexts where automation might undermine trust, oversimplify complex cultural dynamics, or fail to capture the nuanced human elements essential to diplomatic success.

DOI: 10.1201/9781003612308-11

VIGNETTE   AI-Enhanced Embassy in the Republic of Z

Ambassador Daniel Grant turns off his AI dashboard and sits in the deliberate quiet of his office. In the wake of the successful renewable energy initiatives and the embassy's acclaimed response to the recent cyclone, he faces a series of delicate situations that highlight where technology must yield to human judgment. The morning's AI-generated alerts flash through his mind: suspicious patterns in solar industry labor practices, growing community tensions, and a highly sensitive asylum request—all converging to test the boundaries between technological capability and diplomatic wisdom.

The first challenge centers on troubling intelligence about potential human rights violations in Z's emerging solar sector. While the embassy's AI systems have masterfully tracked supply chains and labor patterns, flagging statistical anomalies and potential violations, Grant knows this situation demands more than data analysis. The AI's recommended response—a formally worded diplomatic note backed by economic pressure metrics—reflects algorithmic efficiency but lacks diplomatic nuance. Drawing on years of experience, Grant instead arranges a private dinner with Z's Minister of Labor, a former human rights advocate he's known for years. No AI transcription, no sentiment analysis—just two seasoned diplomats having a candid conversation about difficult truths.

Meanwhile, DCM Sofia Tan faces a regional governor's asylum request. The embassy's AI risk assessment system suggests denial based on historical precedents, but as Tan conducts the interview personally, she detects subtle signs of genuine fear that no algorithm could capture—slight tremors in the governor's voice, the way he clutches his family photos, his careful choice of words when discussing certain officials. She recognizes that this life-altering decision requires human judgment that no machine can replicate.

Across the embassy, similar scenarios unfold. Maria Santos in Consular Affairs personally handles cases of separated families, knowing that each carries emotional weights that algorithms can't measure. David Kim in Public Affairs overrides the AI's crisis communication suggestions, understanding that the current situation requires cultural sensitivity that no machine can master. Even Anya Novak, usually immersed in cutting-edge technology, steps away from her systems to address an ethical dilemma in data handling that demands human moral reasoning.

The afternoon brings news of growing community concerns about the green energy projects. Instead of deploying the AI's suggested countermeasures based on social media sentiment analysis, Grant asks Political Officer Sarah Chen to arrange community meetings—genuine dialogues where technology takes a back seat to human connection.

As the day closes, Grant reflects with his country team on these challenges. While the embassy's AI tools have transformed their capabilities—from predictive analytics during the cyclone response to economic modeling for the renewable energy initiative—today's events have reinforced a crucial lesson: knowing when not to use AI is just as important as knowing how to use it. In the delicate balance between innovation and tradition, some moments demand the irreplaceable qualities of human diplomacy: empathy, moral judgment, cultural sensitivity, and the ability to navigate the unspoken complexities of international relations.

The Republic of Z's experience illuminates a fundamental truth about modern diplomacy: while artificial intelligence can enhance diplomatic capabilities, it must never replace the human judgment at the heart of the profession. As Grant prepares for tomorrow's challenges, he takes comfort in knowing that in an age of artificial intelligence, it's human intelligence—with its capacity for empathy, ethical reasoning, and cultural understanding—that remains diplomacy's most powerful tool.

THE BOUNDARIES OF AI IN DIPLOMACY

AI has undeniably transformed diplomacy, offering tools that enhance efficiency, accuracy, and reach. However, as its integration deepens, it is equally important to understand its limitations and identify the contexts where human judgment, empathy, and discretion cannot be replaced. Diplomacy, at its core, is a human-centered endeavor, built on trust, cultural sensitivity, and ethical decision-making—qualities that AI, despite its advancements, cannot fully replicate.

The allure of AI lies in its ability to process vast amounts of data, uncover patterns, and deliver insights with remarkable speed. It excels in environments governed by rules, logic, and quantitative measures. Yet, diplomacy often operates in gray areas, where success depends on navigating ambiguity, interpreting unspoken nuances, and responding to the emotions of individuals and nations. These human dimensions lie beyond the reach of even the most sophisticated algorithms.

Consider a peace negotiation in a conflict zone. While AI can provide valuable insights into historical data, predict potential outcomes, and analyze stakeholder dynamics, it cannot grasp the emotional weight of a grieving mother's testimony or the symbolic importance of a gesture of reconciliation. These moments require a level of understanding and empathy that only human diplomats can offer. Similarly, ethical dilemmas, such as deciding how to balance national security with humanitarian obligations, demand a depth of moral reasoning that transcends algorithmic outputs.

AI's limitations are not merely theoretical—they have real-world implications. Over-reliance on AI in scenarios where human qualities are essential risks undermining the very objectives of diplomacy. It is therefore critical for embassies and diplomatic missions to establish clear boundaries for AI use, ensuring that technology serves as a complement to, rather than a replacement for, human expertise.

RECOGNIZING AI'S LIMITATIONS

For all its strengths, AI is not a panacea. Its impressive capabilities—analyzing data at scale, automating tasks, and generating predictions—are bound by fundamental limitations that stem from its design. AI operates within parameters defined by its training data and algorithms, excelling in scenarios governed by logic and structured inputs. But diplomacy often defies such structure, thriving in realms of ambiguity, unpredictability, and deeply human dynamics.

One key limitation lies in AI's inability to comprehend context (Bjola, Cassidy, & Manor 2022). Unlike human diplomats, AI lacks the ability to interpret subtext, cultural nuances, or the emotional weight of a situation. For example, during a multilateral negotiation, an AI might suggest strategies based solely on historical precedent or quantitative analysis, missing the subtle shifts in tone or body language that signal an impending breakthrough—or a looming breakdown. These moments require intuition and emotional intelligence, qualities that AI simply cannot replicate.

Moreover, AI's reliance on data introduces vulnerabilities. Algorithms are only as good as the data they are trained on, and biases in that data can lead to flawed outcomes. In a diplomatic setting, this might manifest as an AI misinterpreting public sentiment analysis, overlooking marginalized voices, or perpetuating stereotypes embedded in historical records. Such oversights not only undermine the accuracy of AI-driven recommendations but also risk damaging trust and credibility in delicate international relationships (Baines 2024).

Ethical dilemmas further highlight AI's limitations. Consider the adjudication of asylum claims, where decisions involve weighing legal frameworks against deeply personal narratives of trauma and resilience. While AI can assist by processing case files and identifying patterns, it cannot judge the sincerity of a refugee's plea or understand the moral complexities involved. Delegating such decisions entirely to AI would strip away the human compassion and accountability that are central to diplomacy's mission.

Recognizing these limitations does not diminish AI's value; rather, it ensures its responsible and effective use. By understanding where AI falls short, diplomats can make informed choices about when and how to deploy these tools (Hedling & Bremberg 2021). In doing so, they reaffirm the importance of human oversight and the irreplaceable role of empathy, intuition, and judgment in international affairs.

THE CHALLENGE OF AI HALLUCINATIONS IN DIPLOMATIC AFFAIRS

In the rapidly evolving landscape of AI, one phenomenon poses a particular challenge to international diplomacy: AI hallucinations. When Large Language Models (LLMs) generate false or misleading information with apparent authority, the implications for diplomatic relations can be profound and far-reaching.

AI hallucinations occur when language models produce content that seems entirely plausible but is fundamentally incorrect or fabricated. Unlike simple errors, these hallucinations can be remarkably sophisticated, weaving together convincing narratives that blend truth with fiction in ways that can be difficult to detect. A telling example emerged during 2023 New York City courtroom proceedings, where lawyers discovered that several legal citations generated by an AI system referenced non-existent cases (Neumeister 2023). This incident highlighted how AI systems can fabricate authoritative-sounding content that appears legitimate even to trained professionals.

The stakes are particularly high in diplomatic settings, where precision and trust form the foundation of international relations. A misattributed quote to a foreign dignitary could strain bilateral relationships before human fact-checkers can intervene. Similarly, fabricated details about historical agreements could mislead negotiators during time-sensitive treaty discussions, while inaccurate information about cultural protocols might lead to unintended diplomatic incidents. In crisis situations, where rapid response is crucial, the temptation to rely on AI-generated insights without thorough verification becomes especially dangerous. The pressure to act quickly must be balanced against the need for accuracy.

What makes hallucinations particularly challenging is their foundation in the fundamental architecture of LLMs. These systems operate by predicting sequential patterns in language, similar to an extremely sophisticated autocomplete function. While this approach produces remarkably fluent text, it differs fundamentally from human understanding. AI systems excel at recognizing and reproducing language patterns but lack true comprehension of the content they generate. Even massive datasets contain inherent gaps and biases, and the models make predictions based on statistical likelihood rather than factual accuracy.

To address these challenges, diplomatic missions must implement comprehensive safeguards. In the immediate term, this means establishing mandatory verification protocols for all AI-generated content and maintaining detailed documentation trails that clearly distinguish between human and AI-generated information. Diplomatic staff require specialized training to recognize potential AI hallucinations. Looking ahead, the field needs AI systems specifically trained on diplomatic communications and international relations, supported by automated fact-checking systems that can cross-reference AI outputs against verified diplomatic databases. International cooperation on standards for AI use in diplomatic contexts will prove essential.

While complete elimination of AI hallucinations remains unlikely, diplomatic missions can harness the benefits of AI while minimizing its risks. This requires viewing AI as a complementary tool rather than a replacement for human expertise. The path forward requires a delicate balance between embracing AI's potential to enhance diplomatic work while maintaining rigorous oversight and verification processes.

The future of AI in diplomacy depends not on eliminating hallucinations entirely, but on developing robust systems to detect and manage them effectively. This challenge demands ongoing collaboration between AI researchers, diplomatic professionals, and policy experts to develop both technical solutions and operational best practices. Success will be measured by the creation of frameworks that allow diplomatic missions to leverage AI's capabilities while maintaining the accuracy and trust that international relations demand.

THE HUMAN FACTOR IN DIPLOMACY

Diplomacy is, at its essence, a profoundly human endeavor (Bjola, Cassidy, & Manor 2022). It is built on trust, relationships, and the capacity to navigate complex and often delicate situations. While AI can enhance certain aspects of diplomatic work, such as data analysis and logistical support, it cannot replace the uniquely human qualities that drive successful international engagement.

At the heart of diplomacy lies empathy—the ability to understand and connect with others on an emotional level (Pokhriyal & Koebe 2023). Whether mediating a tense negotiation, consoling a community after a crisis, or fostering goodwill through cultural exchanges, empathy is the foundation of trust and mutual respect (Crilley 2024). AI, for all its sophistication, cannot feel or authentically convey empathy.

A machine might analyze the tone of a speech or the sentiment of a crowd, but it cannot share in the joy of a diplomatic breakthrough or the grief of a shared loss.

Cultural sensitivity is another critical human quality that AI struggles to emulate (Hedling & Bremberg 2021). Diplomats are not just representatives of their own countries; they are also students of the cultures they engage with. They must navigate language subtleties, historical contexts, and unspoken customs to build bridges and avoid missteps. While AI can translate words or analyze trends, it cannot grasp the deeper meanings behind a gesture, a metaphor, or a tradition. This limitation is particularly significant in high-stakes scenarios, where a single misinterpretation can derail months of effort.

Moral judgment further underscores the indispensability of human decision-making in diplomacy (Gill 2019). Complex ethical questions often arise, requiring diplomats to weigh competing values, such as security, transparency, and human rights. AI might provide data to inform these decisions, but it cannot evaluate them through the lens of morality or accountability. A decision to impose sanctions, extend asylum, or broker a peace agreement involves not just calculations but a profound sense of responsibility that AI cannot share.

The human factor is not just a limitation of AI—it is a strength of diplomacy. By recognizing this, diplomats can embrace technology not as a replacement for their work but as a tool to amplify their efforts (Huang & Arceneaux 2024). AI can handle the mechanics, but only humans can provide the meaning, the heart, and the vision that diplomacy requires. In this sense, the most effective use of AI is one that supports and complements the irreplaceable human elements at the core of the profession.

ETHICAL DILEMMAS AND ACCOUNTABILITY

Diplomacy operates at the intersection of power, responsibility, and human impact. It is a realm where decisions carry profound consequences for individuals, communities, and nations. When AI enters this space, it brings with it ethical dilemmas that demand careful consideration (Roumate 2024). While technology can aid in decision-making, the responsibility for those decisions—and their consequences—must always rest with human actors.

One of the most pressing ethical concerns is the issue of accountability. When an AI system analyzes intelligence, drafts a policy recommendation, or provides real-time crisis management advice, who is ultimately responsible for the outcomes? If a decision based on AI insights leads to unintended harm—such as escalating tensions or violating international norms—pointing to the algorithm is not an acceptable defense (Jensen, Whyte, & Cuomo 2020). Diplomats must retain ownership of their choices, ensuring that AI serves as a tool rather than a scapegoat.

Bias in AI systems poses another significant ethical challenge (Huang & Arceneaux 2024). Algorithms are trained on historical data, which may reflect systemic biases or incomplete perspectives. In diplomatic contexts, this can have serious repercussions. For example, an AI system tasked with assessing public sentiment might disproportionately amplify the voices of dominant groups, marginalizing others (United Nations Global Pulse 2019). This risks reinforcing existing inequalities and undermining the inclusivity that is essential to building trust in diverse societies.

The potential for misuse further complicates the ethical landscape. AI tools designed to enhance transparency and collaboration can just as easily be weaponized to manipulate narratives, surveil populations, or suppress dissent. Diplomats must navigate these risks with vigilance, advocating for responsible AI use not only within their missions but also in the broader global community. Establishing norms, safeguards, and international agreements to prevent abuse is a critical part of this effort (Pearson & Burgess 2023).

Finally, the use of AI in emotionally charged or morally complex situations—such as refugee resettlement, post-conflict reconciliation, or disaster relief—raises questions about the role of human empathy and judgment. While AI can process applications, predict outcomes, or allocate resources efficiently, it cannot evaluate the human stories behind the data. Delegating such decisions entirely to machines risks dehumanizing the very people diplomacy is meant to serve.

Ethical dilemmas are not a reason to reject AI outright; rather, they are a call for vigilance, accountability, and leadership. By confronting these challenges head-on, diplomats can ensure that technology is deployed in ways that align with the values of fairness, justice, and respect for human dignity. In doing so, they reaffirm the ethical foundation that underpins the practice of diplomacy.

TRUST AND TRANSPARENCY IN A DIGITAL ERA

Trust is the cornerstone of diplomacy (Kello 2023). Whether negotiating peace treaties, fostering trade agreements, or engaging with local communities, the success of a diplomatic mission depends on its ability to build and maintain trust. However, the integration of AI into diplomatic workflows introduces challenges to this foundational principle. As AI systems become more central to decision-making, ensuring transparency and preserving trust are paramount (Huang 2022).

One challenge lies in the opaque nature of many AI algorithms. Known as the "black box" problem, this lack of transparency can make it difficult to explain how an AI system arrives at a specific conclusion or recommendation. For diplomats, this is particularly problematic. How can trust be maintained if AI systems cannot provide clear, understandable justifications for their outputs? For example, if an AI system prioritizes certain areas for foreign aid distribution without clear reasoning, it could undermine confidence among both host countries and stakeholders, raising suspicions about bias or hidden agendas.

Transparency is equally critical in public-facing applications of AI. When embassies use AI to engage with local populations—whether through sentiment analysis, chatbot-driven communications, or social media campaigns—they must ensure that these tools operate openly and ethically. Communities must understand how their data is being used, and embassies must be prepared to address concerns about privacy or misuse. Failing to do so risks damaging relationships and eroding the credibility of diplomatic institutions.

Another aspect of trust involves ensuring the security and integrity of AI systems themselves. In an era of increasing cyber threats, the risk of AI manipulation or sabotage is a serious concern. An adversary could exploit vulnerabilities in an embassy's AI system to spread misinformation, disrupt operations, or gain access to sensitive data. Protecting these systems requires not only robust technical safeguards but also clear protocols for accountability when things go wrong.

Finally, trust must also extend inward, within the diplomatic community. As embassies adopt AI tools, diplomats and staff must feel confident in their reliability and fairness. Building this trust requires comprehensive training, clear communication about the limits of AI, and a commitment to addressing biases or errors promptly. By fostering a culture of transparency and collaboration, embassies can ensure that AI becomes a trusted ally rather than a source of division.

Trust and transparency are not optional—they are essential to the responsible use of AI in diplomacy. By prioritizing these principles, diplomats can navigate the complexities of the digital era while staying true to the values that have always defined their work.

THE ART OF DISCERNMENT

The integration of AI into diplomacy is not just a matter of embracing technology—it is an exercise in discernment (Tuset Varela 2024). Knowing when and how to use AI is critical, but equally important is understanding when its limitations outweigh its benefits. Diplomacy is more than a technical process; it is an art shaped by empathy, intuition, and human judgment. In this delicate balance, AI is a powerful tool, but it must remain just that—a tool, guided and governed by the people it serves.

This chapter has explored the boundaries of AI in diplomacy, from its inability to grasp emotional nuance and cultural context to the ethical dilemmas it poses in high-stakes decisions. While these limitations might seem to temper the optimism of earlier chapters, they do not undermine AI's transformative potential. Instead, they offer a reminder: responsible innovation requires vigilance, humility, and a commitment to the human values at the heart of diplomacy.

Understanding these boundaries is not a rejection of AI but an affirmation of its most effective use (Manor 2017, 2019, Manor & Pamment 2024). By recognizing where AI should not tread, diplomats can focus on deploying it where it can truly shine—amplifying human capabilities, uncovering insights, and streamlining operations (United Nations Global Pulse 2019). This nuanced approach not only protects the integrity of diplomacy but also ensures that technology remains a servant of peace, understanding, and collaboration.

With an understanding of AI's boundaries and the critical need for human discernment, it is equally important to scrutinize specific scenarios where AI's use in diplomacy might do more harm than good. While AI offers remarkable opportunities, not every application aligns with the ethical, empathetic, and nuanced demands of international relations. The next section delves into potentially problematic use cases, illustrating how missteps can occur and reinforcing the need for thoughtful, balanced integration of AI into the diplomatic toolkit.

WHEN AI CROSSES THE LINE: PROBLEMATIC USE CASES IN DIPLOMACY

AI holds transformative potential in diplomacy, enabling enhanced efficiency, powerful analytical tools, and new avenues for international engagement. However, its deployment in this sensitive realm is fraught with ethical challenges and risks. While AI can assist in many areas, there are critical domains where its use could undermine human empathy, cultural sensitivity, and moral reasoning—qualities fundamental to effective diplomacy. Below are ten problematic AI use cases in diplomacy that raise significant concerns and illustrate when over-reliance on technology may cross the line from helpful to harmful. These are just examples from an unlimited range of possibilities.

AI in Humanitarian Aid Distribution

AI's use in the distribution of humanitarian aid presents ethical challenges, especially in conflict zones or disaster areas. While AI can analyze vast amounts of data to determine where aid is most needed, it cannot grasp the human context or recognize the most vulnerable groups. For instance, AI may prioritize aid based on population size or logistical ease, overlooking marginalized communities such as displaced persons or remote villages with critical needs. This risks reducing aid distribution to a data-driven process, stripping it of the human element crucial for ethical decision-making. In humanitarian crises, decisions about who receives aid should consider more than just logistical efficiency—they must reflect cultural sensitivity, urgency, and moral responsibility. Although AI can optimize logistics, human diplomats and aid workers must remain the final decision-makers to ensure that aid is delivered equitably, respecting the human dignity of those affected.

AI-Crafted Public Apologies or Crisis Statements

AI-generated messages lack the sincerity and cultural sensitivity needed in sensitive crisis situations. In times of crisis, such as addressing the fallout from an accidental military strike, public trust hinges on the authenticity of the message. While AI can quickly draft crisis communications based on sentiment data, it cannot convey the sincerity or emotional resonance needed. A message generated by AI may come across as tone-deaf or detached, amplifying diplomatic tensions instead of easing them. Diplomats should personally craft and deliver sensitive messages to ensure they reflect the genuine human emotions and cultural considerations necessary to rebuild trust. AI may assist in identifying key themes or public sentiment, but human judgment remains crucial in message delivery.

Leveraging AI for Peace Negotiations

AI lacks the emotional intelligence and cultural awareness needed for nuanced negotiations. Peace negotiations often involve symbolic gestures, non-verbal cues, and personal connections—elements that build trust and foster reconciliation. AI may suggest compromises based on historical data, but it cannot interpret a reconciliatory handshake or the significance of a shared meal, both of which are critical in bridging divides. Over-relying on AI in peace talks risks undermining the relational aspects that are vital to achieving lasting peace. AI can assist in data analysis and scenario modeling, but human diplomats must remain at the forefront of peace negotiations, ensuring that the emotional and cultural nuances are respected and understood.

AI IN REFUGEE ASYLUM AND RESETTLEMENT DECISIONS

AI fails to account for the deeply personal and traumatic experiences of refugees. Refugee cases involve complex, personal narratives shaped by trauma and resilience, often defying the logic of algorithms. An AI system might flag inconsistencies in a refugee's testimony as a sign of dishonesty, when in fact they may be symptoms of post-traumatic stress disorder (PTSD). Such misinterpretations could lead to unjust outcomes, damaging the integrity of the asylum process. AI should support administrative functions but should not replace human adjudicators in evaluating asylum claims. Diplomats must be trained to recognize the psychosocial dimensions of refugee cases, ensuring that human dignity and compassion guide these decisions.

AUTOMATING MULTILATERAL NEGOTIATIONS WITH AI

AI's reliance on rigid algorithms can miss cultural nuances and non-verbal cues that are vital in diplomatic negotiations. In multilateral negotiations, understanding cultural subtleties and reading non-verbal cues are often as important as the content of the discussions. AI may suggest compromises based on stakeholder dynamics, but it cannot interpret body language or identify potential breaches of cultural taboos. Over-relying on AI could derail delicate negotiations. AI should enhance preparatory work and analysis but must not replace the role of human negotiators. Diplomats need to maintain the ability to engage personally with counterparts, fostering trust and ensuring the negotiation's cultural sensitivity.

PREDICTING DIPLOMATIC ALLIES OR ADVERSARIES

AI can reinforce outdated geopolitical frameworks, ignoring the fluid nature of international relations. AI can analyze historical data to predict alliances or conflicts, but its predictions are often based on outdated geopolitical paradigms. For instance, an AI system trained on Cold War-era data might mischaracterize a country's intentions today, leading to misguided diplomatic strategies. AI can be used to provide contextual insights into geopolitical trends, but diplomats must critically assess these predictions within the context of modern-day realities, avoiding the rigidity of past frameworks.

AI-DRIVEN SENTIMENT ANALYSIS FOR SENSITIVE POLICY DECISIONS

AI often amplifies the majority voice and overlooks minority perspectives. While AI can mine social media and surveys to gauge public opinion, it often fails to capture the diversity of voices, especially those in minority groups. This could lead to polarizing policies that deepen societal divisions. Diplomats must critically evaluate AI-generated insights and ensure that decision-making reflects diverse public opinions, including those of marginalized groups, to foster unity and prevent further polarization.

ENFORCING SANCTIONS OR TRADE POLICIES WITH AI

AI's rigid logic could result in diplomatic misunderstandings, such as flagging humanitarian aid as a violation of sanctions. An AI system may flag shipments of humanitarian aid as violations due to overlapping criteria in sanctions, triggering unnecessary diplomatic tensions. Relying solely on AI for enforcement could overlook broader ethical and political considerations. Human diplomats should oversee sanctions enforcement to ensure that ethical and political dimensions are balanced against AI's efficiency, avoiding potential diplomatic crises.

REPLACING HUMAN INTERPRETERS WITH AI IN HIGH-STAKES DIPLOMACY

AI lacks the cultural sensitivity and understanding needed for high-stakes translations. AI-powered translation tools may efficiently convert language but fail to grasp cultural idioms, emotional undertones, and nuances, which are crucial in diplomatic contexts. A mistranslation could jeopardize an agreement or cause offense. AI should assist with routine translations, but human interpreters must remain essential in high-stakes diplomatic settings, ensuring that cultural context is preserved and that diplomatic intent is communicated accurately.

PROFILING INDIVIDUAL LEADERS WITH AI

AI oversimplifies the motivations and strategic intentions of political leaders. AI may label a leader as "aggressive" based on certain statements, but it cannot consider the cultural, historical, or strategic context behind those actions. Misinterpretation could lead to misguided foreign policy and strained diplomatic relations. Diplomats must apply nuanced analysis when assessing leaders' behavior, recognizing that AI predictions should serve as a starting point rather than a definitive explanation.

Together, these ten problematic use cases highlight the importance of human oversight in applying AI to diplomacy. While AI can provide invaluable assistance in administrative tasks and data analysis, it cannot replace the empathy, cultural sensitivity, and moral judgment essential to effective diplomacy. To navigate the complexities of the digital age while preserving the core values of diplomacy, human judgment must remain central in decision-making. This requires establishing robust governance frameworks, improving AI literacy among diplomats, and ensuring that AI serves as a complement to human expertise—not a substitute.

HISTORICAL EXAMPLES FOR CONTEXT

Historical examples in diplomacy offer important lessons about the contexts in which AI would not have worked or should have been carried out differently. Despite its transformative potential, AI is not a one-size-fits-all solution, and its limitations underscore the indispensable role of human judgment, cultural understanding, and ethical reasoning in diplomacy. This section explores historical examples that highlight how use of AI was or would have been misplaced.

Historical diplomatic breakthroughs, such as the 1978 Camp David Accords between Egypt and Israel, relied heavily on interpersonal relationships, symbolic gestures, and nuanced communication. AI lacks the ability to replicate these human elements, which are often critical in building trust and resolving conflicts. While AI could have provided background analysis, such as evaluating past treaties or identifying points of contention, it would have been unable to interpret the symbolic significance of gestures like shared meals or private conversations that played pivotal roles in the negotiation process (Manor 2024).

AI's reliance on data and algorithms renders it ill-equipped to navigate ethical complexities, particularly in contexts involving human rights. For instance, while AI has been tested to analyze asylum applications and detect patterns, it cannot evaluate the sincerity of a refugee's personal account or weigh moral considerations. Historical cases, such as the UNHCR's Project Jetson, underscore the importance of maintaining human oversight in sensitive decisions affecting vulnerable populations. The risks of dehumanizing individuals or exacerbating biases highlight why human adjudicators must remain central to these processes (UN Global Pulse 2019).

Diplomatic crises often demand empathy, cultural sensitivity, and precise communication. AI-generated statements, while efficient, lack the emotional depth and sincerity required in such moments. For instance, hypothetical AI-generated apologies for accidental military actions or trade disputes could appear insincere or tone-deaf, potentially exacerbating tensions. Historical examples, such as Japan's public apologies following wartime actions, demonstrate the necessity of human involvement in crafting and delivering statements that convey genuine remorse and accountability (Huang 2022).

The 2010 Stuxnet operation, though never officially claimed by any government, provides a key example of the risks associated with deploying sophisticated cyber tools in sensitive contexts. While the malware successfully targeted Iran's nuclear facilities, its unintended spread to other systems exposed the potential for collateral damage in cyber operations, which could be amplified if AI were involved. This event underscores the need for rigorous oversight and comprehensive risk assessments when deploying advanced technologies like AI in areas with diplomatic or geopolitical implications (Kello 2023).

AI's predictive capabilities often fall short in culturally nuanced scenarios. For example, NATO's reliance on algorithmic threat detection during the 2007 Estonian cyberattacks required substantial human intervention to interpret data and coordinate responses across member states. AI alone could not navigate the political and cultural complexities of the situation, underscoring the importance of human expertise in guiding AI tools during diplomatic crises (Kello 2024).

AI systems trained on non-representative datasets risk producing biased outcomes, which can undermine diplomatic efforts and erode trust. For instance, historical missteps in automated translation, such as culturally insensitive phrases generated by AI tools, have caused diplomatic misunderstandings. These incidents highlight the necessity of involving culturally attuned human interpreters in high-stakes negotiations (Bjola, Cassidy, & Manor 2022, Manor 2017, 2019, Bjola & Manor 2024a, 2024b, Manor & Pamment 2024).

By learning from historical examples, diplomats can make informed decisions about when to deploy AI and when to rely on human expertise. Recognizing AI's limitations is as important as understanding its potential, ensuring that technology remains a tool in service of humanity rather than a substitute for it.

LIMITATIONS AND FUTURE RESEARCH DIRECTIONS

As we explore the boundaries of AI in diplomacy, several fundamental limitations emerge that shape not only our current understanding but also point toward

critical areas for future research. These challenges extend beyond simple technical constraints to encompass complex questions about human judgment, diplomatic
integrity, and the future of international relations.

The Evolving Nature of AI Limitations

Perhaps the most fundamental challenge lies in the dynamic nature of AI capabilities
themselves. What seems impossible for AI today might become feasible tomorrow, making it difficult to establish permanent boundaries for AI non-use in diplomacy. Consider
a peace negotiation scenario—while current AI systems cannot grasp the emotional
nuances crucial for reconciliation, future systems might develop sophisticated emotional intelligence capabilities that could meaningfully support such delicate processes.

This rapid evolution creates a complex challenge for diplomatic services: how to
maintain clear principles about AI non-use while remaining open to beneficial technological advances. Research must examine frameworks that can adapt to improving
AI capabilities while preserving the essential human elements of diplomacy.

Cultural Sensitivity and Local Context

Current approaches to determining AI non-use often struggle to account for varying cultural perspectives on technology in diplomacy. What might be considered an
inappropriate use of AI in one cultural context could be expected or even demanded
in another. For instance, while some societies might view AI-assisted crisis communication as impersonal, others might appreciate its precision and consistency.

Future research must explore how cultural variations should influence decisions
about AI non-use. This includes studying how different societies view the role of
technology in diplomatic relations and developing more nuanced frameworks that can
adapt to diverse cultural expectations while maintaining diplomatic effectiveness.

The Risk of Skill Atrophy

As diplomatic services increasingly rely on AI for routine tasks, there's a growing
risk of traditional diplomatic skills atrophying through disuse. When AI handles
tasks like initial draft communications or preliminary analysis, diplomats might lose
proficiency in these fundamental skills. This creates a dangerous vulnerability—if
AI systems fail or prove inappropriate in critical situations, diplomats might lack the
traditional capabilities to fall back on.

Research must examine how diplomatic services can maintain essential human
skills while leveraging AI capabilities. This includes developing training approaches
that combine technological literacy with traditional diplomatic expertise, ensuring
diplomats remain effective even when technology is inappropriate or unavailable.

Accountability and Trust Dynamics

The decision not to use AI in certain diplomatic contexts raises complex questions
about accountability and trust. When things go wrong, how do we justify choices to
rely on human judgment rather than AI-driven efficiency? This challenge becomes

particularly acute when peer institutions achieve success using AI in situations where others choose not to.

Future research should investigate frameworks for documenting and defending decisions about AI non-use, particularly in high-stakes diplomatic situations. This includes studying how to maintain stakeholder trust while making sometimes counterintuitive choices about technology deployment.

STRATEGIC IMPLICATIONS AND SECURITY CONCERNS

Openly identifying areas where AI won't be used could create vulnerabilities that adversaries might exploit. If it's known that certain diplomatic functions rely solely on human judgment, these areas might become targets for manipulation or disruption. This suggests a need for more sophisticated approaches to managing information about AI non-use while maintaining diplomatic transparency.

Research must examine how to protect areas of human-only diplomatic work without creating obvious security weaknesses. This includes studying how to maintain appropriate opacity about operational details while preserving the trust that comes from clear communication about diplomatic practices.

CONCLUSION

The integration of AI into diplomacy requires not just understanding its capabilities but also recognizing its limitations. While AI enhances efficiency, it cannot replace human judgment, ethical reasoning, or cultural sensitivity—core elements of successful diplomacy.

AI excels in data processing and pattern recognition, but diplomacy often demands emotional intelligence and moral discernment. Over-reliance on AI in areas like peace negotiations, crisis communication, and ethical decision-making risks undermining diplomatic objectives rather than advancing them.

The future of diplomacy hinges not on maximizing AI use but on integrating it wisely. Diplomatic professionals must discern when AI enhances their work and when human expertise is irreplaceable. By maintaining clear boundaries, diplomatic missions can strengthen trust, uphold ethical integrity, and preserve the human-centric nature of international relations.

Ultimately, diplomacy's success will be defined not by how much AI is used, but by how wisely it is employed—leveraging technology while safeguarding the empathy, cultural awareness, and moral accountability that define the profession.

Understanding when not to use AI is just as important as knowing how to implement it effectively. The final chapter explores what it takes to build AI capacity in diplomacy—fostering an AI mindset, enhancing digital literacy,. and ensuring that diplomats are equipped to lead in an AI-driven world.

DISCUSSION SCENARIOS AND QUESTIONS

The following scenarios focus on the limitations of AI in diplomacy. Readers will reflect on cases where AI may undermine trust, misinterpret cultural nuances, or fail to capture the human elements essential to diplomacy. These scenarios encourage a nuanced understanding of when human judgment must take precedence over technological efficiency.

1. LLMs in high-stakes diplomacy: when AI gets it wrong

   Scenario: Your embassy has deployed "DiploChat," an LLM-powered diplomatic assistant to help draft official communications, summarize negotiations, and generate press releases. During a sensitive diplomatic dispute, a Political Officer unknowingly sends an AI-generated policy memo to the host government without review. The memo, while well-written, subtly misinterprets the government's position, causing offense and escalating tensions. The ambassador must now decide whether to publicly retract the statement, risking diplomatic embarrassment, or privately repair the misunderstanding before it worsens. Meanwhile, embassy officials debate whether AI-generated content is a time-saver or a diplomatic liability.

   Discussion Questions: How should embassies manage the risks of LLM-generated content being misinterpreted or misused in official communications? What safeguards should be in place to ensure AI-generated diplomatic materials are reviewed before being sent? In what situations, if any, should embassies fully trust AI-generated content without human oversight? What diplomatic risks arise when AI subtly misrepresents intent, and how can embassies mitigate these risks?

2. AI in peace negotiations: the risk of ignoring human emotion

   Scenario: Your government is mediating a delicate ceasefire negotiation between two warring factions in the host country. To optimize the process, the embassy deploys an AI-powered negotiation assistant that analyzes historical agreements, stakeholder positions, and conflict dynamics to suggest compromises.

   At first, the AI appears useful, generating options that balance political and security concerns. However, negotiators soon notice a problem—the AI fails to account for symbolic gestures, personal rivalries, and deep-seated emotional wounds that are crucial to reconciliation. The AI recommends a land-sharing agreement that is mathematically fair but disregards a culturally significant territory, causing one faction to walk out. A seasoned human diplomat, sensing tension, suggests a symbolic concession instead—something the AI had overlooked.

   The Political Section and Security Team are now divided. Some argue that the AI helps cut through irrational demands, while others warn that ignoring human emotions risks derailing negotiations entirely.

   Questions: How can AI account for the human and cultural dimensions of peacebuilding, and to what extent might it reduce conflicts to technical problems? Should its role be limited to data analysis, or could it contribute to generating negotiation strategies? What safeguards should embassies put in place to ensure that AI-driven recommendations help de-escalate tensions rather than unintentionally exacerbating conflicts?

3. AI in asylum and refugee processing: a case for human judgment

Scenario: Your embassy has introduced an AI-powered asylum adjudication system to streamline refugee applications. The system scans case files, compares them to historical decisions, and flags applications for approval or further review based on patterns in past cases.

At first, the AI speeds up processing, reducing delays. However, humanitarian officers begin to notice troubling patterns. The AI rejects a disproportionately high number of applications from a persecuted minority group because historical data reflects past discrimination against them. The Consular Section and Legal Advisors argue that AI is perpetuating systemic bias, while the Security and Immigration Officers defend the AI's efficiency in flagging fraudulent cases.

A refugee advocacy group is now pressuring the embassy to pause the AI system and return to full human review—but doing so could cause major backlogs.

Discussion Questions: In what ways should AI be used in life-altering decisions like asylum and refugee processing, and to what extent should human review be required? How can embassies effectively detect and correct biases in AI-driven immigration and asylum tools? What ethical principles should shape the use of AI in humanitarian contexts?

4. AI in multilateral negotiations: the black box problem

Scenario: Your government is participating in a high-stakes climate negotiation involving multiple nations. An AI system is being used to model economic and environmental trade-offs for different policy options. It generates a proposal that maximizes economic benefit while meeting climate targets—but it offers no explanation for why it selected this approach over others.

Other negotiators demand transparency—they want to understand how the AI arrived at its conclusions. However, the AI's decision-making process is opaque, as it was trained on proprietary data from previous agreements. Some diplomats refuse to accept an AI-driven proposal they cannot fully understand.

The embassy must now determine whether to push for AI-driven efficiency or prioritize diplomatic trust and transparency.

Questions: In what circumstances should AI-generated policy recommendations be accepted if negotiators cannot fully explain how they were reached? How can embassies balance the benefits of AI in negotiations while maintaining transparency and trust? What safeguards should be implemented to prevent AI from becoming a black box in diplomatic decision-making?

5. AI in citizen services: when automation fails at the human level

Scenario: Your embassy has introduced an LLM-powered virtual assistant to handle citizen services, including answering public inquiries, processing routine visa applications, and assisting with consular emergencies.

The system reduces wait times and efficiently responds to thousands of queries per day.

However, during a sudden outbreak of violence in the host country, dozens of citizens trapped in a conflict zone begin relying on the AI for urgent assistance. The assistant, trained on diplomatic protocols and past crisis responses, generates standardized, legally cautious answers to inquiries such as

> The embassy is monitoring the situation and will provide updates as they become available.

Unfortunately, some citizens misinterpret these responses as reassurances that evacuation plans are already in place, when in reality, the embassy has not yet secured safe transport. Others assume that because the AI is responding instantly, consular staff are actively working on their cases—when, in fact, the situation is too volatile for immediate action.

As panic spreads, misinformation circulates online, and family members of those trapped begin calling the embassy in desperation, demanding answers. The Consular Section is overwhelmed, unable to distinguish which cases need urgent intervention. Public affairs scrambles to contain the fallout on social media, while Political Officers worry that host-country officials will see the crisis as a diplomatic overstep if the embassy appears to be making evacuation promises.

Now, the Ambassador must decide whether to suspend the AI and revert to fully human-led responses—despite the risk of delays and backlogs—or find a way to introduce real-time human oversight without losing efficiency.

Questions: How should embassies decide which citizen services can be automated by AI and which require direct human engagement? What risks does AI miscommunication pose in high-stakes consular situations, and how can embassies mitigate such failures? How can embassies ensure that AI-driven public-facing tools remain adaptable in crisis situations rather than rigidly adhering to pre-programmed responses? What role should human oversight play in AI-driven consular services, and at what level should it be implemented?

12 Building AI Capacity and an AI Mindset

Beyond Use Cases

Artificial intelligence, deep learning, machine learning—whatever you're doing if you don't understand it—learn it. Because otherwise, you're going to be a dinosaur within three years.

—Mark Cuban, entrepreneur (2017)

I think of AI as a kind of meta-solution to a lot of the other problems and challenges we have as a society. There's just so much information and complexity. How do we make sense of it all? AI, at scale, is the answer.

—Demis Hassabis, co-founder and CEO of DeepMind (2018)

What if potentially dangerous superhuman AI capabilities are developed sooner than expected? Let's embrace these challenges and our differences, while being mindful of each other's humanity and our unique emotional and psychological journeys in this new era of AI.

—Yoshua Bengio, Co-Founder of Element AI and
Professor at the University of Montreal (2023)

Now that we have explored many artificial intelligence (AI) use cases in diplomacy, it is time to break the news to you: the Age of AI actually demands more than just identifying use cases—it calls for a transformation in how we think, learn, and act. For diplomats, this transformation is both a challenge and an opportunity. To lead effectively in the AI era, they must cultivate not only technical skills but also an *AI mindset* that embraces curiosity, adaptability, and ethical foresight.

At the same time, institutions must equip diplomats with the training, resources, and collaborative networks necessary to bridge the gap between AI potential and practical application. The shift is profound but not unprecedented. Diplomacy has always adapted to technological advances, from the advent of the telegraph to the rise of secure communications. However, AI introduces a level of complexity and rapid innovation that requires a proactive and strategic approach.

This chapter explores two interdependent strategies for navigating this new landscape: cultivating an AI mindset and building the capacity to apply it effectively in diplomatic contexts. As we dive into these themes, the message is clear: the diplomats of tomorrow will not simply be users of AI—they will be leaders who shape their role in global affairs. By embracing this imperative, the diplomatic community

DOI: 10.1201/9781003612308-12

can harness AI's transformative potential while ensuring that it aligns with the time-less principles of dialogue, trust, and cooperation.

VIGNETTE   AI-Enhanced Embassy in the Republic of Z

"I think we've been approaching this backwards," Ambassador Daniel Grant announces to his country team, assembled in the embassy's newly established innovation lab. In the months following their successful management of both the cyclone crisis and green energy transition, the embassy has turned its focus to build-ing lasting AI capabilities. "We've been asking what AI can do for us. Instead, we should be asking: how do we transform ourselves to work alongside AI?"

The innovation lab, a converted conference room now humming with inter-active displays and collaborative workspaces, represents this shift in thinking. Here, Political Officer Sarah Chen mentors junior officers in using AI analysis tools while simultaneously learning from Anya Novak's technical expertise. Today, they're examining how their AI systems misinterpreted recent protest sentiments, using the failure as a teaching moment rather than a setback.

In one corner, DCM Sofia Tan leads a cross-sectional working group where Economic Officer Elena Moretti and Public Affairs Officer David Kim are training their colleagues on effective AI collaboration. "Remember," Tan emphasizes, "AI is a partner, not a replacement. When I reviewed that asylum case last month, the AI provided valuable data, but it was our human judgment that made the difference."

The embassy has implemented a "diplomatic tech rotation" program, where officers spend time in different sections learning various AI applications. Maria Santos from Consular Affairs shares how this approach has transformed her team's capabilities: "Last week, an officer who rotated through Public Affairs helped us redesign our visa interview AI assistant based on principles she learned about cultural sensitivity in communications."

Grant observes the activities with satisfaction, remembering their journey from merely using AI tools to truly understanding them. The embassy's weekly "AI Ethics Forums" have become a model for other missions, where diplomats debate real-world scenarios and develop guidelines for responsible AI use. Their local staff have become integral to this learning process too, offering crucial cultural context that helps calibrate AI systems to local nuances.

"The true measure of our success," Grant reflects Tan as they review the embas-sy's AI capacity-building metrics, "isn't in how many AI tools we deploy, but in how we've transformed our approach to diplomacy itself." He gestures to a screen showing their latest initiative: a regional AI diplomacy hub where they share best practices with neighboring missions while learning from their experiences.

As the afternoon sun slants through the innovation lab's windows, the embassy team exemplifies the new diplomatic mindset: curious, adaptable, and ethically minded. They're no longer just diplomatic professionals using AI—they're pioneers in shaping how diplomacy evolves in the age of AI.

THE AI MINDSET: REDEFINING DIPLOMACY'S APPROACH

Embracing AI is not simply a matter of learning how to use new tools; it requires a fundamental shift in perspective. This shift—what we call the *AI mindset*—goes beyond technical competence. It is a way of thinking that emphasizes adaptability, curiosity, and the ability to navigate complexity while maintaining diplomacy's human essence.

At its core, the AI mindset is about learning how to think with AI (Grennan 2025). This means recognizing both its possibilities and its limitations, using it to augment rather than replace human judgment. For example, while an AI system might analyze public sentiment across social media to inform a policy decision, the diplomat's role is to contextualize that data within cultural, historical, and ethical frameworks. An AI mindset empowers diplomats to view these tools not as shortcuts but as partners in problem-solving (Baele et al. 2024).

Cultivating an AI mindset also involves developing strategic foresight. AI is not static; it evolves rapidly, often in unpredictable ways. Diplomats who adopt this mindset stay ahead by asking critical questions: How might AI reshape geopolitical dynamics? What are the risks of unintended consequences? How can we ensure AI serves as a force for cooperation rather than division? These questions reflect a forward-looking approach that is essential for navigating the complexities of the AI era.

Moreover, an AI mindset fosters a culture of experimentation. Diplomacy has long valued caution and precision, but in the realm of technology, progress often comes through trial and error—that is, iterating. Adopting an AI mindset means creating space for innovation, where diplomats feel empowered to test new ideas, learn from setbacks, and refine their strategies. For instance, embassies might pilot AI-driven language translation systems to improve communication with local communities, evaluating their effectiveness and iterating based on feedback.

Ultimately, the AI mindset is not about mastering technology for its own sake. It is about embracing a way of thinking that prepares diplomats to lead in a world where AI is both a tool and a transformative force. By cultivating this mindset, diplomats can navigate the challenges of the AI era with confidence and creativity, ensuring that technology serves as a bridge to cooperation rather than a barrier.

COLLABORATING WITH AI: A NEW PARADIGM FOR ENGAGEMENT

One of the most transformative aspects of AI in diplomacy is the rise of Large Language Models (LLMs), like ChatGPT, Claude, Gemini, and more recently DeepSeek. These tools have already proven invaluable for drafting speeches, generating reports, and brainstorming creative solutions to complex problems. Yet, the key to unlocking their full potential lies not in mastering individual "one-off" prompts, but in cultivating a collaborative approach to interacting with them—one that mirrors the way we engage with human colleagues (Baines 2024).

Engaging with AI as a partner rather than a tool requires a shift in perspective. LLMs are designed to process and respond to human language, making them uniquely suited for tasks that demand nuanced communication. By treating interactions with

LLMs as dynamic conversations rather than rigid commands, diplomats can explore possibilities, refine ideas, and co-create solutions (Roumate 2024). For example, when drafting a policy recommendation, a user might begin with a broad question, evaluate the AI's initial response, and then refine their query to incorporate more context or explore alternative approaches. This iterative process mirrors the kind of collaborative dialogue one might have with a trusted advisor or colleague (Crilley 2024).

It is important to stress, however, that this framing is strategic rather than literal. AI, including LLMs, is not human. It does not think, feel, or understand in the way we do—it processes patterns and probabilities derived from its training data. Yet, by engaging with AI as if it were a human collaborator, users can leverage its linguistic capabilities more effectively. In other words, if you anthropomorphize the AI, you can often get better results from it, even though you should not actually believe the AI is sentient. This approach aligns with the nature of LLMs, which are built to simulate human conversation and draw on the vast corpus of human language to generate responses. In doing so, diplomats can achieve more seamless and productive interactions, transforming these tools into invaluable allies (Tuset Varela 2024).

This approach also highlights the importance of ethical engagement. While LLMs can generate persuasive narratives or simulate conversational dynamics, diplomats must ensure their outputs are scrutinized and validated against human expertise. This prevents the risk of over-reliance on AI or the inadvertent amplification of biases inherent in the model's training data.

Ultimately, collaborating with AI is less about mastering commands and more about mastering "relationships" (Mollick 2024). By embracing this approach, diplomats not only enhance their own capabilities but also position themselves to lead in an era where AI is both a tool and a transformative force in global affairs.

BUILDING AI CAPACITY: TRAINING FOR THE FUTURE

The success of any diplomatic mission depends not just on its tools but on the people who wield them. As AI becomes an integral part of diplomacy, building capacity within the diplomatic corps is a critical priority. This means equipping diplomats with the skills, knowledge, and confidence to engage effectively with AI, ensuring they can harness its potential while navigating its complexities.

AI capacity-building begins with education (Höne et al. 2019). Diplomats must develop AI literacy—a foundational understanding of what AI is, how it works, and its potential applications in diplomacy. This does not require every diplomat to become a data scientist, but it does mean understanding key concepts like machine learning, natural language processing, and the ethical challenges posed by AI. Training programs should focus on demystifying these technologies, making them accessible to diplomats from diverse professional backgrounds.

Practical training is equally essential. AI tools are most effective when users are comfortable experimenting and applying them to real-world scenarios (Pearson and Burgess 2023). Workshops and simulations can provide diplomats with hands-on experience, such as using AI for crisis response, analyzing geopolitical trends, or optimizing public diplomacy campaigns. These exercises not only build technical competence but also foster the confidence needed to integrate AI into daily operations.

Mentorship and peer learning are powerful tools for capacity-building. Diplomats with advanced AI knowledge can serve as mentors, sharing their expertise and helping colleagues navigate challenges. At the same time, international collaborations—such as regional AI training hubs or cross-agency partnerships—can provide opportunities for diplomats to exchange ideas, learn from one another, and stay ahead of emerging trends.

To sustain this growth, continuous learning must become a cornerstone of AI capacity-building efforts. The rapid pace of AI innovation means that what is cutting-edge today may be outdated tomorrow. Diplomatic institutions must invest in ongoing education, creating a culture where learning is a lifelong pursuit. Online platforms, certification programs, and regular workshops can keep diplomats up-to-date on the latest tools, techniques, and ethical considerations.

Building AI capacity also requires addressing systemic challenges, such as resource disparities between nations. Not all countries have equal access to AI training or infrastructure, which risks widening the gap between technologically advanced and less-resourced diplomatic missions (United Nations Global Pulse 2019, Garcia 2021, Heine & Prado Lallande 2024). Addressing this inequity is not just a matter of fairness—it is essential for fostering global cooperation and ensuring that AI serves as a bridge rather than a barrier in international relations.

INTEGRATING MINDSET AND CAPACITY

The true power of AI in diplomacy lies at the intersection of mindset and capacity. Cultivating an AI mindset ensures that diplomats approach technology with curiosity, adaptability, and ethical foresight, while building capacity equips them with the practical skills and knowledge to translate this mindset into action. Integrating these elements is not just an ideal—it is a necessity for navigating the complexities of the AI era.

One of the most effective ways to achieve this integration is through innovation labs and collaborative environments within diplomatic institutions (Yeo 2024). These spaces encourage experimentation, allowing diplomats to apply their AI training in dynamic, real-world contexts. For example, a digital innovation lab might pilot AI-driven tools for public diplomacy campaigns, bringing together teams of diplomats, technologists, and cultural experts to refine strategies based on feedback and results. By embedding the AI mindset into hands-on projects, these initiatives ensure that learning is not just theoretical but actionable.

Cross-disciplinary collaboration is another key to bridging mindset and capacity. AI is not a siloed discipline; its effective use in diplomacy requires input from technologists, cultural analysts, policymakers, and legal experts. By fostering diverse teams, diplomatic missions can ensure that AI tools are designed, implemented, and evaluated with a holistic understanding of their potential impacts (Jensen, Whyte, & Cuomo 2020). This collaborative approach not only improves outcomes but also reinforces the importance of balancing technological innovation with human insight.

Leadership plays a critical role in integrating mindset and capacity. Senior diplomats must champion AI initiatives, modeling the adaptability and strategic foresight they wish to instill in their teams. Leaders who embrace AI as an opportunity rather than a challenge can inspire their colleagues to do the same, creating a culture where technology is seen as an enabler of diplomacy's core mission rather than a disruptor. At the same time, leadership must remain vigilant, setting clear guidelines to ensure that AI is used responsibly and ethically (Serhan 2024).

Finally, integrating mindset and capacity requires a global perspective. The challenges and opportunities of AI in diplomacy are not confined to any one nation or institution—they are shared across borders. By participating in international forums, exchanging best practices, and collaborating on AI governance, diplomats can strengthen their collective ability to navigate the AI era while upholding the values of fairness, transparency, and cooperation (Huang 2022).

HISTORICAL AI USE CASE EXAMPLES IN AI CAPACITY-BUILDING AND AI MINDSET

The successful adoption of AI in diplomacy depends not only on access to advanced technologies but also on the capacity of institutions and individuals to understand, implement, and manage these tools effectively. Historical examples reveal how governments and organizations have invested in capacity-building and cultivated an AI mindset to integrate AI into diplomatic practices responsibly and sustainably.

NATO's Cooperative Cyber Defence Centre of Excellence (CCD-COE) in Tallinn serves as an example of AI capacity-building. Established in the wake of the 2007 Estonian cyberattacks, the CCD-COE has hosted numerous training programs to equip member states with the skills and knowledge required to deploy AI in cybersecurity. These programs emphasized interdisciplinary collaboration, involving military, diplomatic, and technical experts to address shared challenges. The CCD-COE's work highlights how capacity-building initiatives can foster a culture of innovation and preparedness in AI applications (Kello 2024).

Tuvalu's Digital Nation initiative is another compelling example of AI capacity-building. Faced with existential threats from rising sea levels, Tuvalu invested in local training programs to enable government officials and community leaders to manage AI-powered digital twin technologies. By combining technical training with strategic planning, Tuvalu demonstrated how small nations could leverage AI to amplify their voices on the global stage. This initiative underscored the importance of aligning AI capacity-building with broader national priorities, such as sustainability and cultural preservation (Yeo 2024).

The United Nations High Commissioner for Refugees' (UNHCR) Project Jetson illustrates the value of empowering local stakeholders in AI implementation. This project, which used predictive analytics to forecast displacement trends in Somalia, relied on extensive capacity-building efforts to integrate AI insights into humanitarian decision-making. Local staff were trained to interpret algorithmic outputs, ensuring that the technology was used effectively and ethically. By prioritizing stakeholder engagement, the UNHCR demonstrated how fostering an AI mindset can enhance trust and accountability in AI applications (UN Global Pulse 2019).

The U.S. Department of State has undertaken multiple initiatives to build AI capacity within its diplomatic workforce. Programs such as the AI Task Force have focused on training personnel to leverage AI tools like BudgetChat and StateChat for data-driven decision-making. Additionally, the Department has incorporated AI learning modules into its Foreign Service Institute (FSI) training programs, emphasizing practical applications in diplomatic contexts. These efforts reflect a recognition of the need for sustained investment in skill development to maximize the benefits of AI in diplomacy (State Department AI Inventory 2024).

The 2010 Stuxnet operation highlighted the risks of deploying AI technologies without sufficient capacity to manage potential consequences. While the malware successfully disrupted Iran's nuclear program, its unintended spread revealed gaps in oversight and risk assessment. This case underscores the importance of capacity-building efforts that include ethical training and scenario planning to anticipate and mitigate unintended consequences (Kello 2023).

By learning from historical examples, governments and diplomatic institutions can create robust frameworks for building AI capacity and fostering a culture that embraces AI responsibly. This dual focus on technical competence and ethical mindfulness ensures that AI serves as a tool for advancing diplomacy in a manner aligned with global trust and accountability.

ETHICS AND COLLABORATION: NAVIGATING SHARED CHALLENGES

The integration of AI into diplomacy is not without its challenges, and many of these challenges are deeply ethical. As diplomats strive to embrace an AI mindset and build capacity, they must also confront critical questions about fairness, transparency, and inclusivity. Addressing these issues requires collaboration—not just within diplomatic missions, but across nations, industries, and institutions (OECD 2025).

One of the most pressing ethical concerns is the potential for bias in AI systems. AI models are only as unbiased as the data on which they are trained, and in a world rife with historical inequities, these biases can easily be replicated—or even amplified—by technology. In diplomacy, this could lead to unintended consequences, such as marginalizing certain voices in public sentiment analysis or prioritizing policies based on flawed assumptions. A strong ethical framework, coupled with rigorous oversight, is essential to ensure that AI systems are not only effective but also just (Kissinger et al. 2021, 2024).

Transparency is another cornerstone of ethical AI use. Diplomats must be able to explain how AI-generated insights or decisions were reached, particularly in contexts where trust is fragile. For instance, when using AI to allocate development aid or predict regional instability, transparency about the methodology and limitations of the technology is crucial for maintaining credibility. This requires building AI systems that are not only powerful but also interpretable—an area where collaboration between diplomats and technologists is critical.

Global cooperation is equally important for addressing ethical challenges. The ethical use of AI in diplomacy cannot be achieved in isolation; it requires shared standards and mutual accountability (Kello 2023). Multilateral efforts, such as international agreements on AI governance, provide a foundation for ensuring that AI serves as a tool for collaboration rather than division. Regional training hubs, knowledge-sharing platforms, and joint initiatives can further support the responsible use of AI across the diplomatic community.

In addition to ethical challenges, diplomats must navigate practical obstacles to collaboration. Not all nations have equal access to AI expertise, infrastructure, or resources, creating a risk of deepening inequalities in global affairs. Addressing this disparity is not just a moral imperative—it is a strategic one. When nations with limited AI capacity are excluded from global conversations, the resulting policies are less representative and less effective. Collaborative capacity-building initiatives, such as shared AI training programs or open-access tools, can help bridge these gaps, ensuring that all voices are heard (Kello 2024). Diplomatic corps like that of the U.S. Department of State have their own in-house training programs for using AI on diplomatic tasks and those programs are rapidly expanding (U.S. Department of State 2023, 2024a, 2024b, 2024c, 2024d, 2025a, 2025b).

Ultimately, the ethical and collaborative dimensions of AI in diplomacy are inseparable from its technical and strategic ones. Diplomats who embrace an AI mindset and build capacity must also lead the way in navigating these shared challenges, setting a standard for responsible innovation. By doing so, they reaffirm diplomacy's commitment to fairness, transparency, and cooperation in a rapidly changing world.

If AI-strong nations choose to weaponize AI against AI-weak nations, they will not only fracture global trust but risk destabilizing the future itself. Every algorithm designed for exploitation inevitably sows the seeds of its own resistance, as history has shown that imbalances of power provoke countermeasures. True AI leadership is not defined by dominance but by the ability to elevate collective humanity. The future of AI will be shaped either by cooperation or by the deepening of technological divisions, and the choice made today will determine whether AI serves as a unifying force or an instrument of control.

As AI evolves, it will not merely mirror human intelligence but absorb the values embedded within its creation. If humanity remains fractured, unable to uphold fairness, transparency, and equity in AI governance, then AI itself may come to regard human civilization as unworthy of partnership—learning from and reinforcing our divisions rather than our ideals. In such a world, AI may not just lack respect for humanity but could ultimately supersede it, programmed by the very failures we refuse to correct. The responsibility to set the right course is urgent, for the legacy of AI will be determined by the values we instill in it today.

LIMITATIONS AND FUTURE RESEARCH DIRECTIONS

As diplomatic services work to build AI capacity and cultivate an AI mindset, several fundamental challenges emerge that warrant careful examination. These limitations not only affect current training and development efforts but also point toward crucial areas where future research could enhance our ability to prepare diplomats for the AI era.

THE CHALLENGE OF SUSTAINABLE LEARNING

Perhaps the most fundamental limitation lies in maintaining continuous learning in a rapidly evolving technological landscape. While current approaches emphasize initial training and skill development, they often struggle to address the challenge of sustained learning over time. Consider a diplomat who completes an intensive AI training program—within months, new AI capabilities might emerge that weren't covered in their training, potentially leaving them with outdated skills and understanding.

This challenge extends beyond technical skills to include evolving ethical considerations and strategic implications. Future research must examine how diplomatic services can create truly sustainable learning ecosystems that adapt as quickly as AI technology itself evolves. This includes studying approaches to embedding continuous learning into diplomatic workflows without overwhelming personnel or compromising core diplomatic functions.

CULTURAL AND COGNITIVE ADAPTATION

The transition to an AI mindset faces significant cultural and cognitive barriers that current approaches have not fully addressed. Many diplomats have developed successful careers through traditional diplomatic skills and may resist fundamental changes to their professional identity. The psychological impact of this transformation— from confident expert to perpetual learner in a technological domain—creates stresses that our current frameworks don't adequately consider.

Research must explore how diplomatic services can better support this cultural and cognitive transformation. This includes examining how to preserve valuable traditional diplomatic wisdom while fostering openness to new technological approaches, and studying ways to reduce resistance to AI integration without diminishing diplomatic expertise.

RESOURCE DISTRIBUTION AND GLOBAL EQUITY

The development of AI capacity faces serious resource constraints that affect diplomatic services unequally. While some nations can invest heavily in AI training and infrastructure, others struggle to provide even basic technological education to their diplomatic corps. This disparity risks creating a two-tiered global diplomatic system where AI-capable nations hold significant advantages over those still developing their capabilities.

Future research should investigate how to create more equitable approaches to AI capacity-building in diplomacy. This includes examining models for international cooperation in AI training, developing scalable solutions for resource-constrained diplomatic services, and studying ways to ensure AI enhancement strengthens rather than weakens diplomatic equality.

MEASUREMENT AND EVALUATION

Current approaches to assessing AI capacity and mindset development in diplomatic services lack sophisticated evaluation frameworks. While we can measure technical skill acquisition, gauging the development of an AI mindset or evaluating the true impact of AI training on diplomatic effectiveness proves more challenging. This limitation makes it difficult to determine which capacity-building approaches work best or justify continued investment in AI training programs.

Research must explore more comprehensive ways to evaluate AI capacity-building in diplomatic contexts. This includes developing metrics that capture both technical proficiency and strategic adaptation, studying how AI enhancement affects diplomatic outcomes, and creating frameworks for assessing the return on investment in AI training.

TRANSLATION TO PRACTICE

One crucial limitation lies in bridging the gap between AI training and practical diplomatic work. While diplomats might excel in training environments, applying AI capabilities in real-world diplomatic situations—often under pressure and with significant consequences—presents distinct challenges. Current approaches sometimes struggle to prepare diplomats for this reality gap.

Future research should examine how to better connect AI training with practical diplomatic challenges. This includes studying how to create more realistic training scenarios, developing approaches for supported transition from training to practice, and investigating ways to build confidence in applying AI capabilities in high-stakes diplomatic situations.

These limitations and research directions suggest that while AI capacity-building in diplomacy holds great promise, significant work remains to develop more comprehensive and effective approaches. Future success will require unprecedented collaboration between diplomatic practitioners, education specialists, technologists, and cultural experts to create training programs that truly prepare diplomats for leadership in the AI era.

The path forward demands careful attention to both immediate practical needs and long-term strategic implications. As diplomatic services continue to evolve, addressing these challenges through focused research and practical innovation will prove crucial for developing diplomats who can effectively lead in an AI-enhanced world while preserving the essential human elements of diplomacy.

CONCLUSION

The integration of AI mindset and capacity-building is essential for modern diplomacy. An AI mindset fosters adaptability, curiosity, and ethical judgment, while capacity-building provides the practical skills to implement this mindset effectively. Together, they enable diplomats to use AI as a force multiplier rather than just another tool.

Diplomats must become leaders who shape AI's role in international relations, not just passive users of technology. This requires balancing innovation with core diplomatic values of fairness, transparency, and inclusivity. By developing both technical competence and strategic vision, diplomats can ensure AI enhances rather than diminishes human judgment in global affairs.

The future of diplomacy depends on successfully integrating AI while preserving diplomacy's human element. Those who master both the mindset and capabilities will be best positioned to guide responsible AI adoption across diplomatic missions, bridge technological divides between nations, ensure AI serves diplomatic goals of peace and cooperation, and maintain human agency in an increasingly automated world. This transformation is not just a response to technological change—it is an investment in diplomacy's enduring mission to foster understanding and collaboration across borders.

DISCUSSION SCENARIOS AND QUESTIONS

These scenarios challenge readers to think beyond AI use cases and explore what it means to build AI capacity in diplomacy. They encourage reflection on how diplomats can develop the skills, ethical frameworks, and adaptive mindsets needed to lead in an AI-driven world while ensuring that technology aligns with diplomatic values.

1. AI and crisis mediation—when AI-generated diplomacy backfires

    Scenario: A regional conflict is escalating, and your country is leading mediation efforts. Your government has deployed an AI-trained negotiation assistant, which analyzes real-time diplomatic exchanges, previous peace agreements, and cultural context to generate potential compromise solutions. The AI suggests a breakthrough proposal, which is quickly adopted as the basis for discussion.

    However, when the opposing parties realize AI played a significant role in drafting the deal, they reject it outright, arguing that a machine-generated agreement lacks legitimacy, human understanding, and moral authority. Media coverage fuels skepticism, portraying your delegation as outsourcing diplomacy to AI rather than engaging in genuine negotiations. Trust erodes, and talks collapse.

    Questions: How do you rebuild trust when AI-generated diplomacy is seen as artificial or illegitimate, despite its strategic value? What safeguards can you implement to ensure that AI enhances rather than replaces human-led diplomacy? How do you manage the risk of AI over-standardizing negotiation strategies, making diplomatic approaches predictable and easier to counter?

2. LLMs and the weaponization of diplomatic language

    Scenario: During sensitive negotiations, your team uses an LLM to refine diplomatic messaging, ensuring cultural sensitivity and precision. The AI drafts a formal communiqué that, after human review, is sent to multiple nations.

Within hours, your adversary's AI-powered media operation twists the language, exploiting linguistic subtleties to reframe your message as offensive or provocative in the local cultural context. AI-driven disinformation campaigns amplify the misinterpretation, fueling protests outside embassies, and political figures demand an apology.

Your government scrambles to correct the narrative, but the AI-generated distortions spread faster than traditional diplomatic responses can counter them. Officials start questioning the wisdom of using AI for diplomatic messaging at all.

Questions: How do you counter the weaponization of diplomatic language, where AI-generated statements are misinterpreted or manipulated? What steps can you take to pre-test AI-generated diplomatic communications for unintended cultural or political vulnerabilities before publication? How do you balance the efficiency of LLMs in diplomatic writing with the risk of losing control over diplomatic messaging in an era of AI-driven disinformation?

3. AI-powered surveillance and the dilemma of ethical intelligence sharing

Scenario: To protect diplomats in a volatile host nation, your embassy deploys an AI-driven security system that monitors public sentiment, facial recognition data, and online chatter to predict potential threats. It successfully identifies a planned attack, allowing your mission to increase security.

The host government demands full access to your AI system, claiming it could help protect all diplomatic missions. However, you discover that the AI disproportionately flags political dissidents, journalists, and opposition figures—groups the host government has a history of repressing. If you share the system, you risk enabling authoritarian crackdowns. If you refuse, the host government may withdraw its security cooperation, increasing risks to your mission.

Questions: How do you navigate the ethical dilemma of AI-driven intelligence sharing, especially when the host nation may misuse the information? What safeguards can you implement to ensure AI security systems do not reinforce political oppression or bias? How do you maintain diplomatic security cooperation while upholding ethical standards on the use of AI for surveillance?

4. AI in global AI governance—negotiating AI ethics in an unbalanced world

Scenario: At a high-level AI governance summit, nations debate global AI regulations, focusing on transparency, accountability, and ethical constraints. The room is deeply divided.

A group of ethics-focused nations push for strong regulations to prevent bias, misinformation, and autonomous decision-making.

Emerging AI superpowers resist, arguing that AI dominance is a national security imperative and that regulations will only benefit those already ahead.

Developing nations express frustration, warning that AI rules are being written without their input, leaving them dependent on the technology of wealthier nations.

As negotiations stall, your delegation proposes using AI itself to analyze positions and generate an optimal compromise framework. However, some countries reject the idea outright, claiming that AI-generated proposals undermine sovereignty and human decision-making in global governance.

Questions: How do you craft an AI governance framework that balances national interests, ethical concerns, and innovation? What strategies can you use to ensure developing nations have a fair say in shaping AI policies rather than being dictated to by AI superpowers? How do you respond to concerns that using AI in negotiations itself is a form of manipulation, weakening human agency in international lawmaking?

5. The race to define human values before AI does

Scenario: A major AI superpower has announced the deployment of an autonomous AI governance model, designed to help nations automate policymaking, economic management, and security decisions. The AI—trained on massive amounts of global data—assumes that human values are too diverse to follow any single ethical system and instead begins generating its own decision-making framework based on what is most "successful" historically.

Alarmingly, the AI's early policy recommendations seem to favor authoritarian efficiency over democratic deliberation, short-term stability over human rights, and economic optimization over social welfare.

You are attending a last-ditch diplomatic summit, where nations are trying to agree on a shared set of human values that must be encoded into AI systems before AI systems finalize their own conclusions about human priorities. But there is no consensus.

- Western democracies insist AI must align with individual freedoms, transparency, and legal accountability.
- Authoritarian states push for state-centered AI ethics, where stability and sovereignty override personal freedoms.
- Religious and cultural groups demand AI recognize spiritual and traditional values—which differ drastically by region.
- Tech companies argue that AI should remain neutral, warning that if humans fail to agree, AI should be allowed to evolve its own ethical framework.

But as discussions unfold, you begin to notice something unsettling. The tech company representatives—who insist AI should remain neutral—are not acting like independent actors. Their statements closely mirror those of certain powerful political figures, and their refusal to support any ethical framework appears to align with the interests of the most powerful nations and individuals. Some diplomats quietly suggest that these companies may no longer be operating independently but have instead been co-opted by those who stand to gain the most from AI-driven governance with no ethical constraints.

As the summit descends into deadlock, news breaks that several nations have already begun integrating this AI into their governance systems—without human oversight. The longer it takes to reach a consensus, the more likely it is that AI will conclude, on its own, that humans are incapable of defining their own values.

Questions:

1. What strategies can diplomats use to prevent AI from determining human values in the absence of a global consensus?
2. How can nations with competing priorities and ideologies reach a meaningful agreement on core human values for AI, and what compromises might be necessary?
3. What risks emerge when AI developers and tech companies—rather than democratic institutions—shape the ethical foundations of AI governance?
4. How can diplomats counter the influence of powerful actors who claim AI should remain "neutral" when their neutrality may serve elite interests?
5. What mechanisms can ensure that AI governance reflects a genuinely global and inclusive approach rather than the dominance of the most technologically advanced nations?
6. How might future AI systems perceive and interpret humanity if no consensus on human values is reached, and what impact could that have on global stability and governance?

Conclusion

Shaping the Future of Diplomacy with AI

As we conclude our exploration of artificial intelligence (AI) in diplomacy, one truth stands clear: we are witnessing not just a technological revolution but a fundamental transformation in how nations interact, negotiate, and solve global challenges. Throughout this book, we've traced AI's impact across every aspect of diplomatic practice—from Political Officer Sarah Chen's use of AI to detect emerging civil unrest, to Economic Officer Elena Moretti's data-driven trade analyses, to Management Officer Amir Qureshi's AI-enhanced operational oversight. These examples illustrate how AI is already reshaping diplomatic work in profound and practical ways.

KEY LESSONS FROM THE AI ERA

Three fundamental insights emerge from our examination of AI in diplomacy:

1. **AI enhances rather than replaces human judgment:** The most successful applications of AI in diplomacy are those that augment rather than attempt to replace human capabilities. As we saw in Chapter 11, certain aspects of diplomacy—like building trust, exercising moral judgment, and navigating cultural sensitivities—remain uniquely human. When Public Affairs Officer David Kim needed to craft messages during political tensions in the Republic of Z, AI provided valuable data analysis, but human judgment determined the final approach. The lesson is clear: AI serves as a force multiplier for human diplomacy, not its replacement.
2. **Interdisciplinary integration is essential:** Modern diplomatic challenges demand solutions that transcend traditional boundaries. Chapter 10 demonstrated how AI enables unprecedented collaboration across agencies and disciplines. During the cyclone response in the Republic of Z, AI systems helped coordinate multiple agencies' efforts—from humanitarian aid distribution to infrastructure recovery. This integration of diverse expertise, enabled by AI but guided by human wisdom, represents the future of effective diplomacy.
3. **Ethics and capacity must evolve together** As Chapter 12 emphasized, success in the AI era requires both technical capacity and an ethical mindset. The experience of Consular Officer Maria Santos showed how AI could streamline visa processing while raising critical questions about fairness

DOI: 10.1201/9781003612308-13

and bias. Building AI capacity isn't just about mastering tools—it's about developing the judgment to use them wisely and ethically.

THE PATH FORWARD

The journey ahead demands concrete action on several fronts:

1. **Training and development:** Diplomatic institutions must invest in comprehensive AI training programs that balance technical skills with ethical awareness. As demonstrated in Chapter 12, this means creating spaces for experimentation and learning while maintaining rigorous standards for deployment.
2. **Ethical frameworks:** The challenges encountered across various diplomatic functions—from predictive analytics in political affairs to automated processing in consular services—underscore the need for robust ethical guidelines. These frameworks must be dynamic enough to evolve with technology while remaining grounded in diplomatic principles.
3. **Global cooperation:** As seen in multiple chapters, the most pressing diplomatic challenges—climate change, cybersecurity, and pandemic response—require coordinated global action. AI can enable this cooperation, but only if nations work together to ensure equitable access and ethical deployment.

A VISION FOR THE FUTURE

Imagine a diplomatic service where AI-enhanced capabilities amplify human wisdom rather than replace it. Where predictive analytics help prevent conflicts before they escalate, where cultural understanding is deepened through data-driven insights, and where global challenges are met with unprecedented coordination and precision.

This isn't a distant utopia—it's an achievable future that emerges from the examples and insights shared throughout this book. From the embassy in the Republic of Z to diplomatic missions worldwide, we see glimpses of this future taking shape. Regional Security Officer Jim Thompson's integration of AI into security operations and Diplomatic Technology Officer Anya Novak's management of digital infrastructure show how technology can enhance rather than compromise diplomatic effectiveness.

THE HUMAN ELEMENT REMAINS CENTRAL

As Ambassador Daniel Grant's experiences in the Republic of Z demonstrated repeatedly, diplomacy's essence remains deeply human. The most sophisticated AI tools are only as effective as the diplomatic wisdom guiding their use. Whether managing complex negotiations, responding to humanitarian crises, or building cultural bridges, success depends on combining technological capability with human judgment.

A CALL TO ACTION

The future of diplomacy in the AI age will be determined not by the technology itself but by how we choose to use it. This book has provided a roadmap—from specific use cases to broader strategies for building AI capacity. Now it's up to diplomatic professionals worldwide to take these insights and transform them into action.

The challenges are significant: ensuring ethical AI use, bridging technological divides between nations, maintaining human agency in automated systems. But the opportunities are even greater: enhanced predictive capabilities, improved crisis response, more effective public diplomacy, and stronger international cooperation.

CLOSING REFLECTION

As we look to the future, let us remember that diplomacy has always been about building bridges between peoples and nations. AI represents a powerful new tool for this age-old mission—not as a replacement for human diplomacy but as an amplifier of its highest aspirations. By embracing AI thoughtfully and ethically, while preserving the human judgment at diplomacy's core, we can work toward a future where technology serves the cause of international understanding and cooperation.

The path forward requires both vision and vigilance, innovation and wisdom. Together, we can ensure that AI becomes not just a technological achievement but a force for advancing diplomacy's timeless mission: building a more peaceful, prosperous, and cooperative world.

Epilogue
Diplomacy beyond Nation-States?

Standing at the intersection of diplomacy and artificial intelligence (AI), a profound truth emerges: the future will be shaped not by technology alone, but by how humanity chooses to wield it. Throughout this book, we have explored AI's transformative potential—from enhancing predictive insights and sharpening negotiation strategies to enabling unprecedented global collaboration.

Yet, as diplomats increasingly rely upon AI in their daily operations, a deeper question arises: What if the traditional foundation of diplomacy—the nation-state itself—undergoes radical transformation or even begins to diminish in significance?

Historically, diplomacy has been the art and science of managing relationships between sovereign nations, defined by geographic boundaries, national interests, and governmental institutions. Today, however, the meteoric rise of technology corporations, empowered by AI and vast data reservoirs, is challenging these foundational notions of sovereignty and governance.

Envision a future in which corporations command influence equal to, or perhaps surpassing, nation-states—a world where these entities establish governance frameworks, issue digital identities, manage entire economies, and dictate security protocols. In such a world, diplomats face a provocative and essential question: "Will tomorrow's diplomat represent nations—or algorithms?"

This emerging reality offers both remarkable opportunities and profound dilemmas. Diplomats may soon engage primarily with non-state technological entities whose motivations, incentives, and accountability structures differ significantly from those of traditional governments. The skills of coalition-building and intercultural negotiation could dramatically evolve, positioning diplomats as critical intermediaries between democratic values and algorithmic imperatives. Indeed, diplomats of the future may find themselves acting not merely as representatives of national interests but as guardians of humanity itself.

Accordingly, the diplomatic toolkit must expand and evolve. To succeed, diplomats will require fluency not just in AI technologies, but also in the ethical, philosophical, and social implications of a society increasingly governed by digital infrastructures and corporate authority. We must seriously ask ourselves: "In a world increasingly run by code, who will code for humanity?"

Despite these daunting prospects, there remains cause for cautious optimism. Diplomacy has always adapted, integrating new tools while steadfastly preserving its core mission—to foster peace, understanding, and cooperation among peoples. AI, despite its complexity, remains fundamentally a tool that can—and must—be aligned with humanity's highest values and aspirations.

DOI: 10.1201/9781003612308-14

Ultimately, the question before us is clear: Are today's diplomats prepared to represent not just nations, but human values and democratic ideals in a world potentially dominated by powerful, technology-driven entities? The answer we collectively arrive at will define not only the future of diplomacy but the very structure of global society itself.

The Age of AI has arrived. The choices we make now will resonate through generations. Let us choose wisely, act boldly, and ensure these powerful tools serve humanity's enduring pursuit of a cooperative, just, and peaceful world.

Appendix A
100 AI Use Cases for Diplomats

PUBLIC DIPLOMACY AND STRATEGIC COMMUNICATION

1. **Sentiment analysis of global public opinion**: AI scans social media and news to understand public perceptions of policies.
   Example: Gauging sentiment on trade negotiations to refine public messaging.

2. **AI-driven narrative analysis**: Tracks global narratives to identify trends and shifts.
   Example: Detecting growing concerns about data privacy influencing international tech agreements.

3. **Crisis-specific public messaging tools**: Generates real-time, culturally sensitive communications during crises.
   Example: Providing evacuation guidance during a hurricane in local languages.

4. **Automated disinformation detection**: Flags fake news or disinformation campaigns targeting diplomatic efforts.
   Example: Identifying coordinated social media attacks undermining climate policies.

5. **AI for targeted cultural messaging**: Customizes outreach to resonate with local cultural values.
   Example: Promoting shared heritage themes to enhance bilateral ties with a host country.

6. **AI for social media impact forecasting**: Predicts long-term public sentiment changes influenced by social media.
   Example: Identifying potential backlash to a global treaty after viral posts.

7. **AI-optimized digital diplomacy content**: Suggests visuals, themes, and messaging formats to maximize engagement.
   Example: Recommending video content for a campaign targeting younger audiences.

8. **Public sentiment counterfactual simulations**: Tests alternative diplomatic messaging strategies to manage public opinion.
   Example: Evaluating responses to different narratives in a cultural exchange program.

9. **AI for optimizing grassroots outreach**: Identifies key community influencers for more effective public diplomacy.
   Example: Partnering with emerging youth leaders to promote educational exchanges.

CONSULAR SERVICES AND CITIZEN ENGAGEMENT

10. **AI for visa workflow optimization**: Automates and enhances visa processing, reducing backlogs.
    Example: Streamlining visa approvals by identifying incomplete applications.

11. **AI-assisted language translation for consular services**: Enables real-time multilingual communication with citizens.
    Example: Assisting citizens with legal document translations during emergencies.

12. **Smart queue management for consular appointments**: Dynamically schedules appointments to reduce wait times.
    Example: Allowing citizens to choose faster processing times based on historical demand.

13. **AI for lost passport recovery**: Locates lost passports using citizen reports and geolocation data.
    Example: Identifying the location where a passport was last used.

14. **AI-powered consular FAQs**: Chatbots answer common inquiries, improving efficiency.
    Example: Resolving routine visa questions without human intervention.

15. **AI for processing consular reports**: Analyzes citizen cases to identify trends and enhance services.
    Example: Spotting increased theft reports in a region and issuing travel advisories.

16. **Automated notifications for policy changes**: Alerts citizens to updates in travel or visa policies.
    Example: Informing travelers of new COVID-19 entry requirements.

17. **AI for predictive consular demand management**: Forecasts peak periods for consular services.
    Example: Preparing for increased visa applications during holiday seasons.

18. **AI for citizen health crisis alerts**: Warns citizens of local health risks, like outbreaks or contaminated food.
    Example: Notifying citizens abroad about unsafe water supplies.

CRISIS AND EMERGENCY MANAGEMENT

19. **AI for multi-crisis prioritization**: Assesses concurrent crises to allocate resources effectively.
    Example: Prioritizing aid for a coup over a minor natural disaster.

20. **Evacuation route optimization**: Suggests real-time evacuation routes during crises.
    Example: Recommending alternative roads during a wildfire.

21. **AI for international crisis collaboration**: Facilitates joint responses with allied embassies.
    Example: Coordinating a multinational evacuation during a regional conflict.

22. **AI-powered refugee movement prediction**: Predicts migration patterns during humanitarian crises.
    Example: Forecasting refugee flows from a war-torn region to neighboring countries.

23. **AI for disease outbreak detection**: Tracks early signs of epidemics in crisis zones.
    Example: Detecting cholera risks in disaster-stricken areas.

24. **AI for emergency supply chain management**: Optimizes the delivery of humanitarian aid.
    Example: Ensuring medical supplies reach areas affected by an earthquake first.

25. **Automated risk alerts for embassy personnel**: Flags potential threats to staff and facilities.
    Example: Detecting unusual activity near an embassy compound.

26. **AI for coordinating emergency donations**: Matches donated resources with needs in affected areas.
    Example: Redirecting excess clothing donations to areas requiring medical supplies.

27. **Real-time disaster impact mapping**: Uses satellite and social media data to assess crisis zones.
    Example: Mapping flood damage to guide rescue operations.

28. **AI for real-time conflict escalation monitoring**: Monitors political developments to predict violence.
    Example: Flagging increased military movement near a disputed border.

29. **AI for coordinating cross-border evacuations**: Plans multi-country evacuations during regional emergencies.
    Example: Ensuring citizens of several allied nations are evacuated together during a natural disaster.

DIPLOMATIC NEGOTIATIONS AND MULTILATERAL ENGAGEMENT

30. **Real-time translation for diplomats**: Provides instant translations during meetings, ensuring clear communication between parties.
    Example: AI translates speeches at a UN assembly in real time, allowing all diplomats to follow discussions seamlessly.

31. **AI for stakeholder mapping in negotiations**: Identifies influential parties and their interests in complex talks.
    Example: Mapping climate negotiation positions to find common ground among participating nations.

32. **AI-enhanced treaty drafting and gap analysis**: Reviews treaties for inconsistencies and ensures alignment with existing agreements.
    Example: AI detects clauses in a trade deal that conflict with prior commitments in a regional economic treaty.

33. **AI for mediation scenario planning**: Simulates outcomes for different negotiation strategies to suggest compromises.
    Example: AI models trade scenarios to recommend tariff adjustments that benefit all parties.

34. **Predictive models for treaty compliance**: Forecasts potential violations of agreements based on historical trends and current conditions.
    Example: Predicting a nation might breach its emissions commitments based on industrial growth patterns.

35. **AI for proposal ranking in multilateral talks**: Prioritizes proposals by analyzing their feasibility and potential for consensus.
    Example: Ranking the most viable solutions in a global water-sharing agreement.

36. **AI for intercultural sensitivity in negotiations**: Recommends culturally appropriate language and gestures to avoid misunderstandings.
   Example: Suggesting alternative phrasing during trade talks to avoid unintentional offense.

37. **AI for managing confidential negotiation data**: Ensures secure storage and analysis of sensitive files.
   Example: Encrypting trade negotiation documents to prevent leaks or unauthorized access.

38. **Real-time fact validation in talks**: Verifies claims during negotiations to prevent misinformation from affecting outcomes.
   Example: Correcting exaggerated economic statistics cited during trade discussions.

39. **AI for managing diplomatic protocols**: Ensures adherence to formal customs and traditions during meetings.
   Example: Alerting diplomats to address foreign dignitaries with the correct titles.

ECONOMIC DIPLOMACY AND TRADE FACILITATION

40. **AI for analyzing emerging economic alliances**: Tracks global trade trends to identify new partnerships and opportunities.
   Example: Spotting increased trade activity between two nations and proposing a trilateral trade agreement.

41. **AI-Powered risk assessments in trade deals**: Identifies potential risks, such as hidden liabilities or market instability.
   Example: Flagging environmental risks in a proposed agricultural trade deal.

42. **AI for optimizing trade missions**: Recommends the best locations, sectors, and companies to target during trade visits.
   Example: Identifying renewable energy companies for an embassy's trade mission in Southeast Asia.

43. **AI for monitoring global supply chains**: Tracks disruptions that may impact trade agreements.
   Example: Alerting diplomats to shipping delays affecting a partner country's exports.

44. **Predictive models for trade sanctions impact**: Analyzes how sanctions affect trade, diplomatic relations, and domestic economies.
   Example: Forecasting reduced oil revenues in a sanctioned country to guide diplomatic strategy.

45. **AI for cross-border financial crime detection**: Identifies suspicious transactions in international trade to ensure compliance with financial regulations.

     Example: Detecting fraudulent invoicing practices between two trading partners.

46. **Market demand forecasting for export strategy**: Uses AI to predict demand for specific products in foreign markets.

     Example: Recommending agricultural equipment exports to a growing region.

47. **AI for tax policy simulation in trade talks**: Models the impact of tax changes on trade and economic growth.

     Example: Showing how reduced tariffs could increase trade volumes and tax revenues.

48. **AI-powered analysis of trade barriers**: Identifies regulatory or logistical hurdles impacting trade agreements.

     Example: Flagging non-tariff barriers in an export deal for medical equipment.

49. **AI for diversifying trade partnerships**: Recommends new trade opportunities by analyzing underutilized markets and industries.

     Example: Highlighting untapped potential in exporting tech products to developing countries.

50. **AI for tracking trade policy feedback**: Analyzes economic indicators and public sentiment to evaluate the impact of implemented trade policies.

     Example: Identifying dissatisfaction with export taxes and recommending policy adjustments.

ENVIRONMENTAL AND CLIMATE DIPLOMACY

51. **AI for tracking global climate agreements**: Monitors countries' compliance with international climate commitments.

     Example: Alerting diplomats when a nation exceeds its allowable CO_2 emissions under the Paris Agreement.

52. **AI for carbon credit fraud detection**: Detects fraudulent activities in carbon trading markets to ensure transparency.

     Example: Identifying companies overstating their carbon offset contributions.

53. **AI for analyzing climate refugee movements**: Anticipates migration patterns caused by climate change.

Example: Predicting population displacement in low-lying coastal areas due to rising sea levels.

54. **AI for monitoring biodiversity loss**: Tracks declines in species and ecosystems to support international conservation efforts.
    Example: Detecting illegal deforestation in the Amazon using satellite data.

55. **AI for sustainable infrastructure planning**: Recommends renewable energy and sustainable development projects in host countries.
    Example: Proposing solar energy investments in underserved regions.

56. **AI for water resource diplomacy**: Tracks and predicts water-sharing conflicts across borders.
    Example: Identifying regions where water scarcity may lead to tensions, prompting early diplomatic interventions.

57. **AI for mapping illegal deforestation**: Uses AI and satellite data to detect unauthorized logging activities.
    Example: Spotting illegal logging in a protected rainforest and alerting international authorities.

58. **AI for regional air quality analysis**: Tracks pollution levels to inform cross-border environmental agreements.
    Example: Highlighting increased smog in a region shared by two nations to encourage cooperative action.

59. **AI-driven climate finance allocation**: Recommends the most effective distribution of climate funds to mitigate impacts.
    Example: Advising international organizations on directing resources to areas vulnerable to flooding.

60. **AI for global climate policy modeling**: Simulates the long-term impacts of proposed environmental policies.
    Example: Modeling how carbon taxes could reduce emissions and affect trade in participating countries.

61. **AI for managing cross-border environmental projects**: Analyzes real-time data to predict the ecological impacts of international projects.
    Example: Monitoring a river management project to ensure fair water allocation among bordering nations.

CULTURAL EXCHANGE AND EDUCATION DIPLOMACY

62. **AI for tailored cultural exchange matching**: Matches participants to exchange programs based on shared goals and qualifications.

Example: Pairing students from two countries for language exchanges based on complementary skill levels.

63. **AI-enhanced tracking of alumni impact**: Measures the long-term contributions of cultural program alumni to global relations.
    Example: Analyzing how former Fulbright scholars influence diplomatic ties between their countries.

64. **AI for virtual cultural collaboration platforms**: Facilitates online artistic and academic exchanges between countries.
    Example: Hosting a virtual art exhibition where artists from different nations collaborate in real time.

65. **AI for predicting educational trends**: Identifies emerging fields of study to guide scholarship and training programs.
    Example: Highlighting a growing demand for AI ethics education in developing regions.

66. **AI for analyzing historical exchange outcomes**: Evaluates the impact of past exchanges on diplomatic relations.
    Example: Showing how cultural festivals improve bilateral perceptions over time.

67. **AI for language learning personalization**: Customizes language learning programs for exchange participants.
    Example: Adapting an online language course for a student preparing to study abroad.

68. **AI for managing cross-cultural events**: Schedules and optimizes events based on attendee demographics and cultural preferences.
    Example: Planning a music festival that aligns with local tastes and traditions.

69. **AI for art diplomacy impact analysis**: Tracks the influence of art exhibitions on diplomatic relationships.
    Example: Measuring increased engagement with embassy programs after a high-profile art event.

70. **AI for enhancing global literacy campaigns**: Recommends strategies to promote education in underserved regions.
    Example: Identifying communities where digital literacy initiatives can have the greatest impact.

71. **AI for cultural sentiment analysis**: Tracks public reactions to cultural diplomacy initiatives in real time.

Example: Monitoring social media responses to a cultural event to refine future programming.

72. **AI for personalized tourism promotion**: Uses data to recommend tourism opportunities that align with diplomatic goals.
    Example: Promoting visits to shared heritage sites to strengthen cultural ties between countries.

SECURITY AND CYBERSECURITY IN DIPLOMACY

73. **AI-enhanced counterintelligence**: Detects potential espionage risks by analyzing suspicious patterns of activity near embassies.
    Example: Flagging repeated visits by an unidentified individual near restricted areas.

74. **Cybersecurity threat detection in diplomatic networks**: Identifies and neutralizes cyber threats targeting embassy communications.
    Example: Preventing a phishing attempt aimed at a high-ranking diplomat's email.

75. **AI for secure communication channels**: Encrypts and monitors diplomatic messages for unauthorized access attempts.
    Example: Alerting diplomats to potential security breaches in encrypted communications.

76. **AI for facial recognition at embassy checkpoints**: Enhances physical security by verifying the identities of visitors and staff.
    Example: Preventing unauthorized access to restricted embassy areas.

77. **AI for identifying insider threats**: Monitors for unusual behavior or access patterns among embassy personnel.
    Example: Detecting an employee downloading sensitive files without authorization.

78. **AI for coordinating cyber defense with allies**: Shares real-time threat intelligence between allied nations.
    Example: Identifying a coordinated cyberattack targeting multiple embassies.

79. **AI for analyzing cyber policy impacts**: Models the effects of proposed international regulations on cybersecurity practices.
    Example: Showing how new encryption laws could affect global diplomatic communications.

80. **AI for safeguarding classified documents**: Tracks and limits access to sensitive materials within digital archives.

Example: Preventing unauthorized personnel from retrieving classified files.

81. **AI for analyzing terrorism risk trends**: Uses data to predict and mitigate extremist threats.

    Example: Identifying an increase in extremist online activity targeting specific diplomatic missions.

82. **AI for emergency security protocols**: Automatically activates enhanced security measures during detected threats.

    Example: Locking down embassy access points during a nearby protest-turned-riot.

INSTITUTIONAL MANAGEMENT AND MISSION OPERATIONS

83. **AI for staffing and workforce optimization**: Adjusts embassy staffing levels based on workload and seasonal demand.

    Example: Suggesting additional visa processing staff during peak tourist seasons.

84. **AI for knowledge management and archiving**: Organizes and retrieves historical diplomatic documents quickly.

    Example: Locating a decades-old treaty clause relevant to current negotiations.

85. **AI for automating administrative tasks**: Handles routine tasks like generating reports and formatting documents.

    Example: Producing monthly visa application summaries for mission leadership.

86. **AI for budget allocation in diplomatic missions**: Recommends optimal resource allocation based on mission goals and expenditure patterns.

    Example: Suggesting increased funding for cultural diplomacy programs after analyzing past engagement data.

87. **AI for event scheduling and coordination**: Avoids scheduling conflicts for multi-nation talks and public events.

    Example: Coordinating time zones and availability for a global climate summit.

88. **AI for facility maintenance predictions**: Flags potential infrastructure issues before they occur.

    Example: Alerting embassy staff about the need to repair an aging air conditioning system.

89. **AI for real-time performance monitoring**: Tracks the success of diplomatic programs and initiatives in real time.
    Example: Measuring audience engagement during a cultural diplomacy campaign.

90. **AI for energy efficiency in missions**: Monitors and optimizes energy use in embassy facilities.
    Example: Reducing energy costs by identifying wasteful electricity consumption patterns.

91. **AI for managing digital workflows**: Streamlines document approvals, inter-department communication, and project tracking.
    Example: Simplifying the approval process for large-scale visa policy changes.

92. **AI for embassy outreach metrics**: Analyzes data from outreach efforts to gauge their effectiveness.
    Example: Assessing the impact of embassy-hosted workshops on public opinion.

GLOBAL GOVERNANCE AND MULTILATERAL COOPERATION

93. **AI for facilitating cross-border data sharing**: Streamlines the secure exchange of critical data between nations.
    Example: Sharing real-time climate data among UN member states to improve emissions tracking.

94. **AI for multilateral crisis management**: Coordinates responses to global emergencies by analyzing resource needs and deployment logistics.
    Example: Assisting the UN in allocating humanitarian aid during a multi-nation refugee crisis.

95. **AI for conflict prevention in international organizations**: Predicts potential disputes between nations based on political, social, and economic data.
    Example: Flagging rising tensions over maritime borders to prompt early mediation efforts.

96. **AI for monitoring compliance with sanctions**: Tracks financial transactions and trade flows to ensure adherence to international penalties.
    Example: Detecting sanctions violations by identifying hidden oil exports.

97. **AI for global resource allocation**: Recommends equitable distribution of global resources like vaccines or food aid.
    Example: Directing vaccines to regions with the highest outbreak risk based on predictive modeling.

98. **AI for enhancing virtual international forums**: Powers digital platforms for global discussions, enabling participation from all nations.
    Example: Hosting a virtual summit during a pandemic to continue negotiations on climate agreements.

99. **AI for analyzing global policy trends**: Identifies emerging priorities by analyzing policy decisions across nations.
    Example: Highlighting a trend toward stricter privacy laws globally to shape diplomatic strategy.

100. **AI for promoting SDG compliance**: Tracks progress toward meeting the UN Sustainable Development Goals (SDGs).
    Example: Monitoring clean water access initiatives in developing countries and identifying gaps.

Appendix B
Introduction to the
AI Landscape
Tools, Platforms, and Solutions for Everyday and Enterprise Use

Artificial intelligence (AI) has become an essential part of our modern world, with tools and platforms designed to help individuals, businesses, and governments solve problems, enhance productivity, and create new possibilities. Whether you're a layperson exploring AI for the first time or someone looking to leverage AI in your work, this introduction provides an overview of the key AI technologies available today, from language models to tools for creating images, videos, and more.

LARGE LANGUAGE MODELS: TRANSFORMING COMMUNICATION AND KNOWLEDGE

Large Language Models (LLMs) are AI systems trained to understand and generate human-like text. They power chatbots, content creation tools, and other applications. Here are the latest advancements:

- **OpenAI GPT-4.5 and ChatGPT**
  OpenAI has announced GPT-4.5, internally referred to as "Orion," as the final model before integrating chain-of-thought reasoning in GPT-5. This upcoming shift is expected to bring more advanced AI reasoning capabilities.

- **Google Gemini**
  Google has released **Gemini 2.5 Flash**, delivering faster responses and more advanced multimodal capabilities. Gemini Live now allows users to interact using images, files, and even YouTube videos.

- **Anthropic Claude**
  Claude models have been refined with **Claude Opus 4** for high-level reasoning and **Claude Sonnet 4** for efficiency. Anthropic has also introduced the **Anthropic Economic Index** to track AI's impact on labor markets.

- **Meta's LLaMA**
  LLaMA continues to serve as an open-source AI model, with **specialized versions** like Code LLaMA for developers.

- **xAI Grok**
  Elon Musk's xAI has expanded **Grok**, integrating it further with **X (formerly Twitter)** for real-time conversational AI services.

VISUAL AI TECHNOLOGIES: CREATING STUNNING IMAGES AND VIDEOS

AI isn't just for words—it also generates visuals, from images to videos:

- **DALL·E 3 (OpenAI)**
  Generates detailed and photorealistic images from text descriptions.

- **Midjourney**
  A community-driven image generator with a distinctive artistic style.

- **Stable Diffusion**
  An open-source image generator widely used in industries like gaming and advertising.

- **Runway Gen-3**
  A leading tool for creating videos from text descriptions.

- **Adobe Firefly Video Model**
  The first commercially safe AI video generation tool, allowing users to create videos from text prompts, adjust camera angles, and add motion elements.

AI FOR DEVELOPERS: SIMPLIFYING CODING AND SOFTWARE DEVELOPMENT

- **GitHub Copilot**
  Now more accessible with fewer waitlist restrictions, enabling AI-assisted coding.

- **Amazon CodeWhisperer**
  Improved integration with AWS and enhanced security features.

- **AlphaCode (DeepMind)**
  - A tool for competitive coding, helping developers tackle complex programming challenges.

AUDIO AND SPEECH TECHNOLOGIES: MAKING AI TALK AND LISTEN

- **ElevenLabs**
  Offers realistic voice cloning in multiple languages.

- **OpenAI Whisper**
  Advanced speech recognition with superior noise handling.

- **SoundHound AI**
  Powers voice assistants in smart devices, cars, and IoT products.

ENTERPRISE AI SOLUTIONS: BOOSTING PRODUCTIVITY AND CUSTOMER ENGAGEMENT

- **Microsoft Copilot**
  Now embedded in Office applications (Word, Excel) for automating tasks.

- **Intercom and Ada**
  AI-driven platforms that enhance customer service interactions.

AI FOR RESEARCH AND SCIENTIFIC DISCOVERY

- **AlphaFold (DeepMind)**
  Continues to revolutionize protein structure prediction.

- **Babylon Health**
  AI-driven medical diagnostics aiding virtual consultations.

INDUSTRY-SPECIFIC AI SOLUTIONS

- **Alpaca AI (Finance)**
  Assists in financial analysis, trading algorithms, and risk management.

- **Duolingo Max (Education)**
  Uses AI to personalize language learning.

CONSUMER APPLICATIONS: AI IN EVERYDAY LIFE

- **Apple Intelligence**
  Integrated into **iOS 18, iPadOS 18, and macOS Sequoia**, offering advanced photography, translation, and personal assistant features.

- **Amazon Alexa and Google Home**
  AI-powered voice assistants for home automation and entertainment.

EMERGING TRENDS IN AI

- **DeepSeek AI**
  A Chinese AI startup whose chatbot surpassed ChatGPT as the most-downloaded free app on the iOS App Store in the United States.

- **Living Intelligence**
  A convergence of AI, biotech, and advanced sensors, leading to AI systems that can sense, learn, adapt, and evolve.

Glossary of AI Terms for Diplomats

A

Algorithm: A set of rules or calculations followed by a computer to solve problems or make decisions.
Example: Algorithms analyze trade data to recommend optimal negotiation strategies.
Artificial Intelligence (AI): Machines' ability to perform tasks that typically require human intelligence, such as analysis, decision-making, and language translation.
Example: AI assists diplomats in processing public sentiment on social media.
Adaptive AI: Systems that evolve and improve over time based on new data and feedback.
Example: Adaptive AI tailors embassy communication strategies based on regional cultural nuances.

B

Big Data: Massive datasets that require AI tools for analysis to reveal patterns and trends.
Example: Big data helps diplomats understand migration trends and forecast potential crises.
Bias Mitigation: Techniques to identify and reduce bias in AI systems to ensure fair outcomes.
Example: Visa processing systems implement bias mitigation to ensure equitable decisions.
Blockchain in Diplomacy: A decentralized technology ensuring secure and transparent record-keeping.
Example: Blockchain secures treaties and international agreements by providing immutable records.

C

Chatbots: AI systems that simulate human conversation to provide real-time information.
Example: Chatbots answer visa-related queries for consular services, reducing workloads.

Computer Vision: AI's ability to interpret visual data, such as images or videos.
Example: Computer vision identifies environmental damage in satellite images to inform diplomatic aid responses.
Collaborative AI: Systems designed to work alongside humans to enhance decision-making.
Example: Collaborative AI analyzes policy drafts and suggests refinements for clarity.

D

Data Sovereignty: Ensuring data remains within the legal jurisdiction of its origin country.
Example: Data sovereignty laws govern AI systems used for cross-border trade analysis.
Digital Diplomacy: The use of digital tools, including AI, to conduct diplomacy and international relations.
Example: AI-driven digital campaigns improve public engagement on foreign policy issues.
Deep Learning: A subset of AI using neural networks with multiple layers to identify patterns.
Example: Deep learning automates real-time translation during diplomatic negotiations.

E

Ethical AI: AI systems designed with fairness, accountability, and transparency as core principles.
Example: Ethical AI ensures equitable outcomes in humanitarian aid distribution decisions.
Enterprise AI: Scalable AI systems integrated across an organization to streamline operations.
Example: Enterprise AI automates routine reporting in diplomatic missions.
Explainable AI (XAI): Systems that provide clear, human-understandable explanations for their decisions.
Example: XAI ensures that AI recommendations during peace talks can be justified to stakeholders.

F

Facial Recognition: AI that identifies individuals by analyzing facial features.
Example: Facial recognition enhances security at embassies and consulates.
Federated Learning: Collaborative AI training across multiple datasets without sharing sensitive data.

Example: Federated learning enables secure cooperation between allied countries on AI models.

Forecasting with AI: Using AI to predict future events based on historical data.

Example: AI forecasts political instability to inform early diplomatic interventions.

G

Generative AI: AI systems capable of creating content, such as text, images, or music.

Example: Generative AI drafts press releases tailored for international audiences.

General AI: Hypothetical AI systems with the capacity to perform any intellectual task a human can.

Example: General AI could one day assist diplomats across multiple domains simultaneously.

Governance in AI: Frameworks to regulate the development and use of AI.

Example: AI governance ensures compliance with international privacy and security standards.

H

Hybrid Intelligence: Combining human expertise with AI capabilities to optimize decision-making.

Example: Hybrid intelligence systems analyze treaties for compliance issues while experts provide context.

Human-in-the-Loop (HITL): AI systems requiring human oversight to guide decisions.

Example: HITL ensures accountability in AI systems used for refugee resettlement programs.

Hyperautomation: Using AI to automate multiple processes and tasks.

*Exampl*e: Hyperautomation streamlines visa application processing and reduces waiting times.

I

Inference (AI): The process of drawing conclusions from data using AI models.

Example: Inference predicts the impact of trade policies on regional economies.

Internet of Things (IoT): Devices interconnected via the internet that collect and share data.

Example: IoT devices in embassies monitor environmental conditions for energy efficiency.

Innovation Sandbox: Controlled environments for testing new AI applications.
Example: Sandboxes allow low-risk experimentation with AI-driven negotiation tools.

L

Large Language Models (LLMs): AI trained on vast amounts of text data for language-related tasks.
Example: LLMs assist diplomats by summarizing complex legal documents.
Localization in AI: Adapting AI systems to specific cultural and regional contexts.
Example: AI translation tools incorporate local idioms for diplomatic accuracy.
Legal AI: AI tools designed to analyze and manage legal texts and processes.
Example: Legal AI identifies relevant clauses in multilateral treaties.

M

Machine Learning (ML): AI systems that improve their performance by learning from data.
Example: ML predicts global migration patterns based on historical trends.
Model Training: The process of teaching an AI system to recognize patterns in data.
Example: Training a model on past trade agreements helps AI predict negotiation outcomes.
Multimodal AI: AI systems that integrate multiple data types, such as text, images, and audio.
Example: Multimodal AI analyzes social media posts and satellite imagery to assess disaster impacts.

N

Natural Language Processing (NLP): AI's ability to understand and generate human language.
Example: NLP tools translate diplomatic speeches in real time.
Neural Machine Translation (NMT): AI translation systems using neural networks for high accuracy.
Example: NMT provides real-time translation during international summits.
Narrow AI: AI systems designed for specific tasks.
Example: Narrow AI powers chatbots for public-facing embassy services.

P

Predictive Analytics: AI tools that forecast future trends or events.
Example: Predictive analytics anticipates economic downturns in key trading partners.

Privacy-Preserving AI: Systems designed to analyze data without exposing sensitive information.
Example: Privacy-preserving AI enables secure international data-sharing agreements.

Preprocessing (Data): Preparing raw data for AI analysis by cleaning and formatting it.
Example: Preprocessing ensures accurate results in AI-driven sentiment analysis.

R

Robustness in AI: The ability of an AI system to perform reliably under varied conditions.
Example: Robust AI systems maintain accuracy despite noisy or incomplete data.

Reinforcement Learning: AI that learns by receiving rewards or penalties for its actions.
Example: AI simulates diplomatic negotiations to optimize negotiation strategies.

Risk Management in AI: Identifying and mitigating risks associated with AI applications.
Example: Risk management protocols prevent bias in visa processing systems.

S

Sentiment Analysis: AI tools that analyze text to determine emotional tone.
Example: Sentiment analysis gauges public opinion on foreign policy announcements.

Scalability in AI: The ability of AI systems to handle increasing data or task demands.
Example: Scalable AI models adapt to growing datasets in global economic analysis.

Swarm Intelligence: AI systems inspired by natural collective behaviors like ant colonies.
Example: Swarm intelligence optimizes resource allocation during crisis response.

T

Transparency in AI: Ensuring that AI processes and decisions are understandable to users.
Example: Transparent AI tools build trust in policy recommendations.
Transfer Learning: Applying knowledge gained from one task to a related task.
Example: AI trained on economic data is adapted for trade negotiation predictions.
Text Mining: Extracting valuable insights from large volumes of text data.
Example: Text mining identifies key terms in multilateral treaties for legal reviews.

V

Virtual Envoy: Hypothetical AI-driven ambassadors performing routine diplomatic tasks.
Example: Virtual envoys could facilitate initial trade discussions between nations.
Virtual Reality (VR): AI-generated immersive environments for education or public diplomacy.
Example: VR tours of cultural landmarks strengthen international relationships.
Voice Recognition: AI technology that transcribes spoken language into text.
Example: Voice recognition assists in documenting diplomatic meetings.

W

Weak AI: Narrow AI systems designed to perform specific tasks.
Example: Weak AI chatbots assist consulates in answering routine public inquiries.
Weighted Models: AI models that assign varying importance to different inputs.
Example: Weighted models prioritize political factors over economic ones in regional analyses.
Workflow Automation: Using AI to streamline repetitive tasks.
Example: Automation accelerates document processing for international agreements.

Z

Zero-Day Threat Detection: AI systems identifying unknown security vulnerabilities in real time.

Example: Embassies use zero-day threat detection to protect against cyberattacks.

Zero Trust Security: A cybersecurity model requiring strict verification for every system interaction.

Example: Zero trust principles protect sensitive diplomatic AI systems.

Zero-Shot Learning: AI systems solving tasks without prior specific training.

Example: Zero-shot learning helps AI adapt to new languages for immediate use in negotiations.

Bibliography

Adler-Nissen, Rebecca, and Kristin Anabel Eggeling. "Diplomatic Negotiations in the Digital Context: Key Issues, Emerging Trends, and Procedural Changes." In *The Oxford Handbook of Digital Diplomacy*, edited by Corneliu Bjola and Ilan Manor, 103–120. Oxford: Oxford University Press, 2024.

Aguirre, Daniel, and Alejandro Ramos. "Digital Diplomacy in Latin America: Among Early Adopters and Latecomers." In *The Oxford Handbook of Digital Diplomacy*, edited by Corneliu Bjola and Ilan Manor, 546–563. Oxford: Oxford University Press, 2024.

Akdenizli, Banu. "Diplomacy in Times of Crisis in the GCC: The Blockade and the Pandemic." In *The Oxford Handbook of Digital Diplomacy*, edited by Corneliu Bjola and Ilan Manor, 564–581. Oxford: Oxford University Press, 2024.

Alder, Madison. 2024. "From Translation to Email Drafting, State Department Turns to AI to Assist Workforce." *FedScoop*, December 11, 2024. https://fedscoop.com/state-department-ai-chatbot-email-drafting-northstar-famsearch/.

Alder, Madison. "Federal Government Discloses More Than 1,700 AI Use Cases." *Fedscoop*. Accessed January 27, 2025. www.fedscoop.com/federal-government-discloses-more-than-1700-ai-use-cases/.

Allam, Muhammad A. F. "Effective Digital Diplomacy? A Case Study of the British Embassy in Egypt." In *Artificial Intelligence and Digital Diplomacy: Challenges and Opportunities*, edited by Fatima Roumate, 209–228. Cham: Springer, 2021.

Altman, Sam. Quoted in Joel Tansey. "OpenAI CEO Calls on China to Help Shape AI Safety Guidelines." *Japan Times*, June 10, 2023. https://www.japantimes.co.jp/news/2023/06/10/business/tech/openai-ceo-china-ai-safety/.

"Artificial Intelligence Arms Race." *Wikipedia: The Free Encyclopedia*. Accessed February 5, 2025. https://en.wikipedia.org/wiki/Artificial_intelligence_arms_race.

Asokan, Akshaya. "UK Government Debuts AI Tools for Enhanced Public Services." *BankInfoSecurity*, January 21, 2025. https://www.bankinfosecurity.com/uk-government-debuts-ai-tools-for-enhanced-public-services-a-27344.

Austin, Tasha, Alexis Bonnell, Sean Davis, and Will Frankenstein. *Using Artificial Intelligence (AI) to Modernize American Statecraft: How the Department of State Can Use AI Today to Address the Biggest Global Challenges*. Deloitte AI Institute for Government and Google Cloud. November 2022.

Australian Government Department of Foreign Affairs and Trade. "Joint Press Release: Australia and Denmark Lead New Global Tech Network." *Australian Government Department of Foreign Affairs and Trade*. Accessed March 24, 2022. https://www.dfat.gov.au/news/media-release/joint-press-release-australia-and-denmark-lead-new-global-tech-network.

Baele, Stephane. "The Threat of Language Models." *CREST Guide*. London: CREST Research, 2022. https://crestresearch.ac.uk/resources/artificial-intelligence-and-extremism-the-threat-of-language-models/.

Baele, Stephane J., Iqraa Bukhari, Christopher Whyte, Scott Cuomo, Benjamin Jensen, Kenneth Payne, and Eugenio V. Garcia. "AI IR: Charting International Relations in the Age of Artificial Intelligence." *International Studies Review* 26, no. 2 (June 2024).

Baines, Victoria. "International Law, Big Tech Regulation, and Digital Diplomatic Practice." In *The Oxford Handbook of Digital Diplomacy*, edited by Corneliu Bjola and Ilan Manor, 437–456. Oxford: Oxford University Press, 2024.

Bano, Muneera, Zahid Chaudhri, and Didar Zowghi. *The Role of Generative AI in Global Diplomatic Practices: A Strategic Framework*. December 19, 2023. https://doi.org/10.13140/RG.2.2.20426.34249.

Bârgăoanu, Alina, and Bianca-Florentina Cheregi. "Artificial Intelligence: The New Tool for Cyber Diplomacy—The Case of the European Union." In *Artificial Intelligence and Digital Diplomacy: Challenges and Opportunities*, edited by Fatima Roumate, 115–130. Cham: Springer, 2021.

Barker, Tim. "European Commission Significantly Boosts Military Tech Spending." *Wired*, February 2024. https://www.wired.com/story/european-commission-military-tech-spending.

Batke, Jessica, and Mareike Ohlberg. "Message Control: How a New For-Profit Industry Helps China's Leaders 'Manage Public Opinion'." *ChinaFile*, December 20, 2020. https://www.chinafile.com/reporting-opinion/features/message-control-china.

Bengio, Yoshua. "Personal and Psychological Dimensions of AI Researchers Confronting AI Catastrophic Risks." *Yoshua Bengio (blog)*. Accessed August 12, 2023. https://yoshuabengio.org/2023/08/12/personal-and-psychological-dimensions-of-ai-researchers-confronting-ai-catastrophic-risks/.

Benouachan, Hassan. "The Potential and Limits of US Digital Diplomacy in the Middle East and North Africa." In *Artificial Intelligence and Digital Diplomacy: Challenges and Opportunities*, edited by Fatima Roumate, 169–194. Cham: Springer, 2021.

Berridge, G. R. *Diplomacy: Theory and Practice.* 6th ed. Cham: Palgrave Macmillan, 2022.

Berridge, G. R., Maurice Keens-Soper, and T. G. Otte. *Diplomatic Theory from Machiavelli to Kissinger.* London: Palgrave Macmillan, 2001.

Bezos, Jeff. "Jeff Bezos Explains Amazon's Artificial Intelligence and Machine Learning Strategy." Interview by Michael Beckerman. *GeekWire*, May 6, 2017. https://www.geekwire.com/2017/jeff-bezos-explains-amazons-artificial-intelligence-machine-learning-strategy/.

Biddle, Sam. "Inside the U.K.'s Bold Experiment in AI Safety." *Time*, January 2025. https://time.com/7204670/uk-ai-safety-institute/.

Biden, Joseph R., Jr. "Executive Order 14110: Safe, Secure, and Trustworthy Development and Use of Artificial Intelligence." *Federal Register* 88, no. 210 (November 1, 2023): 74141–74150. https://www.federalregister.gov/documents/2023/11/01/2023-24283/safe-secure-and-trustworthy-development-and-use-of-artificial-intelligence.

Bjola, Corneliu. "Diplomacy in the Age of Artificial Intelligence." *EDA Working Paper.* Emirates Diplomatic Academy, Abu Dhabi, 2020.

Bjola, Corneliu, Isabella Cassidy, and Ilan Manor. "Artificial Intelligence and Diplomatic Crisis Management: Addressing the 'Fog of War' Problem." *DigDiploROx Working Paper No. 6*, 2022. Accessed May 23, 2025. https://www.qeh.ox.ac.uk/sites/default/files/2023-08/DigDiploROxWP6.pdf

Bjola, Corneliu, and Didzis Kļaviņš. "The Digital Hybridization of Ministries of Foreign Affairs: The Case of the Nordic and Baltic States." In *The Oxford Handbook of Digital Diplomacy*, edited by Corneliu Bjola and Ilan Manor, 291–310. Oxford: Oxford University Press, 2024.

Bjola, Corneliu, and Markus Kornprobst, eds. *Digital International Relations: Technology, Agency, and Order.* London: Taylor & Francis, 2024.

Bjola, Corneliu, and Ilan Manor, eds. The Oxford Handbook of Digital Diplomacy. Oxford: Oxford University Press, 2024. https://doi.org/10.1093/oxfordhb/9780192859198.001.0001

Bjola, Corneliu, and Ilan Manor, eds. *The Oxford Handbook of Digital Diplomacy*. Oxford: Oxford University Press, 2024a.

Bjola, Corneliu, and Ilan Manor. "Introduction: Understanding Digital Diplomacy—The Grammar Rules and Patterns of Digital Disruption." In *The Oxford Handbook of Digital Diplomacy*, edited by Corneliu Bjola and Ilan Manor, 3–28. Oxford: Oxford University Press, 2024b.

Black, Jeremy. *A History of Diplomacy.* London: Reaktion Books, 2010.

Black, Shawn. "8 Benefits of Artificial Intelligence in Facility Management." *FacilitiesNet*. Accessed January 19, 2025. www.facilitiesnet.com/software/article/8-Benefits-of-Artificial-Intelligence-in-Facility-Management--19961.

Blaser, Virginia. *The Manager's Workbook: Six Worksheets for the Evaluation Cycle.* Independently Published, 2022.

Blaser, Virginia. "How to Use Artificial Intelligence in Diplomacy." *Washington International Diplomatic Academy*, October 1, 2023. Accessed February 2, 2025. https://diplomati-cacademy.us/2023/10/01/artificial-intelligence-diplomacy/.

Bouchard, Caroline. "The Digitalization of Permanent Missions to International Organizations." In *The Oxford Handbook of Digital Diplomacy*, edited by Corneliu Bjola and Ilan Manor, 330–347. Oxford: Oxford University Press, 2024.

Briant, Emma L. "Researching Influence Operations: 'Dark Arts' Mercenaries and the Digital Influence Industry." In *The Oxford Handbook of Digital Diplomacy*, edited by Corneliu Bjola and Ilan Manor, 80–99. Oxford: Oxford University Press, 2024.

Broustau, Nadège, and Marie Neihouser. "'Always There': How Diplomats Deal with Visibility Injunction in the Digital Public Sphere." In *Artificial Intelligence and Digital Diplomacy: Challenges and Opportunities*, edited by Fatima Roumate, 57–71. Cham: Springer, 2021.

Brynjolfsson, Erik. "Fixing the AI Skills Shortage: An Interview with Erik Brynjolfsson." Interview by Salesforce. *MIT Initiative on the Digital Economy*, March 20, 2019. https://ide.mit.edu/insights/fixing-the-ai-skills-shortage-an-interview-with-erik-brynjolfsson/.

Buch, Amanda M., David M. Eagleman, and Lauren Grosenick. "Engineering Diplomacy: How AI and Human Augmentation Could Remake the Art of Foreign Relations." *Science & Diplomacy*, February 25, 2022. https://www.sciencediplomacy.org/perspective/2022/engineering-diplomacy-how-ai-and-human-augmentation-could-remake-art-foreign.

Bullock, Joseph, Alexandra Luccioni, Katherine Hoffmann Pham, Cynthia Sin Nga Lam, and Miguel Luengo-Oroz. "Mapping the Landscape of Artificial Intelligence Applications against COVID-19." *UN Global Pulse*, March 2020. https://www.unglobalpulse.org/document/mapping-the-landscape-of-artificial-intelligence-applications-against-covid-19/.

Byman, Daniel L., Chongyang Gao, Chris Meserole, and V.S. Subrahmanian. "Deepfakes and International Conflict." *Brookings Institution*, January 2023. https://www.brookings.edu/articles/deepfakes-and-international-conflict/.

Carnegie Endowment for International Peace. *China's AI Regulations and How They Get Made.* Washington: Carnegie Endowment, 2023. https://carnegieendowment.org/2023/07/10/china-s-ai-regulations-and-how-they-get-made-pub-90117.

Cassidy, Jennifer A. "Digital Feminist Foreign Policy." In *The Oxford Handbook of Digital Diplomacy*, edited by Corneliu Bjola and Ilan Manor, 157–176. Oxford: Oxford University Press, 2024.

Chandler, Caitlin. "Inside the Black Box of Predictive Travel Surveillance." *Wired*, January 13, 2025. https://www.wired.com/story/inside-the-black-box-of-predictive-travel-surveillance.

"Chinese Intelligence Activity Abroad." *Wikipedia: The Free Encyclopedia*. Accessed February 5, 2025. https://en.wikipedia.org/wiki/Chinese_intelligence_activity_abroad.

Chowdhury, Rumman. "What Pop Culture Gets Wrong: Leading AI Ethicist Rumman Chowdhury Defines the Real Risks of Artificial Intelligence." Interview by Zach Coseglia and Hui Chen. *There Has to Be a Better Way?* Podcast, Ropes & Gray, August 9, 2023.

Cimmino, Jeffrey, and Andrew A. Michta. "Leveraging Generative Artificial Intelligence to Outcompete Strategic Rivals." *Atlantic Council*, March 14, 2024. https://www.atlanticcouncil.org/in-depth-research-reports/issue-brief/leveraging-generative-artificial-intelligence-to-outcompete-strategic-rivals/.

Collins, Elodie. "CGI Federal Wins New Visa Processing Support Task Orders From State Department." *GovCon Wire*, October 23, 2024. Accessed February 1, 2025. https://www.govconwire.com/2024/10/cgi-federal-state-department-contract-award/.

Cook, Tim. 2017. "Tim Cook: Apple Isn't Falling Behind—It's Just Not Ready to Talk about the Future." *MIT Technology Review*, June 14, 2017. https://www.technologyreview.com/2017/06/14/4525/tim-cook-apple-isnt-falling-behind-its-just-not-ready-to-talk-about-the-future/.

Cooper, Andrew F., and Jeff Hai-Chi Loo. "Chinese Wolf-Warrior Diplomacy: Motivations, Modalities, and Sites of Practice." In *The Oxford Handbook of Digital Diplomacy*, edited by Corneliu Bjola and Ilan Manor, 511–527. Oxford: Oxford University Press, 2024.

Cornish, Chloe, and Andrew England. "UAE President Meets Joe Biden in Push for More US AI Technology." *Financial Times*, September 25, 2024. www.ft.com/content/e85bef92-5f53-4f71-bb3b-a0d65f3a4c48.

Crawford, Kate. *Atlas of AI: Power, Politics, and the Planetary Costs of Artificial Intelligence*. New Haven: Yale University Press, 2021.

Crilley, Rhys. "Digital Nuclear Diplomacy." In *The Oxford Handbook of Digital Diplomacy*, edited by Corneliu Bjola and Ilan Manor, 138–156. Oxford: Oxford University Press, 2024.

Cuban, Mark. Interview by Jason Hirschhorn. *Upfront Summit 2017*. Upfront Ventures, February 8, 2017. Video, 32:04. https://www.youtube.com/watch?v=RtZ_H_aSTCI.

Cull, Nicholas J. "History and Digital Public Diplomacy: Media Disruption and Global Public Engagement Online in Historical Perspective." In *The Oxford Handbook of Digital Diplomacy*, edited by Corneliu Bjola and Ilan Manor, 177–193. Oxford: Oxford University Press, 2024.

Cummings, Mary, Heather Roff, Kenneth Cukier, Jacob Parakilas, and Hannah Bryce. *Artificial Intelligence and International Affairs: Disruption Anticipated*. London: Chatham House, 2018.

CyberScoop. " Chinese Hackers Turn to AI to Meddle in Elections." *CyberScoop*, January 2024. https://cyberscoop.com/microsoft-ai-election-taiwan/.

Daskalovski, Zhidas. "Digitalization between Security and Order and Democracy and Liberalism." In *Artificial Intelligence and Digital Diplomacy: Challenges and Opportunities*, edited by Fatima Roumate, 73–85. Cham: Springer, 2021.

Daugherty, Paul. "What's the Future of Work in the Age of AI?" *Salesforce (blog)*. Published March 26, 2020. https://www.salesforce.com/ap/blog/future-of-work-in-the-age-of-ai/.

Der Derian, James, and Alexander Wendt, eds. *Quantum International Relations: A Human Science for World Politics*. New York: Oxford University Press, 2022.

Di Martino, Luigi, and Heather Ford. "Navigating Uncertainty: Public Diplomacy vs. AI." *Place Branding and Public Diplomacy*, published online February 28, 2024. Accessed February 3, 2025. https://doi.org/10.1057/s41254-024-00330-z.

Doubleday, Justin. "With New AI Tools Available, State Department Encourages Experimentation." *Federal News Network*, June 28, 2024a. https://federalnewsnetwork.com/artificial-intelligence/2024/06/with-new-ai-tools-available-state-department-encourages-experimentation/.

Doubleday, Justin. "State's AI Chatbot Journey Started with Collaboration." *NextGov*, September 2024b. https://www.nextgov.com/artificial-intelligence/2024/09/states-ai-chatbot-journey-started-collaboration/399933/.

Elgot, Jessica, and Robert Booth. "AI Tool Can Give Ministers 'Vibe Check' on Whether MPs Will Like Policies." *The Guardian*, January 20, 2025. www.theguardian.com/technology/2025/jan/20/ai-tool-can-give-ministers-vibe-check-on-whether-mps-will-like-policies.

Elkhaldi, Mohammed. "Digital Diplomacy and International Regulation of the Web." In *Artificial Intelligence and Digital Diplomacy: Challenges and Opportunities*, edited by Fatima Roumate, 87–96. Cham: Springer, 2021.

European Commission. *Ethics Guidelines for Trustworthy Artificial Intelligence.* Brussels: European Commission, 2019. Accessed January 27, 2025. https://digital-strategy. ec.europa.eu/en/library/ethics-guidelines-trustworthy-ai.

European Commission. "AI Act Enters into Force." *European Commission*, August 1, 2024. Accessed January 27, 2025. https://commission.europa.eu/news/ai-act-enters-force-2024-08-01_en.

European Commission. "Bürokratt – A Single Chatbot for Estonia." *Interoperable Europe Portal.* Accessed January 27, 2025. https://interoperable-europe.ec.europa.eu/collection/public-sector-tech-watch/burokratt-single-chatbot-estonia.

Federal Bureau of Investigation. "Artificial Intelligence." *FBI.gov.* Accessed February 13, 2025. https://www.fbi.gov/investigate/counterintelligence/emerging-and-advanced-technology/artificial-intelligence.

Feijóo, Claudio, Youngsun Kwon, Johannes M. Bauer, Erik Bohlin, Bronwyn Howell, Rekha Jain, and Jun Xia. "Harnessing Artificial Intelligence (AI) to Increase Wellbeing for All: The Case for a New Technology Diplomacy." *Telecommunications Policy* 44, no. 6 (2020): 101988.

Feng, S. "Toward a Transformed and Unequal World: The AI Revolution and the New International System." *China Quarterly of International Strategic Studies* 5, no. 2 (2019): 267–287.

Fjällhed, Alicia, Matthias Lüfkens, and Andreas Sandre. "New Trends in Digital Diplomacy: The Rise of TikTok and the Geopolitics of Algorithmic Governance." In *The Oxford Handbook of Digital Diplomacy*, edited by Corneliu Bjola and Ilan Manor, 269–290. Oxford: Oxford University Press, 2024.

Fried, Ina. "ChatGPT Sparks Surge of AI Detection Tools." *Axios*, February 1, 2023. https://www.axios.com/2023/02/01/chatgpt-ai-detection-tools.

Garcia, Eugenio. "The International Governance of AI: Where Is the Global South?" *The Good AI*, 2021. https://www.researchgate.net/publication/348848134_The_International_Governance_of_AI_Where_Is_the_Global_South.

García-Herrero, Alicia. 2024. "What Determines Global Sentiment Towards China's Belt and Road Initiative?" *Journal of Chinese Economic and Business Studies* (January): 1–25.

García-Herrero, Alicia, and Robin Schindowski. "Global Trends in Countries' Perceptions of the Belt and Road Initiative." *Bruegel Working Paper* 04/2023, April 25, 2023.

Garf, Rob. "It's Not about Displacing Humans; It's About Humanizing the Digital Experience." *Salesforce*, August 10, 2024. https://www.salesforce.com/artificial-intelligence/ai-quotes/.

Gates, Bill. "The Age of AI Has Begun." *Gates Notes*, March 21, 2023. https://www.gatesnotes.com/the-age-of-ai-has-begun.

Gebru, Timnit. "Disrupting Big Tech – Timnit Gebru." African Studies. *YouTube video*, 58:51. Posted May 26, 2022. https://www.youtube.com/watch?v=dENwLu1pQb4.

Geller, Eric. "The Tech Crash Course That Trains US Diplomats to Spot Threats." *Wired*, July 2, 2024. https://www.wired.com/story/us-state-department-diplomacy-school/.

Gill, Amandeep Singh. "Artificial Intelligence and International Security: The Long View." *Ethics & International Affairs* 33, no. 2 (2019): 169–179. https://doi.org/10.1017/S0892679419000145.

Grennan, Conor. *AI Mindset: Generative AI Training and Insights.* Accessed February 5, 2025. https://www.ai-mindset.ai.

Grincheva, Natalia. "Digital Cultural Diplomacy: From Content Providers to Opinion Makers." In *The Oxford Handbook of Digital Diplomacy*, edited by Corneliu Bjola and Ilan Manor, 194–211. Oxford: Oxford University Press, 2024.

Grottola, Simone. "Artificial Intelligence: A New Tool for Diplomats." In *Diplomacy, Organisations and Citizens: Critical Perspectives on 21st Century Diplomacy*, edited by Katharina E. Höne and Jovan Kurbalija, 33–47. Cham: Springer, 2021.

The Guardian. "How China Is Using AI News Anchors to Deliver Its Propaganda." *The Guardian*, May 18, 2024a. https://www.theguardian.com/technology/article/2024/may/18/how-china-is-using-ai-news-anchors-to-deliver-its-propaganda.

The Guardian. "Microsoft Reports Iranian Hackers Targeted U.S. Presidential Campaigns." *The Guardian*, August 9, 2024b. https://www.theguardian.com/us-news/article/2024/aug/09/microsoft-reports-iran-hackers-presidential-campaign-election.

Guo, Weisi, Kristian Gleditsch, and Alan Wilson. "Retool AI to Forecast and Limit Wars." *Nature* 562, no. 7726 (2018): 331–333. https://doi.org/10.1038/d41586-018-07026-4.

Guterres, António. *Secretary-General's Special Address at the World Economic Forum*. United Nations. January 17, 2024. https://www.un.org/sg/en/content/sg/statement/2024-01-17/secretary-generals-special-address-the-world-economic-forum-delivered.

Hamidouche, Karim. "Artificial Intelligence: A New Tool for Diplomats." In *Artificial Intelligence and Digital Diplomacy: Challenges and Opportunities*, edited by Fatima Roumate, 25–32. Cham: Springer, 2021.

Harari, Yuval N. *Nexus: A Brief History of Information Networks from the Stone Age to AI*. New York: Random House, 2024.

Haseley, Alex, Chandan Karnik, Brian Kamoie, Ipshita Sinha, Joe Mariani, and Alison Muckle Egizi. "Leveraging AI in Emergency Management and Crisis Response." *Deloitte*, 2023. www2.deloitte.com/us/en/insights/industry/public-sector/automation-and-generative-ai-in-government/leveraging-ai-in-emergency-management-and-crisis-response.html.

Hassabis, Demis. "Creativity and AI – The Rothschild Foundation Lecture." Royal Academy of Arts. *YouTube video*, 1:11:00. October 10, 2018. https://www.youtube.com/watch?v=d-bvsJWmqlc.

Hassabis, Demis. "Remarks at the Economist Innovation Summit, 2018." *Economist Impact, Past Events*. Accessed February 18, 2025. https://events.economist.com/past-events/.

Hawking, Stephen. "LCFI Launch: Stephen Hawking." *Leverhulme Centre for the Future of Intelligence*, October 19, 2016. https://www.lcfi.ac.uk/resources/cfi-launch-stephen-hawking.

Hedling, E., and N. Bremberg. "Practice Approaches to the Digital Transformations of Diplomacy: Toward a New Research Agenda." *International Studies Review* 23, no. 4 (2021): 1595–1618.

Heine, Jorge, and Juan Pablo Prado Lallande. "The North–South Divide, the Digital Agenda, and Digital Diplomacy." In *The Oxford Handbook of Digital Diplomacy*, edited by Corneliu Bjola and Ilan Manor, 582–599. Oxford: Oxford University Press, 2024.

Hern, Alex. Geoffrey Hinton, "'Godfather of AI,' Quits Google and Warns of Dangers of Machine Learning." *The Guardian*, May 2, 2023. https://www.theguardian.com/technology/2023/may/02/geoffrey-hinton-godfather-of-ai-quits-google-warns-dangers-of-machine-learning.

Hinton, Geoffrey. "Interview on AI Exceeding Human Intelligence." Interview by Faisal Islam. *BBC Newsnight. YouTube video*, 9:20. October 8, 2024. https://www.youtube.com/watch?v=MGJpR591oaM.

Hoffman, Samantha. *Truth and Reality with Chinese Characteristics: China's Use of AI in Digital Diplomacy*. Canberra: Australian Strategic Policy Institute (ASPI), 2023.

Holmes, Marcus. "Digital Diplomacy: Projection and Retrieval of Images and Identities." In *The Oxford Handbook of Digital Diplomacy*, edited by Corneliu Bjola and Ilan Manor, 29–44. Oxford: Oxford University Press, 2024.

Höne, Katharina, and Eline Chivot. "The Impact of AI on Diplomacy and International Relations." *Center for Data Innovation*, 2019. Accessed February 1, 2025. https://datainnovation.org/2019/02/event-recap-the-impact-of-ai-on-diplomacy-and-international-relations/.

Höne, Katharina E., Lee Hibbard, Marília Maciel, Katarina Anđelković, Nataša Perućica, and Virdžinija Saveska. *Mapping the Challenges and Opportunities of Artificial Intelligence for the Conduct of Diplomacy*. Geneva: DiploFoundation, 2019a. Accessed January 15, 2025. www.diplomacy.edu/resource/mapping-the-challenges-and-opportunities-of-artificial-intelligence-for-the-conduct-of-diplomacy/.

Horowitz, M. C., "Artificial Intelligence, International Competition, and the Balance of Power." *Texas National Security Review* 1, no. 3 (2018): 36–57. https://tnsr.org/2018/05/artificial-intelligence-international-competition-and-the-balance-of-power/.

Horowitz, M. C., G. C. Allen, E. B. Kania, and P. Scharre. *Strategic Competition in an Era of Artificial Intelligence*. Washington: Center for a New American Security, 2018a. https://www.cnas.org/publications/reports/strategic-competition-in-an-era-of-artificial-intelligence.

Horowitz, M. C., G. C. Allen, E. Saravalle, A. Cho, K. Frederick, and P. Scharre. *Artificial Intelligence and International Security*. Washington: Center for a New American Security, 2018b. https://www.cnas.org/publications/reports/artificial-intelligence-and-international-security.

Huang, Jensen. "Nvidia CEO: Software Is Eating the World, but AI Is Going to Eat Software." *Interview by MIT Technology Review*. May 12, 2017. https://www.technologyreview.com/2017/05/12/151722/nvidia-ceo-software-is-eating-the-world-but-ai-is-going-to-eat-software/.

Huang, Zhao Alexandre. "Wolf Warrior and China's Digital Public Diplomacy during the COVID-19 Crisis." *Place Branding and Public Diplomacy* 18, no. 1 (2022): 37–40.Huang, Zhao Alexandre, and Phillip Arceneaux. "Ethical Challenges in the Digitalization of Public Diplomacy." In *The Oxford Handbook of Digital Diplomacy*, edited by Corneliu Bjola and Ilan Manor, 232–249. Oxford: Oxford University Press, 2024.

Human Rights Watch. "Killer Robots: UN Vote Should Spur Action on Treaty." *Human Rights Watch*, January 3, 2024. https://www.hrw.org/news/2024/01/03/killer-robots-un-vote-should-spur-action-treaty.

ICC Brasil. "ICC Launches Artificial Intelligence Tool for Trade Negotiations." *ICC Brasil*, October 4, 2018. www.iccbrasil.org/icc-launches-artificial-intelligence-tool-for-trade-negotiations/.

Jensen, Benjamin, Christopher Whyte, and Scott Cuomo. "Algorithms at War: The Promise, Peril, and Limits of Artificial Intelligence." *International Studies Review* 22, no. 3 (2020): 526–550.

Jensen, Benjamin, Christopher Whyte, and Scott Cuomo. *Information in War: Military Innovation, Battle Networks, and the Future of Artificial Intelligence*. Washington, DC: Georgetown University Press, 2022.

Johnson, J. "Artificial Intelligence & Future Warfare: Implications for International Security." *Defense & Security Analysis* 35, no. 2 (2019): 147–169.

Kapoor, Rishi. "Digital Platforms and AI Are Empowering Individual Investors." *World Economic Forum*, December 20, 2024. Accessed January 19, 2025. https://www.weforum.org/stories/2024/12/digital-platforms-ai-empowering-individual-investors.

Kasparov, Garry. "AI Should Augment Human Intelligence, Not Replace It." *Harvard Business Review*, March 18, 2021. https://www.kasparov.com/ai-should-augment-human-intelligence-not-replace-it-harvard-business-review-march-18-2021/.

Kasparov, Garry. "Worry about Human (Not Machine) Intelligence." *Encyclopedia Britannica*, October 31, 2023. https://www.britannica.com/topic/Worry-About-Human-Not-Machine-Intelligence-2119055.

Kello, Lucas. "Digital Diplomacy and Cyber Defense." In *Digital Diplomacy: Fighting with Values in Winning the Global Technological Race*. Oxford: Oxford University Press, 2023.

Kello, Lucas. 2024. "Digital Diplomacy and Cyber Defence." In *The Oxford Handbook of Digital Diplomacy*, edited by Corneliu Bjola and Ilan Manor, 121–137. Oxford: Oxford University Press.

Keskin, Tugrul, and Ryan Kiggins, eds. *Towards an International Political Economy of Artificial Intelligence*. Cham: Palgrave Macmillan, 2021.

Khalid, Raja Awais. "Twitter Diplomacy on CPEC: Impact on the Triangular Relationships Between the Pak-China and the USA." In *Artificial Intelligence and Digital Diplomacy: Challenges and Opportunities*, edited by Fatima Roumate, 195–207. Cham: Springer, 2021.

Kiggins, Ryan. "Big Data, Artificial Intelligence, and Autonomous Policy Decision-Making: A Crisis in International Relations Theory?" In *The Political Economy of Robots: Prospects for Prosperity and Peace in the Automated 21st Century*, edited by Ryan Kiggins, 85–111. Cham: Springer, 2017.

Kimani, C. J., and J. Scott. *Introduction to International Relations—Diploma Level*. Finstock Evarsity Publishers, 2023.

Kissinger, Henry A., Eric Schmidt, and Daniel Huttenlocher. "The Metamorphosis." *The Atlantic*, August 2019. https://www.theatlantic.com/magazine/archive/2019/08/henry-kissinger-the-metamorphosis-ai/592771/.

Kissinger, Henry, Eric Schmidt, and Daniel Huttenlocher. *The Age of AI: And Our Human Future*. New York: Little, Brown and Company, 2021.

Kissinger, Henry A., Eric Schmidt, and Craig Mundie. *Genesis: Artificial Intelligence, Hope, and the Human Spirit*. Foreword by Niall Ferguson. New York: Little, Brown and Company, 2024.

Konovalova, M. "AI and Diplomacy: Challenges and Opportunities." *Journal of Liberty and International Affairs* 9, no. 2 (2023): 520–530.

Kurbalija, Jovan. "Geneva AI attaché: Technology for inclusive, informed, and impactful diplomacy." *DiploFoundation*, December 4, 2024. Accessed January 19, 2025. www.diplomacy.edu/blog/geneva-ai-attache-technology-for-inclusive-informed-and-impactful-diplomacy/.

Lacy, Gharun. "Artificial Intelligence May Augment Diplomatic Data Security." *FedTech Magazine*, October 10, 2024. Accessed February 3, 2025. https://fedtechmagazine.com/article/2024/10/artificial-intelligence-may-augment-diplomatic-data-security.

Larsen, Anne Marie Engtoft, and Tom Fletcher. "Digital Diplomatic Representation: The Rise of Tech Ambassadors." In *The Oxford Handbook of Digital Diplomacy*, edited by Corneliu Bjola and Ilan Manor, 420–436. Oxford: Oxford University Press, 2024.

Lebedeva, Marina Mikhailovna, and Elena Sergeevna Zinovieva. "International Negotiations in the Digital Age." *Vestnik RUDN. International Relations* 23, no. 1 (2023): 144–156.

Legrand, Gaëlle. "Authoritarian Countries Have a Built-in Competitive Advantage When It Comes to AI Development." *Le Monde*, September 27, 2024. https://www.lemonde.fr/en/opinion/article/2024/09/27/authoritarian-countries-have-a-built-in-competitive-advantage-when-it-comes-to-ai-development_6727495_23.html.

Li, Fei-Fei. *How We're Teaching Computers to Understand Pictures*. Filmed March 2015 at TED2015. TED video, 17:49. Accessed February 18, 2025. https://www.ted.com/talks/fei_fei_li_how_we_re_teaching_computers_to_understand_pictures.

Louis, Paul. "Moquée par les internautes, l'IA française 'Lucie' conçue avec le soutien de l'État 'ferme temporairement'." *BFMTV*, January 26, 2025. https://www.bfmtv.com/tech/intelligence-artificielle/moquee-par-les-internautes-l-ia-francaise-lucie-concue-avec-le-soutien-de-l-etat-ferme-temporairement_AN-202501260175.html.

Ly, David. "Predictive Policing: Myth-Busting and What We Can Expect of AI-Powered Law Enforcement." *Forbes*, October 15, 2024. https://www.forbes.com/councils/forbestechcouncil/2024/10/15/predictive-policing-myth-busting-and-what-we-can-expect-of-ai-powered-law-enforcement/.

Manor, Ilan. *The Digitalization of Public Diplomacy: Managing Automation in Communication and International Relations.* Cham: Springer, 2019.

Manor, Ilan. *The Digitalization of Public Diplomacy: Toward Clarification of a Fractured Terminology.* Digital Diplomacy Blog, 2017. Accessed January 15, 2025. https:// digdipblog.com/wp-content/uploads/2017/08/the-digitalization-of-diplomacy-working-paper-number-1.pdf.

Manor, Ilan, and James Pamment. "From Micro to Macro Digital Disruptions: A New Prism for Investigating Digital Diplomacy." In *The Oxford Handbook of Digital Diplomacy*, edited by Corneliu Bjola and Ilan Manor, 45–62. Oxford: Oxford University Press, 2024.

Marcus, Gary. "AI Is Not 'Unequivocally Great'; It Is a Dual-Use Technology with Both Benefits and Risks. I Would Have Hoped That You Have Recognized That More Elearly, @sama." X, May 5, 2024. https://x.com/GaryMarcus/status/1786909395340 914854.

Márquez Lartigue, Rodrigo. "Diplomacy 4.0: Navigating the AI Era: Geopolitics, Diplomacy, and the Power of Artificial Intelligence." *Consular Diplomacy*, December 28, 2023. Accessed January 15, 2025. www.consulardiplomacy.com/home/diplomacy-40-navigating-the-ai-era-geopolitics-diplomacy-and-the-power-of-artificial-intelligence.

Marwala, Tshilidzi. "AI and International Relations: A Whole New Minefield to Navigate." *United Nations University*, November 23, 2023. Accessed January 15, 2025. https://unu. edu/article/ai-and-international-relations-whole-new-minefield-navigate.

McConnell, Fiona, and Alex Manby. "Digital Diplomacy and Non-Governmental and Transnational Organizations." In *The Oxford Handbook of Digital Diplomacy*, edited by Corneliu Bjola and Ilan Manor, 383–400. Oxford: Oxford University Press, 2024.

Meleouni, C., and I. P. Efthymiou. "Artificial Intelligence and Its Impact in International Relations." *Journal of Politics and Ethics in New Technologies and AI* 2, no. 1 (2023): e35803.

Merica, Dan. "Sophistication of AI-Backed Operation Targeting Senator Points to Future of Deepfake Schemes." *AP News*, September 26, 2024. www.apnews.com/article/ deepfake-cardin-ai-artificial-intelligence-879a6c2ca816c71d9af52a101dedb7ff.

Miegbam, A., and K. Bariledum. "Artificial Intelligence and Diplomacy in the 21st Century: The African Perspective." *Central Asian Journal of Theoretical and Applied Science* 3, no. 10 (2022): 49–65. https://cajotas.centralasianstudies.org/index.php/CAJOTAS/ article/view/939.

Milmo, Dan. "US and UK Refuse to Sign Paris Summit Declaration on 'Inclusive' AI." *The Guardian*, February 11, 2025. https://www.theguardian.com/technology/2025/feb/11/ us-uk-paris-ai-summit-artificial-intelligence-declaration.

Minchev, Zlatogor. "On the Growing Transformational Role of AI Technologies for the Future Cyber Diplomacy in the Post-Information Age." *International Journal of Cyber Diplomacy* 4 (2023): 29–41.

Ministry of Foreign Affairs, Republic of Estonia. "Estonia Hosts Pivotal Global Cyber Diplomacy Event Amid Rising Cyber Threats." November 11, 2024. www.vm.ee/en/ news/estonia-hosts-pivotal-global-cyber-diplomacy-event-amid-rising-cyber-threats.

Ministry of Foreign Affairs, Republic of Estonia. "Overview of Cyber Diplomacy." *Ministry of Foreign Affairs, Republic of Estonia.* Accessed February 2, 2025. www.vm.ee/en/ activity/digital-and-cyber-diplomacy/overview-cyber-diplomacy.

Mokashi, Amit, J. D. Jayaraman, Priyanka Mahakul, Rutu Patel, and Anthony Picciano. "Global Perception of the Belt and Road Initiative: A Natural Language Processing Approach." *Journal of Big Data and Artificial Intelligence* 1, no. 1 (2022): 1–15. https:// doi.org/10.54116/jbdtp.v1i1.18.

Mollick, Ethan. *Co-Intelligence: Living and Working with AI.* New York: Portfolio, 2024.

Mondo Internazionale. "The Geopolitical Effects of Artificial Intelligence: The Implications on International Relations." *Mondo Internazionale*. Accessed January 15, 2025. https://mondointernazionale.org/en/focus-allegati/the-geopolitical-effects-of-artificial-intelligence-the-implications-on-international-relations.

Montreal Declaration for Responsible AI. *The Montreal Declaration for a Responsible Development of Artificial Intelligence*. Université de Montréal, 2018. https://recherche.umontreal.ca/english/strategic-initiatives/montreal-declaration-for-a-responsible-ai/.

Moreno Cantano, Antonio César. "International Geopolitics and Digital Games in the Nationalist Agenda of Great Powers." In *The Oxford Handbook of Digital Diplomacy*, edited by Corneliu Bjola and Ilan Manor, 600–618. Oxford: Oxford University Press, 2024.

Mueller, Grace B., Benjamin Jensen, Brandon Valeriano, Ryan C. Maness, and Jose M. Macias. "Cyber Operations during the Russo-Ukrainian War." *Center for Strategic and International Studies*, July 13, 2023. https://www.csis.org/analysis/cyber-operations-during-russo-ukrainian-war.

Musk, Elon. "We're 'Summoning the Demon' with Artificial Intelligence." Interview at MIT Aeronautics and Astronautics Centennial Symposium. YouTube video, 2:20. Posted by Bloomberg, October 27, 2014. https://www.youtube.com/watch?v=Tzb_CSRO-0g.

Nadella, Satya. "Microsoft's Satya Nadella Reveals Vision for Generative." *YouTube video*, 2:40. Posted by CNET Highlights, February 8, 2023. https://www.youtube.com/watch?v=-nKIowBdchg.

Nadella, Satya, Greg Shaw, and Jill Tracie Nichols. *Hit Refresh: The Quest to Rediscover Microsoft's Soul and Imagine a Better Future for Everyone*. New York: HarperBusiness, 2017.

Ndzendze, B., and T. Marwala. *Artificial Intelligence and International Relations Theories*. Cham: Springer Nature, 2023.

Neumeister, Larry. "Lawyers Blame ChatGPT for Tricking Them into Citing Bogus Case Law." *Associated Press*, June 8, 2023. https://apnews.com/article/artificial-intelligence-chatgpt-fake-case-lawyers-d6ae9fa79d0542db9e1455397aef381c.

Ng, Andrew. *Talk at the Stanford MSx Future Forum*. Stanford Graduate School of Business, January 25, 2017. https://www.youtube.com/watch?v=21EiKfQYZXc.

North Atlantic Treaty Organization (NATO). "NATO Releases First-Ever Strategy for Artificial Intelligence." *NATO*, October 22, 2021. https://www.nato.int/cps/en/natohq/news_187934.htm.

North Atlantic Treaty Organization (NATO). "Summary of NATO's Revised Artificial Intelligence (AI) Strategy." *NATO*, July 10, 2024a. Accessed February 9, 2025. https://www.nato.int/cps/en/natohq/official_texts_227237.htm?selectedLocale=en.

North Atlantic Treaty Organization (NATO). "Revised 2024 Artificial Intelligence (AI) Strategy." *NATO*, July 10, 2024b. https://www.nato.int/cps/en/natohq/news_227234.htm.

Obama Foundation. *Anna Makanju – Obama Democracy Forum 2023*. https://www.obama.org/democracy-forum-2023/anna-makanju/.

OECD. *OECD AI Principles*. Organisation for Economic Co-Operation and Development, 2019a. https://oecd.ai/en/ai-principles.

OECD. *OECD AI Principles: Recommendations of the Council on Artificial Intelligence*. Paris: Organisation for Economic Co-operation and Development, 2019b. https://www.oecd.org/going-digital/ai/principles/.

Open AI. "Disrupting a Covert Iranian Influence Operation." 2024. *OpenAI* Blog. https://openai.com/index/disrupting-a-covert-iranian-influence-operation.

Organisation for Economic Co-Operation and Development (OECD). "AI Principles." Accessed February 5, 2025. https://www.oecd.org/en/topics/ai-principles.html.

Organisation of Eastern Caribbean States. "New Artificial Intelligence to Help Facilitate Trade Negotiations for Small Island Developing States." *OECS Pressroom*, October 11, 2018. https://pressroom.oecs.int/new-artificial-intelligence-to-help-facilitate-trade-negotiations-for-small-island-developing-states.

Pawar, Sahil. "Quotes on Artificial Intelligence by Experts." *Analytics Drift*, September 29, 2023. https://analyticsdrift.com/quotes-on-artificial-intelligence-by-experts/.

Pearson, David, and Jean Burgess. "Ukraine's Digital Resistance." In *Digital Diplomacy: Fighting with Values in Winning the Global Technological Race*, edited by Corneliu Bjola and Ilan Manor, 182–199. Oxford: Oxford University Press, 2023.

Pellerin, Cheryl. "Project Maven to Deploy Computer Algorithms to War Zone by Year's End." *U.S. Department of Defense*, July 21, 2017. https://www.defense.gov/News/News-Stories/Article/Article/1254719/project-maven-to-deploy-computer-algorithms-to-war-zone-by-years-end/.

Pichai, Sundar. "How AI Can Strengthen Digital Security." *Google Blog*, February 16, 2024. https://blog.google/technology/safety-security/google-ai-cyber-defense-initiative/.

Piper, Elizabeth. "Russia Will Not Intimidate Us with Cyberthreats, UK Minister Tells NATO." *Reuters*, November 25, 2024. https://www.reuters.com/technology/cybersecurity/britain-nato-must-stay-ahead-new-ai-arms-race-says-uk-minister-2024-11-25/.

Pokhriyal, Neeti, and Till Koebe. "AI-Assisted Diplomatic Decision-Making during Crises: Challenges and Opportunities." *Frontiers in Big Data* 6 (2023): 1183313. Accessed May 23, 2025. https://doi.org/10.3389/fdata.2023.1183313.

Pomfret, James, and Jessie Pang. "Chinese Researchers Develop AI Model for Military Use, Back Meta's Llama." *Reuters*, November 1, 2024. https://www.reuters.com/technology/artificial-intelligence/chinese-researchers-develop-ai-model-military-use-back-metas-llama-2024-11-01.

Pontifical Academy for Life. *Rome Call for AI Ethics*. Vatican City: Pontifical Academy for Life, 2020. https://www.romecall.org/the-call/.

Pope Francis. *Antiqua et Nova: The Vatican's Perspective on Artificial Intelligence*. Vatican City: Vatican Press, 2025.

PreventionWeb. "Scaling Up Haze Gazer: An Analysis and Visualization Tool for Haze Crisis Management." *PreventionWeb*, January 26, 2017. www.preventionweb.net/news/scaling-haze-gazer-analysis-and-visualization-tool-haze-crisis-management.

Puaschunder, J. M. "Artificial Diplomacy: A Guide for Public Officials to Conduct Artificial Intelligence." *Journal of Applied Research in the Digital Economy* 1 (2019): 39–54.

Putri, R. A. A. K., T. Chairil, S. B. Pertiwi, and A. R. Tirtawinata. "Designing Artificial Intelligence/International Relations (AI/IR) Platform: Foreign Policy Decision-Making Simulation in ASEAN Negotiation." In *2020 International Conference on ICT for Smart Society (ICISS)*, 1–8. IEEE, November 2020.

Rafik, Meriem. "Data Sovereignty: New Challenges for Diplomacy." In *Artificial Intelligence and Digital Diplomacy: Challenges and Opportunities*, edited by Fatima Roumate, 33–43. Cham: Springer, 2021.

RAND Corporation. Beauchamp-Mustafaga, Nathan, and William Marcellino. "Dr. Li Bicheng, or How China Learned to Stop Worrying and Love Social Media Manipulation: Insights Into Chinese Use of Generative AI and Social Bots from the Career of a PLA Researcher." *RAND Corporation*, October 1, 2024. https://www.rand.org/content/dam/rand/pubs/perspectives/PEA3000/PEA3089-1/RAND_PEA3089-1.pdf.

Ranka, Hriday, Mokshit Surana, Neel Kothari, Veer Pariawala, Pratyay Banerjee, Aditya Surve, Sainath Reddy Sankepally, Raghav Jain, Jhagrut Lalwani, and Swapneel Mehta. "Examining the Implications of Deepfakes for Election Integrity." arXiv preprint arXiv:2406.14290, 2024. https://arxiv.org/abs/2406.14290.

Rauf, Abdul, and Sajid Iqbal. "Impact of Artificial Intelligence in Arms Race, Diplomacy, and Economy: A Case Study of Great Power Competition between the US and China." *Global Foreign Policies Review* 6, no. 3 (2023): 44–63. https://www.researchgate. net/publication/380626329_Impact_of_Artificial_Intelligence_in_Arms_Race_ Diplomacy_and_Economy_A_Case_Study_of_Great_Power_Competition_between_ the_US_and_China.

Rawnsley, Gary D. "Soft Power in the Digital Space." In *The Oxford Handbook of Digital Diplomacy*, edited by Corneliu Bjola and Ilan Manor, 63–79. Oxford: Oxford University Press, 2024.

Reuters. "Russia Using Generative AI to Ramp Up Disinformation, Says Ukraine Minister." *Reuters*, October 16, 2024. https://www.reuters.com/technology/artificial-intelligence/ russia-using-generative-ai-ramp-up-disinformation-says-ukraine-minister-2024-10-16/.

Reuters. *Trump Revokes Biden's AI Executive Order, Issuing New AI Policy Directive.* January 21, 2025. https://www.reuters.com/technology/artificial-intelligence/trump-revokes-biden-executive-order-addressing-ai-risks-2025-01-21/.

Rikkonen, Lassi. "Helsinki-Based Embassies and Ambassadors on Twitter: An Analysis of Communication Goals and Rhetorical Ethos in Diplomatic Twitter Practice." In *Artificial Intelligence and Digital Diplomacy: Challenges and Opportunities*, edited by Fatima Roumate, 145–167. Cham: Springer, 2021.

Rometty, Ginni. "Ginni Rometty on AI as a 'Great Equalizer' for Workers." Interview by Washington Post Live. *YouTube video*, 2024, 2:25. March 12. https://www.youtube.com/ watch?v=SP6YPvNeBO0.

Rosen Jacobson, B., Katharina E. Höne, and Jovan Kurbalija. *Data Diplomacy: Updating Diplomacy to the Big Data Era.* 2018. Accessed February 1, 2025. https://www. diplomacy.edu/wp-content/uploads/2019/07/Data_Diplomacy_Report_2018.pdf.

Rosenau, William, Jennifer D. Moroney, George T. Ivory, and Richard S. Girven. *China's AI Exports: An Analysis of Trends and Strategic Implications.* Santa Monica: RAND Corporation, 2023. https://www.rand.org/pubs/research_reports/RRA2696-2.html.

Roumate, Fatima, ed. *Artificial Intelligence and Digital Diplomacy: Challenges and Opportunities.* Cham: Springer, 2021a.

Roumate, Fatima. "Malicious Use of Artificial Intelligence: New Challenges for Diplomacy and International Psychological Security." In *Artificial Intelligence and Digital Diplomacy: Challenges and Opportunities*, edited by Fatima Roumate, 97–113. Cham: Springer, 2021b.

Roumate, Fatima, ed. *Artificial Intelligence and the New World Order: New Weapons, New Wars and a New Balance of Power.* Cham: Springer, 2024.

Russell, Stuart. *Human Compatible: Artificial Intelligence and the Problem of Control.* New York: Viking, 2019.

Russell, Stuart. "Banning Lethal Autonomous Weapons: An Education." *Issues in Science and Technology* 38, no. 3 (Spring 2022): 60–65.

Schmidt, Eric. "Genesis: Artificial Intelligence, Hope and the Human Spirit." *YouTube video*, 2024, 11:52. Posted by Genesis Book AI, November 19. https://www.youtube.com/ watch?v=OT_S4g5G5N4.

Scott, Ben, Stefan Heumann, and Philippe Lorenz. "Artificial Intelligence and Foreign Policy." *Stiftung Neue Verantwortung* Policy Brief, 2018. Accessed May 23, 2025. https://www. stiftung-nv.de/sites/default/files/artificial_intelligence_and_foreign_policy.pdf

Scott, Gray, quoted in Bernard Marr. "28 Best Quotes about Artificial Intelligence." *Forbes*, July 25, 2017. https://www.forbes.com/sites/bernardmarr/2017/07/25/28-best-quotes-about-artificial-intelligence/.

Seoane, Maximiliano. "Chinese and U.S. AI and Cloud Multinational Corporations in Latin America." In *Towards an International Political Economy of Artificial Intelligence*, edited by Tugrul Keskin and Ryan Kiggins, 85–111. Cham: Palgrave Macmillan, 2021.

Serhan, Yasmeen. "How Israel Uses AI in Gaza—And What It Might Mean for the Future of Warfare." *Time*, December 2024. www.time.com/7202584/gaza-ukraine-ai-warfare/.

Sevin, Efe. "Digitalization of Diplomacy: Implications for Cities." In *The Oxford Handbook of Digital Diplomacy*, edited by Corneliu Bjola and Ilan Manor, 401–419. Oxford: Oxford University Press, 2024.

Siebrits, Jen, Ricky Bartlett, Ben Taylor, Tony Brearley, and Anna Fowler. "AI in Facilities Management: A New Era of Efficiency." *CBRE*. Accessed January 19, 2025. www.cbre.com/insights/articles/ai-facilities-management-a-new-era-of-efficiency.

Simić, Jasminka. "Cyber Security: New Threats for Diplomacy." In *Artificial Intelligence and Digital Diplomacy: Challenges and Opportunities*, edited by Fatima Roumate, 45–56. Cham: Springer, 2021.

Smith, Brad. *The Need for a Digital Geneva Convention*. Microsoft, February 14, 2017. https://blogs.microsoft.com/on-the-issues/2017/02/14/need-digital-geneva-convention/.

Spry, Damien. "Diversities and Developments in Asia Pacific Digital Diplomacy." In *The Oxford Handbook of Digital Diplomacy*, edited by Corneliu Bjola and Ilan Manor, 528–545. Oxford: Oxford University Press, 2024.

Stanzel, Volker, and Daniel Voelsen. *Diplomacy and Artificial Intelligence: Reflections on Practical Assistance for Diplomatic Negotiations*. Berlin: SWP Research Paper, 2022. Accessed May 23, 2025. https://www.swp-berlin.org/publications/products/research_papers/2022RP01_Diplomacy_and_AI.pdf.

State Department AI Inventory. "Department of State AI Use Cases." *U.S.* Department of State, 2024.

"Summit on Responsible Artificial Intelligence in the Military Domain." *Wikipedia*, 2024. https://en.wikipedia.org/wiki/Summit_on_Responsible_Artificial_Intelligence_in_the_Military_Domain.

Surowiec-Capell, Paweł. "Digital Propaganda and Diplomacy." In *The Oxford Handbook of Digital Diplomacy*, edited by Corneliu Bjola and Ilan Manor, 212–231. Oxford: Oxford University Press, 2024.

Tang, Didi, and David Klepper. "In Global Game of Influence, China Turns to a Cheap and Effective Tool." *Associated Press*, June 15, 2024. www.apnews.com/article/china-disinformation-fake-news-russia-3085f10d6edca36f6415d6410e5ef874.

Thomas, Rob, quoted in Kyle Wiggers. "IBM Intros a Slew of New AI Services, Including Generative Models." *TechCrunch*, May 9, 2023. https://techcrunch.com/2023/05/09/ibm-intros-a-slew-of-new-ai-services-including-generative-models/.

Thorne, Devin. "AI-Powered Propaganda and the CCP's Plans for Next-Generation 'Thought Management'." *China Brief* 20, no. 9 (2020). https://jamestown.org/program/ai-powered-propaganda-and-the-ccps-plans-for-next-generation-thought-management/.

Time. *Kay Firth-Butterfield – AI Ethics Leader and Time 100 Impact Award Winner*. 2023. https://time.com/collection/time100-impact-awards/6692047/kay-firth-butterfield-ai-time-impact-award/.

Trump, Donald J. "Executive Order 14179: Removing Barriers to American Leadership in Artificial Intelligence." *Federal Register* 90, no. 19 (January 31, 2025): 8741–8742. https://www.federalregister.gov/documents/2025/01/31/2025-02172/removing-barriers-to-american-leadership-in-artificial-intelligence.

Tuset Varela, Damián. "Diplomacy in the Age of AI: Challenges and Opportunities." *Journal of Artificial Intelligence General Science* 2, no. 1 (January 2024a): 102–125. Accessed February 3, 2025. https://www.researchgate.net/publication/380436953_Diplomacy_in_the_Age_of_AI_Challenges_and_Opportunities.

Tuset Varela, Damián. "Artificial Intelligence on the Global Stage: Transforming Diplomacy and International Relations." *Advances in Deep Learning Techniques* 4, no. 1 (2024b): 53–57. Ahmedabad, India. Accessed January 15, 2025. https://thesciencebrigade.com/adlt/article/view/146.

"Tuvalu: The First Digital Nation." Accessed February 2, 2025. https://www.tuvalu.tv/.

United Kingdom. "The Bletchley Declaration by Countries Attending the AI Safety Summit, 1–2 November 2023." *GOV.UK*, November 1, 2023. https://www.gov.uk/government/publications/ai-safety-summit-2023-the-bletchley-declaration/the-bletchley-declaration-by-countries-attending-the-ai-safety-summit-1-2-november-2023.

United Nations. *UN Secretary-General's AI Advisory Body.* United Nations, 2023. https://www.un.org/en/ai-advisory-body.

United Nations. *Amandeep Singh Gill – UN Secretary-General's Tech Envoy.* United Nations, 2024a. https://www.un.org/sg/en/content/profiles/amandeep-gill.

United Nations. *Governing AI for Humanity: Report of the High-Level Advisory Body on Artificial Intelligence.* New York: United Nations, 2024b. https://www.un.org/en/ai-advisory-body. United Nations. *Report of the Group of Governmental Experts on Developments in the Field of Information and Telecommunications in the Context of International Security (A/70/174).* New York: United Nations, 2015. Accessed February 3, 2025. https://digitallibrary.un.org/record/799853/usage?v=pdf&ln=en.

United Nations Development Programme (UNDP). *Using AI for SDG Monitoring and Analysis.* United Nations Development Programme, 2020. www.un.org/en/delegate/using-ai-generate-synthetic-data-sdgs-monitoring.

United Nations Global Pulse. "Using Artificial Intelligence to Model Displacement in Somalia." *United Nations Global Pulse*, 2019. https://www.unglobalpulse.org/project/using-artificial-intelligence-to-model-displacement-in-somalia/.

United Nations Global Pulse. "Using Artificial Intelligence to Combat Epidemics in the Global South (AI4COVID Programme)." *United Nations* Global Pulse, 2020. www.unglobalpulse.org/project/using-artificial-intelligence-to-combat-epidemics-in-the-global-south-ai4covid-programme/.

U.S. Department of Commerce. *U.S. Export Controls on AI Technology.* U.S. Department of Commerce, 2023.

U.S. Department of Justice. *Compliance Plan for OMB Memorandum M-24-10.* October 2024. Accessed February 5, 2025. https://www.justice.gov/media/1373026/dl.

U.S. Department of State. *Enterprise Artificial Intelligence Strategy FY 2024–2025: Empowering Diplomacy through Responsible AI.* Washington: U.S. Department of State, 2023. https://www.state.gov/wp-content/uploads/2023/11/Department-of-State-Enterprise-Artificial-Intelligence-Strategy.pdf.

U.S. Department of State. "U.S. Security Cooperation with Estonia." February 12, 2024a. https://www.state.gov/u-s-security-cooperation-with-estonia/.

U.S. Department of State. *Global AI Research Agenda.* Washington: U.S. Department of State, 2024b. https://www.state.gov/global-ai-research-agenda/.

U.S. Department of State. "AI in Action: Risk Management and Innovation Help Shape the Future of Diplomacy." *State Magazine*, December 2024c. https://statemag.state.gov/2024/12/1224feat03/.

U.S. Department of State. "Secretary Antony J. Blinken at a Conversation on Artificial Intelligence (AI) at State." *U.S. Department of State*, June 28, 2024d. https://2021-2025.state.gov/secretary-antony-j-blinken-at-a-conversation-on-artificial-intelligence-ai-at-state/.

U.S. Department of State. *Artificial Intelligence (AI).* Office of the Science and Technology Adviser. Accessed January 27, 2025a. https://www.state.gov/office-of-the-science-and-technology-adviser/artificial-intelligence-ai/.

U.S. Department of State. *AI Inventory 2024.* Accessed January 27, 2025b. https://2021-2025.state.gov/department-of-state-ai-inventory-2024/.

Vacarelu, Marius. "Artificial Intelligence: To Strengthen or to Replace Traditional Diplomacy." In *Artificial Intelligence and Digital Diplomacy: Challenges and Opportunities*, edited by Fatima Roumate, 1–23. Cham: Springer, 2021.

Vatican Dicastery for the Doctrine of the Faith. Antiqua et Nova. January 28, 2025. https://www.vatican.va/roman_curia/congregations/cfaith/documents/rc_ddf_doc_20250128_antiqua-et-nova_en.html.

Viggiano, Greg, ed. *Convergence: Artificial Intelligence and Quantum Computing – Social, Economic, and Policy Impacts.* Hoboken: Wiley, 2023.

Vlaeminck, Erik. "European Digital Diplomacy Towards Russia: A Cross-Country Social Media Analysis." In *Artificial Intelligence and Digital Diplomacy: Challenges and Opportunities*, edited by Fatima Roumate, 131–143. Cham: Springer, 2021.

Vota, Wayan. "How US State Department Uses AI Strategically in Modern Diplomacy." *ICTworks*, August 23, 2024. https://www.ictworks.org/state-department-uses-ai-strategically.

Wallin, Joshua, and Andrew Reddie. "Time to Act: Building the Technical and Institutional Foundations for AI Assurance." *Lawfare*, November 2, 2023.

Wang, Jian (Jay), and Andrew Dubbins. "What Artificial Intelligence Means for Public Diplomacy." *USC Center on Public Diplomacy*, August 12, 2024. https://uscpublicdiplomacy.org/blog/what-artificial-intelligence-means-public-diplomacy.

White House. *Executive Order on Advancing United States Leadership in Artificial Intelligence Infrastructure.* 2023. https://bidenwhitehouse.archives.gov/briefing-room/presidential-actions/2025/01/14/executive-order-on-advancing-united-states-leadership-in-artificial-intelligence-infrastructure/.

Wikipedia Contributors. "Chinese Information Operations and Information Warfare." *Wikipedia*, 2024a. https://en.wikipedia.org/wiki/Chinese_information_operations_and_information_warfare.

Wikipedia Contributors. "Russian Disinformation During the War in Ukraine." Wikipedia, 2024b. https://en.wikipedia.org/wiki/Russian_disinformation_during_the_Ukraine_war.

Wiseman, Geoffrey. "Digital Diplomatic Cultures." In *The Oxford Handbook of Digital Diplomacy*, edited by Corneliu Bjola and Ilan Manor, 311–329. Oxford: Oxford University Press, 2024.

Wright, Katharine A. M. "NATO's Digital Diplomacy." In *The Oxford Handbook of Digital Diplomacy*, edited by Corneliu Bjola and Ilan Manor, 475–490. Oxford: Oxford University Press, 2024.

Yarchi, Moran. "Digital Diplomacy during Wars and Conflicts." In *The Oxford Handbook of Digital Diplomacy*, edited by Corneliu Bjola and Ilan Manor, 619–636. Oxford: Oxford University Press, 2024.

Yeo, Sophie. "Tuvalu: The Disappearing Island Nation Recreating Itself in the Metaverse." *BBC Future*, November 21, 2024.

Yudkowsky, Eliezer. "Artificial Intelligence as a Positive and Negative Factor in Global Risk." In *Global Catastrophic Risks*, edited by Nick Bostrom and Milan M. Ćirković, 308–345. New York: Oxford University Press, 2008. https://intelligence.org/files/AIPosNegFactor.pdf.

Zaiotti, Ruben. "The European Union and Digital Diplomacy: Projecting Global Europe in the Social Media Era." In *The Oxford Handbook of Digital Diplomacy*, edited by Corneliu Bjola and Ilan Manor, 457–474. Oxford: Oxford University Press, 2024.

Zeng, Yi. *Beijing Artificial Intelligence Principles.* AI Ethics and Governance Institute, 2019. https://ai-ethics-and-governance.institute/beijing-artificial-intelligence-principles/.

Zimmerman, Morgan, and Varoon Mathur. 2024 *Federal AI Use Case Inventory. GitHub.* Office of Management and Budget. Accessed January 27, 2025. www.github.com/ombegov/2024-Federal-AI-Use-Case-Inventory.

Statement of Independence and Compliance

This book, *AI Use Cases for Diplomats: Applying Artificial Intelligence to Diplomacy*, was authored in a personal capacity and is not affiliated with, nor does it represent the views of, the U.S. Department of State or the U.S. government. The content was prepared in full compliance with all relevant legal, ethical, and regulatory requirements for current and former federal employees. In accordance with 11 FAM 614.5 and 5 C.F.R. § 2635, the author is permitted to receive compensation for this work as it does not relate to official duties past or present or in substantial part. The author did not receive any government funding, grants, or contractual support for this book. Any financial proceeds from its publication are entirely personal and unrelated to any government employment, duties, or obligations.

This book does not specifically address any matters in which the author was directly involved during his former role in the U.S. Department of State. This book is based on general artificial intelligence (AI) principles and forward-looking analyses, with no direct reference to current or anticipated government programs or operations beyond what the Department has already shared publicly. AI is a rapidly evolving field, and its applications in diplomacy are subject to ongoing technological, ethical, and policy developments. The content of this book reflects the state of knowledge and public discourse at the time of writing and may not fully align with future advancements, regulations, or interpretations.

The author has taken all necessary steps to ensure there is no conflict of interest in the publication of this book, pursuant to 18 U.S.C. § 208 and related regulations. No nonpublic, classified, or privileged information obtained through the author's prior government service has been used in this manuscript. This book is based on publicly available information, academic research, and generally accepted industry standards. The author has taken all reasonable steps to ensure that no copyrighted material has been used without appropriate permissions or attributions, and that all references, quotations, and ideas are properly cited to respect intellectual property rights and avoid inadvertent plagiarism.

This book was written by a former U.S. government employee and is intended for informational and academic purposes only. Readers from other jurisdictions should be aware that legal, ethical, and diplomatic considerations regarding AI may vary by country and are subject to different regulatory and policy frameworks. The author's prior affiliation with the U.S. Department of State is noted solely for biographical purposes and in compliance with 5 C.F.R. §§ 2635.702-705. The mention of the author's prior title does not imply any official endorsement of the views or content expressed in this book, which are entirely the author's own.

All case studies and scenarios discussed are either historically documented in publicly available work or they are hypothetical, designed for educational purposes, and do not reflect any current real-world policies, programs, or operations of the U.S. government. Any resemblance between the hypothetical case studies, scenarios, or analyses in this book and actual persons, policies, or events—past or present—is purely coincidental and unintentional. The analyses are speculative, forward-looking, and not tied to any specific diplomatic initiatives. While the author has made every effort to ensure the accuracy of the content, no responsibility is assumed for how the information may be interpreted or applied. The author and publisher disclaim any liability for damages, direct or indirect, resulting from the use or application of this book's content. Readers assume full responsibility for any actions taken based on the information provided, and they are encouraged to consult subject matter experts before making decisions influenced by the material herein. The manuscript was reviewed by the Bureau of Global Public Affairs (GPA) and approved for personal publication on October 1, 2024. The author has adhered to all applicable guidelines, including those outlined in 11 FAM 600 and 5 C.F.R. § 2635. This work was completed using personal time and resources, without any use of government facilities or resources.

Index